EC COMPETITION LAW
AND
INTELLECTUAL PROPERTY RIGHTS

WITHDRAWN

EC Competition Law
and
Intellectual Property Rights

The Regulation of Innovation

STEVEN D. ANDERMAN

OXFORD
UNIVERSITY PRESS

OXFORD

UNIVERSITY PRESS

Great Clarendon Street, Oxford OX2 6DP

Oxford University Press is a department of the University of Oxford.
It furthers the University's objective of excellence in research, scholarship,
and education by publishing worldwide in

Oxford New York

Athens Auckland Bangkok Bogotá Buenos Aires Cape Town
Chennai Dar es Salaam Delhi Florence Hong Kong Istanbul Karachi
Kolkata Kuala Lumpur Madrid Melbourne Mexico City Mumbai Nairobi
Paris São Paulo Shanghai Singapore Taipei Tokyo Toronto Warsaw

with associated companies in Berlin Ibadan

Oxford is a registered trade mark of Oxford University Press
in the UK and in certain other countries

Published in the United States
by Oxford University Press Inc., New York

British Library Cataloguing in Publication Data
Data available

Library of Congress Cataloging in Publication Data
Anderman, S. D. (Steven D.)
EC competition law and intellectual property rights/
S. D. Anderman
p. cm.
Includes bibliographical references and index.
1. Intellectual property—European Union countries.
2. Competition, Unfair—European Union countries. I. Title.
KJE 2636.A95 1988
341.7'58'094—dc21
ISBN 0-19-825977-8
ISBN 0-19-829924-9 (Pbk)

3 5 7 9 10 8 6 4 2

Printed in Great Britain
on acid-free paper by
Bookcraft Ltd., Midsomer Norton, Somerset

Contents

Preface   xi

Table of Cases   xiv

Table of Legislation   xxiv

PART I
INTRODUCTION

1 General Introduction   3
    1.1   EC Competition Law as a System of Regulation of
           Intellectual Property Rights   3
    1.2   Competition Policy and Intellectual Property Rights:
           the Policy Context   8

**2 The Relationship between Intellectual Property Rights and
Competition Law under the Treaty**   8
    2.1   Introduction   8
    2.2   Grant and 'Existence'   11
    2.3   Permitted and Prohibited Exercise of Intellectual
           Property Rights   12
           2.3.1   Normal Exercise   12
           2.3.2   A Functional Test for Permitted
                   Exercise?   13
    2.4   The Objectives of the Rules on Competition in
           the Treaty   16
    2.5   Effective Competition   16
    2.6   The Goal of Fair Competition   19
    2.7   The Goal of Integration   21
    2.8   Negative or Positive Integration   23

PART II
ARTICLE 85 AND INTELLECTUAL PROPERTY LICENSING

**3 Introduction: Intellectual Property Right Licensing
and Competition Policy Generally**   27

4 The Structure of Article 85 and Licensing Agreements   34
    4.1   Introduction   34
    4.2   The Requirements of the Exemption Process   37

4.3   The Clearance of Licensing Agreements under
       Article 85(1)   40
       4.3.1   Agreements between independent
                undertakings   40
       4.3.2   Effect upon Interstate Trade   43
       4.3.3   Agreements of Minor Importance:
                De Minimis and Article 85(1)   45
       4.3.4   The Object of Effect or Preventing, Restricting
                or Distorting Competition   48

5   **The Development of the Concept of Restriction of
    Competition and Intellectual Property Right Licensing**   **52**
    5.1   The Scope of the Patent Doctrine and Restriction on
           Competition   52
    5.2   The Commission's Change to *per se* Prohibitions in
           Licensing Agreements   55
           5.2.1   The *Grundig* Decision   55
           5.2.2   The Commission's Change of Policy   57
    5.3   The Court's Application of the Appreciability Test to
           Intellectual Property Rights   63
           5.3.1   Exclusive Territoriality   63
           5.3.2   The Scope of the Exception for Open
                    Exclusive Licences   65
    5.4   The New Technology/Market Opening Test   66
    5.5   Non-territorial Restraints and Restrictions on
           Competition   73

6   **The Development of the Commission's Block Exemption
    Policy for Technology Licensing Agreements**   **76**
    6.1   The Patent Licensing Block Exemption (2349/84)   76
    6.2   The Know-how Block Exemption Regulation
           (556/89)   78
    6.3   The Technology Transfer Block Exemption
           Regulation (240/96)   81

7   **The Regulation of Territorial Restraints in Intellectual
    Property Right Licensing Agreements under Article 85**   **90**
    7.1   The Court's Approach   91
           7.1.1   Non-Restrictive Exclusive Licences   91
           7.1.2   Exemptible Exclusive Territoriality   93
    7.2   The Duration of Territorial Protections   95
    7.3   Closed Licences and Intellectual Property Rights   97

8   The Regulation of Non-Territorial Restraints in
     Licensing Agreements   **100**
     8.1   Introduction   100
     8.2   Protecting the Integrity of the Innovation: the
            Indispensable Provisions in Licensing Agreements   102
            8.2.1   Introduction   102
            8.2.2   The Low Risk Indispensable Restraints   103
            8.2.3   Quality Controls and Licensing   106
     8.3   The Limits of Indispensability   107
            8.3.1   Tie-ins and Quality Specifications   107
            8.3.2   Improvements and Grant Backs   109
     8.4   Field of Use Provisions   118
     8.5   The Regulation of Royalties   120
            8.5.1   Duration   120
            8.5.2   The Base for Calculating Royalties   122
     8.6   No-challenge Clauses   123
     8.7   Exclusive Territoriality, Minimum Quantities, and
            Non-competition clauses   125
            8.7.1   Minimum Royalties and Minimum
                     Quantities   125
            8.7.2   Non-Competition Clauses   127

9   Conclusions   **130**
     9.1   The US Antitrust Guidelines   136
     9.2   The Relevance of the US Guidelines for EC
            Competition Law   139

PART III
ARTICLE 86 AND INTELLECTUAL PROPERTY RIGHTS

10 Introduction   **147**

11 The Relevant Market and Intellectual Property Rights   **151**
     11.1 The Relevant Product Market   151
            11.1.1 Defining the Relevant Product   153
            11.1.2 Narrow Product Markets and Commission
                     Practice   157
            11.1.3 Dependence, 'Essential Facility', and Market
                     Definition   160
     11.2 The Relevant Geographic Market   165

12 The Concept of Dominance and Intellectual Property
     Rights   **168**
     12.1 Introduction   168
     12.2 Dominance and Intellectual Property Rights   169

12.3 Dominance, Intellectual Property Rights, and Barriers
to Entry   172

13 The Concept of Abuse and Intellectual Property Rights   **180**
13.1 The Expansion of the Concept of Abuse under Article 86
from Exploitive to Anticompetitive Conduct   181
    13.1.1 Weakening Levels of Competition in
Markets   182
    13.1.2 Methods of Normal Competition   184
13.2 The Expanded Concept of Abuse and Restrictions on
Intellectual Property Rights   187
    13.2.1 Structural Abuse and Intellectual Property
Rights in the Primary Market   188
    13.2.2 Specific Abuses, Second Markets and
Intellectual Property Rights   190
    13.2.3 The Concept of Related Markets under
Article 86   191

14 Refusals to Supply and Intellectual Property Rights   **195**
14.1 Refusals to Supply: the Court and Commission   195
14.2 From Refusal to Supply to Refusal to License: the
Commission Decisions   199
    14.2.1 New Entrants and Commission Decisions   201
    14.2.2 The Commission's 'Essential Facility'
Doctrine   202
14.3 *Magill*   204
    14.3.1 *Magill* and the Commission   204
    14.3.2 The Judgment of the Court of First Instance
in *Magill*   206
    14.3.3 The Advocate General's Opinion in *Magill*   207
    14.3.4 The Judgment of the Court of Justice
in *Magill*   208
    14.3.5 Some Implications of *Magill*   211
14.4 The Pricing of Compulsory Licensing   214

15 Tie-ins and Intellectual Property Rights   **221**

16 Excessive Pricing and Intellectual Property Rights   **224**
16.1 Introduction   224
16.2 Article 86(A) generally   225
16.3 Article 86(A) and Intellectual Property Rights   228
16.4 Dual Markets, Intellectual Property Rights, and
Unfair Trading   231

17 Discriminatory Pricing and Intellectual Property Rights **232**
  17.1 The Concept of Equivalent Transactions 232
  17.2 Discriminatory Discounts and Rebates in a Single
     Market 233
     17.2.1 Non-Equivalent Transactions: Different
          Quantities 234
     17.2.2 The Effects of the Discriminatory Practice 235
  17.3 Separate Markets and Price Discrimination 235
     17.3.1 Intellectual Property Rights and Separate
          Markets 236
  17.4 Geographic Price Discrimination 239
  17.5 Article 86(C) as a Regulatory Framework for an
     Essential Facility 242

18 Predatory Pricing **244**

19 Conclusions **246**
  19.1 The Exceptional Circumstances Test and Normal
     Exploitation 246
  19.2 The Effect of the Competition Rules upon Incentives 247
  19.3 Appropriation of Value and Market Power 248
  19.4 Balancing Access to Markets and Exclusivity 250

APPENDICES

**Appendix I—Excerpts from the Treaty establishing the
European Community** **255**
Appendix II—Commission Regulation (EC) No. 240/96 **258**
**Appendix III—Antitrust Guidelines for the Licensing of
Intellectual Property (USA)** **276**

Bibliography 305
Index 311

Preface

European competition Law is a field in which law and policy are almost indivisible. A case before the Commission can rarely be conducted on the basis of a purely legalistic reading of the case-law; the underlying policy arguments must also be marshalled. The Commission's regulations must be interpreted in the light of the policies expressed in the recitals. The decisions of the Court of First Instance and the European Court of Justice are heavily influenced by the policies expressed in the European Treaties.

This book is an attempt to stress the policy reasons underlying the application of EC competition law to the exercise of intellectual property rights. It is influenced by my fifteen-year period of association with the Economic and Social Committee of the European Union in the capacity of Expert. In particular it draws upon my work as Expert to the Rapporteur for the Patent Licensing Regulation (1984), the Technology Transfer Regulation (1996), and the Green Paper on Vertical Restraints (1997), as well as Expert to Group I for the Know-how Regulation (1989), the Franchising Regulation (1986), and the Merger Control Regulation (1989). The process by which the Committee engages in line by line scrutiny of a regulation with representatives of the Commission present in the sessions offers a particularly useful vantage point to discover the evolution of the policies to which the regulations give legal expression. I have particularly benefited from conversations with Hartmut Johannes, Helmut Schroter, John Temple Lange, Sebastiano Guttuso, and Luc Peeperkorn.

I also owe a debt of gratitude to my colleagues at Essex, Dan Goyder, now of Linklaters and Paines, to Val Korah, of University College London and Fordham Law Schools, and to Richard Whish of Kings College London and Watson Farley and Williams, for opening up the pathways to the subject of EC Competition Law in their books and articles. I am indebted to John Kallaugher of Wilmer Cutler and Pickering and University College London for sharing his profound understanding of the case-law interpreting the Articles of the Treaty. I also owe thanks to Guy Leigh and John Angel of Theodore Goddard & Co. and to Nick Green, Paul Lasok QC, Thomas Sharpe QC, and John Vickers, Professor of Economics at Oxford University, for conversations about the subject and, in the case of the latter two, for reading part of the manuscript.

My thanks also go to the members of the Law Faculty at Essex University, Peter Stone, Nick Bernard, Janet Dine, and Sheldon Leader, whose willingness to talk through issues and read drafts contributes to the lively research culture in the School of Law at Essex.

To those who have helped me along much thanks; any errors which remain are entirely my own responsibility.

Finally, a book is always written at the expense of those close to the author. I thank my wife Gunilla and son Benjamin for their resigned but gracious tolerance.

Steve Anderman

Addendum to the Preface

Since the hardback edition was published, at least three new developments have occurred which are particularly relevant to this field. The first is the way the *Microsoft* case has awakened interest in the use of extensive market power based on IPR protection to exclude competitors who attempt to introduce new applications of protected platforms or infrastructures. Although, the *Microsoft* case was initially brought by the Antitrust Division of the US Justice Department, it involved a breach of an undertaking made both to the European Commission and the US Justice Department *inter alia* not to 'tie-in' sales of its Windows platform to other applications. Much of the analysis of the second part of this book offers a template to analyse how, under Article 82 of the Treaty, the competition authorities are likely to view the conduct of Microsoft towards competitors in software applications markets, particularly in the web browser market, whilst possessing a near monopoly in the platform market created by their Windows 95 and 98 versions. The fact that the EU Commission is now looking into complaints against Microsoft because its Windows 2000 creates difficulties of access for other firms providing Windows compatible software makes such an analysis more than merely a historical exercise.

The second development is the judgment of the ECJ in *Oscar Bronner GMbH & Co.KG v Mediaprint* [1999] 4 CMLR 112. The decision has been viewed in some quarters as limiting the reach of the *Magill* case, particularly in view of the comments of the Advocate-General in the case. Nevertheless, a careful reading of *Oscar Bronner* suggests that it essentially reaffirmed the judgment of the Court of Justice in *Magill*. It reminded parties of the requirement stipulated by the ECJ in *Magill* in paragraph 56 that a crucial condition for the test of abuse for a refusal to supply by an owner with a monopoly of an essential input for a secondary market is that the input must be indispensable; mere commercial disadvantage is not sufficient. *Oscar Bronner* also re-emphasized the point made by the Court in *Magill* that the effect of the refusal to supply an essential input must be to allow the input owner to reserve the secondary market to itself by excluding all competition to it. By reminding the parties of these requirements, the Court could said to be re-emphasizing that it will require truly 'exceptional circumstances' before Article 82 can be used to limit the scope of the otherwise lawful exercise of IPRs.

The third development is the European Commission's reform of the law relating to Article 81. The new EU Block Exemption Regulation on Vertical Agreements, accompanied by the Guidelines on Vertical Restraints, applies primarily to distribution agreements including franchising agreements and specifically rules out IPR licensing agreements falling within the scope of the Technology Transfer Regulation. However, it widens the scope of the block exemption to include new categories of vertical distribution agreements combined with IPRs which are used by the distributor. This reform, with its shift from form-based regulation to a more economics-based regulation, when taken together with the White Paper on Modernization, suggests that changes in the nature of regulation of Technology Transfer agreements cannot be entirely ruled out in the next few years.

S. D. Anderman
6 April 2000

Table of Cases

TABLE OF EC CASES (ALPHABETICAL)

AEG Telefunken *v* Commission Case 107/82 R [1983] ECR
3151 .... 42, 43
AKZO *v* Commission [1993] 5 CMLR 215 .... 20, 170–171, 181,
182, 184, 185, 192, 244

Basset *v* SACEM Case 402/85 [1987] ECR 1747, [1987] 3 CMLR
173 198
BMW Belgium *v* Commission Cases 32, 36–82/78 [1979] ECR
435 42
BPB Industries and British Gypsum *v* Commission [1993] ECR
II–389 .... 187, 192, 236
Brasserie de Haecht I Case 23/67 [1967] ECR 407, [1968]
CMLR 26 46
Brasserie de Haecht II *v* Wilkin Case 48/72 [1973] ECR 77 36
British Leyland *v* Commission Case 226/84 [1986] ECR 3263 .... 225, 230
British Plasterboard [1995] ECR I–865, [1997] 4 CMLR 238 233
  see also BPB Industries and British Gypsum *v* Commission
BRT *v* SABAM and Fonior Case 127/73 [1974] ECR 51 .... 36, 186

Centrafarm *v* Sterling Drug Case 15/74 [1974] ECR 1147 .... 12, 41
Centre Belge d'Etudes de Marche (CBEM) *v* Télémarketing Case
113/84 [1985] ECR 3261 ....162, 169, 174, 177, 187,
92, 195, 202, 203, 221
CICRA et Maxicar *v* Renault Case 53/87 [1988] ECR 299 .... 9, 173,
181, 189, 205, 216, 228, 231
Cimenteries Joined Cases 8–11/66 [1967] ECR 75 85
Coditel I Case 62/79 [1980] ECR 881 .... 68, 69
Coditel II Case 262/81 [1982] ECR 3381 .... 13, 35, 68
Commercial Solvents case *see* ICI and Commercial Solvents *v*
  Commission
Commission *v* Solvay and La Porte Case 85/74 [1985] 1 CMLR 481 ... 41
Consten Grundig *v* Commission [1966] ECR 235 .... 9, 10, 12, 15,
16, 21, 22, 34, 41, 50, 52, 55–57, 63, 71
Continental Can *v* Commission [1973] ECR 215 .... 17, 19, 170,
171, 181, 182, 184, 188, 191

Corinne Bodson *v* Pompes Funebres de Rehgion Liberees SA
[1985] ECR 2479, [1989] 4 CMLR 984 41
Corsica Ferries Italia SRL *v* Corpo del Piloti del Porto di Genova
Case C–18/93, 17 May 1994 166

Delimitis *v* Henniger Brau AG Case C–234/89 [1991] ECR I–935,
[1992] 5 CMLR 210 . . . . 38, 46, 47, 88
Deutsche Grammophon Gesellschaft mbH *v* Metro-SB-
Grossmarketete GMbH & Co Case 78/70 [1971] ECR
487, [1971] CMLR 631 . . . . 6, 12, 35, 169
Deutsche Grammophon [1974] ECR 1147 . . . . 8, 9

ECS *v* AKZO [1983] 3 CMLR 694 185
EMI *v* CBS (UK) Ltd Cases 51, 86, 96/75 [1976] ECR 811 12
Erauw-Jacquery *v* La Hesbignonne Case 27/87 [1988] ECR
1919 . . . . 24, 70, 71, 72
Europemballage and Continental Can *v* Commission Case 6/72
[1973] ECR 215 182
Europort AIS *v* Denmark [1993] CMLR 457 (Port of Rødby) 203

Ford Werke AG & Ford of Europe *v* Commission Cases 25 and
26/84 [1985] ECR 2725 42

General Motors Continental *v* Commission Case 26/75 [1976]
ECR 1367 . . . . 177, 225
Grundig case *see* Consten Grundig *v* Commission
GVL *v* Commission Case 7/82 [1983] ECR 483 241

Hilti AG *v* Commission [1991] ECR II–1439 . . . . 3, 164, 172, 180,
184, 186, 221, 222, 234, 236, 238
Hoffman La Roche *v* Commission Case 102/77 [1978] ECR
1139 . . . . 13, 15, 168, 170, 171, 172, 182, 183, 186, 233, 234, 235
Hugin *v* Commission Case 22/78 [1979] ECR 1869 . . . . 164, 166, 168,
173, 174

ICI and Commercial Solvents *v* Commission Cases 6 and 7/73
[1974] ECR 223 . . . . 41, 168, 170, 173, 182, 184, 187, 191,
192, 195, 201, 202, 203, 209, 211, 213, 221
Irish Continental Group *v* CCI Morlaix [1995] 5 CMLR 177 203
Italian Flat Glass Case T–68, 77 and 78/89 [1990] 4 CMLR 535 166

Keurkoop *v* Nancy Kean Gifts Case 144/81 [1982] ECR 2653 . . . . . 11, 12,
197, 211

Lucazeau *v* SACEM Case 395/87 [1989] ECR 2811 . . . . 34, 198

Magill case *see* RTE *v* Commission
Merci Conventzionale Porto di Genoa Case 179/90 [1991] ECR
   I–5889 166
Merck *v* Prime Crown [1997] 1 CMLR 83 9
Metro *v* Commission Case 26/76 [1977] ECR 1875 17
Michelin *v* Commission Cases 322/81 [1983] ECR 3461 . . . . . 19, 166, 168,
                               170, 172, 178, 179, 180, 182, 233
Ministère Publique *v* Tournier Cases 110/88, 241/88, 242/88
   [1989] ECR 2565 . . . . 186, 198
Ministère Publique *v* Tournier Case 395/87 [1991] 4 CMLR 248 226

Nungesser *v* Commission Case 258/78 [1982] ECR 2015 . . . . . . 24, 64, 71,
                                            72, 76, 79

Parke Davis *v* Probel Case 24/67 [1968] ECR 55 . . . . 8, 9, 10, 12, 16,
                                         34, 35, 224, 228
Port of Rødby case *see* Europort AIS *v* Denmark
Pronuptia de Paris *v* Schillgalis Case 161/84 [1986] ECR 353 . . . 44, 71, 74

Remia BV & Verenidge Bedrijven Nutricia *v* Commission Case
   42/84 [1987] 1 CMLR 1 74
RTE *v* Commission [1991] ECR II–485 . . . . 11, 15
RTE *v* Commission (Magill)[1995] ECR I–743 . . . . 3, 9, 11, 15, 164,
           166, 169, 177, 179, 180, 181, 188, 191, 203, 204–214, 215

SACEM case *see* Ministère Publique *v* Tournier and Lucazeau
   v SACEM
Sirena *v* Eda Case 40/70 [1971] ECR 3169 . . . . 34, 224, 230
Solvay *v* Commission; British Plasterboard and British Gypsum
   v Commission [1993] ECR II–389 166
STM *v* Maschinenbau Ulm [1966] ECR 235, [1966] CMLR 357 . . . . . 43, 44,
                                         50, 51, 63

Tetra Pak Rausing SA *v* Commission (Tetra Pak I) Case T–51/89
   [1990] ECR II–309, [1991] 4 CMLR 334 . . . . 3, 85, 172, 179, 180,
                                            181, 189
Tetra Pak *v* Commission (Tetra Pak II) Case C–333/94 P, [1994]
   ECR II–755, [1997] 4 CMLR 602 . . . . 3, 164, 167, 170, 179, 184, 186,
                         193, 212, 222, 223, 234, 236, 237, 240, 244
Tierce Ladbroke SA *v* Commission Case T–504/93 12 June 1997
   (CFI) 210, 214
Tournier case *see* Ministère Public *v* Tournier

United Brands *v* Commission Case 27/76 [1978] ECR 207 . . . . 19, 165,
    168, 171, 185, 186, 187, 202, 224, 225, 226, 232, 235, 239, 240, 241, 242

Viho Europe *v* Commission [1995] ECR–II 217 41
Volk *v* Vernaeke Case 5/69 [1969] ECR 295, [1969] CMLR 277 44
Volvo *v* Veng (UK) Ltd Case 238/87 [1988] ECR 6211 . . . . 9, 11, 12,
                    14, 15, 164, 173, 185, 197, 198, 199, 205, 207, 210

Walt Wilhelm *v* BundesKartelamnt Case 14/68 [1969] ECR 1 43
Windsurfing International Inc *v* Commission Case 193/83 [1986]
    ECR 611 73
Woodpulp Cases 89, 104, 114, 116, 117, 125–129/85 [1988] ECR
    5193, [1988] 4 CMLR 901 43

Zuiker Unie *v* Commission [1975] ECR 1663, [1976] 1 CMLR
    295 . . . . 43, 49, 53, 73

TABLE OF EC CASES (NUMERICAL)

Joined cases 8–11/66 Cimenteries [1967] ECR 75 85

Case 23/67 Brasserie de Haecht I [1967] ECR 407, [1968] CMLR 26 46
Case 24/67 Parke Davis *v* Probel [1968] ECR 55 . . . . 8, 9, 10, 12, 16,
                                            34, 35, 224, 228
Case 14/68 Walt Wilhelm *v* BundesKartelamnt [1969] ECR 1 43
Case 5/69 Volk v Vernaeke [1969] ECR 295, [1969] CMLR 277 44
Case 40/70 Sirena vEda [1971] ECR 3169 . . . . 34, 224, 230
Case 78/70 Deutsche Grammophon Gesellschaft mbH *v* Metro-
    SB-Grossmarketete GmbH & Co [1971] ECR 487, [1971]
    CMLR 631 . . . . 6, 12, 35, 169
Case 6/72 Europemballage and Continental Can *v* Commission
    [1973] ECR 215 182
Case 48/72 Brasserie de Haecht II *v* Wilkin [1973] ECR 77 36
Cases 6 and 7/73 ICI and Commercial Solvents *v* Commission
    [1974] ECR 223 . . . . 41, 168, 170, 173, 182, 184, 187, 191,
                            192, 195, 201, 202, 203, 209, 211, 213, 221
Case 127/73 BRT *v* SABAM and Fonior [1974] ECR 51 . . . . 36, 186
Case 15/74 Centrafarm *v* Sterling Drug [1974] ECR 1147 . . . . 12, 41
Case 85/74 Commission *v* Solvay and La Porte [1985] 1 CMLR 481 . . . 41
Case 26/75 General Motors Continental *v* Commission [1976] ECR
    1367 . . . . 177, 225
Cases 51, 86, 96/75 EMI *v* CBS (UK) Ltd [1976] ECR 811 12
Case 26/76 Metro *v* Commission [1977] ECR 1875 17

Case 27/76 United Brands *v* Commission [1978] ECR 207 . . . . . . .19, 165,
  168, 171, 185, 186, 187, 202, 224, 225, 226, 232, 235, 239, 240, 241, 242
Case 102/77 Hoffman La Roche *v* Commission [1978] ECR
  1139 . . . . .13, 15, 168, 170, 171, 172, 182, 183, 186, 233, 234, 235
Case 22/78 Hugin *v* Commission [1979] ECR 1869 . . . . 164, 166, 168,
  173, 174
Cases 32, 36–82/78 BMW Belgium *v* Commission [1979] ECR 2435 . . . 42
Case 258/78 Nungesser *v* Commission [1982] ECR 2015 . . . . . . 24, 64, 71,
  72, 76, 79
Case 62/79 Coditel I [1980] ECR 881 . . . . 68, 69
Case 144/81 Keurkoop *v* Nancy Kean Gifts [1982] ECR
  2653 . . . . 11, 12, 197, 211
Case 262/81 Coditel II [1982] ECR 3381 . . . . 13, 35, 68
Case 322/81 Michelin *v* Commission [1983] ECR 3461 . . . . 19, 166,
  168, 170, 172, 178, 179, 180, 182, 233
Case 7/82 GVL *v* Commission [1983] ECR 843 241
Case 107/82 R AEG Telefunken *v* Commission [1983] ECR 3151 . . . 42, 43
Case 193/83 Windsurfing International Inc *v* Commission [1986]
  ECR 611 73
Case 25, 26/84 Ford Werke AG & Ford of Europe *v* Commission
  [1985] ECR 2725 42
Case 42/84 Remia BV & Verenidge Bedrijven Nutricia *v*
  Commission [1987] CMLR 1 74
Case 113/84 Centre Belged'Etudes de Marche (CBEM) *v*
  Télémarketing [1985] ECR 3261 . . . . 162, 169, 174, 177, 187,
  192, 195, 202, 203, 221
Case 161/84 Pronuptia de Paris *v* Schillgalis [1986] ECR 353 . . . 44, 71, 74
Case 226/84 British Leyland *v* Commission [1986] ECR 3263 . . . . 225, 230
Cases 89, 104, 114, 116, 117, 125–129/85 Woodpulp [1988] ECR
  5193, [1988] 4 CMLR 901 43
Case 402/85 Basset *v* SACEM [1987] ECR 1747, [1987] 3 CMLR
  173 198
Case 27/87 Erauw-Jacquery *v* La Hesbigonne [1988] ECR
  1919 . . . . 24, 70, 71, 72
Case 53/87 CICRA et Maxicar *v* Renault [1988] ECR 299 . . . . 2, 173,
  181, 189, 205, 216, 228, 231
Case 238/87 Volvo *v* Veng (UK) [1988] ECR 6211 . . . . 9, 11, 12, 14,
  15, 164, 173, 185, 197, 198, 199, 205, 207, 210
Case 395/87 Lucazeau *v* SACEM [1989] ECR 2811 . . . . 34, 198
Cases 110, 241, 242/88 Ministière Publique *v* Tournier [1989] ECR
  2565 . . . . 186, 198
Case T–51/89 Tetra Pak Rausing SA *v* Commission (Tetra Pak I)
  [1990] ECR II–309, [1991] 4 CMLR 334 . . . . 3, 85, 172, 179, 180, 181, 189

Case 68, 77 and 78/89 Italian Flat Glass [1990] 4 CMLR 535 166
Case C–234/89 Delimitis *v* Henniger Brau AG [1991] ECR I–935,
    [1992] 5 CMLR 210 . . . . 38, 46, 47, 88
Case 179/90 Merci Conventzionale Porto di Genoa [1991] ECR
    I–5889 166
Case C–18/93 Corsica Ferries SRL *v* Corpo del Piloti sel Porto di
    Genova 17 May 1994 166
Case T–504/93 Tierce Ladbroke SA *v* Commission 12 June
    1997 . . . . 210, 214
Case C–333/94 P Tetra Pak *v* Commission (Tetra Pak II) [1994]
    ECR II–755, [1997] 4 CMLR 602 . . . . 3, 164, 167, 170, 179, 184, 186,
                                    193, 212, 222, 223, 234, 236, 237, 240, 244

TABLE OF EC DECISIONS

Adalat [1996] 5 CMLR 416 42
AOIP/Beyrand OJ EC L6/8 (1976) 59, 60
Association of Plant Breeders of the EEC (Comasco) [1990] 4 CMLR
    259 72
AT&T/NCR Merger [1992] 4 CMLR M41 . . . . 163, 175

BBI/Boosey & Hawkes OJ [1987] L286/36; [1971] CMLR D35 . . . 196, 202
Bendix/Ancien Ets. Mertons & Strae 1.6.64 5 OJ EC 1496 (1964) 49
Boussois/Interpane [1988] 4 CMLR 124 . . . . 79, 87
Breeders: Roses [1988] 4 CMLR 193 46
British Midland/Aer Lingus [1993] CMLR 596 . . . . 201, 202
Bronmemaling-Heidemaat (no ref given) 60
Burroughs-Delplanque OJ EC L 13/50 (1972) 58
Burroughs-Geha-Werke OJ L 13/53 (1972) 58

Campari [1978] 2 CMLR 397 81

Davidson Rubber OJ EC L 143/31 (1972) 58
DDD/Delta Chemie [1989] 4 CMLR 535 . . . . 72, 91
Decca Navigation Systems EC Comm. Dec. 89/113 (1989); [1990]
    4 CMLR 627 . . . . 163, 176, 200
Digital Kienzle [1992] 4 CMLR M99 163

GEMA [1971] ECR 791; [1971] CMLR D 35 . . . . 198, 241
GEMA [1979] ECR 3173 . . . . 186, 198

HOV-SVZ/MCN [1994] OJ L104/34 232

IBM Corp *v* Commission EC Comm. Dec. 84/233 (1984); [1981] ECR
2639 .... 162, 175, 196, 199, 202, 212
IGR Stereo Television EC Comm. XIth Competition Policy Rep.
(1982), p. 63 200
Ideal Standard [1994] ECR I–2789 34

Johnson and Johnson [1981] 2 CMLR 287 41

Kabelmetal/Luchaire OJ EC L (222) 34 (1975) 59, 60

London European/Sabena OJ N L317/47, 24 Nov. 1988 201

Mannesman/Vallourec/Ilva [1994] OJ L 102/15 .... 166, 171
Moosehead/Whitbread [1991] 4 CMLR 391 .... 37, 81, 87

Pelican *v* Kyocera, Competition Policy Newsletter Vol. 1, No. 6 250
Pilkington-Technint/SIV OJ No L 158, 25 June 1994 166
Polypropylene [1988] 4 CMLR 34 41

Reuter/BASF [1976] 2 CMLR D 44 73
Rhone Poulenc/SNIA OJ C 212/23 [1992] 170
Rich Products/Jus Rol [1988] 4 CMLR 527 .... 72, 79

Sandoz [1990] ECR 145 42
Sea Containers *v* Stena Sealink [1995] 1 CMLR 84 .... 176, 202, 203
Soda Ash-Solvay et Cie [1991] OJ L152/21; [1995] ECR
II–1775 .... 233, 234
Sugar case [1975] ECR 1663 170

Vacuum Interrupters [1977] 1 CMLR D 67 43
Vaessen/Morris (no ref. given) 61
Velcro/Aplix [1989] 4 CMLR 157 72

TABLE OF US CASES

Abbot Laboratories *v* Brennan 952 F 2d 1346 (Fed. Cir. 1991), cert.
denied 112 S. Ct. 2993 (1992) 279
American Cyanamid Co. 72 FTC 632 (1967), affd. *sub nom.* Charles
Pfizer & Co. 401 F 2d 574 (6th Cir. 1968), cert. denied 394 US
920 (1969) 303
Argus Chemical Corp. *v* Fibre Glass Evercoat Inc 812 F 2d 1381
(Fed. Cir. 1987) 303

Atari Games Corp. *v* Nintendo of America Inc 897 F 2d 1572 (Fed.
Cir. 1990) 278

Barber-Colman Co. *v* National Tool Co. 136 F 2d 339 (6th Cir. 1943) . . 298
Beltone Electronics Corp. 100 FTC 68 (1982) 299
Broadcast Music Inc. *v* Columbia Broadcasting System Inc. 441
US 1 (1979) 290, 300
Brook Group Ltd *v* Brown and Williamson Tobacco Group 405
US 209 (1993) 245

Continental TV Inc. *v* GTE Sylvania Inc. 433 US 36 (1977) 29, 31
Cummer-Graham Co. *v* Stariaght Side Basket Corp. 142 F 2d 646
(5th Cir.), cert. denied 323 US 726 (1944) 298
CVD Inc. *v* Raytheon Co. 769 F 2d 842 (1st Cir. 1985), cert. denied
475 US 1016 (1986) 303

Digidyne Corp. *v* Data General Corp. 734 F 2d 1336, (9th Cir. 1984),
cert. denied 473 US 908 (1985) 279
Dr. Miles Medical Co. *v* John D. Park & Sons Co. 220 US 373
(1911) 298

Eastman Kodak Co. *v* Image Technical Services Inc. 112 Sup. Ct.
Rep. 2072 (1992) 250, 298
Ethyl Gasoline Corp. *v* United States 309 US 436 (1940) 298

Federal Trade Commission *v* Indiana Federation of Dentists 476 US
477 289–290
Federal Trade Commission *v* Superior Court Trial Lawyers
Assocn. 493 US 411 (1990) 290

Handgards Inc. *v* Ethicon Inc. 743 F 2d 1282 (9th Cir. 1984), cert.
denied 469 US 1190 (1985) 303
Handgards Inc. *v* Ethicon Inc. 601 F 2D 986 (9th Cir. 1979), cert.
denied 444 US 1025 (1980) 303

International Salt Co. *v* United States 332 US 292 (1947) 30, 298

Jefferson Parish Hospital District No 2 *v* Hyde 466 US 2 (1984) 279

Kewanee Oil Co. *v* Bicron Corp. 416 US 470 (1974) 278

Mercoid Corp. *v* Mid Continent Investment Co. 320 US 661 (1943) 52

Michael Anthony Jewellers Inc. *v* Peacock Jewelry Inc. 795 F
Supp. 639 (SDNY 1992) 303
Morton Salt Co. *v* G S Suppiger Co. 314 US 488 (1941) 61

National Society of Professional Engineers *v* United States 435
US 679 (1978) 290
NCAA *v* Board of Regents of the University of Oklahoma 468
US 85 (1984) 290, 300
Newburgh Moire Co. *v* Superior Moire Co. 237 F 2d 283 (3rd Cir.
1956) 298
Northwest Wholesale Stationers Inc. *v* Pacific Stationary and
Printing Co. 472 US 284 (1985) 300

Professional Real Estate Investors Inc. *v* Columbia Pictures
Industries Inc. 113 S Ct 1920 (1993) 303

Royal Indus. *v* St Regis Paper Co. 420 F 2d 449 (9th Cir. 1969) 298

Tampa Electric Co. *v* Nashville Coal Co. 365 US 320 (1961) 299
Transparent Wrap Machine Corp. *v* Stokes & Smith Co 329 US 637
(1947) 302

United States *v* Aluminium Co. of America 148 F 2d 416 (2nd Cir.
1945) 280
United States *v* Automobile Manufacturers Asscn. 307 F. Supp.
617 (CD Cal. 1969), appeal dismissed *sub nom* City of New
York *v* United States 397 US 248 (1970), modified *sub nom.*
United States *v* Motor Vehicles Mfrs. Asscn. 1982–83
Trade Cas. (CCH)¶ 65,088 (C D Cal. 1982) 285, 301
United States *v* General Electric Co. 272 US 476 (1926) 298
United States *v* General Motors Corp. Civ. No. 93–530 (D.Del. filed
Nov. 16 1993) 285
United States *v* Grinnell Corp. 384 US 563 (1966) 280
United States *v* Jerrold Electronics Corp. 187 F. Supp. 545 (E.D.Pa.
1960), affd. per curiam 365 US 567 (1961) 295
United States *v* Manufacturers Aircraft Asscn. Inc. 1976–1
Trade Cas. (CCH) ¶60,810 (SDNY 1975) 301
United States *v* New Wrinkle Inc. 342 US 371 (1952) 300
United States *v* Paramount Pictures Inc. 334 US 131 (1948) 298
United States *v* Singer Manufacturing Co. 374 US 174 (1963) 300
United States *v* United States Gypsum Co. 333 US 364 (1947) 61
United States *v* Univis Lens Co. 316 US 241 (1942) 298

Walker Process Equipment Inc *v* Food Machinery & Chemical Corp.
382 US 172 (1965) 303

OTHER CASES

Catnic Components Ltd and another *v* Hill & Smith Ltd [1983]
PSR 512 (Ch. Pat.Ct.) 216
Chemidis Wavin *v* TERI (1978) CMLR 514 36

Telecom Corpn of New Zealand *v* Clear Communication Ltd
[1995] 1 NZLR 385 217

Table of Legislation

EC LEGISLATION

The pre-Amsterdam numbering system will continue to be used in this paperback edition, Art. 85 is now 81 and 86 is now 82.

Treaties

EC Treaty 255–257
  Art. 2 . . . . .8, 16
  Art. 3 . . . . .8, 16, 17, 23, 24, 181
    (a) 8, 23
    (c) 23
    (f) 19
    (g) 8, 16, 17, 23, 148
    (h) 23
    (j) 16
    (l) 23
    (m) 16, 23
  Art. 30–36 . . . . .8, 10, 97
  Art. 30 . . . . .12, 24, 97, 99
  Art. 36 . . . . .10, 11, 12, 13, 14, 24, 97, 99, 198
  Art. 59 68
  Arts. 85, 86 . . . . .4, 8, 9, 10, 11, 12, 18, 19, 21, 24
  Art. 85 . . . . .10, 12, 13, 15, 16, 17, 22, 32, 33, 34–51, 55, 56, 69,
              86, 89, 90–99, 115, 120, 125, 134, 143, 147, 149, 162, 200, 236
    (1) 10, 11, 21, 22, 34, 35, 36, 37, 40, 41, 42, 43
             44, 45–48, 49, 50, 51, 52, 53, 54, 55, 56, 57, 58, 59, 60, 61, 63,
             64, 65, 66, 67, 68, 69, 70, 71, 72, 73, 74, 75, 76, 79, 80, 83, 91
             92, 93, 94, 95, 97, 99, 100, 101, 102, 103, 104, 105, 106, 107,
             111–112, 113, 114, 115, 116, 117, 119, 120, 121, 122, 123, 124,
                    126, 127, 128, 131, 139, 140, 141
    (1)(c) 221
    (2) 36, 38, 74
    (3) 21, 22, 35, 38, 39, 54, 57, 58, 60, 61, 63, 64, 66, 72, 73,
                  76, 77, 83, 84, 91, 93, 94, 97, 100, 101, 103,
                  107, 122, 123, 126, 128, 131, 186
  Art. 86 . . . . .11, 13, 14, 16, 20, 40, 77, 120, 147, 148, 149, 150, 151,
            154, 155, 156, 157, 161, 162, 163, 164, 165, 166, 168, 169, 172,
            175, 177, 178, 179, 180, 181, 182, 183, 185, 186, 188, 189, 190,
            191, 193, 196, 197, 198, 199, 200, 202, 203, 205, 206, 207, 208,
             210, 211, 214, 215, 221, 223, 226, 233, 241, 244, 246

(a) 14, 148, 197, 198, 214, 215, 224, 225, 226, 227,
228, 229, 230, 231, 235
(b) 14, 15, 148, 191, 197, 198, 205, 209, 214, 215, 218
(c) 14, 148, 191, 195, 197, 214, 232, 233, 235, 236,
237, 238, 239, 240, 241, 242, 243
(d) 14, 148, 191, 197, 213, 214, 221, 222, 223
Art. 90 204
Art. 177 .... 124, 197, 226
Art. 222 .... 10, 24

Regulations

Regulation 17 OJ C 204/62 (1962) 36, 44, 195
Art. 3 210
Art. 4   (1) 37
          (2) 53, 101
Art. 15 36
Regulation 1963/63 Patent Licensing agreements 59
Regulation 1983/83 Exclusive Distribution and Purchasing
Agreements 37, 86
Regulation 1983/84 Exclusive Distribution and Purchasing
Agreements 37
Regulation 2349/84 Patent Licensing Agreements Regulation 37,
76–78, 81, 88, 99, 131, 135
Art. 1   (1) 77
          (2) 78
Art. 2   (1)(1) 106
          (5) 104
          (8) 124
          (9) 106
Art. 3   (1) 124
Art. 3   (7) 119
Art. 5   (1) 78
Regulation 417/85 Block Exemption for Specialization
Agreements 37, 81, 130
Regulation 418/85 Block Exemption for R & D Agreements 37, 81,
86, 130
Regulation 4087/88 Block Exemption for Franchise Agreements 37,
81, 86, 130
Regulation 4064/89 EC Merger Reg OJ 1990 L257/14 .... 81, 130, 143
Regulation 556/89 Know-How Regulation 78–81, 113, 115, 127, 128
Art. 2   (1)(2) 104
          (4) 114, 117

          (5) 106–107
          (7) 80, 124
   Art. 3 (4) 124
          (6) 000
   Recital 1 79
   Recital 6 79
   Recital 15 80
Regulation 151/93 (amending 417/85 and 418/85) 37, 81, 130
Regulation 240/96 Technology Transfer Agreements 3, 81–89,
                    99, 108, 109, 113, 117, 119, 134, 135, **258–275**
   Art. 1 . . . . 84, 94, 118, 131, 140
          (1) 87, 133
   Art. 1.3 95
   Art. 1.5 81
   Art. 2 . . . . 102, 131, 140
          (1) 102, 104, 105
          (1)(2) 104
          (1)(3) 105
          (1)(4) 110, 111, 112
          (1)(5) 84, 107, 108, 132
          (1)(7) 122, 127
                    (a) 122
                    (b) 122
          (1)(8) 120
          (1)(9) 83
          (1)(10) 126
          (1)(12) 83
          (1)(14) 97, 99
          (1)(17) 83, 126, 128
          (1)(18) 126, 128
          (2) 102, 104
          (3) 104
   Art. 3 . . . . 131, 132, 140
          (1) 84
          (2) 83, 84, 104, 121, 128
          (3) 84
                    (a), (b) 84
          (4) 83, 84, 120
          (5) 84
          (6) 83, 84, 118
          (7) 118
          (9) 115
   Art. 4 132

(1) 108
    (a) 109
    (b) 125
Art. 5 . . . . 86, 93, 131, 132
    (1)(1) 86
    (1)(3) 86
    (1)(4) 87, 133
Art. 7 . . . . 84, 85, 86, 93, 129, 131, 132, 140
    (4) 126, 129
Art. 8 81
    (3) 83, 114, 118
Art.. 10 (1)–(4) 93
    (2) 105
    (5) 88, 93, 96
    (10) 94
    (15) 87, 133
Recital 3 . . . . 83, 131
Recital 6 . . . . 81, 88, 132
Recital 9 93
Recital 10 92
Recital 11 134
Recital 14 . . . . 114, 118
Recital 19 84
Recital 20 . . . . 105, 110, 111, 114
Recital 21 . . . . 120, 122, 123
Recital 22 120
Recital 23 120

Directives

EC Software Directive 91/250
    s. 5 250
    s. 6 250
    Recital 27 213

Notices

Commission Notice OJ C 139/2921 (1962) 43, 102
Commission Notice OJ C 75/3 (1968) 43, 45, 46, 48
Commission Notice on Agreements of Minor Importance Doc.
    Com (96) 722 Final 46

OTHER LEGISLATION

GERMANY

Act Against Restraints of Competition (GWB)
s 20(1) 52
s 23(a) 135

NEW ZEALAND

Commerce Act
s 36 . . . . 217, 218
Part IV 218

UNITED KINGDOM

Broadcasting Act 1992 215

UNITED STATES

Antitrust Guidelines 136–139, **276–303**
s 3.4 137
s 4.1.2 137
s 4.2 137
s 5.4 138

Sherman Act 227

PART I

Introduction

1

General Introduction

EC Competition law in recent years has quite dramatically demonstrated its capacity to regulate the exercise of intellectual property rights (IPRs). In *Magill*,[1] the Court of Justice confirmed that the European Commission has the power to end an abusive refusal to licence by imposing a compulsory copyright license. In other recent cases, the Court of Justice has held that the competition rules in the Treaty may be used as the basis to prevent IPR owners from acquiring competitor firms with similar technology,[2] using aggressive discounting and pricing schemes,[3] and engaging in 'product bundling'.[4] Moreover, the European Commission has developed an array of block exemptions, including the new Technology Transfer Regulation,[5] which provide a detailed regulation of the clauses in intellectual property licensing agreements.[6]

These developments provide strong evidence that the rights of IPR owners are subject to a second tier of regulation provided by the competition rules of the Treaty. Yet IPR specialists have argued strenuously that IPR legislation and EC competition law should be viewed as of equal weight and status under EC law, or even that EC competition law should defer to IPR legislation in the interests of innovation.[7]

The purpose of this book is to provide a counterweight to such arguments by demonstrating how both under the Treaty and as a matter of economic policy, EC competition law provides a set of outer limits to the exploitation and licensing of intellectual property rights by IPR owners

---

1 *RTE* v. *Commission* [1995] EC I–743.
2 See e.g. *Tetra Pak Rausing SA* v. *Commission (Tetra Pak I)* [1990] ECR II–309.
3 See e.g. *Tetra Pak II* [1997] 4 CMLR 662.
4 Ibid. See also *Hilti AG* v. *Commission* [1991] ECR II–1439.
5 Reg. 240/96.
6 Furthermore, the R&D regulation and the Joint Venture Guidelines make it plain that the choices of intellectual property rightholders to exploit their rights by resort to joint ventures are also curbed and constrained by EC Competition Law.
7 See e.g. I. Govaere, *The Use and Abuse of Intellectual Property Rights in EC Law* (Sweet & Maxwell, 1996). See too Advocate Gulman's argument in *RTE* v. *Commission* op. cit. n. 1; A. Reindl, 'Intellectual Property and Intra-Community Trade' [1996] *Fordham Corp. Law Inst.* 453.

which can override their entitlements under IPR legislation. It shows how in defining the borderline between permitted and prohibited conduct by IPR owners, the case-law of the Community Courts and the decisions of the Commission create a framework of rules which regulates the exercise of IPRs. The book argues that the key to understanding the way the framework established by the cases affects IPRs is to appreciate how the exercise of IPRs is viewed within the logic of EC competition law.

By identifying the existing ground rules in EC competition law which are relevant for its regulation of IPRs, and the basis upon which they are generated, the book provides a useful template of the rules of EC competition law. It will of course require some adaptation to the different types of IPR as well as to new technologies supported by intellectual property protection not yet regulated by EC competition law in the form of block exemptions, such as computer programs[8] and telecommunications.[9]

The book has a second aim, to assess the 'interface' between EC competition law and IPRs in the light of the established criteria of modern competition policies relating to IPRs. It makes use, in particular, of the criterion that the rules of EC competition policy should be designed and applied to minimize its interference with the process of IPR exploitation and the incentives it offers to investment in innovation while pursuing competition policy objectives. By assessing the role of competition policy in the light of this criterion, the book will provide a basis for new legal arguments and hopefully make a contribution to legal and regulatory reform. The field of EC competition law is at present undergoing a process of far-reaching re-evaluation. In the field of vertical restraints in distribution,[10] basic assumptions are being questioned. Moreover, the Commission is looking at issues raised by the application of the rules in Articles 85 and 86 to new technologies in telecommunications and information software.[11]

This study does not attempt to cover the entire field of EC competition law and IPRs. Instead, it concentrates upon two main areas of interest: Article 85 and licensing agreements (Part II); and Article 86 and the regulation of product markets (Part III). Before looking at these two

---

[8] See e.g. J. Derbyshire, 'Computer Programs, and Competition Policy' [1994] 9, *EIPR* 374; J. Hendricks, 'The Information Technology Revolution: The Next Phase' [1995] *Fordham Corp. Law Inst.* 549.

[9] See e.g. H. Ungerer, 'EU Competition Law in the Telecommunications, Media and Information Technology Area' [1995] *Fordham Corp. Law Inst.* 465; T. Ramsay, 'The EU Commission's Use of the Competition Rules in the Field of Telecommunications: A Delicate Balancing Act' [1995] *Fordham Corp. Law Inst.* 561.

[10] See e.g. EC Commission's Green Paper on Vertical Restraints in EU Competition Policy, Com. (96) 721.

[11] See *XXVIth Report on Competition Policy* (1996).

fields, it is necessary to examine in greater detail the relationship between competition policy and IPRs in two contexts: the economic policy context (next section) and in the context of the EC Treaty (Chapter 2).

Many, if not most, legal systems today monitor the exercise of IPRs within the framework of their competition policies.[12] Even though the exercise of IPRs is already extensively regulated by IPR legislation,[13] an extra tier of regulation is added by competition law to ensure that the grant of exclusivity by IPR legislation is not misused by being incorporated into cartels and market sharing arrangements or monopolistic practices which deny access to markets.

In this second tier of regulation, competition authorities attempt to balance the aim of preserving competition on markets with the aim of IPR legislation to reward investment in innovation. There were periods in the past, in both the USA[14] and the EC,[15] when assumptions that the exclusivity of an IPR itself created the market power of a monopoly and that all IPR licences allowed collaboration between competitors, led to judicial and administrative competition rules which paid inadequate attention to their effects upon investment in R&D and innovation.

The evidence has now accumulated, however, that the grant of an exclusive right for a limited period of time to the inventor to exploit the invention is a necessary incentive for investment in R&D, innovation, and imitation.[16] Whilst not a guarantee, it offers the prospects of a reward to the inventor because it reduces the risk that free riders can

---

[12] See e.g. *OECD Report on Competition Policy and Intellectual Property Rights* (Paris, 1989). Hereinafter cited as 'OECD Report'.

[13] Such legislation regulates by limiting the period of exclusivity, applying compulsory licences for non-use, etc. See e.g. W. Cornish, *Intellectual Property: Patents, Copyright, Trade Marks and Allied Rights* (Sweet & Maxwell, 3rd edn; 1996).

[14] See e.g. Kaplow, 'The Patent/Antitrust Intersection: A Reappraisal [1983–4] *Harvard Law Review* 1813–32.

[15] See e.g. H. Johannes, 'Technology Transfer under EEC Law—Europe between the Divergent Opinions of the Past and a New Administration: A Comparative Law Approach' [1982] *Fordham Corp. Law Inst.* 65.

[16] See e.g. C. Taylor and Silberstone, *The Economic Impact of the Patent System* (Cambridge, 1984) at p. 198. There are other methods of protecting such investment (see e.g. F. M. Scherer, *Industrial Market Structure and Economic Performance* (2nd. edn. 1980) at pp. 444–7 who points out that some firms rely on imitation lags, oligopolitic markets, and methods of differentiation to secure protection from rivals) but economists have found that IPRs are particularly useful for most firms in certain sectors of industry, such as pharmaceuticals and engineering (see e.g. Taylor and Silberstone above), and to small and medium sized firms in most sectors of industry. (See Scherer above.)

devalue the investment in R&D and provides an opportunity for the IPR owner to recoup investments at a higher level than would have been the case in a fully competitive market. IPR licensing helps by offering an opportunity for exploitation in situations where the inventor has insufficient means to exploit the invention itself.[17]

Moreover, IPRs are now recognized as an asset to trade.[18] By encouraging investment in R&D and innovation,[19] they stimulate economic growth and increased competitiveness.[20] In recent years, many of the specific industries whose development is currently crucial to economic growth and competitiveness in world trade—information technology, telecommunications, biotechnology, and new materials—have been shown to be dependent on IPR protection for investment.[21]

Nevertheless, the need for adequate incentives for innovation cannot justify a complete immunity to IPRs from the rules designed to protect effective competition in markets. While there is no longer an assumption of an inherent conflict between the two policies, certain forms of exercise of IPRs, including certain types of licensing agreements, entail real risks to competition. Indeed, many of the practices which help to stimulate investment are also used as devices to engage in anti-competitive conduct.

For example, it is true that the exclusive rights granted to IPRs in the form of patents, copyright, design rights, and particularly trade marks are not necessarily monopolies. They do not confer market power as long as there are adequate substitutes for the protected product or process.[22] There are situations, however, where an IPR owner does possess real market power and in such a case, if the licensor attempts to extend that power by using an IPR, for example by 'tying-in' the sale of non-patented products to patented products or preventing third parties from entering product markets which are dependent upon that IPR, this creates a competition concern.

Similarly, most licensing arrangements today are viewed as beneficial to competition, particularly where the licensee and licensors are not existing competitors. They introduce a new competitor into the market and they help to diffuse the invention throughout the economy. Nevertheless, a licensing agreement can be used to conceal a market sharing arrangement or be incorporated in a scheme to prevent new technologies from entering a market.

---

[17] See e.g. F. J. Contractor, 'Technology Licensing Practices in U.S. Companies: Corporate and Public Policy Implications' [1983] *Col. Jnl. Of World Business* 80.

[18] See e.g. I. Govaere, *The Use and Abuse of Intellectual Property Rights in EC Law* (Sweet & Maxwell, 1996) at p. 2.

[19] See e.g. J. Schmookler, *Invention and Economic Growth* (1996) 206.   [20] Id.

[21] See e.g. *Competition Policy and Intellectual Property Rights* (OECD, 1989).

[22] See e.g. *Deutsche Grammophon Gesellschaft mbH* v. *Metro-SB-Grossmarkte GMbH & Co.* [1971] ECR 487.

The task for competition policy today, therefore, is to ensure that it uses an appropriate balancing mechanism in drawing a line between the two interests. The rules of competition policy must not be designed so tightly in the effort to protect effective competition in markets, that they unnecessarily reduce the incentives to invest in R&D.[23] It is in this policy context that the relationship between EC competition law and IPRs can be evaluated.

[23] See e.g. OECD Report at p. 13.

2

The Relationship between Intellectual Property Rights and Competition Law under the Treaty

2.1 INTRODUCTION

Under EC law, the way the balance is struck between competition law and intellectual property rights (IPRs) has been shaped by the structure of the EC Treaty and the interpretation it has been given by the Community Courts and the European Commission. Article 2 of the Treaty provides that: 'The Community shall have as its task, by establishing a Common market ... and by implementing the Common policies or activities referred to in Articles 3 and 3a, to promote throughout the Community a harmonious and balanced development of economic activities.' Article 3(g) of the Treaty requires the institution of a system to ensure that competition in the internal market is not distorted. Articles 85 and 86 are then set out as the two main means of achieving this goal.[1]

Article 85 regulates 'all agreements between undertakings which have the object or effect of preventing, restricting or distorting competition'. IPR licensing agreements fall within its scope. Article 86 regulates unilateral action by undertakings, prohibiting abuses of a dominant position. This can apply to various forms of exercise of an IPR by its owner.

The Treaty ensures that the reconciliation between IPR legislation, which is predominantly national legislation,[2] and EC competition law occurs within the framework of Articles 85 and 86. The Court has regularly reaffirmed that the exercise of intellectual property rights must in principle be compatible with the rules of competition (Articles 85 and 86) as well as the rules of free movement of goods (Articles 30–6).[3] In the case of the rules concerning the free movement of goods, the Treaty offers a guide to the appropriate balancing mechanism in Article 36 which provides that 'the protection of industrial and commercial property' can justify a prohibition on imports or exports between member

---

[1] A merger control regulation was added to the armoury of competition policy measures in 1989. Since this is a paperback version of the original book the pre-Amsterdam Treaty numbering system will perforce, continue to be used, eg Art 85 is now 81 and 86 is now 82.

[2] IPR legislation is still predominantly national, although Community legislation and the harmonization process is slowly building towards a Community legislative framework for IPRS.

[3] *Parke Davis* v. *Probel* [1968] ECR 55; *Deutsche Grammophon* [1974] ECR 1147.

states as long as they are not 'a means of arbitrary discrimination or a disguised restriction on trade'.[4]

In the case of Articles 85 and 86, the Treaty contains no comparable provision. Yet the Court of Justice has regularly given the reassurance to IPR owners that the Treaty rules will not interfere with the 'normal exercise' of IPR rights.[5] Thus, in *Maxicar*, the Court stated that 'the mere fact of securing the benefit of an exclusive right granted by law, the effect of which is to enable the manufacture and sale of protected products by unauthorised third parties to be prevented, cannot be regarded as an abusive method of eliminating competition'.[6] In *Volvo,* the Court also pointed out that to be abusive some 'additional factor' was required in addition to the elimination of competition from other manufacturers in respect of the protected product since that corresponds to the substance of the protected right.[7] Further, in *Magill*, the Court held that 'exceptional circumstances' must be found before the exercise of an IPR can be held to be contrary to the Articles of the Treaty.[8]

The argument has been made that because the Court has tended to decide these issues on a case by case basis, it is difficult to discern the framework the Court uses to distinguish between the permitted and prohibited exercise of IPRs.[9] Moreover, it is also claimed that the function of IPRs should figure prominently in the demarcation even to the point of requiring the competition rules to defer to the logic of reward and incentive built into the IPR legislation.[10]

A close reading of the Community Court's decisions, however, suggests neither assertion is tenable. The Court's judgments do suggest that it uses a framework to define the borderline between permitted and prohibited exercise of IPRs based on the competition rules of the Treaty and the Court has long maintained that the prohibitions in Articles 85 and 86 are unyielding restrictions upon the exercise of intellectual property rights.[11] The Court has regularly held that the exercise of IPRs must defer to the competition rules in cases where the two are in conflict.

The foundations for the current form of reconciliation between IPRs and the competition rules were established in the early case of *Consten*

---

4 This in turn has led to a body of case-law in which doctrines such as 'consent', 'exhaustion', and 'discrimination' provide ground rules drawn with reference to the specific functions of the IPRs as well as the board policy of Art. 30. See e.g. *Merck* v. *Prime Crown* [1997] 1 CMLR, 83; see I. Govaere op. cit. at ch. 4.

5 *Parke Davis* v. *Probel* [1968] ECR 55; *Deutsche Grammophon* [1974] ECR 1147.

6 *CICRA et Maxicar* v. *Renault* [1988] ECR 299.

7 *Volvo* v. *Veng (UK) Ltd.* [1988] ECR 6211 para. 15.

8 *RTE* v. *Commission* [1995] ECR I–743.

9 See e.g. I. Govaere op. cit. at p. 104.

10 See Sources at n. 7 in Ch. 1 *supra*. Govaere alone argues for a redefinition of the function of IPRs to enable it to be reconciled with Arts. 85 and 86 (at p. 69).

11 See e.g. *Grundig* v. *Commission* [1966] ECR 99; *Parke Davis* v. *Probel* [1968] ECR 55.

Grundig.[12] In *Grundig*, a trade mark was used to reinforce a sole distribution agreement between a German manufacturer, Grundig, and a French distributor, Consten. As part of that agreement, Consten was allowed to register the Grundig trade mark, GINT, in France. When it was discovered that another French distributor, UNEF, had bought Grundig appliances in Germany and tried to sell them in France, Consten used its trade mark to stop the infringing exports. In response to UNEF's complaint, the Commission investigated and ordered Consten to stop its exercise of the trade mark licence. On appeal, the ECJ upheld the Commission's decision. To do otherwise, it said, would make the prohibition under Article 85 meaningless; the exercise of an intellectual property right could not be used to frustrate the rules of competition law.[13] The Court found that neither Article 36 nor Article 222 could operate to exclude 'any influence whatever of Community law on the exercise of national intellectual property rights'.

The Court was concerned to ensure that the enforcement of Article 85 would not interfere with the grant of the intellectual property right by the member state. It emphasized that 'the injunction . . . does not affect the grant of those rights but only limits their exercise to the extent necessary to give effect to the prohibition under Article 85(1)'.[14]

The Court clearly indicated, however, that if an IPR was linked to an agreement which was contrary to Article 85, then the Commission could prohibit this form of exercise. As the Court pointed out, it was the agreement which enabled Consten to register the trade mark in the first place and 'the prohibition would be ineffective if Consten could continue to use the trade-mark to achieve the same object as that pursued by the [unlawful] agreement'.[15]

In *Parke Davis* v. *Probel*,[16] this distinction between grant and exercise was reaffirmed. The issue in the case was whether Articles 85 and 86 would limit the use of a patent to prevent the importation of an antibiotic product into Holland from Italy where the product had been manufactured without the consent of the Dutch patentee. The Court ruled that under those Treaty provisions,[17] the patent could be used to block the import. Again it referred to the distinction between grant and exercise. The patent taken by itself was merely the expression of a legal status granted by a member state to products under certain conditions. The Court used the expression the 'existence' of the grant of rights by a member state to the holder of a patent and stated that this was not affected by the prohibitions contained in Articles 85(1) and 86 of the

---

[12] *Consten Grundig* v. *Commission* [1966] ECR 299.   [13] Ibid. at p. 346.
[14] Ibid. at p. 345.   [15] Ibid. at p. 345.   [16] [1968] ECR 55.
[17] The Court did not deal with the issue of Arts. 30–6.

Treaty; it then went on to add that the 'exercise' of such rights cannot of itself fall either under Article 85(1), in the absence of any agreement, decision or concerted practice prohibited by this provision, or under Article 86, in the absence of any abuse of a dominant position.[18]

At this stage, the Court could be seen to have marked out three legal categories in the interface between EC competition law and IPRs.[19] The first category, 'existence', was the authority of member states to determine the conditions for granting IPRs. This was beyond the reach of Articles 85 and 86. The second category 'permitted forms of exercise' of IPRs, was defined by a combination of the powers granted by IPR legislation and the limits imposed by Articles 85 and 86 (and 36). The third category, 'prohibited forms of exercise' of IPRs, was defined by the prohibitions in Articles 85 and 86 (and 36). This book limits itself to the treatment of these categories under Articles 85 and 86.

2.2 GRANT AND 'EXISTENCE'

The early judgments of the ECJ clearly indicated that there was no competition law interest in regulating the conditions upon which the member states conferred the legal status of IPRs. Nor did it have any role to play in the harmonization of IPRs in the common market. This position was steadily maintained by the Court over the years.[20] By the time of *Magill*, the Court felt that it was so well established that the point could be stated without reference to earlier authority: 'in the absence of Community standardisation or harmonisation of laws, determination of the conditions and procedures for granting protection of an intellectual property right is a matter for national rules'.[21]

In later years assertions were made that the concept of the 'existence' of the IPR could be widened beyond the concept of the conditions which had to be fulfilled to qualify for the grant to extend to the exercise of the legal prerogatives which were the entitlement of the IPR owner. These included the claims that the 'existence' should be expanded to include the 'essential function' or 'specific subject matter' of the intellectual right.[22] These claims appeared to be unwarranted attempts to use the

---

[18] Since the act was that of the patentee alone Art. 85(1) was not applicable. Moreover, since the act was the normal use of the IPR it could not be treated as an abuse of a dominant position under Art. 86. It was only if the use of the patent were for another purpose it could be curbed by Art. 86 as an abuse.

[19] See e.g. Govaere op. cit. at p. 65. See too chs. 4 and 6 re Art. 36.

[20] See e.g. *Keurkoop* v. *Nancy Kean Gifts* [1982] ECR 2653; *Volvo* v. *Veng (UK) Ltd.* [1988] ECR 6211.

[21] *RTE* v. *Commission* [1995] ECR I–743 at para. 49.

[22] See discussion by AG Gulman in *RTE* v. *Commission* [1991] ECR II–485.

concepts of 'existence', which is effectively only the basis for the grant, and 'permitted exercise' interchangeably under Article 85, a confusion which appears to have also occurred in the context of Article 36.[23]

2.3 PERMITTED AND PROHIBITED EXERCISE OF INTELLECTUAL PROPERTY RIGHTS

The earlier Competition law cases also established that the rules in Articles 85 and 86 created a set of outer limits to the lawful exercise of IPRs. In *Consten Grundig*, the Court was unwilling to allow the exercise of the trade mark to frustrate the rules of competition law.[24] In *Parke Davis*, the Court upheld the entitlement to exercise the patent but only because it was not contrary to rules on competition law.[25]

2.3.1 Normal Exercise

The Court's frequent statement that the 'normal exercise' of the IPR was not caught by either Article 85 or 86, hinted at a core of lawful exploitation rights for IPRs under the rules of competition law.[26] Thus, in *Parke Davis*, the Court stated that the exercise of the rights arising under the patent in accordance with the legislation of a member state does not *of itself* constitute an infringement of the rules on competition laid down in the Treaty.[27] In *Deutsche Grammophon*,[28] the Court stated that, in principle, the owner of an intellectual property right does not occupy a dominant position merely by exercising his exclusive right to distribute the protected articles.[29] In *Volvo*[30] the Court of Justice went so far as to declare that a refusal to grant an intellectual property right licence cannot in itself constitute an abuse of a dominant position under Article 86 of the Treaty.

These statements by the Court were meant in the first place to reassure that the exclusivity of an IPR and its exercise are not in themselves regarded as anti-competitive despite the prohibitions on restrictions and distortion of competition in Articles 85 and 86. They were designed to suggest a basis of accommodation between the statutory grant of

[23] *Centrafarm* v. *Sterling Drug* [1974] ECR 1147; see F.-K. Beier, 'Industrial Property and the Free Movement of Goods in the Internal Market' [1990] *IIC* 131.

[24] Ibid. at p. 346.   [25] [1968] ECR 55.

[26] The Court prefaced that remark by saying that this was 'for similar reasons' to the effect of Art. 36 on Art. 30, i.e. that Art. 36 in its first sentence presupposed that the normal exercise of IPRs could be justified.

[27] [1968] ECR 55. The Court has held this to be true of trade marks (*EMI* v. *CBS (UK) Ltd.* [1976] ECR 811 at para. 26) and design rights (*Keurkoop* v. *Nancy Kean Gifts* [1983] ECR at para. 27.   [28] *Deutsche Grammophon* v. *Metro* [1971] ECR 487.

[29] Ibid. at para. 16.   [30] *AB Volvo* v. *Erik Veng (UK) Ltd.* [1988] ECR 6211.

exclusivity which is literally a restriction of competition in pursuit of a wider objective and the strictures of Article 85 which prohibits agreements which prevent, restrict or distort competition, and Article 86 which prohibits dominant undertakings from weakening the competitive structure in markets. In themselves, they do not provide a springboard for asserting that the function of the IPR can offer protection against the prohibitions of Articles 85 and 86, or a basis for narrowing the scope of the Treaty provisions. They are essentially a statement of the residual area of exercise permitted under the rules of EC competition law.

The basis for the test of permitted exercise of IPRs under Article 86 was spelt out by the Court in *Hoffman La Roche*.[31] Assuming that it is in accordance with Article 36, 'the exercise of a trade mark right is ... not contrary to Article 86 of the treaty on the sole ground that it is the act of an undertaking occupying a dominant position on the market if the trade mark right has not been used as an instrument for the abuse of such a position'.[32]

Hence, the mere exercise of the exclusive right is not automatically abusive. To be unlawful the exercise of the IPR must be linked in some way to a commercial practice which is itself unlawful under Articles 85 and 86. As the Court described it in *Hoffman La Roche*, an IPR must be used as an 'instrument of abuse' of a dominant position to be unlawful under Article 86.[33]

Similarly, under Article 85, before an IPR licence, even an exclusive licence, is unlawful, it must 'serve to give effect to', or 'be the means of' an agreement, decision or concerted practice which itself is prohibited as a restriction of competition under that Article 85.[34]

It is thus only in unusual circumstances that the exercise of an IPR will be limited by Articles 85 and 86. However, if the exercise of the IPR is associated with a commercial practice which is unlawful under Articles 85 and 86, it cannot be saved by the fact that it is lawful under national law.[35]

2.3.2 A Functional Test for Permitted Exercise?

It is true that certain statements made by the Court in competition cases have offered support for the view that the delineation between permitted and protected exercise should be made by reference to the specific function of the individual IPR.

---

[31] [1978] ECR 1139.   [32] Ibid. at para. 16.

[33] *Hoffman La Roche* [1978] ECR 1139 at para. 16. This also implicitly indicates that, even if an act is lawful under Art. 36, it may nevertheless be unlawful under Art. 86.

[34] *Coditel II* [1982] ECR 3381 at para. 14.

[35] See *Hoffman La Roche* v. *Commission* [1978] ECR 1139.

Thus in *Volvo* the Court stated that: 'the right of the proprietor of a protected design to prevent third parties from manufacturing and selling and importing, without his consent, products incorporating the design constitutes the very subject-matter of his exclusive right'. It followed that an obligation imposed on the proprietor of an intellectual property right, in this case a protected design, to grant a licence would constitute a deprivation of 'the substance of his exclusive right, and that a refusal to grant such a license cannot in itself constitute an abuse of a dominant position'.[36]

This statement, taken in isolation, might suggest that the Court accepts that there is a core of IPR exploitation rights defined by reference to the substance or specific subject-matter which is protected from the rules of competition law. It is reminiscent of the assertions made about the protective scope of specific subject-matter or essential function concepts under Article 36.[37] The difficulty with this interpretation is its selectivity; it does not give sufficient weight to the contradictory statements by the Court in the same judgments.

For example in *Volvo*, whilst the above statement appeared on its own to suggest an unqualified test of permitted exercise, the Court went on to add in the very next paragraph, the following qualifications:

It must however be noted that the exercise of an exclusive right by the proprietor of a registered design in respect of car body panels may be prohibited by Article 86 if it involves . . . certain abusive conduct such as the arbitrary refusal to supply spare parts to independent repairers, the fixing of prices for spare parts at an unfair level or a decision no longer to produce spare parts for a particular model even though many cars of that model are still in circulation . . .[38]

The significance of these qualifications is that they refer to examples of specific abuse under Article 86[39] and imply limits to the scope of exclusive exploitation in secondary markets, such as maintenance markets. They also imply limits to the concept implicit in IPR legislation of charging what the market will bear for a product incorporating an exclusive IPR.

Unfortunately, at the time of the decision, these qualifications were not interpreted as qualifications of the rights of normal exercise of the IPR effectively curbing their specific subject-matter or substance.[40]

---

[36] *Volvo* v. *Veng Ltd.* [1988] ECR 6211, para. 8.

[37] The decision appeared consistent with the law under Art. 36 which places great emphasis upon the rightholder's consent to the manufacture or marketing of the protected goods.   [38] Op. cit. n. 36 para. 9.

[39] The first is an abuse under Art. 86(b) or (c); the second is an abuse under Art. 86(a); the third is an abuse under Art. 86(d).

[40] See e.g. Friden (1989): 'It is submitted that one should not read too much into them . . . the court probably felt obliged, after having given an example of what was not abusive conduct, to give a few examples of what would be considered as abusive'. 'Recent Developments in EEC Intellectual Property Law: The Distinction Between Existence and Exercise Revisited' [1989] *CMLRev.* 193. At p. 210.

Instead, the general statements of principle in the previous paragraph were given excessive weight, particularly in the light of the decision of the Court that the IPR could be enforced in an infringement proceeding. The case was thought by many to signal recognition of the specific functions of IPR as protected against the prohibitions of the rules of competition law even in secondary markets.[41]

In *Magill*,[42] however, the Court made it clear that the exceptions mentioned in *Volvo* were to be given considerable weight. It acknowledged that a refusal to grant a licence, even by an undertaking in a dominant position, cannot in itself constitute an abuse, adding however that the exercise of the exclusive right by the proprietor may in exceptional circumstances involve abusive conduct.[43] It then went on to hold that where the refusal of the TV companies to license Magill prevented him from introducing a new product for which there was a potential demand and which was not provided by them, this was an abuse under Article 86(b) where no objective justification was offered by the TV companies.[44]

The *Magill* judgment confirmed that the Court regarded the specific abuses in Article 86 as outer limits to the exercise of IPRs in the sense that if an IPR was used as an instrument of such an abuse by a dominant firm,[45] then the fact that it was lawful under national law was not an obstacle to 'review in relation to Article 86 of the Treaty'.[46] The ground rules established in the earlier case-law were reiterated. The concept of normal exploitation of IPRs which was built into the legislative policy for each type of IPR could not be used to override the competition rules.

In *Consten Grundig*,[47] Advocate General Roemer attempted to define the relationship between Article 85 and the trade mark in terms of whether or not the Commission's injunction 'interfered with the function of the trade mark', which he defined as guaranteeing the origin of the product to the consumer. The Court of Justice refused to accept that conceptual approach to the reconciliation between IPRs and the competition rules in the Treaty. It stated that the concept of specific function could not provide an immunity from unwarrantable interference when its exercise was contrary to Article 85.

In *Magill*, Advocate General Gulman also attempted to define an irreducible minimum level of protection for IPRs against the strictures of competition law. He conceded that the specific subject-matter was

---

41 See e.g. opinion of AG Gulman in *RTE* v. *Commission* [1995] ECR I–743 at para. 111.
42 *RTE* v. *Commission* [1995] ECR I–743.   43 Ibid. at paras. 49–50.
44 Ibid. at paras. 54–5.
45 In *Hoffman La Roche*, the Court said that 'the exercise of an IPR could be a violation of Article 86 when a dominant undertaking uses its IPR as an instrument for the abuse of such a position'. [1978] ECR 1139.   46 Ibid. at para. 48.
47 [1966] ECR 299 at 366.

subject to regulation by Article 86, but he maintained that the 'essential function' of the IPR should be treated as equivalent to the 'existence' of the IPR and not subject to Article 86.[48] The Court of Justice, however, showed no interest in a test of the 'function' of the IPR as the decisive criterion for 'exceptional circumstances'. As in the earlier cases of *Grundig* and *Parke Davis*, it preferred the line to be drawn by the competition rules.[49]

2.4 THE OBJECTIVES OF THE RULES ON COMPETITION IN THE TREATY

Since Articles 85 and 86 provide a framework for the regulation of IPRs, a closer look at their objectives is necessary to understand how they can be used to generate rules limiting the exploitation of IPRs. EC competition policy differs from other competition law systems, such as the USA[50] and Japan,[51] largely because of the influence of the Treaty in infusing political economic objectives into EC competition policy.

The starting-point for understanding the objectives of EC competition law is the position of the competition rules in the EU Treaty. As we have seen, 'a system ensuring that competition in the internal market shall not be distorted',[52] Article 3(g), is listed as one of the activities of the Community to promote the purposes of Article 2.

This 'system' has been interpreted to have three distinct objectives under the Treaty. The first is the maintenance of 'effective competition'. The second is the application of the principle of fair competition, most particularly in the form of special protections for small and medium sized businesses. The third is the use of the rules of competition to help integrate the individual national markets of the member states into a single market. Each objective has had an effect on the interpretation of Articles 85 and 86 which in turn has influenced the interface between EC competition law and IPRs.

2.5 EFFECTIVE COMPETITION

In referring to the goal of Articles 85 and 86 under the Treaty as 'the maintenance of effective competition within the common market' in

---

[48] In this he drew some assistance from the Court of First Instance which had made reference to the essential function of the IPR as a desiteratum, but the CFI had qualified its remarks by defining the essential function as itself being subject to the rules in the Treaty.

[49] [1995] ECR I–743 at para. 48.   [50] See e.g. OECD Report at para. 42.

[51] OECD Report at p. 36.

[52] Other 'activities' in Art. 3 appear to vie for constitutional parity with Art. 3(g). For example, Art. 3(m) calls for the promotion of research and technical development; Art. 3(j) insists that the activities must include a strengthening of the competitiveness of Community. Both arguably could be used as indirect treaty support for IPRs.

Continental Can,[53] the Court had in mind two separate but related concepts. The first was the view that markets should have a competitive structure. Thus in *Continental Can,* the Court stated that undistorted competition under what is now Article 3(g) requires the limitation of practices which affect consumers 'through their impact on an effective competition structure'.[54]

The goal of an effective competitive structure entails acceptance of the economists' paradigm that if the structure of a market is competitive, this will affect the conduct of companies on that market as well as their economic performance.[55] Economists, particularly, those of the Chicago school,[56] have extensively criticized the structure/conduct/performance paradigm, but these criticisms have not persuaded the Community Courts to abandon their acceptance of the structural goal for competition policy.

The maintenance of effective competition also embodies a concept of a particular process of competition, i.e., the competition rules are designed to regulate the forces of supply and demand on markets to preserve a process of 'workable competition'. As the Court of Justice said in *Metro v. Commission:*[57] '[t]he requirement contained in Article 3 and 85 of the EEC Treaty that competition shall not be distorted implies the existence on the market of workable competition'.

The objective of 'workable competition', although not defined in the Treaty, is generally taken to refer to a degree of competition which, whilst not being 'perfect', embodying all of the assumptions of the economists' textbook, is nevertheless able to achieve the three main effects of a competitive economy. The first effect is 'allocative efficiency', which presupposes that the price mechanism will ensure that producers will produce the products that consumers want. This is an important feature of the 'invisible hand' of the market at work. The second is 'productive efficiency' which presupposes that producers will produce at near optimum costs because the competition from other producers will drive down prices close to costs. The third effect, somewhat more contentiously, is that workable competition will also produce 'innovative efficiency'. The idea is that producers will respond to the pressures of competition by continuously seeking to innovate as well as to examine means of lowering productive costs using existing levels of technology.

The concept that fierce competition breeds innovation has been challenged by economists arguing the need for a more dynamic view of

---

[53] [1973] ECR 215.   [54] Ibid. at p. 245.

[55] See e.g. Scherer and Ross, *Industrial Market Structure and Economic Performance* (3rd edn., 1990) chs. 3 and 4.

[56] See e.g. Landes and Posner, 'Market Power in Antitrust Cases', 94 *Harv. Law Rev.* 937.   [57] [1977] ECR 1875.

competition. Schumpeter[58] for example has suggested that innovation is better achieved in conditions of monopoly because that condition provides the best profit incentive for investments in R&D and high rewards for innovation will encourage other competitors to attempt to match innovative efforts. A more common distinction is that between the short term and static model of micro-economic markets and the long term, dynamic efficiency effects on innovation of IPRs.[59] Moreover, in recent years, the costs of research, particularly high technology research, seem to require a scale of capital that presupposes either large enterprise or co-operation between enterprises rather than atomistic competition. Furthermore, the concept of scale of operation has also been suggested as an important element of competitiveness in global competition, leading to cries for 'Eurochampions' from several quarters.[60] However, EC competition law has resisted weakening its concept of workable competition to embrace either Schumpeterian models of monopoly,[61] or the value of size for its own sake. It remains a belief that workable competition will provide the breeding ground for innovation and competitiveness. As the Commission stated in its *XXVIth Report on Competition Policy*:

The Commission does not believe that [globalization] calls for less strict application of the competition rules. Its experience, through its decision making practice in all the areas covered by competition policy, shows that competition-mindedness and efficiency required to be an effective competitor internationally are acquired through competition between firms on domestic markets.[62]

Since workable competition presupposes that the pricing mechanism must be in good working order, competition policy is aimed at preventing any pair or group of firms from controlling output and prices by co-ordinating their activities to establish cartels or other market sharing arrangements. Competition policy also attempts to maintain effective competition structures by preserving access to markets by preventing abuses of market power by firms in dominant or near-monopoly positions and by preventing mergers or joint ventures which will result in a market structure which is too concentrated to allow workable competition to exist.

These concerns to protect workable competition and competitive

---

[58] See e.g. J. Schumpeter, *Capitalism, Socialism and Democracy* (George Allen & Unwin, 1976).   [59] See e.g. OECD Report.

[60] See e.g. White Paper on Growth, Competitiveness, Employment [1993] *Bulletin of the EC* Supp. 6/93.

[61] Insofar as EC competition law accepts that the normal exercise of IPRs under national legislation is acceptable under Arts. 85 and 86, it might be said to be accepting a limited Schumpeterian view built into IPR legislation.

[62] *XXVIth Report on Competition Policy* (1996) Brussels 1997 SEC(97) 628 Final at p.5.

market structures have led to a concept of abuse of power which has been widened to include conduct which threatens to eliminate competitors in primary and secondary, particularly, downstream markets, even if the market power is only present in the primary market, a result with profound implications for IPRs.

The Court has proceeded on the theory that the Treaty requires a protection of levels of competition in markets which have already been weakened by the presence of a dominant firm. As the Court put it in *Continental Can*, 'if Article 3(f) provides for the institution of a system ensuring that competition in the Common Market is not distorted, then it requires a fortiori that competition must not be eliminated'.[63]

Conduct aimed at driving existing competitors from markets or denying entry to competitors to markets, such as refusals to supply and license, discriminatory pricing, predatory pricing, and tie-ins in the form of product bundling,[64] has been held to be abusive, limiting certain forms of exploitation of exclusive IPRs in secondary markets.[65]

2.6 THE GOAL OF FAIR COMPETITION

The protective functions of Articles 85 and 86 have been reinforced by their second goal; the goal of ensuring that there is a degree of fairness on the market. The concept of undistorted competition has been interpreted to require a set of Marquis of Queensbury rules for competition so that smaller and medium sized firms in particular are not driven out or excluded from markets by illegitimate means, unrelated to business efficiency or innovation. This applies particularly to market dominance, but it is also relevant to cartels and market sharing agreements.[66]

The inclusion of this goal was first suggested in *United Brands* when the Court found the decision of United Brands to stop dealing with a long-term distributor abusive because it was an excessive or 'disproportionate' penalty for the actions of the small distributor's minor transgressions. The Court held that the refusal to continue to sell to the distributor amounted 'to a serious interference with the independence of small and medium-sized firms in their commercial relations with the undertaking in a dominant position'. The Court objected to the use of excessive force because such conduct could have a 'serious adverse effect on competition . . . by allowing only firms dependent upon the dominant undertaking to stay in business'.[67]

---

[63] *Continental Can* v. *Commission* [1973] ECR 215 at para. 24.
[64] See *Michelin* v. *Commission* [1983] ECR 3461 at para. 70.   [65] See Part III.
[66] See e.g. *Ninth Report on Competition Policy* [1979] Luxembourg at pp. 9–10.
[67] [1978] ECR 207.

The case introduced into EC competition law the general principles of 'proportionality' and 'dependence'. Thus, where a dominant undertaking has dealings with a dependent customer, it must be 'proportionate' in its treatment, i.e. it must not behave unreasonably or unfairly, even where the dominant undertaking is not actually operating in the secondary market. Secondly, the concern of the Court with the need to preserve the independence of small and medium sized firms in their dealings with dominant undertakings incorporates an assumption that the damage to the individual competitor is invariably accompanied by damage to the economy.[68]

The Commission and Court's concern with the protection of the independence of small and medium sized firms is also in evidence in the *AKZO* case, a case of predatory pricing by a Dutch chemical multinational against a small English competitor. The Commission's view was that 'Any unfair commercial practices on the part of the dominant undertaking intended to eliminate, discipline or deter smaller competitors would . . . fall within the scope of the prohibition of Article 86 if other conditions are fulfilled'.[69]

The Commission was, however, prepared to include within the notion of fairness, a concept of legitimate competition by performance:

A dominant firm is entitled to compete on the merits . . . The maintenance of a system of effective competition does, however, require that a small competitor be protected against conduct by a dominant undertaking designed to exclude it from the market not by virtue of greater efficiency or superior performance, but by abuse of power. If a dominant undertaking uses its market power to obtain a competitive advantage other than competition on the merits, and it has a substantial effect on the structure of competition, it is abusive.[70]

The concern with the protection and preservation of small and medium sized firms is part of a wider concept of EC competition law which is designed to encourage their development because of their potential to contribute to innovation and employment. In the *XXIInd Report on Competition Policy* (1992), the Commission referred to 'the active policy towards SMEs which the Commission has been pursuing for many years. . . . that SMEs are an engine for economic growth . . . and that the development of SMEs should be encouraged'.[71] In the competition context, this policy has translated into special treatment on state aid, a special

---

[68] The concept of dependence derives from German law but has been enacted into French law. It reflects a concern with the vulnerability of small firms to exploitation by dominant firms. See J. Kallaugher and J. Venit, 'Essential Facilities: A Comparative Law Approach [1994] *Fordham Corp. Law Inst.* 315 at pp. 325–30. See too D. Gerber, 'Law and the Abuse of Economic Power in Europe', 62 *Tulane Law Rev.* 57 (1987).

[69] *AKZO v. Commission* [1993] 5 CMLR 215.   [70] Id.

[71] Ibid. at para. 78.

exemption from Articles 85 and 86 under the Commission's Notice on Agreements of Minor Importance,[72] and favourable treatment to agreements to SMEs with low market shares in the block exemptions.[73]

2.7 THE GOAL OF INTEGRATION

The third goal of competition policy under the Treaty is that of assisting in the integration of the national markets of the member states into a common market.

The effect on Article 86 of the integration goal has been relatively undramatic. Article 86 in effect presupposes integration because it allows firms to grow internally through efficient performance to a position of dominance in a market.[74] It is only after an undertaking has achieved dominance that it is regulated closely. However, in the definition of abusive conduct, Article 86 is influenced by the integration principle to the extent that it finds certain forms of geographic, or interstate, price discrimination abusive which might on purely economic criteria be of less concern.[75]

The effect of the integration goal on the interpretation of Article 85 has been more fundamental. The Court of Justice in *Grundig*[76] interpreted the objectives of Article 85 to include the prohibition of market partitioning agreements in addition to the prohibitions listed in Article 85. Faced with a sole distribution agreement granted by a German supplier to a French distributor, combined with an exclusive trade mark right, the Court held that the infringement of Article 85(1) consisted of the attempt by the supplier and distributor to 'isolate the French market for Grundig products and maintain ... artificially, for products of a very well known brand, separate national markets within the community'. This was prohibited under Article 85(1) as an attempt to distort competition in the common market and could not be exempted under Article 85(3):

An agreement between producer and distributor which might tend to restore the national divisions in trade between Member states might be such as to frustrate the most fundamental object of the Community. The Treaty, whose preamble and content aim at abolishing the barriers between States, and which in several provisions give evidence of a stern attitude with regard to their reappearance, could not allow undertakings to reconstruct such barriers. Article 85(1) is designed to pursue this aim, even in the case of agreements between undertakings placed at different levels of the economic process.[77]

---

[72] Id.   [73] Ibid. at para. 79.
[74] See e.g. Kauper, 'Article 86, Excessive Prices and Refusals to Deal' [1991] *Antitrust Law Journal* 441, at p. 443.   [75] See ch. 17.
[76] *Consten Grundig* v. *Commission* [1966] ECR 299.   [77] At p. 343.

In *Grundig*, the Court was concerned with three types of barriers to inter-state trade associated with the exclusive distribution agreement conferred on the French distributor: the first was the restriction on sales by the exclusive distributor directly into the territories of other distributors in other member states. The second was the contractual obligations placed on the exclusive distributors to prevent customers from engaging in parallel exports into the territories in other member states, i.e. the export bans. The third was the use of the exclusivity of the trade mark to reinforce the boundaries of the exclusive national territories by use of the infringement proceeding. Although there were strong arguments that the protection for Consten from the competition of other distributors in the Grundig distribution network provided a necessary economic incentive to Consten to invest in the distribution activity, the Court insisted that the costs of the barriers to integration overrode the procompetitive benefits of the arrangement. All these elements in the arrangement were held to be *per se* distortive of competition under Article 85(1) and *per se* not capable of qualifying for exemption under Article 85(3).

The applicability of this reasoning to IPR licences is all too evident. Where an exclusive licensing agreement is part of a wider network of parallel licences, there is always potential for competition between the licensees who have been allocated national territories for the same product or process. The nature of the IPR does not restrict the free movement of the goods made incorporating that right. Under EC law the right of free circulation attaches to goods as soon as they are placed on the market. Consequently, the licensees can engage in direct sales both actively by advertising or passively by responding to unsolicited orders. Moreover, the customer of licensees can engage in parallel trading, exporting or importing the licensed goods and services between the different national territories of the licensees. Insofar as this interpretation of Article 85 stresses the need to protect interstate trade, it insists on the preservation of intrabrand competition even to the point of deterring investment in licensing and the consequent spread in the manufacturing of the technology in new member states. The reconciliation of the integration policies of Article 85 with IPRs has to confront this dilemma in the short term: if it concentrates too heavily on protecting the bridges of trade between national markets it discourages the diffusion of manufacture and new technologies.[78]

In the longer term, as the common market becomes a single continental market, the integration objective will play a less important role in the application of Article 85 to licensing agreements. Until then, it has

---

[78] See e.g. H. Ullrich, 'Patents and Know how, Free Trade, Interenterprise, Cooperation and Competition within the Internal European Market' [1992] *IIC* 583.

resulted in a highly interventionist approach to regulation and creates a direct confrontation with the system of territorial protection which is necessary to convince licensees to accept the risks of investing in the manufacturing and distribution facilities necessary to exploit the licence.

2.8 NEGATIVE OR POSITIVE INTEGRATION

Finally, it is worth noting that the Commission's concept of integration in its application of competition policy to IPRs appears to be somewhat limited. Under the Treaty, the competition rules have been closely identified with the freedom of trade provisions of the Treaty, giving them a key role in promoting the goal of integration by breaking down the separate markets and systems of manufacturing and distribution which existed at the time of the formation of the EC. However, the activities listed in Article 3 of the Treaty in fact include two groups which are relevant to the promotion of integration: first, those which promote the process of 'negative integration',[79] i.e., by attempting to achieve a common market by a process of removing the barriers to free trade and movement between the member states. These clearly include: 3(a) 'the elimination, as between Member States, of customs duties and quantitative restrictions and of all other measures having equivalent effect', and 3(c) 'an internal market characterised by the abolition, as between Member States, of obstacles to the free movement of goods, persons, services and capital'. Article 3(g) with its goal of maintaining undistorted competition has been located within this group.

Article 3 also includes a number of activities which promote the process of 'positive integration',[80] e.g., which attempt to harmonize and improve upon the existing conditions of manufacture and provision of services of the member states throughout the common market. Thus, Article 3(h) calls for the approximation of the laws of the member states to the extent required for the proper functioning of the common market, Article 3(m) calls for 'the promotion of research and technological development', and Article 3(l) refers to the strengthening of the competitiveness of Community industry.

Article (3h) refers to the method of achieving integration by a process of harmonization of systems of national law into a unified European system. Intellectual property legislation is on the whole rooted in the law of the member states, although various Community directives are engaged in the process of harmonizing such legislation as part of the creation of a common market.[81]

[79] Id.
[81] See e.g. Beier op. cit. n. 23.

[80] See Ullrich op. cit. n. 78.

In the translation of the methods mentioned in Article 3 into specific provisions of the Treaty, IPRs are given less explicit treatment than competition law. Article 222 refers to property without mentioning intellectual property explicitly. Article 36 refers to industrial property but only in relationship to Article 30. The role of IPR legislation is, however, implicit in the general concept of harmonization of national legislation and conditions of manufacture.

To judges on the European Court of Justice and the members of the European Commission it has proven difficult to avoid the temptation of using Articles 85 and 86 as well as Article 30 as the driving force to achieve the integration of the common market by keeping open the bridges of trade from one member state to another, particularly as the evidence mounted that the method of integration by harmonization was going to be an agonizingly slow process.[82]

At the same time, as the Court has realized, there are limits to negative integration. There is a need to strike an appropriate balance between integration through trade and integration through diffusion of good manufacturing practice. The Court has led the way in a number of cases emphasizing the 'market opening' characteristics of new technology agreements[83] and other forms of licensing practices, requiring the Commission to build into its application of Article 85 recognition of the need to regard such agreements as not always restrictive of competition.[84]

Consequently, from the viewpoint of the competition rules as a regulatory system for IPRs, it is useful in legal argument and analysis to recognize the way in which a narrow economic definition of the goals of competition policy has been displaced by the goals of fairness and integration in the wider concept of 'distortion' applied by the Court of Justice.

---

[82] See e.g. Ullrich, op. cit. at p. 601.

[83] See e.g. *Nungesser* v. *Commission* [1982] ECR 2015; *Erauw-Jacquery* v. *La Hesbignonne* [1988] ECR 1919. [84] See discussion ch. 5.

PART II

Article 85 and Intellectual Property Licensing

3

Introduction: Intellectual Property Right Licensing and Competition Policy Generally

To the parties to intellectual property right (IPR) licensing agreements, the case for the licensor's entitlement to pass on the exclusivity enjoyed under the statutory grant seems unanswerable. Many inventors who have invested in R&D find themselves unable to exploit the full commercial potential of their investment. Either they cannot enter and manufacture in all territories in the EC or they cannot manufacture all possible technical applications of the invention. In such situations, a licence may be the only acceptable way in which a reward to invention can be obtained.[1] The restrictions on the field of technical application or geographical territory in the licence appear to be merely subdivisions of the original right conferred by legislation; they seem to have no adverse effects on third parties who would otherwise be subject to the exclusive rights of the original right owner.

To a large extent, however, intellectual property right holders have tended to underestimate the importance of the difference between individual exploitation and contractual exploitation from a competition point of view, particularly where the exclusivity of the licensor is shared with the licensee.[2]

The process of IPR licensing is generally regarded as procompetitive because it helps to increase the reward for innovative effort and the incentives for others to invest in R&D and this provides an important justification for restrictions in licences which operate to help the licensor obtain the surplus inherent in the innovation.[3] Moreover, the sharing of exclusivity is meant to give protection to the licensee to take on the risks of investment in the manufacturing and distribution facilities. The problem is that there are certain circumstances in which the same or similar restrictions which provide these benefits can be used as instruments to enforce cartel behaviour, such as price fixing, output limitation, and

---

[1] Outright sale or assignment is another possibility but it would mean a loss of control over the invention itself and improvements made upon it.

[2] See H. Ullrich, Patents and Know how, Free trade, Interenterprise Cooperation and Competition within the Internal European Market, [1992] *IIC* 583 at 604

[3] It is worth noting that these arguments support a reasonable reward for the owner of an IPR.

market sharing. These practices harm consumers and can be used to exclude competitors from markets, either for the products made using the licensed technology or for the technology itself.[4]

This competition concern is common to all competition systems and has resulted in a search for sifting mechanisms which can be used to distinguish between genuine IPR licences and those employed in anti-competitive commercial practices. In recent years, there appears to be some convergence between most systems on the types of indicators of competition concerns as well as the most appropriate methods of measuring their competitive effects.[5]

The first premise now widely accepted in many competition policy systems is that the type of relationship between licensor and licensee is a key indicator. If the relationship between licensor and licensee is 'vertical', i.e. the parties to the licensing agreement operate in different markets and at different levels of economic activity, such as agreements between inventors and manufacturers or between specialist component manufacturers and assembly manufacturers, these are viewed as a significantly smaller risk to competition than 'horizontal' licensing agreements, i.e. those between competitors on the same market or likely potential competitors.[6]

This factor, however, is only an indicator. Horizontal relationships using IPR licences are not always anticompetitive; indeed, R&D joint ventures and new technology production joint ventures are often highly procompetitive.[7] However, agreements between competitors are a more fertile seed-bed for anticompetitive practices. There are greater temptations and opportunities for collusion between competitors in the form of price-fixing or market sharing cartels for goods designed to extract higher returns from customers and to prevent entry by other competitors. Intellectual property rights licences, both genuine and sham, can be used to reinforce such collaborative arrangements. Consequently, the restraints in horizontal agreements such as cross-licences and patent pools are often prime candidates for close examination by competition authorities.[8]

In the case of vertical relationships, examples can be found of anti-competitive collusion: for example, where both licensor and licensee have a manufacturing capacity; or where vertical relationships help to reinforce horizontal collusion.[9] However, the risks are significantly lower

---

[4] See e.g. *Competition Policy and Intellectual Property Rights* (OECD, Paris, 1989).
[5] Id.   [6] See e.g. OECD Report.
[7] See e.g. *OECD Report Competition Policy and Joint Ventures* (OECD, Paris, 1987).
[8] See OECD Report ch. 5 at p. 89.
[9] For example vertical licences can be used to facilitate a cartel arrangement by price-fixing at resale or retail levels and/or tie-ins to prevent cheating by detecting non-compliance. See e.g. P. Demeret, *Patents, Territorial restrictions, and EEC Law; A Legal and Economic Analysis* (Wennheim, New York: Verlag Chemie, 1978).

than in the case of horizontal relationships, and this is so for four main reasons.

First, the motive for licensing is often the need to complement the existing capabilities of each firm. The licensor needs the manufacturing capabilities of the licensee. The licensee needs the R&D results of the licensor. It has often been pointed out by economists that it is only through co-operative relationships such as licensing that the efficiencies of scale and scope can be achieved to allow innovation to occur. There are often good indications when a relationship is essentially vertical. For example, the manufacturing capacity of the licensor at the start of the relationship could make it plain that the possibility that it could be active on the market is unlikely. A second and separate indication would be whether or not the licensee is committed to using the licensor's trade mark for the duration of the contract. The absence of a trade mark obligation does not imply collusion but the use of the licensor's trade mark creates a strong presumption that the relationship is vertical and at least in the latter case is likely to remain so for the period of the contract.[10]

Secondly, vertical agreements, in contrast to horizontal agreements, introduce a new competitor into a market and help to diffuse the licensed product or process throughout the economy.

Thirdly, vertical restraints can promote efficiencies by allowing the licensor to induce the licensee to invest in the new product or process, achieve efficiencies in production and distribution, and compete more effectively in the new market.[11]

Finally, as with all vertical relationships, as long as there is robust competition in the product market between brands, such 'interbrand' competition can operate to regulate the effects on price of the absence of competition within each manufacturing and distribution chain, i.e. 'intrabrand' competition.[12] If there is strong competition in the final product market, market forces operate to limit the amount that any one brand can extract from consumers. The main economic effects of intrabrand collusion in such a case would be limited to influencing the distribution of the overall profit of the brand within the distribution chain itself and possibly improving the quality of interbrand competition.[13] For these reasons, most competition law systems operate with different presumptions about horizontal and vertical agreements.[14]

The second premise of many competition policies is that vertical

---

[10] See e.g. J. Venit, 'In the Wake of Windsurfing: Patent Licensing in the Common Market' [1987] *IIC* 3 at p. 36.

[11] See e.g. *Continental TV Inc.* v. *GTE Sylvania Inc.* 433 US 36 at 54 (1977).

[12] Ibid. at 54

[13] e.g. by giving more feedback to the manufacturer about the weaknesses and strengths of the product. [14] Op. cit. n. 4.

agreements are likely to have anticompetitive effects in only a narrow range of market conditions: i.e. where there is a high degree of concentration in the licensor's market; where a high proportion of licensees in that market are subject to similar restraints; and where access to the market is restricted by entry barriers.[15] Again, these factors are indicators. Even high levels of market concentration are not necessarily conclusive evidence of anticompetitive effect. Much depends upon the overall evaluation.

The third premise of many modern competition policies is that there are certain types of provisions in vertical licensing agreements which are most likely to be evidence of anticompetitive practices. The main candidates are resale price maintenance, tying arrangements, non-competition clauses or exclusive dealing and grant backs. These restrictions in licensing agreements are not always anticompetitive but they are the main categories of provisions in licensing agreements which require the most careful monitoring.[16]

Given these well established premises of regulation of IPR licensing by competition policies, most systems make use of methods of filtering the anticompetitive licensing practices from the procompetitive licensing practices by concentrating on the high-risk categories and subjecting these categories to a balancing test of economic effects in some form.

To a large extent, the way has been led by US antitrust law, which, after a period of formalism by the Courts[17] and regulators,[18] has moved to a rule of reason analysis of contractual restraints generally and in particular in the case of IPR licensing agreements. The system of administrative enforcement of antitrust law in the USA makes use of a set of published guidelines, currently the 'Antitrust Guidelines for the Licensing of Intellectual Property' issued in 1995.[19] The Guidelines start with the core principles that intellectual property licensing is generally procompetitive, that IPRs are comparable to other forms of property, and that there is no presumption that exclusivity of IPRs creates market power in the antitrust context.

They then provide guidance in relation to the factors which are to be used by courts and regulators and the parties in evaluating a particular licensing arrangement. The Guidelines identify the categories of licensing agreements, provisions, and market conditions, which are the likely sources of anticompetitive conduct and subject these to a balancing test

---

[15] OECD Report ch. 4   [16] See e.g. OECD Report ch. 5.

[17] See e.g. *International Salt Co.* v. *United States* 332 US 292 (1947). See generally L. A. Sullivan *Antitrust Law* (1977) 434–7.

[18] See Turner, 'Antitrust and Innovation', 12 *Antitrust Bulletin* 277 at 281 (1967).

[19] 6 Apr. 1995. Issued by the US Department of Justice and the Federal Trade Commission. (See Appendix III, below.)

of risks of harm and possibilities of benefit, a so-called rule of reason approach. They thus follow the practice of the US Courts in moving away from a formalistic *per se* approach to restraints in licensing agreements.[20]

The Guidelines suggest the need for an initial identification of an intellectual property licensing arrangement as primarily 'horizontal' or 'vertical' in nature , or whether it has substantial aspects of both. This identification is meant to be 'merely an aid in determining whether there may be anticompetitive effects arising from a licensing arrangement'. A horizontal arrangement is 'not, in itself, anticompetitive'. A purely vertical arrangement does not 'assure that there are no anticompetitive effects'.[21]

They also indicate that the potential for competitive harm is greater the higher the market rate of concentration. They therefore place great emphasis on identifying the relevant market in 'goods', 'technology' or 'innovations' and establishing conditions of concentration on each market. If the parties to licensing arrangements have a combined market share of less than 20 per cent, then because licensing arrangements often promote innovation and enhance competition, the Guidelines provide an 'antitrust safety zone', in which the Agencies will not normally[22] challenge IPR related restraints in the licensing agreements. If the parties have a combined market share above the 20 per cent level, then the degree of market concentration will be one of the important factors to be taken into account in an assessment of the agreement.

In the vast majority of cases, restraints in IPR licences will be evaluated under the rule of reason. In some cases, however, the courts conclude that a restraint is unlawful *per se*, without the need for an elaborate inquiry into the restraint's likely competitive effect: for example, naked price fixing, output restraints, and market division among horizontal competitors, as well as certain group boycotts and resale price maintenance.[23] Under the Guidelines, the assessment of the economic effects of the agreement using a rule of reason analysis is a two step balancing test. First, there must be an examination to determine whether or not the restraint is likely to have anticompetitive effects. Secondly, if so, an assessment must be made whether the restraint is necessary to achieve procompetitive benefits that outweigh those anticompetitive effects.[24]

Application of the rule of reason generally[25] requires a comprehensive

---

[20] See e.g. *GTE Sylvania*, op. cit. n. 11 above.   [21] Id. See Guidelines at p. 8.

[22] The Agencies reserve their position in the case of facially anticompetitive clauses such as RPM arrangements (see below).   [23] Guidelines at pp. 2–6.

[24] Guidelines at p. 16.

[25] For the exceptions, see Guidelines pp. 16–17.

inquiry into market conditions. However, even when the Guidelines identify situations in which the market structure could have anticompetitive consequences, i.e. 'when a licensing arrangement harms competition among entities that would have been actual or likely potential competitors in a relevant market in the absence of the license',[26] this is not intended to replace the rule of reason approach but merely to identify when antitrust concerns arise in a licensing arrangement for the purpose of applying a rule of reason approach. Thus, even cross-licensing of intellectual property rights involving horizontal competitors is dealt with by balancing the procompetitive with the anticompetitive effects of the arrangement.

Moreover, where the parties to a licensing arrangement would not have been actual or likely potential competitors in a relevant market in the absence of the licence, i.e. the relationship is vertical, the competition concern is limited to whether the licensing agreement includes restraints which harm competition with rivals and in such a case, the two steps of the rule of reason approach are applied solely to the restraint.[27]

If the Agencies conclude, upon an evaluation of the market factors described in Section 4.1., that a restraint in a licensing arrangement is unlikely to have an anticompetitive effect, they will consider whether the restraint is reasonably necessary. The agencies will balance the procompetitive efficiencies and the anticompetitive effects to determine the probable net effect on competition in each relevant market. The Agencies' comparison of anticompetitive harms and procompetitive efficiencies is necessarily a qualitative one. The risk of anticompetitive effects may be insignificant compared to the expected efficiencies, or vice versa. As the expected anticompetitive effects in a particular licensing arrangement increase, the Agencies will require evidence establishing a greater level of expected efficiencies.[28]

The Guidelines add that the test includes a determination of whether a restraint is reasonably necessary to achieve the procompetitive efficiencies, and whether the duration of the restraint is reasonably necessary to achieve them.[29]

This system of regulation in the USA thus requires the parties to make an assessment of the competitive effects of their licensing agreements in the light of the Guidelines. The skills required from legal advisers include the ability to assess the nature of the relationship between the parties, the conditions on the relevant market, and the purpose and economic effects of the restraints in the licensing agreement.

In contrast, the system of regulating IPR licensing which has evolved under Article 85 of the EC Treaty is not concerned solely with balancing

---

[26] Guidelines at p. 7.
[27] Guidelines, s. 3.4 at p. 16.
[28] Guidelines, s. 4.2 at p. 22.
[29] Id.

the economic risks and benefits of licensing. Because of its role under the Treaty, it must concern itself with the effects of licensing on the integration of separate member states into a common market.

Secondly, the EC competition law system is one that is still reliant on the technique of legal assessment of licensing agreements with reference to the form of the provisions in licensing agreements to a greater extent than to their overall economic effects.[30]

Thirdly, Article 85 imposes its requirements in the form of two separate and different tests of anticompetitiveness for IPR licensing agreements. The reasons for these characteristics of its regulatory system can be found in the bifurcated structure of Article 85 and in the judicial and administrative interpretation each part has received.

---

[30] Guidelines, s. 4.1 at p. 20; under the Guidelines, as noted earlier, the focus is placed upon the actual practice and its effects, not on the formal terms of the arrangement.

4

The Structure of Article 85 and Licensing Agreements

4.1 INTRODUCTION

Article 85 contains a two part structure, each part contributing to the determination whether any form of collaboration between two or more undertakings is pro- or anticompetitive. Article 85(1) provides the jurisdictional test to determine whether an agreement or concerted practice comes within the scope of the Article as a whole. It applies to 'all agreements, decisions and concerted practices between undertakings' which have the object or effect of preventing, restricting or distorting competition. In principle it is capable of applying to a wide range of acts of collaboration between two or more undertakings.[1]

Article 85(1) has been held to apply widely in the IPR context to licensing agreements; to concerted practices involving licensing agreements;[2] assignments of intellectual property rights (IPRs) to third parties;[3] and trade mark delimitation agreements.[4] However, an agreement involving an IPR only falls within the scope of Article 85(1) if it meets the jurisdictional conditions of that Article. The first condition is that the agreement or concerted practice concerning the IPR must be made between two or more independent 'undertakings'.[5] Article 85 does not apply to the unilateral conduct of a single undertaking.[6] Indeed, the Court's view that the mere ownership of an intellectual property right is not caught by Article 85 is partly a reflection of the fact that the unilateral enforcement of an intellectual property right is not an agreement or a concerted practice under Article 85(1).[7]

The second condition is whether the agreement or practice has a significant quantitative impact on interstate trade.[8] The third condition

---

[1] See e.g. Goyder, *EC Competition Law* (2nd edn., 1993) at pp. 91 *et seq.*
[2] See e.g. *Lucazeau* v. *SACEM* [1989] ECR 2811.
[3] See e.g. *Sirena* v. *Eda* [1971] ECR 3169.
[4] See e.g. *Ideal Standard* [1994] ECR I–2789.   [5] See s. 4.3.1 below.
[6] The Court of Justice has long maintained that 'the Treaty intended Article 85 to leave untouched the internal organisation of an undertaking and to render it liable . . . only in cases where it reaches such a degree of seriousness as to amount to an abuse of a dominant position'. *Consten Grundig* v. *Commission* [1966] ECR 299 at p. 345.
[7] See e.g. *Parke Davis* v. *Probel* [1968] ECR 55.   [8] See s. 4.3.2 below.

involves an assessment of the pro- or anticompetitive nature of the agreement or practice. It asks whether that agreement or practice has the object or effect of appreciably preventing, or distorting competition.[9] If any one of these jurisdictional conditions is not met, the agreement falls outside the scope of Article 85(1). It is 'cleared'.

The Court has repeatedly stated that an IPR licensing agreement as such is not a 'restriction on competition',[10] but it may fall within the scope of Article 85(1) whenever it is 'the subject, the means or the consequence of',[11] or 'serves to give effect to',[12] a commercial practice which has as its object or exercise the prevention, restriction or distortion of competition in the common market. This means that both the effect and the intention of the agreement or practice with which the IPR is involved will be relevant to determine whether or not it comes within the scope of Article 85(1).

If an agreement falls within Article 85(1), it is prohibited, at least initially, but may be saved by a second method of validation—the process of exemption under Article 85(3). Article 85(3) states that 'Article 85(1) may be declared inapplicable, in the case of any agreement, decision or concerted practice' which meets the following four conditions:

1. if it contributes to improving production and distribution of goods and promoting technical progress;
2. and it allows consumers a fair share of the resulting benefit;

and if it does not

3. impose on the undertakings concerned restrictions which are not indispensable to the attainment of these objectives; or,
4. afford such undertakings the possibility of eliminating competition in respect of a substantial part of the products in question.' [13]

The method of exemption appears to be particularly favourable to IPR licensing because of its contribution to the promotion of technical progress. Exemption can be obtained in two possible ways: notification to the Commission for individual exemption or qualification under one of the group or block exemptions issued by the Commission. As we shall see, however, both roads to exemption contain a number of procedural obstacles which have meant that IPR owners cannot always find a convenient route to legal validity.

---

[9] See s. 4.3.3 below.

[10] See e.g. *Coditel II* [1982] ECR 3381 at para. 14; see too *Parke Davis* v. *Probel* discussed in ch. 2.

[11] See e.g. *Deutsche Grammophon Gesellschaft* [1971] ECR 489 at para. 6.

[12] See e.g. *Coditel II*, op. cit. at para. 14.

[13] Although in practice, the conditions are cumulative, the weight of gravity is placed on conditions (1) and (3).

If Article 85(1) applies and an agreement cannot be exempted, the agreement as a whole, or the offending restriction, is void and unenforceable under Article 85(2) in national courts as well as the Community courts. One possible consequence of this is that the other party to the agreement can treat the restriction or the agreement as no longer binding and use Article 85(2) as a 'Euro-defense' to any action to enforce it.[14] A second possible consequence is that its parties are subject to a risk of fines by the Commission.[15]

Despite these threats of legal invalidity, there has been a tendency for the parties to licensing agreements to prefer methods which avoid formal notification of the agreement to the Commission in order to obtain exemption.[16] The first option sought is to attempt to fit an agreement into a block exemption. If that fails, some prefer to use the block exemption as a model for exemptibility, but refrain from notifying.

Parties will also examine the clearance option, which has its uses despite the difficulties involved. One form of clearance consists of fitting a licensing agreement into the category of agreement cleared by the Commission under one of its Notices which operate as 'group clearances'.[17] If that possibility is precluded, the clearance option requires the parties to licensing agreements to assess their provisions in the light of a considerable body of case-law of the Community Courts and the Commission relating to territorial and non-territorial restraints in licensing agreements.[18] Yet clearance has the advantage that it can be achieved through self assessment of the licensing agreement. Although, the Commission offers the possibility of a formal negative clearance, upon notification, it is not necessary. Moreover, clearance can help to make the agreement enforceable in national courts as well as avoid a fine by the Commission. Finally, it can avoid the need for exemption in the first place.

In the event, the most useful way to analyse Article 85 as a regulatory framework for the IPR licensing process, is to look separately at the two

---

[14] In such cases, it is possible to argue that the prohibition should be limited to the offending provisions with the rest of the agreement remaining valid and enforceable but this presupposes that the provisions are severable. The issue of severability is a matter for national courts to decide. See e.g. *Chemidis Wavin* v. *TERI* (1978) CMLR 514. It might also be possible to bring a restitution claim for the value of the performance under the void contract.

[15] Under Reg. 17, it is not obligatory to notify an agreement. However, if an agreement is caught by Art. 85(1) and has not been notified to the Commission with an application for exemption, a fine could be levied. Only the Commission has the authority to levy fines. Art. 15, Reg. 17/62. Fines are more likely if a complaint is made and the agreement proves to be non-exemptible. If on the other hand the agreement is exemptible, fines are less likely. However, there is no provisional validity until the parties notify formally. See *BRT* v. *SABAM and Fonior* [1974] ECR 51 and 313; *Brasserie de Haecht* v. *Wilkin (Brasserie de Haecht II)* [1973] ECR 77.   [16] See s. 4.2 below.

[17] See e.g. the Notice on Agreements of Minor Importance discussed in s. 4.3.3.

[18] See ss. 5.3–5.5.

methods of assessment: (i) the process of exemption and (ii) the process of clearance.

Since 1984, with the enactment of the Patent Licensing Block Exemption,[19] the favoured method of achieving legal validity is to attempt to fit into a block exemption issued by the Commission. The block exemptions provide automatic exemption from Article 85(1) for specific categories of agreements which meet certain conditions. For intellectual property rights licensing, the new omnibus Technology Transfer Regulation applies to the following categories of agreements: pure patent licences, pure know-how licences, and mixed patent, know-how licences. In addition the Commission has provided specific block exemptions for specialization agreements,[20] research and development agreements,[21] franchise agreements,[22] and exclusive distribution and purchasing agreements.[23]

Provided that the parties can draft their agreement to meet all the preconditions of one of these block exemptions, the advantages of exemption are considerable. Legal validity is automatic; there is no need to notify the Commission.[24] The enforceability of the agreement will be certain from the time it is approved by legal counsel if capable legal counsel can conclude that the licensing agreement is compatible with the block exemption. Furthermore, legal costs will be based on that approval process rather than the process of notification to the Commission. Because of these factors, this option is often examined even before an analysis of clearance under Article 85(1) is explored.

The problem for intellectual property rightholders, however, is that not all agreements can be fitted into an existing block exemption.[25] In the first place, an agreement must fall into the correct category of agreements prescribed by a block exemption and not all licensing agreements can be fitted into a requisite category. Trade mark licences or production franchises,[26] computer program licences,[27] manufacturing subcontracting

---

19 Reg. 2349/84.
20 Reg. 417/85, amended by Reg. 151/93, see [1993] 4 CMLR 155.
21 Reg. 418/85, as amended by Reg. 151/93, see [1993] 4 CMLR 163.
22 Reg. 4087/88.
23 Reg. 1983/83 and 1983/84 respectively.
24 See Art. 4(1) Council Reg. No. 17 OJ C 204/62 (1962).
25 See e.g. R. Whaite, 'Licensing in Europe' [1990] 3 *EIPR* 88.
26 See e.g. *Moosehead/Whitbread* [1991] 4 CMLR 391.
27 See e.g. J. Derbyshire, 'Computer Programs and Competition Policy: A Block Exemption for Software Licensing' [1994] *EIPR* 374.

agreements, and certain types of co-operative joint ventures[28] are all examples of intellectual property licensing arrangements which do not fit within the strict rules of any of the existing block exemptions.

Secondly, even if the category of the agreement is appropriate for a particular block exemption, it is necessary for all the clauses within an agreement to conform to the detailed requirements of the block exemption in respect of permitted and prohibited restrictions under Article 85(3). If an agreement fails to satisfy the conditions of a block exemption, it will lose its protection and could be held to be unenforceable under Article 85(2) until the parties obtain individual exemption.[29] The problems of fitting licensing agreements within a block exemption have been ameliorated by the introduction of 'non-opposition procedures' within certain licensing block exemptions which provide a method to obtain Commission approval for clauses which might otherwise prevent a licensing agreement from qualifying for a block exemption.[30] This procedure requires formal notification to the Commission but in the new Technology Transfer block exemption the Commission faces a time limit of four months in which to oppose it. Otherwise, the provision can be presumed to be valid and together with the rest of the agreement, if in conformity to the block exemption, exempted. The non-opposition procedure, however, is not available for all clauses, particularly those on the blacklist. In the event, not all licensing agreements can be modified to fit within an existing block exemption.

The relationship between the block exemption system and the licensing agreement has been graphically described by Robin Whaite, a noted legal specialist in intellectual property law, in the following terms:

A common process is this: either alone or with their lawyers, the businessmen sketch out a tentative agreement; an eye may perhaps be kept on the competition law points, but they will certainly not be allowed to dominate at this early stage. The slate is clean. Does a body of technology exist? Or are we talking a phased programme of research, development and commercialisation? How should the relationship be structured?—a formal joint venture; a simple license . . . The list of questions is endless; but the first step should be to ascertain the sort of deal that is really wanted, and then the second to analyse the proposals from the competition law point of view.

Then difficult decisions have to be made. In the writer's experience, most proposals for a transaction of substance fail to qualify clearly for the relevant block exemption. The first decision is whether to modify the commercial proposals to fit

---

[28] Co-operative joint ventures are evaluated under Art. 85 using the Commission's Notice Concerning the Assessment of Cooperative Joint Ventures Pursuant to Article 85 of the EEC Treaty OJ C 43 (1993) (Comm'n.)

[29] See e.g. *Delimitis* v. *Henniger Brau AG.* [1991] ECR I–935.

[30] See e.g. C. S. Kerse, *Antitrust Procedure* (Sweet & Maxwell, London, 3rd edn., 1994) at pp. 85 *et seq.*

the straitjacket. If the decision is not to tamper with the proposals, a string of questions follow: whether to notify in a case which is arguably but not plainly, within the Regulation; whether to apply for negative clearance or (more likely) both negative clearance and alternatively, an individual exemption: whether to make use of the opposition procedure (if it is available); or whether a comfort letter from the Commission might be satisfactory.[31]

Once it is clear that the only path to exemption consists of an application for individual exemption, however, the attractions of the exemption method are considerably lessened. This is not because IPR licences are difficult to draft to qualify for individual exemption under the substantive criteria. In fact, as we have seen, the prospects of exemption would be favourable for many licensing agreements because of their contribution to the improvement of production of goods and the promotion of technical progress. The difficulties with applications for individual exemption are almost entirely due to the nature of existing procedures.

In the first place, an application for individual exemption requires the parties to submit a formal notification of the agreement to the Commission. The form (Form A/B) calls for extensive information about the firm and its market as well as the agreement itself.[32] This process, as Mario Siragusa reminds us, involves the firm *voluntarily* submitting commercially sensitive information to scrutiny by public officials, which is seen by many firms as a sacrifice of their autonomy. He adds:

... companies which have a serious policy of compliance with the competition rules find it difficult to accept that in certain cases they cannot make their own determination of the legality of their behaviour subject of course to review by the courts and that they have to substitute for their own judgment, the judgment of an administrative authority.[33]

Secondly, the risks of interference are exacerbated by the degree of discretion enjoyed by the administrators. This creates the possibility that the company may be subjected to lengthy investigation depending upon the particular official receiving the notification. Moreover, there are risks of complex procedures if the official insists on the imposition of conditions and obligations on the parties before exemption is granted.[34] Further, there are no time limits to the notification procedure. Finally, there is no guarantee that the Commission will respond by giving a formal exemption decision. The Commission has the sole authority to grant an exemption under Article 85(3) but it has not been given

---

[31] R. Whaite, 'Licensing in Europe' [1990] *EIPR* 88.
[32] M. Siragusa, 'Notification of Agreements in the EEC: To Notify or Not to Notify?', *Fordham Corp. Law Inst.* [1987] 243 at p. 280.
[33] Ibid.   [34] Ibid., pp. 280–1.

resources commensurate with this task. It is able to give only about 20 formal exemption decisions each year to the more than 300 applications.[35] In the event, parties who notify the Commission in order to obtain exemption are far more often issued with 'comfort letters', i.e. informal, administrative letters informing the parties that on the basis of the facts made available to it, the Commission considers that there is no need to take any action. These 'comfort letters' are probably binding on the Commission unless the factual circumstances change,[36] but cannot tie the hands of courts when applying Article 85 to the licensing agreement.

For these reasons, the parties whose licensing agreements cannot fit within a 'block exemption' are not always prepared to invest in the costs of preparing the requisite information for a formal notification to the Commission,[37] and may be prepared to devote resources to the investigation of the possibilities of 'clearance' under Article 85(1) as part of the process of deciding whether or not to notify an agreement to the Commission.[38]

4.3 THE CLEARANCE OF LICENSING AGREEMENTS UNDER ARTICLE 85(1)

The method of attempting to 'clear' an agreement under Article 85(1), i.e. designing it so that its contents do not come within the scope of Article 85(1), is not an easy option for the parties to licensing agreements. The Commission, preferring to assess the procompetitive and anticompetitive features of an agreement in the exemption process, has construed Article 85(1) widely. Nevertheless, the structure of the Article itself and the case-law of the Court of Justice create the possibility for licences to be 'cleared' based on a showing that the agreement does not meet at least one of the Article's three main conditions for jurisdiction.

4.3.1 Agreements between independent undertakings

The first condition in Article 85(1) is that there must be evidence of agreement or other form of collaboration between two or more 'undertakings'. Insofar as the conduct of an intellectual property rightholder consists of unilateral enforcement of such a right under national law, it will not be caught by Article 85,[39] though it might be regulated by Article 86.

---

[35] See e.g. I. Forrester, 'Competition Structures for the 21st century', [1994] *Fordham Corp. Law Inst.* 445.
[36] See AG Reichl's comments in *L'Oreal* [1980] ECR 3775 at 3803.
[37] See detailed analysis of these issues by M. Siragusa op. cit.
[38] Ibid.
[39] *Deutsche Grammophon Gesellschaft* [1971] CMLR 631 at para. 5.

The concept of an undertaking in Article 85(1) though not defined in the Treaty has been held to apply widely to individuals, partnerships, joint ventures,[40] and companies. The Court of Justice has defined it as 'any entity' engaged on a commercial activity.[41] Public authorities are caught if they are engaged on a commercial or economic activity but are excepted if they are acting as a public authority.[42]

However, an undertaking has also been defined as being an independent entity. If it is part of a wider 'economic unit', consisting of a group of companies, the group rather than the individual company may be the 'undertaking.' The Court of Justice has stated that the concept of undertaking is not identical with the question of legal personality for the purposes of company law. The corporate veil can be lifted[43] to show the underlying economic and commercial reality. If a licensing agreement is made between two companies within the same corporate group it may be viewed as excluded from Article 85(1) because, despite the corporate form, the two parties can be viewed as part of the same 'economic unit', and the agreement is not one between separate undertakings. As the court stated in *Centrafarm* v. *Sterling Drug*,[44] an agreement or concerted practice between a parent and a subsidiary does not fall within the scope of Article 85 where the agreement between two companies is in fact an internal allocation of functions between members of the same economic unit. If, however, the reality is that a subsidiary has a measure of independence in determining its commercial policy, then the subsidiary will be viewed as a separate undertaking for the purposes of Article 85(1).[45]

The effect of this jurisdictional condition is to offer to companies the option of avoiding the regulatory effects of Article 85 by acquiring the licensor, or vertically integrating, rather than obtaining a licensing agreement.[46] In the recent case of *Viho Europe* v. *Commission*,[47] the Court of First Instance was faced by a complaint from a distributor that Parker

---

[40] Joint ventures can also be 'agreements' depending on their structure.

[41] See e.g. *Polypropylene* [1988] 4 CMLR 34 para. 99

[42] *Corinne Bodson* v. *Pompes Funebres de Region Liberees SA* [1985] ECR 2479; [1989] 4 CMLR 984.

[43] It is also lifted to establish the jurisdiction of EC law over the foreign parent of a subsidiary within the EC (see e.g. *Commercial Solvents* v. *Commission* [1974] ECR 223) or when holding a parent company attributable for the guilty conduct of the subsidiary (see e.g. *Johnson and Johnson* [1981] 2 CMLR 287).

[44] *Centrafarm* v. *Sterling Drug Inc. and Winthrop BV* [1974] ECR 1147 at 1183; see too *Kodak* [1970] CMLR D31 (Comm.).

[45] See e.g. *Comm.* v. *Solvay and La Porte* [1985] 1 CMLR 481. The issue of autonomy is raised again in the context of the relationship between parents and joint ventures.

[46] After *Consten Grundig*, for example, Grundig simply acquired Consten and integrated it within the Grundig organization.

[47] [1995] II ECR 217.

Pen had an arrangement with its wholly owned subsidiaries which required them to refer all orders from customers from other EC countries to the subsidiary established in the customer's country. The CFI noted that the arrangement contributed to preserving and partitioning the various national markets, but held that when such a policy is 'followed by an economic unit . . . within which the subsidiaries do not enjoy any freedom to determine their conduct in the market', it 'does not fall within the scope of Article 85(1) of the Treaty'.[48] The Commission was told by the CFI that it cannot fill a gap that may exist in the scheme of regulation by stretching Article 85 to apply to circumstances for which it is not intended.

If the network involves independent dealers, Article 85(1) can apply. For example, when Parker Pen had put a similar contractual clause in its distribution agreement with its independent distributor in Germany, Herlitz, prohibiting all sales to resellers from other EC countries, its practices were subject to a fine of 700,000 ECU.

The Court has on occasion blurred the distinction between unilateral and bilateral action by implying agreement between two independent undertakings in cases where one undertaking issued a unilateral prohibition on exports to which the other undertaking acquiesced. For example in *AEG Telefunken* v. *Commission*, the refusal of a manufacturer to admit a known discount reseller to a selective distributions system was deemed to be by agreement with the other resellers contractually involved in the chain because of their 'tacit' acceptance of its exclusionary policy.[49] In such cases, however, there must be evidence of tacit acceptance by an independent undertaking in order to allow a finding of implied agreement to fall within Article 85(1).

In the recent case of *Adalat*,[50] the Commission attempted to take the process a step further by charging the Bayer company with an infringement of Article 85(1) in a situation where it had established a company policy of monitoring its own subsidiaries to restrict the quantities supplied to independent wholesalers based on national market orders. The Commission concluded that there was a 'quasi contractual arrangement' between the subsidiaries and the wholesalers because the latter were clearly influenced by Bayer's conduct to adapt their own practices to fall into line with Bayer's objectives. The Commission's decision has

---

[48] [1995] II ECR 217 at paras. 52–4; upheld by the ECJ Case C–73/95P.

[49] [1983] ECR 3151 at para. 38; see too *Ford Werke AG & Ford of Europe* v. *Commission* [1985] ECR 2725; *BMW Belgium* v. Commisson [1979] ECR 2435 (unilateral instructions by manufacturers to distributors in the form of a circular); *Sandoz* [1990] ECR I45 (supply of printed invoice stating 'exports prohibited').

[50] [1996] 5 CMLR 416; see H. Lidgard, 'Unilateral Refusal to Supply: An Agreement in Disguise' [1997] *ECLR* 352.

been appealed to the CFI and interim relief has been given by the President of the CFI until judgment.[51]

The requirement of collaboration between two or more independent undertakings has also led to the clearance of certain categories of dependent relationships. Thus, some types of commercial agents have been excepted from Article 85(1) by Commission Notice. As long as the agent has been acting on behalf of a principal, and not on his own behalf, the contract between principal and agent is not caught by Article 85(1).[52] In addition, certain types of manufacturing-subcontractor relationships have been 'cleared' by Commission Notice.[53]

4.3.2 Effect upon Interstate Trade

The second major jurisdictional condition of Article 85(1) is that it applies only to agreements, decisions, and concerted practices which have an 'appreciable' quantitative effect on interstate trade. This condition is essentially a jurisdictional test for the application of the system of EC competition law in two important respects. It first establishes a territorial point: whether an agreement made inside or outside the EU is caught by EU competition law by virtue of its effects.[54] Secondly, it defines the jurisdictional borderline where EC competition law applies alongside the domestic competition law of the member states.[55]

This test of effect on interstate trade has been given an extremely wide interpretation by Court and Commission, applying as long as the agreement 'may have an influence direct or indirect, actual or potential on the pattern of trade between member states'.[56]

The influence can be future as well as present, and possible as well as probable.[57] For example in *Vacuum Interrupters*,[58] the Commission held

---

[51] T–41/96R Order of 3 June,1996. The CFI also stated that 'an agreement between the applicant and the wholesalers concerned only the volume of orders that the latter placed. Such an agreement cannot in principle be interpreted as implicitly comprising an export prohibition . . .' See discussion S. Kon and F. Schaeffer, 'Parallel Imports of Pharmaceutical Products: A New Realism or Back to Basics' [1977] *ECLR* 123.

[52] Commission Notice OJ C 139/2921 (1962).

[53] Commission Notice OJ C 75/3 (1968).

[54] An agreement relating to trade outside the EU, whether made inside or outside the EU, can be caught by Art. 85(1) if its side-effects are to restrict or distort competition. See e.g. *Zuiker Unie* v. *Commission* [1975] ECR 1663; [1976] 1 CMLR 295; see also *Woodpulp* [1988] ECR 5193; [1988] 4 CMLR 901.

[55] The jurisdiction is concurrent in the sense that if Art. 85(1) does not apply for any reason, domestic law can still apply. Moreover, even where Art. 85(1) does apply, it only supervenes where a formal Commission has been taken or where the application of the law by member states will not threaten the full and uniform application of Community law. See *Walt Wilhelm* v. *bundesKartelamnt* [1969] ECR 1.

[56] *STM* v. *Maschinenbau Ulm* [1966] ECR 235 at 249; [1966] CMLR 357 at 375.

[57] See e.g. *AEG Telefunken* v. *Commission* [1983] 3 CMLR 325 para. 60.

[58] [1977] 1 CMLR D 67.

that a joint venture agreement between two British manufacturers was caught by Article 85(1) because it was reasonable to assume that had they proceeded independently they would have each marketed the product in other member states. Similarly, in *Pronuptia*,[59] the Court of Justice held that where clauses in a distribution franchise partitioned markets between licensor and licensee, it *per se* affected interstate trade even if both were in the same member state, insofar as they prevented licensees from setting up in other member states.

There has, however, long been an important quantitative dimension to the test of effect on interstate trade. Even a licence between undertakings in two different member states would only be found to satisfy the condition of affecting interstate trade if its effect were appreciable in terms of volume of trade.[60] The Court of Justice made it clear that for an agreement to fall within Article 85(1), it must have a more than *de minimis* effect upon interstate trade. In *Volk* v. *Vernaeke*,[61] the Court held that an exclusive distribution agreement between a German firm and a Belgian firm was not caught by Article 85(1) because the total market share of Volk in Germany was 0.2 per cent and altogether only 200 machines were sold. The weak position of the parties on the market meant that the agreement had only an insignificant effect. The Court stressed that the point of the appreciability test was that even if the Commission found that the purpose of an agreement was to restrain competition because it was an exclusive dealing imposing absolute territorial protection, if its overall effect on the market was insignificant because of the weak market position of the parties, then Article 85(1) would not apply.

This decision was followed by a Commission Notice on Agreements of Minor Importance which defined the *de minimis* effect in terms of both the market share (5 per cent) of the goods and services which are subject to the agreement and aggregate annual turnover of the undertakings participating in the agreement. The main purpose of the Notice was to reduce the number of applications for negative clearance. Its legal status before national and Community Courts was as 'only a factor which the courts may take into account in a pending case', but the Commission agreed not to open proceedings under Regulation 17 and if an agreement covered by the Notice was in fact caught by Article 85(1), there would be no fine. In its new version of the *de minimis* Notice, the Commission has used the occasion to signal a different approach to appreciability. The Notice has been made with

59 *Pronuptia de Paris* v. *Schillgalis* [1986] ECR 353.
60 See *STM* v. *Maschinenbau Ulm* [1966] ECR 235.
61 [1969] ECR 295; [1969] CMLR 277. The court had also referred to this test in the earlier test of *STM* v. *Maschinenbau Ulm*; see n. 60 above.

the awareness within the Commission of its thorough review of vertical restraints in distribution agreements proposed in its Green Paper and it suggests a new approach to appreciability in five important respects.

4.3.3 Agreements of Minor Importance: *De Minimis* and Article 85(1)[62]

4.3.3.1 *Vertical and Horizontal Agreements*

The Notice introduces a distinction between vertical and horizontal agreements. It states that since vertical agreements pose less of a threat and risk for competition in the internal market, they can be treated more leniently than horizontal agreements. In consequence, the Notice fixes a quantitative appreciability threshold at 10 per cent retaining the current threshold of 5 per cent for horizontal agreements. Paragraph 9 of the Notice states as follows:

The Commission holds the view that agreements between undertakings engaged in the production or distribution of goods or in the provision of services do not fall under the prohibition in Article 85(1) if the market share held together by all of the participating undertakings does not exceed, on any of the relevant markets:
—the 5% threshold, where the agreement is made between undertakings operating at the same level of production or of marketing ('horizontal agreement')
—the 10% threshold, where the agreement is made between undertakings operating at different economic levels ('vertical agreement').

In the case of a mixed horizontal/vertical agreement or where it is difficult to classify the agreement as horizontal or vertical, the 5% threshold is applicable.[63] The Notice continues the practice of giving guidance on the methods to be used to define the relevant market. The Notice also accepts that the *de minimis* standard should not be restricted only to SMEs. The Commission infers from the weak position of the parties on the relevant market that the agreement has no appreciable effect on competition even if the undertakings themselves may be large. It therefore removes the turnover threshold of the parties.

4.3.3.2 *Encouraging Small and Medium Sized Undertakings*

The Notice continues the policy of encouraging SMEs but offers a test of appreciability which is more generous. The new Notice stipulates that even where an agreement between SMEs exceeds the stipulated market

---

[62] Notice on Agreements of Minor Importance 97/C 372/04.

[63] The Commission adds that agreements can exceed these thresholds by no more than 10% for two years in succession and still remain outside the scope of Art. 85(1).

thresholds, they may nevertheless be viewed as too insignificant to warrant any intervention by the competition authorities.[64]

4.3.3.3 Per Se *Prohibitions and* De Minimus

The Notice provides, in paragraph 11, that even below the *de minimis* level, the applicability of Article 85(1) cannot be ruled out in the case of (a) horizontal agreements which have as their object:

1. to fix prices or limit production or sales; or
2. to share markets or sources of supply.

(b) vertical agreements which have as their object:

1. to fix resale prices; or
2. to confer territorial protection on the participating undertaking or third undertaking.

4.3.3.4 *The Notice and Networks of Agreements*

The Notice also stipulates that it does not apply where an agreement is part of a network and there are other parallel networks with other manufacturers distorting competition in a cumulative fashion in a relevant market.[65] This is an elaboration of earlier case-law of the Court in relation to beer distribution,[66] in which national courts were to decide the foreclosure effects of networks of agreements on the basis of the economic evidence.[67]

However, the Notice makes a special point of observing that it is without prejudice to the decisions of the Court of Justice defining the appreciability test in quantitative terms. This would apply to the Court of Justice's recent decisions that if an agreement is part of a network, it is necessary to enquire whether the contribution of the individual agreement to the foreclosing effect is substantial.[68] In the case of *Delimitis*,[69] the Court suggested that to test whether the exclusive purchasing obligations in a tied house agreement between a brewer and a café owner was caught by Article 85(1) it was necessary to meet two conditions:

---

[64] See Point 19. Commission Notice on Agreements of Minor Importance. SMEs are defined by the Commission as *inter alia* undertakings with less than 250 employees and a turnover not exceeding 40 million ECU. See Commission Recommendation of 3 Apr. 1996 concerning the definition of SMEs OJ L107 Vol. 39, 30 Apr. 1996.

[65] Para. 20.

[66] See *Brasserie de Haecht I* [1967] ECR 407; [1968] CMLR 26.

[67] See e.g. *Breeders: Roses* [1988] 4 CMLR 193 in which an agreement between two French firms had an appreciable effect beccause of the cumulative effect of the thousands of parallel agreements.

[68] See *Delimitis* v. *Henninger Brau* [1992] 5 CMLR 210. The Commission responded to this case by issuing a Notice indicating that the economic impact of the particular agreement would be taken into account in the context of beer supply agreements. Yet the point would also appear to apply to other types of agreements such as licensing agreements.

[69] *Delimitis* v. *Henninger Brau* [1991]ECR I–935.

The first is that having regard to the economic and legal context of the agreement at issue, it is difficult for competitors who could enter the market or increase their market share to gain access to the national market for the distribution of beer in premises for the sale and consumption of drinks. The fact that that agreement is one of a number of similar agreements having a cumulative effect on competition constitutes only one factor amongst others in assessing whether access to that market is indeed difficult. The second condition is that the agreement in question must make a significant contribution to the sealing off effect brought about by the totality of those agreements in their economic and legal context. The extent of that contribution made by that agreement depends upon the position of the contracting parties in the relevant market and on the duration of that agreement. [Paragraph 27].

Thus, when assessing the appreciability of the agreement's foreclosing effect on the market, the overall effect of beer supply agreements on that market is taken into account but so too is the actual impact of the individual agreement on that restriction of competition in that market. The Commission responded to the *Delimitis* case by issuing a Notice stating its position on the appreciability of networks of exclusive purchasing agreements in the beer supply sector.[70]

In the more recent case of *Langanese* ([1995] ECR II–1533) the Court made the point that the function of the Notice is to define agreements which in the Commission's view do not have an appreciable effect on competition or trade between member states.

It cannot be inferred that a network of exclusive purchasing agreements is automatically liable to prevent, restrict or distort competition appreciably merely because the ceilings laid down in it are exceeded. Moreover, it is apparent from the actual wording of paragraph 3 of that notice that it is entirely possible, as in the present case, that agreements concluded between undertakings which exceed the ceilings indicated affect trade between Member States only to an insignificant extent and consequently are not caught by Article 85(1) of the Treaty.

Nevertheless, in that case, the Commission had found that the sales of the German distributor Scholler far exceeded both the ceilings defining an agreement of minor importance and that these facts alone were sufficient to establish that there was an appreciable effect on competition. The wide threshold test of jurisdiction was undoubtedly influenced by the Court's concern to ensure that developments affecting the flow of trade and integration were kept under control. In the event, it has provided yet another factor contributing to the wide application of Article 85(1) to licensing agreements.

---

70 OJ [1992] C121/2.

4.3.3.5 The Notice and Qualitative Appreciability

The Notice also lists the major cases of the Court which have held that although certain clauses, when examined in isolation, constitute by their very nature restrictions on competition, they are not caught by Article 85(1) when they are seen in the framework of a procompetitive agreement. This reference in the Notice is significant because it makes the point that the Commission accepts that even above the *de minimis* thresholds the Court's interpretation of qualitative appreciability can mean that a restrictive provision in an agreement is not necessarily a restriction on competition. Indeed, the Notice states that it does not in any way prejudice the future development of the decision making practice in this area. This may also be a reference to the Commission's proposals for reform of vertical restraints in distribution contained in its Green Paper.[71] The Green Paper has suggested *inter alia* a rebuttable presumption of procompetitiveness for vertical agreements below the 20 per cent threshold, with the grounds for rebuttal consisting of market factors.[72] The Notice was drafted at the same time as the Green Paper was prepared but has come into effect pending the resolution of the consultations over suggested reforms.[73] Hence it is to this issue of 'qualitative' appreciability and restriction on competition that we must now turn.

4.3.4 The Object or Effect of Preventing, Restricting or Distorting Competition

Under Article 85(1), if a licence agreement is made between independent undertakings and has an appreciable effect on interstate trade, it is still necessary to show that it has as its object or effect the prevention, restriction or distortion of competition before it is contrary to Article 85(1). This test is jurisdictional in the sense that it constitutes a precondition to the application of Article 85(1). Yet it also involves a preliminary assessment of the pro- or anticompetitive nature of the licensing agreement.

In the case-law defining the statutory concept of restriction on competition, the Court and Commission normally apply a two part test. The first part consists of a threshold test of restriction based on the concept of whether the agreement or provision has as its intention or effect the restriction of the commercial autonomy or 'freedom of action' of the parties. The second test is a test of whether that intention or effect is appreciable. Let us look at each in turn.

---

[71] Green Paper on Vertical Restraints in EC Competition Policy, Com (96) 721 final (1997). [72] See para. 295.
[73] See discussion in Conclusions ch. 9.

4.3.4.1 *Restriction on Competition and 'Freedom of Action'*

The concept of freedom of action as part of the test in Article 85(1) was hinted at in *Grundig* when the Court stated: 'Competition may be distorted within the meaning of Article 85(1) not only by agreements which limit it as between the parties, but also by agreements which prevent or restrict the competition which might take place between one of them and third parties.'

The Commission has been more explicit: 'The exclusive nature of a contractual relationship between a producer and a distributor is viewed as restricting competition since it limits the parties' freedom of action in the territory covered.' (See *XXIIIrd Report* on *Competition Policy* (1993) Com (94) 161 final, page 212.)

Whilst the doctrine of freedom of action originating in German law, derives from the regulation of relationships between competitors, the horizontal dimension,[74] it has been applied under Article 85 to vertical agreements like distributorships.[75] If a distribution agreement is exclusive, it is caught by Article 85(1) and requires exemption because it contains a restriction on the supplier selling to anyone in the contract territory apart from the licensee and bars other distributors in that territory from buying from the supplier.[76] The application of the freedom of action doctrine to exclusive vertical distribution agreements by the Commission has been controversial and has been much criticized because of its schizophrenic approach to the treatment of such agreements,[77] as

---

[74] In the case of horizontal agreements, it can perhaps be defended as a reasonable basis for a rebuttable presumption of anticompetitiveness. Where firms are competitors any restriction on their action is probably a restriction on the process and possibly the structure of competition. As the Court of Justice has acknowledged in *Zuiker Unie*: 'The criteria of coordination and cooperation laid down by the caselaw of the Court ... must be understood in the light of the concept inherent in the competition provisions of the EEC Treaty according to which each economic operator must develop independently the policy which he intends to adopt on the common market including the choice of the person or undertaking to which he makes, offers or sells.' *Zuiker Unie* v. *Commission* [1975] ECR 1663 at 1942. See excellent discussion by J. Kallaugher of Wilmer Cutler and Pickering in 'The German Influence on EC Competition Law', unpublished seminar paper given at Essex University Law Department.

[75] See e.g. *Bendix/Ancien Ets. Mertons & Strae* 1.6.1964 5 OJ EC 1496 (1964).

[76] The ideal agreement from a 'freedom of action' perspective is a non-exclusive distributorship which leaves the supplier free to appoint other distributors in the same territory and to distribute its own products in the same territory.

[77] The Commission, it is said, first condemns in principle an inordinate number of vertical agreements under Art. 85(1) as restrictions on competition, creating a 'drift net' approach to jurisdiction, and requiring inordinate numbers of notifications in order to achieve legal validity. It then exempts considerable numbers of agreements because they readily meet the fourfold balancing test of not on balance restricting competition under Art. 85(3). See contribution to C. Bright, 'Deregulaton of EC Competition Policy: Rethinking Article 85(1)' and I. Forrester, 'Competition Structures for the 21st Century' in [1994] *Fordham Corp. Law Inst.* at pp. 505 and 405 respectively.

well as its excessive formalism.[78] It is currently under review by the Commission in respect of vertical restraints in distribution.[79]

The application of this doctrine has the result that a contractual restraint on the freedom of action of the parties on the market is equated to a restriction of competition without any reference to the actual process of competition on the market or the effects of the agreement on that process. Moreover it can apply to the intention of the agreement as well as to its effects.

Under Article 85(1), an agreement can be unlawful either by virtue of its object or its effects. The test of unlawful object consists of an assessment of whether or not the purpose of the agreement was to harm competition. Intent can be inferred from the content of the provisions of the agreement but must be measured objectively. In principle, as the Court confirmed in *STM* v. *Machinenbau Ulm*,[80] if it can be shown that an agreement was made for an anticompetitive purpose, it is not necessary to show anticompetitive effect. The Commission has made much of this point in its analysis of agreements under Article 85(1).

If no intention to restrain competition can be inferred from the agreement or its provisions, then it is necessary to examine the effects of the agreement to see whether they were restrictive or distortive of competition.[81]

4.3.4.2 Restriction of Competition and 'Appreciability'

The Court, however, has always maintained that the concept of restriction of competition, whether under the object test or the effects test,[82] must not be applied mechanically; it must be accompanied by a second stage test of 'qualitative appreciability' particularly in the case of vertical agreements.[83] The test asks whether the specific clauses in the

---

[78]   Its mode of analysis takes no account of the actual economic effects of an agreement or provision, let alone basic economic arguments that strong interbrand competition in the final product market can operate to curb the effects of anticompetitive restrictions within a vertical chain of manufacturing and distribution. The analysis consists of an examination of the terms of agreements to determine whether they limit, or are intended to limit, the freedom of action of the parties to the agreement or third parties in the market.

[79]   See Green Paper, op. cit. *supra* n. 71.

[80]   [1966] ECR 235.

[81]   Ibid. at n. 80. In both cases effect on competition was to be measured by comparing the results of the agreement with the likely state of affairs which would exist in the absence of that restriction.

[82]   See e.g. *STM* n. 80 above.

[83]   Even at the time of the *Grundig* decision, the Court of Justice had the conviction that the freedom of action concept should not apply as comprehensively to vertical agreements as it should to horizontal agreements. Having insisted in *Grundig* that Art. 85 applied to vertical agreements as well as horizontal agreements, and accepted that a version of the freedom of action test was applicable, the Court was equally insistent that the test of restriction should be subject to a qualitative as well as a quantitative appreciability test.

agreement, though restrictive in form, are, or would be, 'appreciable' in their market and legal context.[84]

The appreciability test was directed by the Court from the outset at the Commission's automatic assumption that territorial exclusivity in a vertical contract such as a licence is a 'restriction of competition'. Thus, in the case of *STM* v. *Maschinenbau Ulm*, the Court stated that 'an agreement whereby a producer entrusts the sale of his products in a given area to a sole distributor cannot automatically fall under the prohibition in Art. 85(1)'. But such an agreement may contain the elements set out in that provision by reason of 'the severity of the clauses protecting the exclusive dealership'.[85]

The Court's insistence on a qualitative test of appreciablity was also concerned with the need to ensure that the restraint was appreciable in terms of the movement of interstate trade. As the Court put it in *STM*, an appreciable restriction was one which restricted sales to and from other member states in the agreement or 'limited the opportunities allowed for other commercial competitors in the same products by way of parallel re-exportation and importation'.[86] If there was no appreciable curb on interstate freedom of action, there was no appreciable anticompetitive effect.

Under Article 85(1), the cases by the Court of Justice applying the reasoning of qualitative appreciability are more commonly described as the 'rule of reason' cases.[87] We shall discuss these cases below in relation to IPRs.

---

[84] The Court in *STM* went on to indicate that the appreciability test also had a qualitative dimension. It extended to '. . . the severity of the clauses intended to protect the exclusive dealership or alternatively the opportunities allowed for other commercial competitors in the same products by way of parallel re-exportation and importation.' This indicated that the appreciability test was also concerned with an analysis of clauses in part to determine the extent of their market partitioning effect. There was a suggestion that the absence of such an effect might help to create a basis for clearance under Art. 85(1) thus foreshadowing the category of 'open' exclusive licence that was recognized in the later *Maize Seed* case.

[85] See n. 80 above.

[86] See n. 80 above.

[87] See e.g. R. Whish and B. Sufrin, 'Article 85 The Rule of Reason' [1987] *Ox. Yrbk. in Eur. Law*; Forrester and Norall, 'The Laicisation of Community Law Self Help and the Rule of Reason' [1984] 21 *CML Rev.* 11.

5

The Development of the Concept of Restriction of Competition and Intellectual Property Right Licensing

The application of the two steps of the test of restriction of competition to intellectual property right (IPR) licensing has required modification in two respects. The first test has been modified by the concept of scope of the patent. The second test of appreciability gives greater weight to the fact that exclusive IPR agreements are licences of manufacturing processes and require protection from the risks of competition if licensees are not be be deterred from investing in the risky costs of entering the markets of other member states. Let us examine each of these factors in turn.

5.1 THE SCOPE OF THE PATENT DOCTRINE AND RESTRICTION ON COMPETITION

IPR licensing historically enjoyed a special position under the test of restriction of competition in Article 85(1). In the period prior to *Grundig*, the Commission accepted that exclusive patent licensing agreements, unlike exclusive distribution agreements, could be viewed as not restrictive of competition as long as the contents of the licence remained within the 'scope of the patent'. During this period, many restrictions in patent licensing agreements were found to be acceptable under Article 85(1), provided that they did not go beyond the scope of the patent rights of the licensor, as patentee.

The concept of scope of the patent was derived from US antitrust law[1] and the German law against restraints on competition,[2] both of which maintained that certain practices which extended the original grant of exclusivity, such as tie-ins of non-patented products with

---

[1] Under US law, the patent misuse doctrine evolved from patent law and was later taken up by antitrust law to find clauses which extended the scope of the original exclusivity beyond the patentee itself to be patent abuse. See e.g. *Mercoid Corpn.* v. *Mid Continent Investment Co.* 320 US 661 (1943).

[2] S.20(1) of the Act Against Restraints of Competition provides that patent licensing agreements are void to the extent that they impose restraints on the licensee which exceed the scope of the patent grant. Certain restrictions are deemed not to exceed the patent right.

patented products; price and territorial restrictions on the sale of a patented product, post expiration royalties; licensee veto of other licensees; territorial restrictions on a sale of unpatented products made with a patented process as misuse of the patent, were illegal *per se*.

The Commission's concept of scope of the patent accepted that certain clauses in IP licences which simply divided and shared the licensor's rights as patentee were not restrictions of competition. At this stage, the Commission was prepared to draw a distinction between provisions in the licensing agreement which flowed from the inherent subject matter of the licensed right and formed part of the right itself and which should be compatible with Article 85(1) and those clauses which were an attempt to extend the economic power of the licensor beyond its inherent scope.[3] This first category formed a notable exception to the Commission's freedom of action concept of restriction on competition which applied more widely to exclusive distribution and other agreements. Implicit in the Commission's reasoning was that because the licence was a subdivision of a right granted by legislation, it deprived no third party of their freedom of action.[4]

The influence of the doctrine of scope of the patent could be seen in the earlier formulation of Article 4(2) of Regulation 17/62 which provided that notification was not required with respect to bilateral agreements which only imposed restrictions on the exercise of the rights of the assignee or user of intellectual property rights. It reached its high point, however, in the Commission's Notice on Patent Licensing Agreements of 1962 (the so called 'Christmas Message'). This Notice provided that a patent licence containing only limitations as to technical applications or fields of use, quantity of products to be manufactured, or restrictions on time, or persons to carry out the licensing role would not be caught by Article 85(1). These restrictions were viewed as essentially divisions of the patentee's grant of exclusive rights. What was particularly significant about the Notice was its acceptance that licensors involved in a single licensing relationship could give an 'exclusive' licence to a licensee for a particular territory, i.e. a licence which restricted the licensor not only from appointing any other licensee in that territory but also from making, using or selling itself in that territory, and not be caught by Article 85(1). At this point in time, the Commission accepted that these obligations and rights of the licensee entailed 'only a partial maintenance of the right of prohibition contained in the patentee's exclusive right in

[3] See e.g. First Report of Competition Policy (1972) at pp. 65–74; Fourth Report on Competition Policy (1974) point 20.

[4] In *Zucker Unie* an analogous argument was attempted that since the government regulation had already restricted competition, the contractual co-operation was not itself restrictive of competiton.

relation to the licensee who in other respects is authorised to exploit the invention'. The implication, at this stage, was that an agreement which divided the right under a patent to manufacture, use, and sell a protected product geographically came within its scope just as much as a division of technical application. Neither provision fell within the prohibition of Article 85(1).

It also accepted that certain other obligations in licensing agreements were not caught by Article 85(1), namely (a) the obligation to mark the products with an indication of the product, (b) the obligation to maintain quality standards or procure supplies of products indispensable to the technically perfect exploitation of the patent, (c) non-exclusive grant backs of know-how or licences of inventions. These were regarded as essential in view of the shared nature of the intellectual property right in a licensing relationship.

The Notice itself indicated that other types of clauses had to be examined individually and did not provide a general clearance for more complex licensing arrangements such as joint ownership of patents, reciprocal licences, multiple parallel licences, or to any clauses attempting to extend beyond the period of validity of the patent. Indeed it implied that agreements with the latter clause might have difficulties in getting through the Article 85(3) barrier.

The Commission's reasons for clearing patent licensing agreements in this way were also pragmatic.[5] It thought at the time that patent licences were 'not likely to affect trade between Member States as things stand in the Community at present'.[6] Moreover, it was preoccupied with the issues of formulating a block exemption for distribution agreements and would not have welcomed a flood of notifications of patent licensing agreements.[7]

In the event, the scope of the patent doctrine as incorporated in the Notice helped to shelter patent licensing from the effects of the Commission's 'freedom of action' doctrine throughout the 1960s.[8]

The application of this doctrine consisted of a formalistic analysis of the restrictions in the licence of the IPR and required no analysis of the

---

[5] See e.g. W. Alexander, 'Patent Licensing Agreements in the EC' [1986] *IIC* 1.

[6] See Goyder, *EC Competition Law* (2nd edn., 1993) at p. 290.

[7] See Alexander, op. cit. n. 5.

[8] During the remainder of the 1960s there were few formal notifications of patent licensing agreements. The first Annual Report refers to two cases. One in 1966 consisted of cross-licensing arrangement between two firms, in which their patent sub-licences contained provisions for requirements for licensees to purchase unpatented products from either of the licensors. The Commission's view was that this was an illegal extension of the patent monopoly and a tie-in which did not meet the test of the 1962 Notice. The second case concerned a licensing agreement in which the licensor had incorporated restrictions on exploitation of the patented products beyond the period of validity of the patent. See discussion in Goyder, *EC Competition Law* (2nd edn., 1993) pp. 290–1.

economic effects of the clause or agreement upon the market. Nevertheless, it provided a basis to reconcile intellectual property licensing with Article 85 which allowed considerable weight to be given to the legislative policy underpinning the IPR.[9] For IPR licensing, particularly patent licensing, during the 1960s and 1970s, the scope of the IPR doctrine helped to neutralize the freedom of action doctrine. Unlike distribution, patent licensing could remain free of the notification/exemption decision under Article 85 because such agreements were not caught by Article 85(1) in the first place. There was little pressure for a block exemption at this stage.

5.2 THE COMMISSION'S CHANGE TO *PER SE* PROHIBITIONS IN
LICENSING AGREEMENTS

By the early 1970s, the attitude of the Commission to licensing of IPRs had dramatically changed. This was in part due to the greater awareness of the potential of IPR licences to seal off markets and limit inter-state competition created by the *Grundig* decision.[10] It was also due, however, to the Commission's overzealous interpretation of its role as protector of the flows of direct and parallel trade between the member states. Instead of drawing a distinction between exclusive territorial manufacturing licences and territorial sales restrictions, it chose to apply *per se* prohibitions to both. It is worth considering each point in greater detail.

5.2.1 The *Grundig* Decision

If one were to read Article 85(1) literally, it would appear to be confined to the type of anticompetitive agreements specified in Article 85(1) (a)–(e)—fixing prices, limiting production, limiting markets, price discrimination, etc. In *Grundig*, however, the Court widened the scope of the prohibition in Article 85(1) by defining it to apply to market partitioning agreements. Thus it stated that the infringement of Article 85 consisted of the attempt by the licensor and licensee to isolate 'the French market for Grundig products and maintain . . . artificially, for products of a very well known brand, separate national markets within the community'. This was prohibited under Article 85 as an attempt 'to distort competition in the common market'.

---

[9] Although directed essentially at patent licensing, it could also have been developed to fit other types of intellectual property licensing such as trade marks, copyright, and design rights. [10] *Grundig* v. *Commission* [1966] ECR 299.

An agreement between producer and distributor which might tend to restore the national divisions in trade between Member States might be such as to frustrate the most fundamental object of the Community. The treaty whose preamble and content aim at abolishing the barriers between States, and which in several provisions gives evidence of a stern attitude with regard to their reappearance, could not allow undertakings to reconstruct such barriers. Article 85(1) is designed to pursue this aim, even in the case of agreements between undertakings placed at different levels of the economic process.

In the course of the judgment in *Grundig*, too, the case was made that the distribution agreement was not a restriction of competition because it added a new competitor to the French market to compete with other brands. Consten and Grundig argued that the Commission should have based its approach on a rule of reason and considered the economic effects of the disputed contracts on competition between the different brands. More specifically, it should have taken into consideration the fact that a vertical sole dealer relationship by introducing a new competitor into the French market increases interbrand competition in that market. The Court accepted that 'competition between producers is generally more noticeable than that between distributors of the same make'. The Court, however, was particularly concerned to exclude this as a mitigating factor in a situation where the agreement inhibited interstate trade. As the Court put it:

The principle of freedom of competition concerns the various stages and manifestations of competition. Although competition between producers is generally more noticeable than that between distributors of the same make, it does not . . . follow that an agreement tending to restrict the latter kind of competition should escape the prohibition in Article 85(1) merely because it might increase the former.[11]

Nevertheless, the decision to group vertical agreements together with horizontal agreements as equal subjects of competition law regulation was a new departure in the practice of competition law systems.

The legacy of *Grundig* was a framework establishing two important parameters for the regulation of IPR licensing both stemming from the constitutional role of Article 85 to promote the integration of the separate markets of the EC into a single market. The first parameter it established was that an agreement which contained measures to partition markets

---

[11] See too the analogous argument on interstate trade: 'what is particularly important is whether the agreement is capable of constituting a threat, either direct or indirect, actual or potential to freedom of trade between Member States in a manner which might harm the attainment of the objectives of a single market between states'. Thus, the fact that an agreement encourages an increase, even a large one, in the volume of trade between States is not sufficient to exclude the possibility that the agreement may not affect trade in the above-mentioned manner.

was restrictive of competition under Article 85(1), thus creating curbs on the scope for the normal exercise of the option of IPR licensing. The second was the creation of a *per se* restriction which was not only prohibited by article 85(1) but was also non-exemptible under Article 85(3), again because of the market integration imperative.

5.2.2 The Commission's Change of Policy

In the period after *Grundig*, and with the exclusive distribution block exemption approved, the Commission decided that it could turn its attentions to the need to monitor restrictions in networks of licensing agreements which affected interstate trade. The large number of licensing agreements which had been notified to it had made it plain that networks of multiple parallel licensing agreements created exclusive territories which coincided with the territory of member states. Yet the exclusive territorial rights to manufacture did not in themselves contribute to the sealing off effects. It was the accompanying territorial sales restrictions.

Where an exclusive licensing agreement restricted to one territory is part of a licensing wider network, there is always the potential for competition between the licensees who have been allocated exclusive territories. The territorial nature of the manufacturing and sales right does not restrict the free movement of goods which incorporate the right. Under EC law, the right of free circulation attaches to the goods as soon as they are placed on the market and possibly as soon as they are manufactured.[12] Consequently, the licensees can engage in direct sales to other licensees' territories, whether actively by advertising or passively by responding to unsolicited orders. Moreover, the customers of a licensee can engage in parallel trading, exporting and importing the licensed goods and services between the different territories of the licensees as well as that of the licensor. In such a situation, the territorial sales restrictions imposed on the licensees might reduce interstate trade but not exclusive territorial restrictions on manufacture by themselves. The only effect of an exclusive licence is to limit the number of licensees with a right to manufacture and sell in the protected area. By itself, an exclusive licence to manufacture and sell has no effect on direct or parallel sales from other member states.[13]

The Commission's *First Report on Competition Policy* summed up the change in position by stating that where the owner of a patent conferred

---

[12] See e.g. B. Van der Asch, 'Intellectual Property Rights under EC Law' [1983] *Fordham Corp. Law Inst.* 539.
[13] Cf. Joliet, 'Trademark Licensing under the EEC Law of Competition' [1984] *IIC* 31.

an exclusive right to another undertaking in an assigned area, 'he loses the freedom to enter into agreements with other applicants. The exclusive character of such a license may amount to a restriction of competition and thus fall within the category of prohibited agreements in so far as it has an appreciable effect on market conditions.'[14]

The Commission was prepared to apply a quantitative appreciability test to such agreements, but not a qualitative appreciability test. It preferred such licensing agreements to be tested under Article 85(3). This change in Commission practice meant that the assumptions of the Notice began to be called into question, resulting in a greater need for patent licensing agreements to be notified to the Commission for exemption.

In *Burroughs-Delplanque*,[15] the Commission was notified of an exclusive patent and know-how manufacturing licence to manufacture plasticized carbon paper in France, combined with a non-exclusive licence to sell and use the trade mark throughout the EC and in other territories, The Commission 'cleared' the agreement but only on the ground that the exclusive licensing rights of the licensees amounted to about 10 per cent of the market. It indicated that if the parties' market shares were higher, an exclusive manufacturing licence to a licensee in a particular territory would be viewed as restricting competition and therefore contrary to Article 85(1).

if [a patent holder] undertakes to limit the exploitation of its exclusive right to a single undertaking in a territory and thus confers on that single undertaking the right to exploit the invention and to prevent other undertakings from using it, it thus loses the power to contract with other applicants for a license. In certain cases, the exclusive character of a manufacturing license may restrict competition and be covered by the prohibition set out in Article 85(1).

The Commission also decided that the no challenge clause in the patent licence was prohibited under Article 85(1).

In *Davidson Rubber*,[16] a licence network involving exclusive licensees in West Germany and France with market shares, measured by output, of 20 per cent and 40 per cent respectively, the Commission found that the agreement was caught by Article 85(1). The Commission reasoned that the restriction on the licensor's ability to appoint other licensees limited the freedom of potential suppliers and exporters of the licensed product. As the Commission saw it, 'but for the exclusive rights Davidson might have granted a license for the same area to someone else and, if it had, the licensee might have exported to other member states.'

---

[14] Annex to the *Fifth General Report on the Activities of the Communities*, Apr. 1972, at pt. 78.

[15] *Burroughs-Geha-Werke* OJ L13/53 (1972); *Burroughs-Delplanque* OJ EC L13/50 (1972).

[16] OJ EC L143/31 (1972).

The Commission was prepared to grant an exemption because the exclusivity was necessary to induce the licensee to take on the risks in investing in the manufacturing facilities for a new product but this meant that the agreement would have had to be notified when made.

With the Commission's Notice made suspect by these decisions, there was no longer an easy method of clearance for patent licences. The parties to licensing agreements now found themselves in a similar position to the parties to exclusive distribution agreements but without the benefit of the exclusive dealing block exemption.[17] Industry now were faced with the need to notify patent licensing agreements to the Commission in order to obtain certainty as to their legal validity, and responded by engaging in intensive lobbying of national governments. There were also efforts made to introduce provisions in the drafting of the Community Patent Convention in 1975 to offset the Commission's policy.[18] Article 43(1) of the draft Convention provided that a Community patent may be licensed in whole or in part for the whole or parts of the territories in which it is effective and that a licence may be exclusive or non-exclusive. Article 43(2) then added that the rights conferred by the Community patent may be invoked against a licensee who contravenes any restriction in his licence which is covered by Article 43(1). These were meant to be a signal that such restrictions were not contrary to the treaty.[19]

The Commission responded to this concern by preparing a new patent licensing block exemption to deal with the expected large numbers of notifications. It also introduced a Notice on Sub-Contracting Agreements to help certain types of subcontracting agreements involving licences to be cleared by a group notice.[20] It was not prepared to bow to the lobbying pressure in respect of territorial exclusivity under Article 85(1).

In AOIP/Beyrard[21] it reiterated its basic position in respect of territorial exclusivity. The case itself involved a classical vertical licensing agreement. Beyrard, a French inventor of rheostats and other devices for motor cars, granted an exclusive patent licence to AOIP to manufacture and sell such products in France and the French territories. The Commission was troubled both by the territorial restrictions and the non-territorial restrictions accompanying the exclusive licence. The Commission decided that the grant of exclusive manufacturing rights in the licensing agreement was caught by Article 85(1).[22] The fact that such

---

[17] Reg. 1963/63. [18] See Alexander, op. cit. n. 5 above.

[19] Alexander, op. cit. n. 5 above.

[20] Notice on Contractors and Subcontractors [1979] 1 CMLR 264.

[21] OJ EC L6/8 (1976).

[22] The Commission held the same in the case of a grant of an exclusive right by a German company to use patented steel formulating methods in France. See *Kabelmetal-Luchaire* OJ EC (L 222) 34 (1975).

exclusivity provided a necessary incentive to the licensee to penetrate a new market which had not been, and could not be, exploited by the licensor was a basis only for exemption under Article 85(3) and not clearance under Article 85(1).

The Commission also decided that the obligation upon the licensor not to sell into the licensed territory and the obligation upon the licensee not to sell the licensed product to any country in which the licensor had licensed or assigned the product were normally prohibited under Article 85(1). The first restriction could be exempted provided it was limited to the first sale and otherwise met the test of the four conditions of Article 85(3). The second could be exempted provided that the prohibition applied to direct sales only, was limited in time and met the test of Article 85(3), in particular the indispensability requirement.[23] In its *Fourth Report on Competition Policy* in 1975, the Commission attempted to reconcile its decisions with the earlier pronouncements of the Court of Justice concerning IPRs:

On a legal plane, the Commission faces the problems exposed by the Court of Justice in its distinction between the existence of nationally protected industrial property rights, which is not to be affected by community law, and the exercise of these rights, which can be subject to the Treaty rules.

The assessment of patent licensing agreements under the Treaty calls upon a consideration of interests and issues which go beyond the field of competition policy . . .[24]

It has been suggested that the policy of the Commission was that it would 'in future . . . regard all export restrictions as needing an exemption under Article 85(3) and thus as not belonging to the "essence"of the patent'.[25] The Commission's policy, however, went further; it seemed to treat the sharing of exclusivity geographically as outside the scope of the patent without applying an appreciability test under Article 85(1).

During this period too the Commission adjusted the concept of the 'essence' or 'scope of the patent' in respect of non-territorial restrictions in order to meet competition concerns. In *AOIP* v. *Beyrard*, for example, the Commission found that certain non-territorial provisions were prohibited by Article 85(1), for example the no-challenge clause, non-competition

---

[23] In *Kabelmetal-Luchaire*, the Commission also held that a contractual prohibition on direct sales by the licensee outside its territory was prohibited by Art. 85(1). OJ EC (L 222) 34 (1975).

[24] Annex to *Seventh General Report on the Activities of the Communities*, 1975, at pts. 19 and 20,

[25] Govaere illustrates the point by reference to statements by the Commission in *Kabelmetal-Luchaire* and *Bronbemaling-Heidemaat* to the effect that the undertaking not to grant licences to other parties 'is not the essence of his right as a patent-holder'. At p. 117.

clause, the obligation to pay royalties during the lifetime of the most recent original or improvement patent, whether or not the original patent was being exploited by the licensee. These were all viewed as going beyond the scope of the patent and not only caught by Article 85(1) but also inherently non-exemptible under Article 85(3).[26]

In its Fourth Report, the Commission indicated that subdivisions of the grant of the IPR could be compatible with Article 85(1) subject to the absence of competition effects. For example, restrictions on the duration of the licence were allowed within the frame of the duration of the original grant. Restrictions on field of use were allowed but only as long as they were not disguised market sharing arrangements. Quantitative output restrictions were caught by Article 85(1).

This restrictive policy towards both territorial and non-territorial restraints in licensing agreements was reflected in the draft block exemption for patent licensing officially published in 1979. It allowed territorial exclusivity to all licensees but restricted all territorial sales restraints and export bans to SMEs only, defining these as undertakings with a turnover of less than 100 million ECU. It incorporated a 'blacklist' of fourteen clauses, the presence of any of which would preclude the application of the block exemption. It also offered a 'whitelist' of nine restraints which would not prevent exemption which were more based on the test of clearance under Article 85(1), stating only that they may or may not be caught under Article 85(1).

A factor that appears to have reinforced the Commission's attitude towards non-territorial restrictions in patent licensing agreements was the knowledge that the Antitrust Division of the US Justice Department, under the influence of the 'patent misuse' doctrine developed by the US Supreme Court,[27] had developed a set of administrative guidelines to antitrust enforcement[28] in the form of Nine No Nos for patent licensing. The following restrictions were viewed as *per se* unlawful:

1. Tie-ins
2. Grant backs
3. Resale restraints
4. Tie-outs

[26] Similarly, in *Vaessen/Morris*, the Commission found that a tie-in of certain products to a patented product and process was prohibited by Art. 85(1) because it was not essential to the proper exploitation of the patent. Other products were perfectly adequate and the effect of the tie-in was to deprive the licensee of its business freedom to obtain its supplies elsewhere, if it chose. We shall explore the development of the law of non-territorial restraints in ch. 8.

[27] Under the impetus of Mr Justice Douglas. See e.g. *Morton Salt Co.* v. *G. S. Suppiger Co.* 314 US 488 (1941); *United States* v. *United States Gypsum Co.* 333 US 364 (1947).

[28] Wilson, Dept. of Justice Luncheon Speech, 'Law on Licensing Practice—Myth or Reality Straight Talk from Alice in Wonderland.'

5. Licensee vetoes
6. Mandatory package licences
7. Royalties not reasonably related to the licensees' sales of the patented product
8. Restrictions on the sale of an unpatented product manufactured with a patented process
9. Price restrictions on sales of a licensed product.[29]

These restraints were not subject to a rule of reason. At this stage, the Justice Department appeared to be unconcerned about the effects of strict antitrust rules upon the process of innovation.[30]

The influence of the Nine No Nos reached into the European Commission in the preparation of the draft block exemption. As Hartmut Johannes, the administrator within DGIV (the Competition Directorate) with responsibility for intellectual property rights, put it in 1978, 'In the art of antitrust, the Americans are the teachers and the Europeans are the pupils.' He indicated that US thinking was not accepted uncritically; in particular its *per se* rules and the horizontal/vertical distinction were not transferable. However, he also acknowledged that when the Commission prepared its draft patent licensing block exemption. 'It knew the no nos but of course not the American critics of these no nos; the critics dated from 1981.'[31]

For intellectual property rightholders in the EC, however, the main worries created by the Commission's policy surrounded its refusal to accept the logic of the need for protection of new licensees against competition from other licensees as well as the licensor during the period the licensee was tooling up and familiarizing itself with the new technology.

---

[29] Oppenheim, Weston and McCarthy, *Federal Antitrust Laws Tenth Commentary* (4th edn., 1981) 885–7.

[30] In 1967, the Assistant Attorney General announced: 'I do not believe that the impact of antitrust on patent licensing restrictions has any effect on innovative activity whatsoever . . . to me it seems probably so even if antitrust law were to go so far as to prohibit not only price fixing but also field of use restrictions, quantity restrictions, territorial restrictions, and any other restriction on the complete freedom of the licensee'. In Turner, 'Antitrust and Innovation', 12 *Antitrust Bulletin* 277 at 281 (1967).

[31] This was a reference to the ground swell in antitrust thinking which had been introduced by a combination of the writings of Chicago School adherents such as Bork and Posner and the experience of the administrators within the Justice Department. See E. Fox, 'The New American Competition Policy—from Antitrust to Pro-Efficiency [1981] 2 *ECLR* 439; see also e.g. R. Bork, *An Antitrust Paradox: A Policy at War with Itself* (Basic Books, New York, 2nd edn. 1978, reissued 1993); R. Posner, *Antitrust Law: An Economic Perspective* (University of Chicago Press, 1976). By 1987 the department's views had begun to change quite radically. It signalled the change by suggesting that there was a need to differentiate between horizontal and vertical restraints and to move away from a formalistic approach to an economic approach consisting of an evaluation of licensing restraints. See Abbot Lipsky, 'Current Antitrust Division Views on Patent Licensing Practices', Antitrust Section of the ABA, 15 Nov. 1981, 1981 *Trade Regulation Reporter* (CCH) ¶ 55, 985.

These were not allayed by the draft block exemption with its relatively low turnover limits.

Industry was uneasy because, until an appropriate block exemption could be prepared, it was faced with a pervasive notification requirement for intellectual property rights licences. The Commission's policy at this stage appeared to be doubly unfriendly to innovation. It insisted upon an automatic prohibition of exclusive territorial licences under Article 85(1), in spite of the costs and delays of notification. Yet in its draft block exemption it appeared to be unwilling to translate Article 85(3) to allow protection for territorial sales restrictions to any but the smallest firms.

Competition policy at that stage was so focused on monitoring exclusivity in licensing agreements that it risked deterring investment in innovation and technology transfer. It appeared to ignore the need under the Treaty to strike a balance between the protection of interstate trade and the promotion of the diffusion of the manufacture of new technologies throughout the common market.

5.3 THE COURT'S APPLICATION OF THE APPRECIABILITY TEST TO INTELLECTUAL PROPERTY RIGHTS

5.3.1 Exclusive Territoriality

In the early 1980s, it fell to the Court of Justice to lead the way in easing the competition law framework for intellectual property rights licensing. The Court had previously indicated that the test for territorial exclusivity in vertical contracts should include a qualitative appreciability test in *STM*.[32] Moreover, a careful reading of *Grundig*[33] would have noted that the decision did not preclude the need for an appreciability test to exclusive licences along the lines proposed by the Court in *STM* a few weeks earlier. It was true that the *Grundig* decision gave support to the freedom of action interpretation of restriction of competition. It was also true that the concern of *Grundig* with the distortion of competition was directed at provisions 'aiming at isolating the French market for Grundig products and maintaining ... separate national markets within the Community'. However, this concern was directed at provisions in the contract such as the obligation to place export bans on wholesalers and the use that Consten could make of the IPR to exclude parallel imports; it was not directed at the agreement to give Consten an exclusive trade mark licence for France as such.

---

[32] *STM* v. *Maschinenbau Ulm* [1966] ECR 235.   [33] [1966] ECR 299.

In the much awaited decision of *Nungesser* v. *Commission*,[34] the Court of Justice was able to apply its qualitative appreciability test to licensing agreements for the first time. The case concerned an assignment of breeders' rights to a maize seed variety by INRA, a French research institution, to Eisele who registered the right in Germany. Under the agreement, Eisele was given an exclusive right to manufacture and sell INRA's maize seed variety in Germany. In addition, INRA agreed itself to refrain, and to prevent others, from importing its maize seed variety in Germany. Eisele had relied upon its intellectual property right to prevent a parallel importer from importing into Germany from another French source and had obtained a court approved settlement. Receiving a complaint, the Commission decided, following its policy of the 1970s, that all provisions of the agreement were caught by Article 85(1) and could not be exempted under Article 85(3). This meant that the Commission was prepared to treat exclusive territorial licences to manufacture and sell as equally anticompetitive as territorial sales restrictions under Article 85(1). Both required exemption under Article 85(3). The Commission's view was that the exclusive territorial licences were restrictive of the freedom of action of the parties to the agreement and had an adverse effect on the freedom of action of third parties to import and export the maize seed between France and Germany.

The Court objected to the Commission's insistence that an exclusivity clause in a vertical agreement such as an intellectual property right licence was by its nature caught by Article 85(1) as a restriction on competition,[35] because this gave insufficient weight to the fact that the new seed technology could only move to new member states if the exclusive territorial restriction was part of the contract and was the only means to promote competition.

It thought that there was a need to distinguish between exclusive licences to manufacture and sell in a particular territory on the one hand, and territorial sales restrictions which consist of a contractual obligation on other licensees not to sell directly into a protected territory on the other. The first case, which it called an 'open exclusive license' was one where 'the exclusivity of the license relates solely to the contractual relationship between the owner of the right and the licensee, whereby the owner merely undertakes not to grant other licenses in respect of the same territory and not to compete himself with the licensee on that territory'. In the second case, which it called a 'closed exclusive license', the exclusive licence is joined with territorial sales restrictions and IPRs to create an absolute territorial protection under which the parties to the contract propose, as regards the products and the territory in question, to

---

[34] [1982] ECR 2015.   [35] Ibid. at para. 2 (c).

eliminate all competition from third parties, such as parallel importers or licensees for other territories.[36]

The Court held that an open exclusive licence, i.e. an exclusive licence to manufacture and sell in a particular territory, was 'not in itself incompatible with Article 85(1)',[37] reasoning as follows:

in case of a license of breeders' rights over hybrid seeds newly developed in one Member State, an undertaking established in another Member State which was not certain that it would not encounter competition from other licensees for the territory granted to it, or from the owner of the right himself, might be deterred from accepting the risk of cultivating and marketing that product, such a result would be damaging to the dissemination of a new technology and would prejudice competition in the Community between the new product and similar existing products.

The Court thus reversed the Commission insofar as it had held that the following two types of territorial restraints were contrary to Article 85(1);

1. the exclusive licence to Eisele to produce and sell in Germany, i.e. the obligation upon INRA, or those deriving rights through INRA, to refrain from producing or selling the relevant seeds in Germany through other licensees; and,
2. the licensor's obligation not to compete, i.e. the obligation upon INRA, or those deriving rights through INRA, to refrain themselves from producing or selling the relevant seeds in Germany.[38]

The Court stated that where an exclusive license of plant seed varieties 'does not affect the position of third parties such as parallel importers and licensees for other territories, the exclusive license' it is not in itself incompatible with Article 85(1) of the EEC Treaty.

5.3.2 The Scope of the Exception for Open Exclusive Licences

The open exclusive licence as defined by the Court allowed for a limited form of protection from the other manufacturers within the licence network. Thus, the licensee could have protection under the contract against either the licensor or other licensees locating manufacturing operations in the territory. The Court reasoned that this limited form of security to the licensee was necessary to induce risky investment and it offered no contractual protection against technical products sold in other territories and imported into the territory.

---

[36] Ibid. at para. 53. [37] At para. 53.
[38] See M. Siragusa, 'Technology Transfers under EEC Law, A Private View' [1983] *Fordham Corp. Law Inst.* 95.

The Court indicated, however,[39] that any attempt to place limits on other licensees, as well as on the more obvious category of parallel importers, not to sell into the territory would take the licence outside the scope of an open licence.[40]

Moreover, where a licence provided absolute territorial protection, consisting of protection from all competition from the licensor, other licensees, and their customers, it would be viewed as a 'closed' exclusive licence and would not only be caught by Article 85(1); it would be incapable of being exempted by Article 85(3).

The Court therefore upheld the rest of the Commission's decision which included a prohibition of the following two obligations:

1. the contractual ban on exports, i.e. the obligation upon INRA, or those deriving rights through INRA, to prevent third parties from exporting the relevant seeds into Germany without the licensee's authorization for use or sale in that territory; and
2. Eisele's use of his exclusive rights, both contractual and under the intellectual property right, to prevent all imports of the seed variety into Germany or exports to other member states.[41]

5.4 THE NEW TECHNOLOGY/MARKET OPENING TEST

Although the Court defined open exclusive licences as a category which is not automatically caught by Article 85(1), it did not hold that all 'open' licences were cleared. Instead, it set out four conditions which an exclusive licence had to satisfy in order to be regarded as compatible with Article 85(1):

first, the product had to be new to the licensee's market.[42] The Court indicated that the maize seed in question would have qualified on that count. What was called for was a new technology and not merely the novelty required to obtain a patent.

Secondly, the technology had to be developed after years of research and experimentation.[43]

Thirdly, without the exclusivity the licensee might not be willing to take on the risks of developing and marketing that new product.[44]

Fourthly, that the absence of intrabrand protection would result in the failure to improve interbrand protection.

---

[39] See Siragusa, 'EEC Technology Transfers—A Private View' [1982] *Fordham Corp. Law Inst.* 116–18.

[40] [1982] ECR 2015, at para. 58.

[41] See discussion in ch. 7.

[42] [1982] ECR 2015, at para. 55.

[43] Ibid. at para. 56.

[44] Ibid. at para. 57.

All four conditions had to be satisfied. Some of the conditions left considerable discretion to the Commission or the courts to define. This was particularly true of the condition of new technology.[45] However, assuming the conditions could be met there would be no need for an exclusive licensing agreement to notify.

In the case of technology which was new and where there were difficulties for the licensee to enter the market without territorial protection, the Court was willing to allow some protection from intrabrand competition in the form of a rival's right to manufacture or sell in the protected territory. It was reluctant, however, to extend its reasoning to a wider form of intrabrand protection, i.e. to protection in the form of territorial sales restrictions placed upon other licensees.

Moreover, its inclusion of interbrand competition as a balancing factor in the assessment of exceptions under Article 85(1) did not indicate a full acceptance of the logic of a 'rule of reason' for vertical restraints.[46] Instead, it signalled quite clearly that the exception was to be carefully circumscribed to cases where the technology was new, the commercial risks would have deterred the licensee in the particular case, and the protection offered consisted only in territorial exclusivity for manufacturing and selling purposes and did not include territorial sales restrictions.[47]

The policy driving the Court was not so much the economic balance between pro- and anticompetitive effects as the integration benefits against the integration costs of the transfer of intellectual property rights in the new technology. Thus, the Court was willing to allow the licensee protection against the licensor in the form of territorial sales restriction, presumably because the licensor had the edge on the licensee in terms of prior experience in manufacture. Yet it drew the line at allowing protection against other licensees, even those who may have gained a competitive edge. That issue was to be left to exemption.

In taking this decision, the Court was not concerned to draw a line between intellectual property rights and competition policy as such, but rather between the need for adequate incentives for the integration of manufacturing processes and the need to protect interstate trade. No mention was made of the existence/exercise distinction or the specific subject-matter issue. The case turned on the specific nature of the technology and the extent of protection against risks that was necessary to achieve its dissemination.[48]

---

[45] See discussion in ch. 7.   [46] See discussion in ch. 7.

[47] See Siragusa, op. cit. n. 39.

[48] See e.g. Jan Peeters, 'The Rule of Reason Revisited: Prohibition on Restraints of Competition in the Sherman Act and the EEC Treaty', Vol. 37 *The American Journal of Comparative Law*, 521 at p. 566.

In *Coditel II*,[49] the Court went a step further and held that an agreement conferring an exclusive right to exhibit a film for a specified period in the territory of the member states with absolute territorial protection is not necessarily caught by Article 85(1).

In the *Coditel* cases, a Belgian company, Cine Vog Films, had obtained exclusive exhibition rights to a French film, *Le Boucher*, for a five year period. It discovered that Coditel, a group of Belgian cable companies, had obtained the film from a transmission broadcast by the German licensee with exclusive rights in Germany. In *Coditel I*,[50] Cine Vog was able to obtain an injunction to prohibit Coditel from transmitting the film on Belgian television without offending Article 59 (free movement of services). Coditel had argued that such exclusive rights limited to member states would result in a partitioning of the common market as regards the undertaking of economic action in the film industry. The Court, however, took note of the specific characteristics of the product, i.e. that it was a literary or artistic work available to the public which may be infinitely repeated and presented problems of copyright different from other works such as books which are circulated in a material form. It also took note of the contract which stipulated that the right to show the film on Belgian television could not be exercised until a fixed number of months after the first showing of the film in cinemas in Belgium. The Court considered that this highlighted the fact that the right of a copyright owner and his assigns to require fees for any showing is part of the essential function of copyright in this type of literary and artistic work. The Court reasoned that the effect of these factors was that:

whilst copyright entails the right to demand fees for any showing or performance, the rules in the Treaty cannot in principle constitute an obstacle to the geographical limits which the parties to a contract of assignment have agreed upon in order to protect the author and his assigns in this regard. The mere fact that these geographical limits may coincide with national frontiers does not point to a different solution in situations where television is organized in the Member States largely on the basis of legal broadcasting monopolies.[51]

The Court held that the assignee could rely on his performing right to prohibit an unauthorized showing by cable television without offending Article 59.

In *Coditel II*, the cable company group Coditel appealed from the decision of a Belgian court awarding damages to Cine Vog for the unauthorized transmission. The theory of Coditel on this occasion was that Article 85 could be applied to the agreement and that its prohibition applied to the exclusive licence or assignment of the copyright as an

---

49 [1982] ECR 3381.   50 [1980] ECR 881.   51 Ibid. at para. 16.

improper exercise as the means of a restrictive agreement. The Court accepted that in principle the exercise of an IPR in the form of an agreement may be incompatible with Article 85 but it held that:

the mere fact that the owner of a copyright in a firm has granted to a sole licensee the exclusive right to exhibit that film in the territory of a Member State and consequently to prohibit, during a specified period, its showing by others is not sufficient to justify the finding that a contract must be regarded as the purpose, the means or the result of an agreement, decision or concerted practice prohibited by the Treaty.[52]

The Court was willing to allow the licensor to bestow absolute territorial protection upon the licensee because the industry was engaged in an integrative activity and investment in licensing the product protected by the IPR could only be secured if the full territorial protection was allowed. The Court reiterated the distinction it drew in *Coditel I*, i.e. between licences of works which are performing rights which can be infinitely repeated without anything physical being put on the market and other types of literary and artistic works such as books or records which cannot be circulated in the market apart from their material form.[53] In the Article 85(1) context, this was not so much an attentiveness to the nature of the IPR; rather, the Court was willing to justify the absolute territorial protection on the basis that it was necessary to prevent the purpose of the licensing agreement from being entirely frustrated.[54]

The Court's concern for the protection of the IPR and a need to ensure a just return on the investment made in developing the industrial property should also be seen as prompted more by the need to ensure that the film industry continued to penetrate national markets than to an insistence upon allowing inventors to appropriate their just return. The Court indicated that its indispensability test for territorial protection was related to the special 'characteristics of the [film] industry and its markets in the Community, especially those relating to dubbing and subtitling for the benefit of different language groups, to the possibilities of television broadcasts, and to the system of financing [film] production in Europe'.[55] In other words, where the financing of the integration of film production through the medium of television throughout Europe would be jeopardized by inadequate IPR protection, and the only adequate protection was absolute territorial protection, the Court was prepared to

---

[52] [1982] ECR 3381. [53] [1982] ECR 3381.
[54] See R. Joliet, 'Territorial and Exclusive Trade Mark Licensing under the EEC Law of Competition' [1984] *IIC* 21; R. Joliet, 'Trademark Licensing Agreements under the EEC Law of Competition' [1983–5] *Northwest Jnl. of Int'l. Law and Business* 755.
[55] [1982] ECR 3381.

allow such protection to ensure that the process of interstate film distribution would actually take place.

The Advocate General had suggested that a just return for IPRs in the film industry related to the specific object of the IPR and was therefore not caught by Article 85(1) but this was not referred to in the Court's judgment. Instead, the Court referred only to a fair return upon the investment made. It was the task of the national court to determine whether the exclusive agreement created barriers which were artificial or unjustifiable in terms of the needs of the industry, of undue duration or based on fees which exceeded a fair return on investment.[56] Moreover, the Court was careful to set limits to the width of the exception it was creating for Community wide film. It would be curtailed where the object or effect was to prevent or restrict the distribution of films or where competition within the film market was distorted.[57] Nevertheless, the Court had created the basis for a further exception in the definition of restraint of competition under Article 85(1).

In *Erauw-Jacquery*,[58] the ECJ showed once again that the width of the exception in Article 85(1) would vary with the type of product protected by an intellectual property right and the industry in which it is used. In this case, the Court was prepared to find an export ban indispensable but the circumstances were unusual. The licence was for basic seed (i.e. seeds used to produce the seeds used by growers for the production of cereals) from the licensor to the propagator and the licensor insisted on an export ban for the purpose of quality control. The export ban and customer restrictions on licensees were held to be compatible with Article 85(1) because they were objectively justified by the need to ensure the proper handling of seeds by the growers who enjoyed a licence only for propagation. The Court stated that 'a person who has made considerable efforts to develop varieties of basic seed which may be the subject matter of plant breeders rights must be allowed to protect himself against any improper handling of those varieties of seed'. The protection against improper handling of seed could only be assured by a restriction of propagation to selected licensees. To that extent the clause prohibiting the licensee from selling and exporting basic seeds does not come within the prohibition laid down by Article 85(1) of the Treaty (paragraph 10).

The Advocate General compared the risk of the technology in the seed finding its way into the hands of rivals as comparable to the risk faced by a franchisor that its franchised know-how might benefit competitors. The Court was also strongly influenced by the substantial

---

[56] [1982] ECR 3381 at para. 19.   [57] Ibid. at para. 20.
[58] [1988] ECR 1919.

financial commitment made in investing in the development of the seed.[59] Although the Court referred to *Nungesser*, this reference was to the financial commitment of the licensor in developing the product and the urgency of the need for protection for the licensor's investment rather than to the need for an adequate incentive of territorial protection for the economic risks undertaken by the licensee.[60]

It would be a mistake to conclude from the indispensability analysis of these exceptions that a general doctrine of ancillary restraints is more widely available to clear territorial IPR restraints, given the Court's concerns with market partitioning under Article 85(1). Instead, the test appears to be twofold: is the degree of territorial protection essential to ensure that the licensing agreement will result in a market opening for the product? Are its effects on intrabrand interstate outweighed by the benefits of the extension of manufacture of goods or provision of service? In the case of *Erauw Jacquery*, for example, the Court placed great weight on the need for protection for quality control purposes. The costs of the ban on exports were outweighed by the penetration benefits of the basic licence. In *Pronuptia*,[61] the Court made it clear in the context of franchise agreements where brands were well-known, territorial exclusivity incentives for franchising were not to be regarded as genuine ancillary restraints for the purposes of Article 85(1). On the other hand if the franchise brand *were relatively unknown*, exclusive territorial constraints would be compatible with Article 85(1).

The Court held that the obligation to sell only from the contractual premises which restrained franchisees from opening a second shop without consent, coupled with exclusive territories, could lead to absolute territorial protection for the individual franchise territories and a consequent partitioning of the market. These clauses which divided markets between franchisor and franchisees or prevented franchisees from engaging in price competition with each other could not be viewed as indispensable for the protection of the know-how or the maintenance of the network's identity or reputation. These provisions resulted in a market sharing arrangement between franchisor and franchisees and restricted competition within the network *if the brand was well-known, as in Grundig*

---

[59] Ibid. at para. 10. It has been argued that the Court did not base its findings on the existence/exercise distinction but rather the value of the IPR. J. Derbyshire, 'Computer Programs and Competition Policy: A Block Exemption for Software Licensing' [1994] 9 *EIPR* at p. 370.

[60] These cases may be applied by analogy to related products protected by IPRs. A number of authors have drawn attention to their possible application to computer software. See e.g. Derbyshire, ibid.; I. Forrester, 'Software Licensing in Light of Current EC Competition Law' 1992 *ECLR* 5; H. W. Moritz, 'EC Competition Law Aspects and Software Licensing Agreements—A German Perspective' [1994] *IIC* 357 and 515.

[61] [1986] ECR 353.

and therefore the risks to the franchisee and need for protection against intrabrand competition were relevant only to Article 85(3). The Court recognized that it was possible that a prospective franchisee would not take the risk of becoming part of a chain, investing its own money, paying a relatively high fee, and undertaking to pay a substantial annual royalty unless he could hope, thanks to a degree of protection against competition on the part of the franchisor and other franchisees, that his business would be profitable. However, in the case of well established brands, this was relevant only to the examination of the agreement in relation to Article 85(3), not Article 85(1). The possibility that exclusive territorial restraints could be compatible with Article 85(1) while the franchise brand *was relatively unknown* could plausibly be seen as a reference to a *de minimis* or quantitative appreciability test.[62] However, it could also be seen as the market opening exception applied to new franchises moving into a member state. At all events, in the context of well established franchise operations, territorial exclusivity as such can place a limit on the extent to which IPR licensing could be compatible with Article 85(1).[63]

Nevertheless, the sequence of cases since *Nungesser* have made the point that the test of 'qualitative' appreciability applies to territorial exclusivity in IPR licensing agreements. The Commission has acknowledged the existence of these as exceptions to their general rule, but applied them sparingly. The new technology exception in *Nungesser* has been strictly construed so that the test of 'newness' can be difficult to meet. For example, in *Velcro/Aplix*, the Commission refused to clear an exclusivity clause because the technology was not new.[64] In *Rich Products/Jus Rol*, the fact that other firms in the UK and in other member states had developed processes for freezing yeast, even though they were not easily accessible, meant that the technology was not 'new' under Article 85(1).[65] In *Delta Chemie* the fact that the licensee had previously acted as the distributor meant that the technology was not new.[66] Moreover, the Commission has stated that the exception in *Erauw Jacquery* is to be limited to licences for the propagation of basic seed.[67]

Notwithstanding, it is the Court and not the Commission which has the final word on appreciability and the case-law of the court can be

---

[62] See e.g. Jan Peeters, 'The Rule of Reason Revisited: Prohibition on Restraints of Competition in the Sherman Act and the EEC Treaty', Vol. 37 *The American Journal of Comparative Law* 521 at p. 566.

[63] This in fact was one major reason for the Commission preparing a block exemption for franchising agreements.   [64] [1989] 4 CMLR 157.

[65] [1988] 4 CMLR 527.   [66] [1989] 4 CMLR 535.

[67] See e.g. *Association of Plant Breeders of the EEC (Comasco)* [1990] 4 *CML Rev.* 259. See too the *Eighteenth Report on Competition Policy* (Brussels, EC Commission, 1989) at para. 103. See *CML Rev.* Korah (1996) at p. 17.

analysed to determine to what extent its reasoning applies to other IPRs. The width of the exceptions, and the extent of their applicability to IPRs, may require careful analysis, but the existence of such exceptions has an importance that goes beyond the immediate facts of the cases. They can apply to other types of IPR and they can be applied to other types of products. They will be particularly useful in their application to new types of technology licences, such as computer program licences.[68] We shall return to this point in chapter 7.

5.5 NON-TERRITORIAL RESTRAINTS AND RESTRICTIONS ON COMPETITION

In the field of non-territorial restraints, there has been more of a consensus between Commission and Court over the concepts applicable to clear the provisions of licensing agreements. The concept of the 'scope of the intellectual property right' has been accepted in relation to non-territorial restrictions as a partial exercise of the intellectual property right granted by legislation and therefore one which deprives no third party of their freedom of action.[69] However, this concept has proved to be a two-edged sword in the sense that a contractual provision which goes beyond the scope of the intellectual property right could not only be caught by Article 85(1); it would also be non-exemptible under Article 85(3).[70]

The earlier importance of scope of the patent in defining restriction on competition has waned owing largely to the growth of the overlapping doctrine of ancillary restraints. The Court's endorsement of the concept of 'ancillary restraints' has led to a second basis for finding clauses in licensing contracts to be not appreciably restrictive of competition.[71] During the 1970s, the Commission began to acknowledge that in the case of certain agreements which were procompetitive, some of their contractual restraints which were objectively indispensable to the nature and purpose of the agreement could be regarded as not being restrictive of competition. The concept originated in transfer of business cases but its logic was soon applied to IPR licences. In *Reuter/BASF*,[72] the Commission was confronted with a non-competition clause contained in the sale of a business which was indispensable if the agreement were to be made. Without it, the buyer would be prey to competition from the seller and

---

68 See e.g. Derbyshire op. cit. n. 59 above.

69 It has an analogy with the argument in *Zuiker Unie* that where government regulation had already restricted competition, the resulting contractual co-operation itself was not restrictive of competition.

70 See *Windsurfing International Inc.* v. *Commission* [1986] ECR 611.

71 See discussion in E. Gonzalez Dias, 'Some Reflections on the Notion of Ancillary Restraints' [1995] *Fordham Corp. Law Inst.* 325.   72 [1976] 2 CMLR D44.

would be deterred from entering the agreement in the first place. Since the sale itself was not an anticompetitive agreement, the Commission was prepared to accept the presence of a necessary contractual restraint as a restriction or distortion of competition, as long as it was of reasonable duration. The Commission also held that a prohibition of the transferor divulging secret know-how was not caught by Article 85(1).

The test of indispensability, while giving recognition to commercial logic, was essentially formalistic in method. If a contractual restraint bore a particular relationship to the overall purpose of an agreement acceptable in competition terms, it could constitute an exception from the category of contractual restraints which are *ipso facto* restrictions on competition.

In *Remia and Nutricia*,[73] the Court of Justice applied similar reasoning to a case where the non-competition clause placed on the seller in the first transaction was then extended to the buyer in the second transaction. Again, the issue under Article 85(1) was not whether the agreement had a procompetitive effect but whether the restriction was necessary to make the transfer of assets fully effective.

In the case of *Pronuptia*,[74] the Court had the occasion to apply ancillary restraints reasoning under Article 85(1) to the licensing of know-how together with a trade mark in a distribution franchising agreement. The basis of such an agreement was the obligation of the franchisee to sell certain products in a shop using the franchisor's business name or symbol. It could be contrasted with the more complex production franchise under which the franchisee manufactures products according to the instructions of the franchisor and sells them under the franchisor's trade mark. The agreement entailed the following reciprocal obligations:

1. The franchisor must undertake to transmit his professional expertise to the franchisee and to provide him with the necessary assistance in order to enable him to apply its methods,
2. The franchisee must undertake to apply the franchisor's methods, to utilize the common sign or business name and to pay royalties.

In the case, the franchisee claimed that the franchise agreement was prohibited by Article 85(1) and was therefore unenforceable under Article 85(2). The Court held first of all that the compatibility of such agreements with Article 85(1) could only be assessed by reference to the provisions in the agreement in their economic context. The franchise system allows a franchisor to profit from its success by extending a business through the exploitation of its know-how without further capital

---

[73] *Remia BV & Verenidge Bedrijven Nutricia* v. *Commission* [1987] 1 CMLR 1.
[74] [1986] ECR 353.

investment. The franchisee obtains access to the methods and name of an established business in return for an upfront payment and a royalty. The effect of the agreement is to allow the franchisor to penetrate new markets with the financial help of independent resellers.

The Court identified two conditions which were indispensable to the proper functioning of the system. The first was 'the franchisor must be able to communicate his know-how to the franchisees and provide them with the necessary assistance in order to enable them to apply his methods without running the risk that his know-how and assistance might benefit his competitors even indirectly'.

This made the following clauses essential:

1. The franchisee's obligation not to open a shop of the same or a similar nature in an area where he may compete with a member of the network, during the period of validity of the contract and for a reasonable period after its expiry (i.e. one year).
2. The franchisee's obligation not to transfer his shop to another party without the prior approval of the franchisor.

The second condition the Court identified as essential was 'the franchisor must be able to take the measures necessary for maintaining the identity and the reputation of the network bearing his business name or symbol'. It followed that provisions which establish the means of control necessary for that purpose were also not restrictions on competition for the purpose of Article 85(1). The Court accepted that there were six provisions justified as ancillary restraints under this criterion.[75] As mentioned, the Court was unwilling to extend the logic of the concept of ancillary restraints to territorial exclusivity incentives for franchising where brands were well-known. The Court noted that territorial restrictions in the franchising agreement were not genuine ancillary restraints nor indispensable. This view reinforced the point that territorial restrictions in franchise agreements, and by implication other types of vertical IPR licensing agreements, normally required exemption.

---

[75] (1) The franchisee's obligation to apply the business methods developed by the franchisor and to use the know-how provided; (2) the franchisee's obligation to sell the goods covered by the contract only in premises laid out and decorated according to the franchisor's instructions; (3) a ban on transfer by the franchisee of his shop to another location without the franchisor's approval; (4) a prohibition on any assignment by the franchisee of his rights and obligations under the contract without the franchisor's approval; (5) the franchisee's obligation to sell only products supplied by the franchisor or by suppliers selected by him, provided that it would be impractical to lay down objective quality specifications; (6) the franchisee's obligation to obtain the franchisor's approval for all advertising so long as it concerns only the nature of the advertising.

6

The Development of the Commission's Block Exemption Policy for Technology Licensing Agreements

6.1 THE PATENT LICENSING BLOCK EXEMPTION (2349/84)

The process of formulating block exemptions requires a translation of the balancing test in Article 85(3) into specific lists of acceptable and unacceptable clauses for particular categories of agreements. In principle, the Commission is supposed to build the block exemption on the basis of experience with those categories of agreement. In designing block exemptions, the Commission has had to strike a difficult balance between two different objectives: the need to create wide enough exemptions for legitimate exclusive technology transfers to receive the legal certainty of qualifying for block exemption, since this will encourage and facilitate investment in technology licensing, and the need not to create exemptions which are too wide that anticompetitive licensing agreements can slip through.

After a long and tortuous history of negotiations between the Commission and the member states, both fiercely lobbied by the business community, the patent licensing block exemption was finally introduced in 1984.[1] This was far more favourable to patent licensing than the 1979 draft, not least because it contained acceptance of the principle the Court had articulated in *Nungesser*. In Recital 11, the Commission announced:

Exclusive licensing agreements ... are not in themselves incompatible with Article 85(1) where they are concerned with the introduction and protection of a new technology in the licensed territory, by reason of the scale of the research which has been undertaken and the risk that is involved in manufacturing and marketing a product which is unfamiliar to users in the licensed territory at the time the agreement is made.

Since the exemption related to agreements which on balance met the criteria of Article 85(3), the Commission felt that it could widen the entitlement

[1] Alexander, 'Block Exemption for Patent Licensing Agreement EC Regulation No. 2349/84' [1986] IIC I; S. Pichard, 'The Commission's Patent Licensing Regulation—A Guide [1984] ECLR 384; V. Korah, *Patent Licensing and the EEC Competition Rules—Regulation 2349/84* (Oxford: ESC Publishing, 1985).

to the degree of exclusivity it exempted to agreements 'concerned with the introduction and protection of a process for manufacturing a product which is already known'.

In fact the policy of the block exemption was to limit the category of technology licences to pure patent licences,[2] or mixed patent know-how technology licences (Article 1(1)).[3] Other intellectual property rights (IPRs) could be included in the licensed technology package but these had to be 'ancillary', i.e. less important, than the patent. The Regulation did not apply to pure know-how licences or mixed licences once the patent had expired. Within these categories, there was no further test of novelty for the licensed technology; under Article 85(3), the grant of the patent could be taken as the assurance that the licensed technology was worthy of protection. Nor was there a limit upon the size of the parties to technology licensing agreements. The turnover threshold had been abandoned as the block exemption progressed through the drafting stages.

If a licence agreement fitted into a category of agreement covered by the block exemption, the licensor could offer exclusive territorial rights to manufacture and sell the licensed product in any territory in the common market including the common market as a whole. It could also offer protection to licensees from other licensees as well as the licensor, consisting of a protection against active sales for a period extending for the duration of the patent protection in the relevant territory. It could in addition offer protection against passive sales for a period of five years from the time of the first licence. The block exemption contained a 'whitelist' of eleven permitted clauses most of which consisted of subdivisions of the patent protection under national law and ancillary restraints. The 'whitelist' was more than matched by a 'blacklist' of fourteen prohibited clauses, many reflecting the policy of the Nine No Nos and many modifying the contents of the whitelist. To vet a licensing agreement under the block exemption required an analysis of pairs of its clauses with the provisions of the agreement.

The abandonment of the turnover restrictions for eligibility for territorial sales restrictions meant that the blacklist was viewed by the Commission as its 'front line' of defence against anticompetitive licences slipping through the net. There was a reserve power to withdraw a block exemption in the event of anticompetitive conduct but this was only available after the agreement had been made and exempted. Article 86 was known to provide a further reserve but the Tetra Pak I case had not

---

[2] 'Patents' we defined to include *inter alia* patents, European patents, patent applications, utility models, *certificats d'utilité* and *certificats d'addition* under French law.

[3] 'Know-how', even if non-ancillary, could be included as long as the patent was necessary to achieve the objects of the technology and the know-how was secret and permitted a better exploitation of the licensee's patents.

brought home its full possibilities. Hence the Commission was conscious of the need to deploy a series of *per se* prohibitions as an effective filter to eligibility in the block exemption itself.

Although the block exemption made a major concession to the economic arguments for protections to new licensees against sales from established licensees and the licensor during the tooling up period, it was inflexible in two important respects. First, the blacklist had to be strictly complied with. A deviation could result in the agreement not being exempted. A non-opposition procedure provided a chance for the parties with doubtful clauses to submit these to the Commission for approval with a six month time limit fixed for the Commission to oppose it.[4] However, the non-opposition procedure could not test whether the agreement could be exempted despite the presence of a blacklisted clause. The blacklisted clauses were regarded as non-exemptible. The non-opposition procedure could only test whether in fact a clause was not of a type to fall within the category of non-exemptible clauses. If the parties wrongly estimated the legal status of clauses in the agreement or indeed the category of the agreement itself, the block exemption did not apply to exempt the agreement.

Secondly, the patent licence block exemption was strict in limiting the category of agreements to which it applied. Its exemption of restrictions did apply only to patent licences or mixed patent know-how licences, if they involved the *manufacture* of the licensed product (Article 1(2)). It did not apply to licences for sales only. It did not apply to patent pools, reciprocal licences or joint ventures (Article 5(1)). It did not apply to mixed technology licensing involving trade mark licences or copyright licences if they were so important that the patents were not necessary. Moreover, the licensee could only be restricted from applying the know-how in the licensor's and other licensees' territories and fields of application only as long as the licensed patents accompanying it were necessary to achieve the objects of the licensed technology and at least one of the parallel patents registered in the licensed territory remained in force (Recital 9).

6.2 THE KNOW-HOW BLOCK EXEMPTION REGULATION (556/89)

By the mid-1980s, the need for a block exemption to apply to know-how licensing had become almost alarmingly strong. There was evidence that particularly US firms were hesitant to grant licences of their valuable technical information in the EC when know-how licensing agreements

---

[4] A non-response could be taken as approval.

were of doubtful legal validity.[5] Moreover, the Commission's decision in *Boussois/Interpane* [6] indicated that the patent licensing block exemption was too inflexible to apply to certain types of mixed technology licences in which the know-how predominated and the licensed patents were not necessary to carry out the licensed process. The Commission's response was to produce a second block exemption for pure know-how licensing agreements and mixed patent know-how technology licensing agreements which could not qualify under the patent licensing block exemption. In Recital 1 it stated that the communication of know-how is often irreversible and greater contractual certainty is necessary so that each party can expect to appropriate to itself the benefits of its investment.

In Recital 6 the Commission emphasized that exclusive territorial licences concerning the introduction and protection of innovative technology are not in breach of Article 85(1) 'by reason of the scale of the research which has been undertaken and of the increase in the level of competition, in particular interbrand competition and in the competitiveness of the undertakings concerned resulting from the dissemination of innovation within the Community'. The Commission was willing to recognize the exemptibility of exclusive licences for know-how but was less receptive to extending the *Nungesser* exception for open exclusive licences of new technology to pure or predominant know-how licences.[7] It defined protectable know-how as 'a body of technical information that is secret, substantial and identified in any appropriate form'. These concepts were carefully defined in the Regulation to provide some guarantee to the Commission that there was know-how of innovative value as the basis for the exempted licence agreement. The Commission could not allow the parties to determine for themselves whether or not the technical information was sufficiently valuable to make the licensing agreement worthwhile. This filter was viewed as a key protection against anticompetitive agreements disguised as know-how licences.

The Commission adopted a structure for the know-how block exemption which was similar to the patent licensing block exemption. Exclusive territorial protection was given to the licensees of know-how agreements against active sales by other licensees[8] and the licensor[9] for ten years

---

5 See e.g, Hoyng and Biesheuvel, 'The Know-how Group Exemption' [1989] *CML Rev.* 219 at 220. See too T. Frazer, 'Vorsprung durch Technik: The Commission's Policy on Know-How Agreements' [1989] *Yearbook of Eur. Law* 1; D. Winn, 'Commission Know-how Regulation 556/89: Innovation and Territorial Exclusivity Improvements and the Quid Pro Quo' [1990] *ECLR* 135.   6 [1988] 4 CMLR 124.

7 See e.g. Commission decision in *Rich Products Ltd/Jus Rol* [1988] 4 CMLR 527.

8 In the case of a licensee, the starting date for the time period is the date of the first licence entered into by the licensor for the same technology *in the EEC*.

9 The starting date for the period of protection against active sales by the licensor was the date of the first licence entered into by the licensor in the territory for the same technology.

from the date of the making of the first licence as long as the know-how remained secret and substantial. Protection against passive sales was allowed for the first five years after the date of the first licence entered into by the licensor for the same technology in the EEC.

The whitelist again contained permitted clauses, all justified by reference to ancillary restraints. Again it was matched by an extensive blacklist which contained major safeguards against anticompetitive clauses using a *per se* prohibition approach partly because of the absence of a market share limit.

There were signs that the Commission was beginning to recognize the need to relax the policy of the block exemptions in certain respects in the interest of encouraging investment in innovation.[10] One example of this was the change in the Commission's policy to royalties stated in Recital 15:[11] 'as a rule, parties do not need to be protected against the foreseeable financial consequences of an agreement freely entered into and should therefore not be restricted in their choice of appropriate means of financing the technology transfer'. Under the patent regulation, the royalties clause had only allowed the parties to agree to spread the upfront payment whilst the patent was still in force. The Commission allowed its fear of extending the royalty payments for non-patented information to interfere with the need to give the parties the flexibility to adjust payments to avoid a prohibitive upfront payment. By the time of the know-how block exemption, the Commission appeared to have accepted the need for a change of approach. The regulation provided[12] that royalties could be paid 'in the amounts and according to the methods freely determined by the parties'. There were still difficulties with compliance with the technical rules of the know-how block exemption,[13] but at least the Commission had begun to reduce the inflexibility in the block exemption policy to royalty payments.

The IPR licensing block exemption policy had improved from that in 1984. However, it continued to presented certain difficulties to the parties to technology licensing agreements:

1. The excessive inflexibility and technicality of its conditions. The blacklisted clauses could now be exempted by a process of individual exemption if the market conditions were right, but the need for

[10] At this time too, the Commission began to relax its approach to the assessment of licensing in joint ventures under Art. 85(1), proclaiming a policy of new realism. See *XIIIth Report on Competition Policy*. See too S. Anderman, 'Co-operation, International Competitiveness and Competition Policy' in S. Deakin and J. Michie (eds.), *Contracts, Co-operation and Competitiveness: Studies in Economics Management and Law* (OUP, 1997).

[11] Other examples could be found in the more relaxed approach to tie-ins and non-severable improvements.   [12] Art. 2.1(7).

[13] See R. Whaite, 'Licensing in Europe' [1990] 3 *EIPR* 88 at 91.

the contents of the licence to conform with exactitude to the requirements of the block exemption remained.

2. Mixed technology licensing agreements had to be drafted to fit either within the patent licensing regulation (2349/84) or the know-how regulation (556/89) and there were some difficulties in choosing which of the two regulations applied.

3. Important gaps remained in the coverage of the block exemptions in relation to major categories of IPR licences. Trade mark and copyright licences could not qualify under a block exemption unless these forms of IPR were 'ancillary' to the know-how or patents. If they were equally important or crucial to the licensing agreement, they did not fit into the category of agreements qualifying for the block exemption.[14]

6.3 THE TECHNOLOGY TRANSFER BLOCK EXEMPTION REGULATION (240/96)

The renewal of the patent licensing block exemption was taken as an occasion to reshape the Commission's policy towards block exemptions for technology licensing.The two regulations were merged into a new, unifying[15] technology transfer block exemption (240/96) which applies to pure patent licences, pure know-how licences, and mixed patent, know-how licences, the most common form of technology licensing agreements.[16] This new Regulation takes its place alongside the regulatory regimes for specialization agreements,[17] research and development agreements,[18] franchise agreements,[19] co-operative joint ventures,[20] and mergers[21] which together provide a second tier of

---

[14] See e.g. the type of production franchise or trade mark licence in *Campari* [1978] 2 CMLR 397, in which the trade mark was too important to the overall agreement to be able to be viewed as ancillary to the know-how. See too *Moosehead/Whitbread* [1991] 4 CMLR 391.

[15] The concept of patents is deemed to include a wide variety of IPRs, e.g. patent applications, utility models and applications, topographies of semiconductor products, and plant breeder rights (see Art. 8). The new Regulation provides that it can apply to agreements which include licensing of other intellectual property rights such as trade marks, copyright, and design rights or as long as such rights are 'of assistance in achieving the object of the licensed technology' (Art. 1.5). In other words they must be 'ancillary' to the patent or know-how (Recital 6). This means that industrial or production franchises may be excluded from the block exemption (see e.g. *Moosehead/Whitbread* [1991] 4 CMLR 391). Moreover, computer software is probably not covered.

[16] See V. Korah, *Technology Transfer Agreements and the EC Competition Rules* (OUP, 1996) (cited as Korah (1996)).

[17] Reg. 417/85, amended by Reg. 151/93; see [1993] 4 CMLR 155.

[18] Reg. 418/85, as amended by Reg. 151/93; see [1993] 4 CMLR 163.

[19] Reg. 4087/88.

[20] See Commission's Notice on Co-operative Joint Ventures OJ [1993] C 43/2.

[21] See EC Merger Reg., Council Reg. 4064/89, OJ 1990 L257/14.

regulation by competition law of transfers of technology in addition to the underlying intellectual property legislation.

This occasion offered the Commission an opportunity to make a substantial adjustment to traditional competition policy objectives in the light of the pressing policy need of increasing the technological competitiveness of the EC in world trade. A 1993 Commission White Paper, 'Growth, Competitiveness and Employment', had drawn attention to the fact that the competitive position of Europe *vis-à-vis* the USA and Japan had 'worsened as regards: employment; our share of market exports; R&D and innovation'.[22] It called for a new balance to be struck between competition and co-operation to allow EC firms to enter into strategic alliances to counterbalance the weight of US and Japanese competition. Moreover, a 1994 Commission Communication, also originating in DGIII, argued that there is a clear need to ensure expansion and take up of R&D efforts and 'to facilitate transfers of experience between businesses, particularly small businesses'[23] to ensure that the EC can compete at increasing levels of technology in world trade. As if in anticipation of resistance by DGIV, the White Paper warned that too strict an application of competition rules can place EC firms at a disadvantage on the world stage.

The logic of the White Paper and Communication suggested that a higher priority ought to be given to encouraging technology licensing because of the spur it provides to international competitiveness. Licensing increases incentives to innovation because the great majority of innovators are smaller firms, requiring an independent injection of risk capital, usually in return for an exclusive licence, to take the technology from the stage of research and development to the next stages of manufacture and distribution. It also helps to raise levels of technology throughout the common market by promoting the transfer of technology between member states. In a situation where knowledge based industries, such as aerospace, computers, communications equipment, drugs and medicines, scientific instruments and electrical machinery constitute both a high and a dramatically increasing proportion of total manufacturing output, a policy to promote technology transfer would appear to command considerable support.

In the Technology Transfer Regulation, the issue that faced the competition authorities was to adjust the regulatory regime so that it had less of an inhibiting effect upon IPR licensing. One way would have been to

[22] See European Commission's White Paper on Growth, Competitiveness, Employment. The Challenges and the Ways Forward into the 21st Century [1993] *Bulletin of the EC* Supp 6/93 p. 9.

[23] See European Commission Communication, 'An Industrial Competitiveness Policy for the European Union', 14 Sept. 1994, III. A/JFM/DB/Com. EN 8 DOC.

design the block exemption to exclude all horizontal relationships and apply solely to vertical relationships. A second way, chosen by the designers of the new block exemption, was to allow it to apply to both types of relationships, i.e. to licences between two manufacturers as well as to those between non-manufacturing inventors and manufacturers. In the event, the block exemption contains a mixed and varying model of whether licensing is predominantly horizontal or vertical. On the one hand, the territorial restraints are designed as if the block exemption applied exclusively to vertical relationships. On the other hand, the block exemption treats all licensing agreements which are initially vertical as potentially horizontal so that they may not contain restraints, such as exclusive grant backs of improvements, which could prevent them blossoming into subsequent competitive relationships. Finally, by providing that its benefit will be withdrawn if technology licensing occurs in a horizontal relationship which shows signs of a malignant tendency, such as cross-licensing or patent pooling, or if the parties have market shares approaching dominance, it implies that all other horizontal licensing relationships are eligible provided they otherwise qualify for the block exemption.

As in the case of the Know-how Regulation,[24] the Commission in the new regulation has clearly acknowledged the need to encourage technology licensing. In Recital 3 it states that the purpose of the reform is 'to encourage the dissemination of technical knowledge in the Community and to promote the manufacture of technically sophisticated goods'. Yet the block exemption did not succeed in a radical reform of the block exemption policy. Instead it made five types of adjustments to the existing structure. First, the time periods for territorial exclusivity were increased in most cases, thus marginally increasing the incentives for investment in technology transfer. Secondly, the block exemption lengthened the 'whitelist' adding to the categories of clauses which were either not caught by Article 85(1) or were exempt under Article 85(3). Thirdly, the blacklist was reduced to a core of seven clauses thus reducing the need to vet contract clauses by reference to pairs of sub-articles in the block exemptions but not removing it entirely. The need for pairing and clustering remains in some cases, notably non-competition clauses;[25] improvements;[26] and quantity restrictions.[27]

---

[24] The Commission indicated that the purpose of the Know-how Regulation was 'to ensure that innovation is developed and spread as quickly as possible on the Community's large market . . .', see Commission's Information Notice P–142, 30 Nov. 1988 [1989] 4 CMLR 95.

[25] Art. 3(2) must be read together with Art. 2(1)(9) (minimum royalties) and 2(1)(17) (best endeavours).

[26] Art. 3(6) must be read together with Art. 8(3) (automatic prolongation).

[27] Art. 3(4) must be paired with Art. 2.1.12 (Restrictions on Use for a Third Party's plant).

The blacklist stands as a modern list of *per se* prohibitions in technology licensing agreements: the restrictions on price-fixing,[28] customer sharing,[29] and quantity limits for licensees[30] are designed to deter cartel and market sharing operations. There are restrictions on provisions which impede parallel trade[31] and non-competition clauses.[32] Feed back provisions which require the licensee to assign in whole or in part to the licensor rights to improvements to or new applications of the licensed technology are also blacklisted.[33] Finally, any clause which automatically prolongs the duration of the licensing agreement by the inclusion of new improvements beyond that allowed in Article 1 of the regulation is blacklisted.

The reduction clearly signals a greater willingness to accept that vertical licensing arrangements can be procompetitive even if they contain restrictions such as tie-ins or minimum quality specifications which are technically necessary for the satisfactory exploitation of the technology or respected by the licensor and other licensees.[34]

The policy of the shortened blacklist is to prevent certain forms of anticompetitive co-operative behaviour between competitors using the cover of a licensing agreement to disguise the horizontal nature of the co-operation. The restrictions on price-fixing (Article 3.1), customer sharing (Article 3.4), and on the specification of quantity limits for the licensee (Article 3.5) are, as mentioned, designed to deter cartel and market sharing operations. According to Recital 19, quantity restrictions are suspect because 'they may have the same effect as export bans'. Article 3.5 is designed to prevent the licensor from stipulating levels of production with a view to co-ordinating the production by licensees of just enough product to supply only the demand in their own territory with little if any left over to export to parallel importers. Related to this is Article 3(3)(a) and (b) which blacklists attempts to accomplish the same objective more openly by the use of clauses which would require licensees to refuse without objective justification to meet the orders of resellers or users in their territory or other territories in the common market who are engaged in parallel importation.

Fourthly, as in the two previous block exemptions for IPR licensing, the Commission has retained a power to withdraw the benefit of the Regulation where it finds that an exempted agreement has effects which are incompatible with Article 85(3). Under Article 7, there are four examples of such cases:

1. Where the effect of the agreement is to prevent the licensed products from being exposed to effective competition in the licensed

---

[28] Art. 3.1.   [29] Art. 3.4.   [30] Art. 3.5.
[31] Art. 3(3)(a) and (b).   [32] Art. 3(2).   [33] Art. 3(6).
[34] Art. 2(1)(5).

territory from identical or substitutable goods or services, 'which may in particular occur where the licensee's market share exceeds 40%'.

2. Where the licensee refuses, without any objectively justified reason, to meet unsolicited orders from users or resellers in the territory of other licensees.

3. Where the parties without any objectively justified reason either refuse to meet orders from users or resellers in their own territories who would market outside that territory, or make it difficult for users or resellers to obtain the products from other resellers in the common market;

4. Where the parties are competing manufacturers at the date of the grant of the licence and the effect of a minimum quantity or best endeavours clause would have the effect of preventing the licensee from using competing technologies.

The Commission can exercise its power of withdrawal under Article 7 only by making a formal decision, since the effect of withdrawal would make unenforceable the restrictive provisions in the licensing agreement and make the parties liable to fines from that date onwards. The decision, and the grounds on which it is based, would be appealable to the CFI and ECJ.[35] Moreover, it would not be open to national courts to apply Article 7, since withdrawal as an incident of the Exemption decision is solely within the power of the Commission.

Not surprisingly, the use of the withdrawal power has been rare. The Commission is conscious that it is an instrument that can be used only sparingly. Nevertheless, the Commission has used the threat of its exercise to obtain changes in conduct by the parties to licensing agreements more often. One famous example is that of *Tetra Pak I*[36] in which the Commission responded to an acquisition of a competitor's exclusive licences by a dominant firm by indicating that it would have withdrawn the exemption until Tetra Pak modified the licences from an exclusive to a non-exclusive licence.

The effect of the withdrawal power in the block exemption is to reduce legal certainty to some extent. However, the power is a necessary back up to a form based system of regulation which would otherwise have limited means to regulate the conduct and market power of the parties to licensing agreements.

[35] See *Cimenteries* [1967] ECR 75 at para. 91. See discussion in V. Korah, *Technology Transfer Agreements and the EC Competition Rules* (Clarendon Press, 1996) (cited as Korah (1996)).

[36] See e.g. *Tetra Pak Rausing* v. *Commission* Case T–51/89 [1991] 4 CMLR 334. Whish *Competition Law* (Butterworths, 3rd edn. 1993) at p. 649 draws attention to the fact that the Commission chose to attack the acquisition of the licence rather than the merger itself which it could have done. See ch. 13 below.

At one stage, the Commission attempted to introduce an additional market share test as a precondition to exclusive territoriality because of its concern that dominant undertakings with exclusive licences 'might prevent access to the market of the technology by third parties and eliminate competition in respect of a substantial part of the products in question'. Initially, these market share tests were wide in scope, applying to all licensing agreements whether horizontal or vertical. In the penultimate version of the Regulation, however, they were limited to agreements between competing manufacturers. In the final version, they were taken out as a precondition and made a basis for withdrawal under Article 7.

The decision to shift the market shares test to Article 7 means that the onus is now on the Commission to investigate high market share cases.

The withdrawal power is also used to regulate the adverse effects of licensing agreements or the conduct of the parties in applying the contractual provisions in what is essentially a form based system. This is done partly with a view to the Treaty role of competition policy under Article 85, and partly with a view to testing the economic effects of certain whitelisted clauses. Again this power is necessary to complement a system of vetting which relies in the first instance upon the form of the provisions in the agreement.

The third line of defence for the Commission is its exclusions policy in Article 5. This Article performs two distinct functions. It first excludes from the block exemption the types of agreements which would require a careful examination of the legal and economic context in order to determine their net effect on competition. Consequently Article 5 excludes patent or know-how pools (Article 5(1)(1)) and cross licensing arrangements (Article 5(1)(3)) between competing firms. These must qualify for exemption, if at all, by individual exemption. Secondly, there are categories of agreements which the Commission sifts under other methods of regulation. For example, while Article 5 excludes licensing agreements between competing firms with interests in a joint venture, such agreements can be exempted under the R&D block exemption[37] and either cleared or exempted under the Commission's guidelines to co-operative joint ventures.[38] Similarly, franchise agreements are excluded from the technology transfer regulation but exempted by the franchising block exemption (4087/88). Licences for sales only are not covered by the Technology Transfer Regulation but can be exempted under the exclusive distribution block exemption (1983/83).

---

[37] Reg. 418/85. See E. White, 'R&D Joint Ventures under EC Competition Law' [1985] *IIC* 663; V. Korah, *R and D and the EC Competition Rules: Regulation 418/85* (ESC, 1986).

[38] Notice on Co-operative Joint Ventures OJ [1993] C 4312.

In the new Technology Transfer Regulation, the Commission has also attempted to meet criticisms about the inflexibility of the earlier block exemptions. For example, it has reduced the blacklist and it has also opened up the opposition procedure to a wider variety of clauses and has reduced its time limit to four months.[39]

Nevertheless, the new block exemption continues to be inflexible in two important respects. First, it creates a divide between certain defined categories of IPR licensing agreement which can come within the block exemption and those which are left to the less user-friendly regulation regime of notification for individual exemption.

Recital 6 sets out the policy of the block exemption to other IPRs in the following terms:

It is appropriate to extend the scope of this Regulation to pure or mixed agreements containing the licensing of intellectual property rights other than patents (in particular, trademarks, design rights, and copyright, especially software protection), when such additional licensing contributes to the achievement of the objects of the licensed technology and contains only ancillary provisions.

Article 5(1)(4) provides that the Regulation shall not apply to licensing agreements containing provisions relating to IPR other than patents which are not ancillary. Art. 1(1) states that the block exemption can extend to licensing agreements containing provisions relating to IPRs other than patents but only if they are 'ancillary'.

Under the patent and know-how regulations, the concept of an ancillary provision relating to other IPRs was translated into a requirement that the other type of IPR must not be as important or more important to the agreement than the patent or know-how. For example, in *Boussois Interpane* the know-how was held to have dominated the patented technology and did not have the effect of merely contributing to the better exploitation of the licensed patents.[40] In *Moosehead/Whitbread*[41] the lager production licence did not qualify under the know-how block exemption because the trade mark was not ancillary to the licensed know-how as required by that exemption. The Commission's view was that the principal interest of the parties was in the exploitation of the trade mark rather than the know-how.

In the new Technology Transfer Regulation, however, the concept of ancillary restraint has been defined in rather different terms. Article 10(15) defines ancillary provisions as: 'provisions relating to the obligation of intellectual property rights other than patents which contain no obligations restrictive of competition other than those also attached to

---

[39] C. Kerse, 'Block Exemptions under Article 85(3): The Technology Transfer Regulation—Procedural Issues' [1996] *ECLR* 331.

[40] [1988] 4 CMLR 124.   [41] [1991] 4 CMLR 391.

the licensed know how or patents and exempted under this Regulation'. As Korah perceptively argues: 'This is a surprising definition, since it does not require the provision to be ancillary in the usual sense that it be of less value than the technology license.'

Under the Technology Transfer regulation it appears that there might be a possibility for other IPRs to be part of a mixed technology licence and nevertheless qualify for exemption provided that they meet the following two tests:

(i) The provisions relating to other IPRs must be ancillary, i.e. contain no obligations restrictive of competition other than those also attached to the licensed know-how or patents used and exempted under the regulation (Article 10(5)); and

(ii) the additional IPRs must contribute to the objects of the licensed technology (Recital 6).

This then is the argument that can be made for the inclusion of trade mark licences and copyright licences in the new block exemption.[42] However, this change does not amount to a universal prescription for the inclusion of mixed technology licences containing other IPRs. The Commission has changed the policy of the block exemptions to be more inclusive. Nevertheless, the conclusion remains that there are limits to the coverage of IPR licences by the block exemption.

Secondly, the new Regulation also retains the requirement that the parties apply the Articles of the block exemption to the clauses of the licensing agreement with a fine-tooth comb. If the parties miscalculate the requirements of the whitelist or blacklist and fail to use the opposition procedure, the block exemption will be non-applicable.[43]

Consequently, while the block exemption accepts a presumption of procompetitiveness in technology licensing and continues the process of progressive liberalization that began with the Patent Licensing Regulation in 1984,[44] it has done little to change the formalistic approach to evaluating the contents of licensing agreements. It has undoubtedly improved the position for those licences qualifying for the block exemption. However, it has only partly dealt with the problems caused by the basic rigidities of the structure. In consequence, it remains open to the

---

[42] See Korah's excellent analysis (1996) at pp. 118–20. See too C. Kerse 'Block Exemptions under Article 85(3): The Technology Transfer Regulation Procedural Issues' [1996] ECLR 331 at 335.

[43] See e.g. *Delimitis* [1991] ECR I–935.

[44] See R. Whish, *Competition Law* (Butterworths, 3rd edn., 1993) pp. 631–43; T. Frazer, 'Vorsprung durch Technik: The Commission's Policy on Know-how Agreements' [1989] *Oxford Yearbook of Eur. Law* 1.

charge of placing an unduly heavy regulatory burden upon the parties to licensing agreements who fail to qualify for the benefits of a block exemption, one which compares unfavourably with competitor systems such as the USA, under the 1995 Guidelines for Intellectual Property Licensing.[45]

For any agreement which does not fit under the block exemption, Article 85 requires an analysis of contractual clauses in licensing agreements, clause by clause, in the light of Commission practice and Court decisions. The way this is best tackled is to look separately at territorial and non-territorial restrictions.

[45] See Conclusions below.

7

The Regulation of Territorial Restraints in Intellectual Property Right Licensing Agreements under Article 85

The degree of territorial exclusivity which the licensor can offer the licensee is at the heart of the commercial exchange in a technology licensing agreement. For the licensee the acquisition of a licence means that it is prepared to take on the risks of investing capital in manufacturing premises and plant and a distribution system rather than the costs of an elaborate in-house R&D programme. However, unless there is some protection from competition from the licensor and other licensees in its home territory it will have little incentive to take on such risks. The licensee's need for time to tool up, to acquaint itself with the technology and to establish itself as a manufacturer with a distribution system before being subjected to competition from the licensor or other prior licensees is often so great that without such contractual protection many licensees would be deterred from making the investment.

If there were no competition policy constraints, the licensing agreement would be used to confer several levels of protection. The first level of protection would be protection against the licensor itself. This would include an obligation not to grant a licence to manufacture to another licensee in the licensed territory and not to sell directly into the licensed territory. The second level of protection also includes protection against the direct sales from other licensees. These direct sales could be 'active' in the sense that the other licensees advertise and establish selling facilities in the territory or 'passive' which would consist of answering orders from inside the territory but stopping short of soliciting orders.

There is a further level of protection which can be provided through contract and that is to bind the buyers from the licensees to an obligation not to export. This is meant to prevent parallel trading, that is, the exports of the buyers from the licensees or their customers to other territories within the licensing network.

To the extent that the licensor can offer these protections to the licensee, it will be able to induce investment despite the risks of introducing new products into a market. The issue that has to be tackled under Article 85 is how far the Court and Commission will be prepared to go in the interests of providing an incentive to technology transfer while not allowing such licences to be used as a device to partition the common market. The Court has acknowledged the importance of territorial exclusivity, as indeed the general procompetitive nature of licensing agreements. However, in its decisions on territorial restraints in licensing agreements, the Court must strike a balance between the benefits of licences in the form of the spread of manufacture throughout the common market as against the costs to the flow of interstate trade caused by exclusive sales licences.

The way the Court and Commission have attempted to resolve this dilemma has differed to some extent.

7.1 THE COURT'S APPROACH

The Court has chosen to divide licensing agreements for the purposes of Article 85 into three categories:

1. Non-restrictive exclusive licences: exclusive licences for a territory which whilst containing restraints on competition nevertheless are not contrary to Article 85(1) because the effects of such restraints are not appreciable in qualitative terms.
2. Non-exemptible exclusive licences: exclusive licences for a territory which are accompanied by restraints which create absolute territorial protection. These are caught by Article 85(1) and cannot be exempted.
3. Exemptible exclusive licences: a middle category of exclusive licensing agreements into which most fall which is caught by Article 85(1) but can be exempted under Article 85(3).[1]

7.1.1 Non-Restrictive Exclusive Licences

The case-law of the Court of Justice creates three main categories of exceptions to exclusive IPR licences under Article 85(1)

The first is the new technology/market opening exception in *Nungesser*. Although this applies in terms to plant seed technology, its reasoning is applicable to other forms of intellectual property rights (IPRs) including patents, trade mark, and design rights. There is a need to show that the technology is new[2] and that the market penetration would not occur unless the degree of IPR protection is provided.[3]

---

[1] Cf. H. Ullrich, 'Patents and Know-how, free trade; Interenterprise Cooperation and Competition within the Internal Marker [1992] *IIC* 583.

[2] *Velcro/Aplix* [1989] 4 CMLR 157.

[3] See e.g. *DDD/Delta Chemie* [1989] 4 CMLR 535.

However, if the right mix of these ingredients is present, there will be an exception for exclusive manufacturing licences for a particular territory as long as they are not accompanied by territorial sales restrictions on other licensees. The second is the exception in *Coditel II* which indicates that in cases where the nature of the product protected by the IPR is only capable of protection by exclusive manufacturing and sales territory combined with territorial sales restrictions, and the industry is integrative, then absolute territorial protection consisting of a ban on further sales or use may be allowed in the contract. This exception too can be extended to other fields reliant on copyright protection. For example, Derbyshire makes the point that: 'While package software falls into the category of "other types of literary and artistic works" in the sense that tangible copies of licensed software are usually handed over at the same time licenses for use are granted, analogies can be drawn between exclusive distribution rights and performing rights.'[4] To fit within the *Coditel* exception, however, the IPR analysis must be combined with an analysis of the indispensability of the degree of IPR protection with the interstate penetration of the industry or product.

Erauw Jacquery[5] offers a third type of exception where the combination of the special characteristics of the product and the market opening character of the industry resulted in a finding that a ban on exports could be compatible with Article 85(1). The Court was prepared to recognize where an export ban in the contract was indispensable to ensure that quality control over propagation could be maintained in the process of exporting basic seed from one member state to another, it could be compatible with Article 85(1). This example could be relevant to an argument based upon quality controls for products covered by other types of IPRs.[6]

The Commission's approach to the definition of non-restrictive exclusive territorial provisions has been to give the Court's case-law a somewhat grudging reception. Such cases are treated as exceptions to its own general approach to Article 85(1) and the Commission applies them fairly strictly. The Commission acknowledges acceptance of *Nungesser* in the recitals to the new Technology Transfer Agreement Regulation:[7]

Exclusive licensing agreements, i.e. agreements in which the licensor undertakes not to exploit the licensed technology in the licensed territory himself or to grant further license there, may not in themselves be incompatible with Article 85(1) where they are concerned with the introduction and protection of a new technology in the licensed territory, by reason of the scale of the research which has been

---

4   [1994] 9 *EIPR* 379.   5   [1988] ECR 1919.
6   See discussion pp. 70–71.
7   Recital 10. This is a virtual repetition of the recital in the patent licensing block exemption 2349/84.

undertaken, of the increase in the level of competition, in particular inter-brand competition, and on the competitiveness of the undertakings concerned resulting from the dissemination of innovation within the Community.

It also accepts the logic of *Erauw Jacquery* in Recital 9 when it states that in the case of new technology even export bans binding on the licensor or the licensees may be compatible with Article 85(1).

However, under Article 85(1) both types of exceptions have long been applied strictly by the Commission. The test of new technology has been strictly defined.[8] And the exception in *Erauw Jacquery* has been stated to be limited to restrictions needed to ensure the appropriate handling of basic seed.[9]

7.1.2 Exemptible Exclusive Territoriality

The Commission's reluctance to accept territorial exclusivity as non-restrictive of competition under Article 85(1) can be contrasted with its more receptive approach to exclusivity under Article 85(3). The scope for qualification for exclusivity in the block exemption is quite wide applying to all pure patent licensing, pure know-how licences, and mixed patent-know-how licences as defined by the block exemption. Moreover, the new Technology Transfer Regulation is extremely generous in its approach to the borderline between new and non-new technology. It provides that exclusive patent, know-how, and mixed patent-know-how licensing agreements, although caught by Article 85(1), will be exempt from Article 85(3) without applying a separate test of whether or not they are concerned with the introduction and protection of new technology in the licensed territory. The block exemption acknowledges the importance of exempting new technology licensing because of the investment in research, the increased interbrand competition, and technological competitiveness and it makes the exemption widely available to patent and know-how licensing. The block exemption subjects exclusive licences to four types of qualifications: (i) the patent and know-how must fit the definitions in the Regulation, i.e., patents must be 'necessary' to put into effect the licensed technology (Article 10(5)) and know-how must be secret, substantial and identified (Article 10(1)–(4)); (ii) if any other intellectual property rights are combined in the licensed package, they must be 'ancillary' to the patent or know-how in the licensing agreement; (iii) the agreements must not be of a category excluded by Article 5; or, (iv) subject to the withdrawal provisions of Article 7.

---

[8] See e.g. *Velcro/Aplix* [1989] 4 CMLR 1570.
[9] See *XVIIIth Report on Competition Policy* (1989) para. 103. See *Assn. of Plant Breeders of the EEC (Comasco)* [1990] 4 CMLR 259.

The only prior tests of the novelty of the licensed technology are the precondition of national patent legislation that the patent be novel and the requirement in the block exemption that the patent be unexpired and the requirement that the know-how is substantial and secret. Otherwise, and subject to the provisions of the agreement conforming to the detailed requirements of the block exemption, the Commission has clearly accepted that under Article 85(3) in a block exemption it is not necessary to create the type of fine distinctions suggested by the case-law of the Court under Article 85(1).

A similar approach is taken in the block exemption to the regulation of the types of territorial protection against intrabrand competition that can be given in the licensing agreement. From the Commission's viewpoint there are four types of contractual protection which can be achieved by contract. The first and most comprehensive is a ban on exploitation. This is defined as 'any use of the licensed technology, in particular in the production, active or passive sales in a territory even if not coupled with manufacture in that territory; or leasing of the licensed products' (Article 10(10)). A lesser form of protection against intrabrand competition is a restriction on active sales, engaging in advertising, establishing any branch or maintaining any distribution depot in the protected territory. Further, there is the restriction on passive sales, supplying the licensed product to the protected territory in response to unsolicited orders. Finally, the contract can ban manufacturing and use in a given territory.

In the block exemption, the Commission has channelled its reservations about these forms of restrictions on intrabrand competition in licensing agreements by setting time limits for their duration rather than prohibiting them entirely. Thus, it allows territorial protection against direct sales by licensees both actively and passively, as well as against other forms of exploitation into the territories of other licensees and the licensor under the contract, to all intellectual property right licences covered by the block exemption, varying the duration of such protections with the type of intellectual property right and the type of territorial protection.

In Article 1, the Regulation exempts the following territorial restrictions:

As between the licensor and licensee, the following restrictions are allowed:

1. An obligation on the licensor not to licence anyone else in the licensed territory (a 'sole' licence) for the permitted period of the agreement.
2. An obligation on the licensor not itself to exploit the technology in the licensed territory (an 'exclusive' licence) for the permitted period of the agreement.

3. An obligation on the licensee not to exploit the technology in territories reserved for the licensor for the permitted period of the agreement.

A licensee in one territory can be restricted from competing with other licensees in the following ways:

4. An obligation can be placed on the licensee not to manufacture or use the product or the process in territories reserved to other licensees.
5. An obligation can be placed on the licensee not to pursue active sales in the territories reserved for other licensees by advertising or maintaining depots in such territories.
6. An obligation can be placed on the licensee not to put the licensed product on the market in territory licensed to other licensees within the common market in response to unsolicited orders (passive sales).

In these respects it continues the policy of the patent and know-how regulations of providing a form of territorial protection that includes and surpasses that which was regarded by the Court of Justice as not caught by Article 85(1) only in respect of new technology.[10]

7.2 THE DURATION OF TERRITORIAL PROTECTIONS

The new block exemption also continues the policy of the previous regulations in varying the duration of the protections with the type of intellectual property right and territorial protection. However, it also increases the period of validity of these territorial restrictions in most cases. Thus, in the case of pure know-how licences, the ten year period of territorial protection now starts from the time that the licence is first put on the market anywhere in the Community by a licensee (Article 1.3). This is a distinct improvement over the rule in the previous know-how regulation that the ten year period must start from the date the first licence is signed in the EC in respect of the same technology. It allows the time needed by the licensee to tool up its manufacturing facilities and establish its distribution network before its period of strong territorial protection begins to toll. In the case of pure patent agreements, the basic period of protection continues to be the life of the patent or patents as long as it or they are 'necessary'[11] for the licensed product or products

---

[10] See Whish, *Competition Law* (Butterworths, 3rd edn. 1993) pp. 207–11; T. Frazer, 'Vorsprung durch Technik: The Commission', Policy on Know-how Agreements' [1989] *Oxford Yearbook of Euro. Law* 1 at pp. 5–6.

[11] The 'necessary patents' requirement is included to prevent the use of 'sham' patents, i.e. those which are not really used or needed for the manufacturing of the product, as the basis of eligibility for the block exemption. The block exemption defines a 'necessary patent' as one without which 'the realisation of the licensed technology would not be

and apply in the licensed territory. In the case of a mixed patent-know-how agreement the longer of the two periods is allowed in the interests of encouraging technology transfer, as long as the patent or patents are necessary for the licensed product and apply in the licensed territory.

Apart from protections against passive sales, the parties are entitled to include contractual provisions restricting either from exploiting the licensed intellectual property in each other's territory. However, the regulation allows an obligation on the licensee to refrain from passive sales into the territories reserved to other licensees for a period of only five years starting from the date of first marketing in the EC by a licensee.

The protection against passive sales offers the major assurance to the licensee that for at least the duration of the period of the restriction it will be free of exports by other licensees in response to orders by commercial firms in the licensed territory. However, this would not completely foreclose competition as it would always be open to parallel importers in other licensees' territories to buy from other licensees, or even the licensor, and then export to the newly licensed territory since the exhaustion principle would apply.[12]

The increase in the allowed periods of exclusivity starting from the date when the licensed product is first put on the market by a licensee in the case of pure know-how, mixed licences, and pure patent licences shows that the Commission recognizes the role of territorial exclusivity as a vital incentive to licensing. However, the fact that the regulation provides a common starting time for all licences means that licensors who do not have the resources to set up a twelve country network immediately are penalized. In the case of smaller licensors, i.e. the great majority, it would be more realistic to recognize that the decision to licence rather than exploit the innovative product oneself often reflects a lack of capital resources and this means that the licensor has the wherewithal to select only one or two countries for a trial run. As a result, for those licensees in the second wave of licences there will be a correspondingly shorter period of territorial exclusivity. It is true that a successful run in one country will be encouraging to later licensees, but this effect will not always offset the disincentive of the shorter period of territorial protection allowed under the block exemption. SMEs may have to take refuge in the *de minimis* rules to obtain a five year period of protection for their second wave licensees.

---

possible or would only be possible to a lesser extent or in more costly conditions' (Art. 10(5)). This is a further safeguard against anticompetitive arrangements even if the drafting causes potential problems, e.g. does the test of necessity apply only at the time of the making of the agreement or throughout?

[12] J. Venit, 'In the Wake of Windsurfing: Patent Licensing in the Common Market' [1986] *Fordham Corp. Law Inst.* 517.

What is left unresolved by the block exemption is its relationship with the Court's case-law in respect of Articles 30–6 and direct sales by licensees of the licensed product outside the licensed territory after the period of protection allowed under the block exemption. In Article 2(1)(14), the Commission states that a licensor can reserve its right to rely on its patent to oppose the exploitation of the licensed technology by the licensees. This would presumably apply to passive sales and active sales after the periods stipulated in the agreement as long as the patent protection itself had not expired. This could be a case of the Commission hedging its bets in the face of the case-law of the Community Courts on this issue.

7.3 CLOSED LICENCES AND INTELLECTUAL PROPERTY RIGHTS

The case of *Nungesser* was clear on the point that a closed exclusive licence which was designed to confer absolute territorial protection by partitioning the markets of licensees could not be exempted under Article 85(3). It was in effect a *per se* violation of Article 85. The closed exclusive licence was defined as consisting of two elements:

1. the contractual ban on exports, i.e. the obligation upon INRA, or those deriving rights through INRA, to prevent third parties from exporting the relevant seeds into Germany without the licensee's authorization for use or sale in that territory; and
2. Eisele's use of his exclusive rights, both contractual and under the intellectual property right, to prevent all imports of the seed variety into Germany or exports to other member states.[13]

The Court's inclusion of the second element as part of a 'closed' licence was somewhat misleading because the right to use an IPR, such as a patent, even if it has been registered in both countries, to stop direct or parallel imports is curtailed by the Community doctrine of exhaustion under Articles 30 and 36. In *Centrafarm* v. *Sterling Drug*,[14] the Court indicated that the effect of Articles 30 and 36 upon national patent rights, could be defined by reference to the concept of the 'specific subject matter' of the patent, which it defined as the guarantee that the patentee shall have the exclusive right to be the first to manufacture and sell the patented product. This definition implies that the patentee cannot assert its patent rights in any one member state to prevent imports from another member state in which patented products have been put on the market by the patentee or with its consent, since the first act of putting

---

[13] See discussion in ch. 5.   [14] [1974] ECR 1147.

the patented product on the market in the second member state 'exhausts' the patent right in the first member state.

One effect of this doctrine, as pointed out in *Centrafarm* v. *Sterling Drug*,[15] is that once a patentee has granted a sales licence in a member state, it may no longer prevent the sale of that patented product throughout the common market by using patent protection and this would be true whatever the contractual obligations of the licensee. The Court has effectively made use of the exhaustion concept to ensure that parallel importers who have purchased the patented goods anywhere in the common market where they have been put on the market by or with the consent of the patentee will not be denied access in cases where higher prices in one territory make such importation possible.

What is less clear from the case-law on the exhaustion concept is its precise effect upon direct sales by a patent licensee into the territory of another licensee or the licensor. The language of *Sterling Drug* in respect of this issue allows the conclusion that direct sales by a licensee will have exhausted the intellectual property protection, but it is not conclusive. In the later case of *Pharmon* v. *Hoechst*,[16] which actually involved a direct sale by a licensee into the licensor's territory, the licensor's use of the patent right was decided by reference to the issue of consent and did not deal explicitly with the direct sales issue. The Advocate General suggested that exhaustion should apply to direct sales but the Court did not pronounce upon the issue. In *Hag II*,[17] the Court has made it plain that exhaustion does not apply in the context of the common origin rule. In *Ideal Standard*,[18] a trade mark assignment did not exhaust exclusive rights because of the loss of control of the product. It is not clear, however, how relevant these trade mark decisions are for patent cases.[19]

Nungesser gave support to the view that a licensor's attempt to protect a licensee from competition from another licensee for another territory would be caught by Article 85(1).[20] The Court's judgment implied that a contractual export prohibition would be prohibited by Article 85(1), and require exemption. However, it left open the question of the licensor's rights under the national patent legislation. In other words, the licensor may still make use of the protection under the national patent legislation to prevent direct sales as well as other forms of exploitation by a licensee outside its licensed territory, even if the contractual restriction is caught by Article 85(1).

One implication of this is that a licensor may be able to rely on its statutory intellectual property right protection even after the period of

---

15 [1974] ECR 1147.   16 [1985] ECR 2281.
17 [1990] ECR I–3711.   18 [1994] ECR I–2789.
19 See e.g. Korah (1996) at p. 75.   20 [1982] ECR 2015 at para. 53.

exclusivity permitted under the contract by the block exemption has expired.

At the time of the Patent Licensing Regulation, the Commission viewed the act of licensing as exhausting the IPR protection. It assumed that the grant of a licence to make, use or sell a product protected by an intellectual property right had the effect of 'exhausting' the owner's rights because, apart from a case of 'new technology', a licensor cannot impose a contractual territorial restriction on manufacture, use or sale by the licensee with respect to any member state outside the licensed territory without violating Article 85(1). As Venit describes it:

In effect, as far as contractual rights are concerned, the Commission in Regulation 2349/84 has legislated a Community-wide license in the absence of a Community-wide patent, although it has also created the possibility for the automatic exemption of territorially limited licenses.[21]

In the Technology Transfer Regulation, the Commission appears to have changed its view. In Article 2(1)(14) it states that a reservation by the licensor of the right to exercise the rights conferred by a patent to oppose the exploitation of the technology by the licensee outside the licensed territory is not restrictive of competition and is whitelisted.

This would appear to suggest that the Commission is relying on the doctrine of exhaustion under Articles 30 and 36 to protect parallel trade in the licensed products or processes, i.e. the trade by customers of the licensees.

The Commission's concession in Article 2(1)(14) is limited to direct trade by licensees outside their licensed territories.

---

[21] J. Venit op. cit. n. 12.

8

The Regulation of Non-Territorial Restraints
in Licensing Agreements

The categorization of non-territorial restraints, by the Commission and Court, has produced more of a consensus in respect of the basis for clearance. As we have seen, both have accepted the concept of the 'scope of the intellectual property right' and the doctrine of ancillary restraints in relation to the status of restrictions in licensing contracts under Article 85(1). However, while the scope of the patent doctrine can justify a wide range of non-territorial clauses, the early cases of *Burroughs Geha*[1] and *AOIP* v. *Beyrard*[2] indicated that certain types of non-territorial clauses could be found to be prohibited under Article 85(1) and incapable of exemption under Article 85(3). Moreover, in *Windsurfing*,[3] the Court of Justice had the occasion to review the Commission's approach to clauses which it found to be beyond the scope of the patent. The case concerned a licensing agreement between a US corporation Windsurfing International Inc. and its six German non-exclusive licensees. The agreements were for the manufacture and sale of windsurfing boards consisting of a rig and a sailboard, though the German patent covered only the rig. The Commission decided that seven clauses in the agreement violated Article 85(1) and imposed a fine of 50,000 ECUs. The Court reduced the fine to 25,000 ECUs and held that fewer clauses were prohibited by Article 85(1). The Court held that a restriction in the form of prior approval by the licensor of the type of unpatented boards that licensees could sell with the rigs and restrictions on licensees' rights separately to supply rigs violated Article 85(1). It also held that obligations to pay royalties on unpatented boards, to attach patent notices to the board, not to challenge the patent, or Windsurfing's trade mark or logo were all prohibited under Article 85(1).[4]

Underlying the Court's judgment was acceptance of the concept of the scope of the patent inquiry for the purpose of Article 85(1). The Court

[1] [1972] CMLR D72.
[3] [1986] ECR 611.

[2] [1976] 1 CMLR D14.
[4] Ibid., paras. 85–7.

held that since the patent applied to the rig alone, the restrictions on the licensee in respect of the sale of sailboards and separate rigs went beyond the scope of the patent and were not indispensable to its exploitation.[5] It also held that the obligation to affix patent notices to unpatented equipment and the no-challenge restriction did not come within the subject-matter of the patent and were therefore caught by Article 85(1). Finally, in its analysis of the restriction on licensees to one manufacturing site in Germany, it viewed this not as a limited licence but a restriction on production outside Germany and in particular in countries without patent protection.[6] In other words, this was a restriction on the contractual autonomy of the licensee. In these decisions the Court lent weight to the analysis of Article 85(1) as an analysis of the licensees' contractual freedom rather than an analysis of anticompetitive effect. The one exception was the Court's treatment of the royalties provision which on its face appeared to go beyond the scope of the patent because it applied to the price of the whole windsurfing board and not the rig alone. The Court, however, was prepared to reverse the Commission on this issue because the practical effect of a lower rate of royalty on the whole sailboard was not very different from a higher rate on the patented product taken on its own.

In *Windsurfing*, the Court found that the non-notified agreements were not cleared under Article 4(2) of Regulation 17 because the contents of the agreements went beyond the definition in that Regulation. The Commission had indicated that the clauses in the agreement which went beyond the scope of the patent could not be exempted. Unlike *Pronuptia*, the Court refrained from speculating about the possibilities of exemption.

In the more recent case of *Bayer & Henneker* v. *Sullhofer*,[7] the Court suggested that it was moving away from the view that no-challenge clauses were always unlawful under Article 85(1) and incapable of exemption under Article 85(3). It analysed no-challenge clauses as restrictions of contractual autonomy rather than as inhibitions on the process of protecting the integrity of the patent process and asked whether the restriction had an appreciable effect on that autonomy. It held that in the circumstances of the case, where the patent licence was royalty free, the no-challenge clause did not create a problem under Article 85(1) because the licensee would not have to bear the competitive disadvantage of having to pay royalties for the use of the patent which may be invalid. The *Bayer Henneker* decision suggested a move to a less formalistic approach to no-challenge clauses than *Windsurfing*. It left

---

[5] Ibid. at para. 57. [6] Ibid. at paras. 85–7.
[7] [1988] ECR 5249.

room for argument about other circumstances in which such clauses could be cleared under Article 85(1).[8]

8.2 PROTECTING THE INTEGRITY OF THE INNOVATION: THE INDISPENSABLE PROVISIONS IN LICENSING AGREEMENTS

8.2.1 Introduction

If a list of non-restrictive, non-territorial provisions in licensing agreements were compiled today in a modern version of the Commission's Notice of 1962, it would start with the whitelist in the new Technology Transfer Regulation. Article 2(1) provides that clauses which come into these categories are 'generally not restrictive of competition'. Recital 18 explains that:

It is desirable to list in the Regulation a number of obligations that are commonly found in licensing agreements, but are normally not restrictive of competition, and to provide that in the event that because of the particular economic or legal circumstances they should fall within Article 85(1), they too will be covered by the exemption. This list in Article 2, is not exhaustive.

Article 2(2) duly provides for their exemption even if they are caught by Article 85(1).

This explanatory statement, however helpful to achieve legal certainty in the context of the block exemption, can have the effect of obscuring the extent to which the whitelisted provisions are not caught at all by Article 85(1) by virtue of not being regarded as 'restrictions of competition' as defined by the Court and Commission in individual cases. A greater awareness of this point is useful because in cases where an agreement cannot be brought within the group exemption, it is possible to argue by analogy that similar provisions in say computer programs or trade mark licences are cleared and require no exemption.[9]

At the same time, the blacklist offers a good indication of the limits to exemptibility; the current line that is drawn between exemptible and non-exemptible clauses in licensing agreements. By examining the interplay between the contents of the two lists together with the case-law it is possible to place individual provisions into one of three categories:

---

[8] *Moosehead/Whitbread* [1991] 4 CMLR 391, discussed in S. Singleton, 'Intellectual Property Disputes: Settlement Agreements and Ancillary Licences under EC and UK Competition Law' [1993] *EIPR* 48; see too R. Subbiotto, 'Moosehead-Whitbread: Industrial Franchises and No Challenge Clauses Relating to Licensed Trade Marks under EEC Competition Law' [1990] *ECLR* 226.

[9] Korah, 'The New EC Group Exemption for Technology Licensing' [1994] *ECLR* 263 at 264.

clauses which are non-restrictive of competition under Article 85(1); those which are prohibited by Article 85(1) but exemptible under Article 85(3); and those which are non-exemptible.

To assist with this categorization exercise, it is helpful to examine the main types of clauses in licensing agreements under three separate heads. The first head consists of the provisions which are absolutely indispensable to intellectual property rights (IPR) licensing agreements because without them the value of the IPRs could be lost. The scope of these restrictions under Article 85(1) is limited largely by the logic of indispensability. The second head consists of the restrictions which are often necessary to allow the licensor to proceed with the licensing decision but take a form which could be misused in predictable ways. These are restricted by specific provisions in the blacklist and must be analysed in pairs or clusters to determine whether a provision is compatible with Article 85(1) as well as whether or not it is exemptible. The third head consists of the special cases of provisions accompanying exclusive territorial licences such as minimum royalties or minimum quantities, best endeavours clauses and non-competition clauses. These too must be analysed in pairs or clusters to determine their legal effect.

8.2.2 The Low Risk Indispensable Restraints

There are three types of provisions recognized as 'indispensable' to intellectual property licences which are not restrictions on competition under Article 85(1), at least in their pure form, either because of the scope of the patent doctrine or the ancillary restraints concept.[10]

8.2.2.1 The Obligation Not to Divulge Secret Know-how

It has long been acknowledged by the Commission that a licensor is entitled to place on the licensee an obligation not to divulge know-how communicated by the licensor during the contract. Moreover, the licensor is entitled to hold the licensee to that obligation for a period after the expiry of the contract until the know-how enters the public domain because in both instances non-disclosure is an indispensable condition of know-how licensing.[11] As the Commission stated in *Delta Chemie*,[12] the commercial value of the know-how rests very largely in its confidential character and each disclosure brings prejudice to the holder of that know-how. Since there is no time limit on the know-how protection through contract, it is legitimate to impose an obligation as long as the

---

[10] See Gonzales Diaz, 'Some Reflections on the Notion of Ancillary Restraints under EC Competition Law' [1995] *Fordham Corp. Law Inst.* 325 at pp. 350–4.

[11] See *Burroughs Delplanque* [1972] CMLR D 67 para. 48.

[12] *Delta Chemie/DDD* 4 CMLR 535.

know-how does not enter the public domain. In *Boussois/Interpane*,[13] the Commission cleared a clause which placed a five year limit on the secrecy obligation on the licensee. The parties had agreed that that represented the average life of the know-how and accepted that the obligation remained only as long as the know-how was not obtained by third parties from other sources. The Commission noted in clearing the clause that the ban did not extend beyond the useful life of the technology.

The formula used in the patent licensing block exemption and know-how block exemption is repeated in the Technology Transfer Regulation. It whitelists an obligation on the licensee not to divulge the know-how communicated by the licensor and adds that the licensee may be held to this obligation after the agreement has expired (Article (2)(1)).

This provision is essential for the licensor; the only issue is whether it offers sufficient protection for sharing secret know-how with the licensee. Often, the licensor attempts to combine a secrecy obligation with other provisions such as a ban on sub-licensing without prior consent,[14] a post-term use ban,[15] and a non-competition clause.[16] As we shall see, EC competition law does not allow the licensor the luxury of all these forms of protection; only some are viewed as objectively indispensable.

8.2.2.2 *The Ban on Sub-Licensing and Assignment*

The obligation not to sub-license the know-how which is communicated under the licence or the patent which is licensed or to assign either is not caught by Article 85(1) even if it extends beyond the term of the licence, as long as the know-how has not entered the public domain and the patents are still in force. In *Burroughs Delplanque*,[17] this protection was regarded as within the scope of the patent. In *Jus-Rol*,[18] the ban on sub-licensing to any undertaking other than a wholly owned subsidiary of either licensor or licensee was cleared because it protects the licensor's right to use the know-how as it sees fit as long as the know-how has not entered the public domain.[19] Competition policy would not countenance a ban once the patent expires or the know-how loses its secrecy because the contract would unfairly restrain the licensee whilst its competitors would be free to use the intellectual property. The Technology Transfer Regulation whitelists in Article 2(1)(2) an obligation on the licensee not to grant sub-licences or assign the licence, repeating the formulae of the earlier block exemptions.[20] The main complication involving the ban on

---

13 [1988] 4 CMLR 124.   14 Art. 2(2).
15 Art. 2(3).   16 Art. 3(2).
17 Op. cit., n. 11 above.   18 *Delta Chemie/DDD* op. cit. n. 12 above.
19 At para. 33; see too *Delta Chemie*.
20 Patent Licensing Reg., Art. 2(1)(5); Know-how Licensing Reg., Art. 2(1)(2).

sub-licensing occurs in the context of grant backs of improvements and post-term use bans which will be discussed below.

8.2.2.3 Post-Term Use Bans

The third indispensable clause in intellectual property licensing is the post-term use ban. The Commission has long accepted that an obligation placed upon the licensee to cease using the licensed technology after the termination of the agreement is not a restriction on competition. As the Commission puts it in Recital 20 of the Technology Transfer Regulation:

> The obligation on the licensee to cease using the licensed technology after the termination of the agreement . . . [does] not generally restrict competition. The post-term use ban may be regarded as a normal feature of licensing, as otherwise the licensor would be forced to transfer the know-how or patents in perpetuity.

The presence of this obligation in the agreement distinguishes the licence from the assignment. In *Jus Rol*[21] the Commission cleared a post-term use ban which applied for ten years following termination noting that it was inherent in this type of agreement. If the owner were to lose its exclusive right to use know-how at the expiry of the licensing agreement it would be less willing to grant a licence and this would be harmful to the transfer of technology.[22]

A post-term use ban becomes anticompetitive only if it persists after the know-how becomes freely available to others through no fault of the licensee. In *Delta Chemie*[23] the Commission reiterated that an obligation upon the licensee to cease using the licensed intellectual property right at the end of an agreement is an 'essential condition'[24] insofar as it has not entered the public domain. The limit in time may remove the licensee from the market for the licensed product at the end of the agreement but it is a necessary condition for the transfer of technical knowledge and should not be prohibited by Article 85(1).

Article 2(1)(3) whitelists 'an obligation on the licensee not to exploit the licensed know-how or patents after termination of the agreement in so far and as long as the know-how is still secret or the patents are in force'.

Secrecy is defined in Article 10(2). Nothing is mentioned in Article 2(1)(3) about the possibility that the licensee could be the source of the know-how entering the public domain. Korah has suggested that remedies must be sought in contract and has suggested that 'care should . . . be taken to inform each licensee before the contract is concluded of the likely loss if the licensee discloses the technology wrongfully and to record such a warning in order to prevent much of the damage being too remote'.[25]

---

[21] Op. cit. n. 18 above.
[23] Op. cit. at n. 12 above.
[25] See Korah (1996) at p. 167.

[22] See para. 34.
[24] At para. 35 ibid.

8.2.3 Quality Controls and Licensing

The concern of the licensor to ensure that the licensee preserves quality standards lies at the heart of the licensing decision, particularly where the licensor's trade mark is associated with the licensed product. In general the insistence on minimum quality specifications by itself as long as they are agreed upon in advance and based on objectively verifiable criteria has not been viewed as restrictive of competition under Article 85(1). Moreover, the licensor can reserve a right to monitor quality standards by carrying out related checks. These provisions are recognized by the Court of Justice and Commission as indispensable to an appropriate exploitation of the invention. Thus, in *Delta Chemie*,[26] quality standards applied to manufacturing and marketing were held not to be caught by Article 85(1) because they were 'inspired by the legitimate desire of the licensor to ensure the strict conformity of the products'.[27] In *Windsurfing*,[28] the Court appeared to accept the Commission's assertion that since quality standards come within the scope of the patent they should fall outside the scope of Article 85(1) only where they are intended to ensure 'that the technical instructions as described in the patent and used by the licensee may be carried into effect'.[29] In the patent licensing block exemption, the Commission insisted on a formulation which stressed that the quality specifications must be 'necessary for a technically satisfactory exploitation of the licensed invention'.[30] This attempt to limit quality standards to the bare minimum required for the technical exploitation of the patent may have derived from a concern of the Commission that such standards could be used to impose an unwanted tie-in but it provided a separate limit on tie-ins.[31] Venit has speculated that it might be caused by a concern to limit quality controls in the case of competing manufacturers and makes the point that it is too restrictive in the case of vertical agreements where higher quality standards should not be caught by Article 85(1), in particular where the licensee distributes under the licensor's trade mark.[32] This point is reinforced by the decision in *Pronuptia*.[33]

In the Know-how Regulation, the Commission commingled the issue of quality standards and tie-ins introducing a further requirement, foreshadowed in *Windsurfing*, that the quality specifications must also be necessary for ensuring that the production of the licensee conforms to

---

[26] Op. cit. at n. 12 above.
[28] See e.g. *Windsurfing* [1986] ECR 611.
[30] Art. 2(1)(9).
[32] J. Venit, 'In the Wake of Windsurfing: Patent Licensing in the Common Market' [1986] *Fordham Corp. Law Inst.* 517.

[27] Ibid. at para. 30.
[29] Ibid. at para. 45.
[31] Art. 2(1)(1).
[33] [1986] ECR 353.

the quality standards that are respected by the licensor and other licensees.[34] Again, this relatively strict test may be applicable to horizontal agreements or to tie-ins justified by quality controls but in vertical agreements it appears to be unduly restrictive as a form of regulation in the interests of competition. It ignores the procompetitive influence of intrabrand restrictions upon interbrand competition.

In the Technology Transfer Regulation it appears as if the Commission has taken these points on board. In Article 2(1)(5) it whitelists an obligation on the licensee to observe minimum quality specifications, including *technical specifications*, for the licensed product[35] or:

> to procure goods and services from the licensor or from an undertaking designated by the licensor, insofar as these quality specifications, products or services are necessary for:
> (a) a technically proper exploitation of the licensed technology; or
> (b) ensuring that the product of the licensee conforms to the minimum quality specifications that are applicable to the licensor and other licensees;

In other words, it deals with tie-ins justified by quality specifications as a special category, applying the restrictions in respect of technical exploitation and conformity with standards for licensor and other licensees to such tie-ins (see next section).

8.3 THE LIMITS OF INDISPENSABILITY

The ancillary restraints doctrine requires a balance to be struck when applying the test of indispensability under Article 85(1) as well as Article 85(3). At a certain point, the licensor may overreach the the limits of indispensability by drafting a particular restraint in terms which are too wide. The blacklist in the block exemption offers examples of limits which in principle operate to determine non-exemptibility. However, the analysis of the pairing or clustering of whitelisted and blacklisted provisions may also be used as guidelines to determine the limits of clauses under Article 85(1). This type of analysis can be exemplified in four main areas.

8.3.1 Tie-ins and Quality Specifications

In the Technology Transfer Regulation, there is a limited right for the licensor to place a tying requirement upon the licensee. Along with the

---

[34] Art. 2(1)(5).
[35] It omits to add that the licensor can reserve a right to carry out related checks. This was whitelisted in the Know-how Regulation and should be a provision which is cleared under Art. 85(1). Cf. Raymond Nagoya [1972] CMLR D45. See Korah (1996) p. 175.

obligation on the licensee to observe any necessary minimum quality specifications for the licensed product, the licensor may require the licensee to
procure certain goods and services only from the licensor where they are
necessary for a technically proper exploitation of the licensed technology
or for ensuring that minimum appropriate quality requirements are met
(Article 2(1)(5)). In other words, exemption is automatically granted to tie-
in obligations only if there are no alternative methods for the licensor to
achieve the technical and quality standards. At one point in the drafting
process, the Commission had inserted a less strict requirement. It provided
that a tying clause could be automatically exempted as long as it merely
contributed to a technically satisfactory exploitation of the licensed technology. In the final version of the Regulation, this formula was dropped
and the requirement of necessity reinstated. However, the new block
exemption provides for the possibility that a tie-in linked to quality specifications, which are not strictly necessary for a technically satisfactory
exploitation of the licensed technology or for ensuring that the production
of the licensee conforms to the quality standards that are respected by the
licensor and other licensees, may be notified to the Commission under the
opposition procedure. Under that procedure, it will be remembered, the
Commission accepts that the exemption will apply to the notified agreement if the Commission does not oppose it within a period of four months
from the date the agreement is notified (Article 4(1)). The main concern of
the Commission in monitoring notified tie-ins will be to distinguish
between licensors with considerable market power and those without such
power in the market for the licensed technology. In the latter case, there
will be little opposition because licensees will have alternative sources of
the technology from other licensors in the event they object to the tie-in.
Alternatively, if the tie-in is accepted voluntarily, there is no restriction on
competition. In the case where the licensor is in a dominant position on the
relevant market, the tie-in will be opposed because of the likelihood that
licensees will be constrained in their freedom of action by the contractual
tie.

In the Technology Transfer Regulation the Commission has come a
long way towards the position of not viewing tie-ins as *per se* anticompetitive but differing in effect depending on the state of competition in
the market for the licensed technology. It even suggests that the
Commission has accepted the possibility that some types of tie-in clauses
are capable of leading to increased efficiencies. In *Velcro/Aplix*[36] the
Commission held that only as long as other suppliers are unable to
provide the product and therefore there was no technically adequate
substitute would a tie-in be viewed as technically necessary.[37]

---

[36] [1989] 4 CMLR 157.   [37] See too *Vaessen/Moris* [1979] 1 CMLR 511.

However, as mentioned the form that the relaxation of Commission policy has taken towards tie-ins in the new Technology Transfer Regulation consists of making the opposition procedure available in cases where the licensor at the time of agreement places an obligation on the licensee to accept quality specifications or further licences or to procure goods or services which are not necessary for technical or quality control reasons (Article 4(2)(a)). This change from the previous block exemptions represents a recognition that in cases where the licensor does not occupy a dominant position and the relationship is predominantly vertical there is no need to prohibit tie-ins. The case-law of the Commission reinforces that view particularly in respect of know-how. In *Jus Rol*,[38] for example, an obligation placed upon the licensee to buy a pre-mix from the licensor was regarded as essential to ensure the proper proportions in the preparation of the mix as well as the correct results in the final product. The tie-in was justified as necessary to ensure 'consistency of quality' in the licensed product. In *Delta Chemie*[39] and *Moosehead/Whitbread*[40] the Commission acknowledged that the tie-ins were justified by the need to ensure consistency of manufacture and marketing in situations where the trade mark figured prominently in the agreement.

In respect of patents too a thaw may be detectible. In *Vaessen Moris*,[41] a manufacturer of sausage making machines was prepared to offer a free licence to use a sausage filling machine if the licensee agreed to buy their skins from him. The tie helped him 'meter' the use of the machine as well as to produce income. The Commission found that the tie had the effect of foreclosing other sausage skin makers. In a situation where the licensor offers the licensee a form of payment for the package of patented and non-patented material which in practice[42] is not dramatically different from the overall amounts which would have been payable on the patented material alone, and includes the advantage of avoiding an upfront payment, there seems to be room for exemption via the non-opposition procedure. As long as the market share is not so high that there are no substitutes, the tie-in can be viewed as efficiency enhancing and not an aggrandizement of market power by the licensor.[43]

8.3.2 Improvements and Grant Backs

The licensing of patents and/or know-how, either separately or together almost inevitably leads to improvements being discovered by licensees.

---

[38] *Rich Products/Jus Rol* (1988) 4 CMLR 527.   [39] [1989] 4 CMLR 535.
[40] *Moosehead Ltd. and Whitbread and Co.* (1991) 4 CMLR 391.
[41] [1979] 1 CMLR 511.   [42] Cf. *Windsurfing* [1986] ECR 611.
[43] Cf. discussion by Korah (1996) pp. 177–9.

Some improvements can themselves be patentable. Most consist of know-how which can be protected through contract. Some improvements are 'severable'; they are products or processes which are capable of being exploited independently of the original intellectual property right. Others are 'non-severable'; they are capable of being used only in conjunction with the protected producer or process in the original licence.

Typically, licensors are reluctant to license without a right of disclosure and use of the licensee's improvements. Disclosure is needed in order to monitor the licensee's development and use of the improvements. The right of use allows the licensor to improve the original product or process for its own use and for the use of other licensees. A number of licensors would prefer such rights to be exclusive or even assigned back, reasoning that the improvements are derived from the original invention. They would view a contractual commitment to granting back improvements as part of the quid pro quo for granting the licence in the first place. Some recognize that there is more of an incentive to the licensee to develop and communicate improvements if the licensee can share in the fruits of their severable improvements by licensing them to third parties but the concern about creating extra competitors often leads to a reluctance to cede too much freedom to licensees.

From the viewpoint of EC competition policy, the issue of the stimulus to innovation provided by improvements is too important to be left to freedom of contract. Unilateral control over improvements by strong licensors and/or licensees in the form of restraints in licensing contracts must be curtailed in the interest of promoting the development and diffusion of technology. The restraints in licensing agreements must not be drawn so widely that they stifle the incentives of licensees to improve the technology and disclose the results of their improvements more widely.

There are two noteworthy features of the regulatory framework which is currently provided by EC competition law. The first is an insistence on the feedback of severable improvements on a non-exclusive basis. The second, which is not always so obvious, is a principle that the flow of information and rights of use to improvements should be mutual. The commitment of EC competition policy to both principles is set out clearly in the Technology Transfer Regulation. Recital 20 sets out two broad principles.

The first principle is that 'the obligations on the licensee to make improvements available to the licensor do not generally restrict competition'. This principle is implemented by Article 2(1)(4) which permits:

an obligation on the licensee to grant to the licensor a license in respect of his own improvements to or his new applications of the licensed technology, provided that in the case of severable improvements, such a license is not exclusive, so that the licensee is free to use his own improvements or to license them to third parties, in so far as that does not involve disclosure of the know how communicated by the licensor that is still secret.

The second principle in Recital 20 is more far-reaching. It states that: 'Undertakings by the licensee to grant back to the licensor a license for improvements to the licensed know how and or patents are generally not restrictive of competition if the licensee is entitled by the contract to share in future experience and inventions made by the licensor.' Article 2(1)(4) implements this by stipulating that any grant back obligation placed on the licensee must be accompanied by a provision 'that the licensor undertakes to grant an exclusive or non-exclusive license of his own improvements to the licensee'. However, as we shall see, this is only a partial implementation of the principle. It may apply in a number of other situations.

8.3.2.1 *Article 85(1) and Grant Backs of Improvements*

The Commission has consistently accepted that as long as the licensor insists only on a grant back of a non-exclusive licence and accepts a reciprocal obligation to grant a licence of his own improvements to the licensee during the contract, there are no restraints on competition under Article 85(1). Such an arrangement allows licensees freely to exploit their own improvements, introduces new players into the process of development and diffusion of new technology, and is therefore generally procompetitive. For example, in *Raymond/Nagoya*[44] the Commission cleared a patent licensing agreement which required Nagoya, the licensee, to grant back non-exclusive licences for patented improvements to Raymond's patented process as well as for any new patents in the field even if unrelated to Raymond's technology. The Commission reasoned that as long as the grant back was non-exclusive and would not prevent Nagoya granting other licences in the EC, it would not be viewed as restricting competition under Article 85(1). The Commission viewed the continuing exchange of information concerning improvements and other know-how as part and parcel of the contractual utilization of property rights and know-how created by the agreement.

8.3.2.2 *Severable Improvements During the Term of the Contract*

In the case of improvements which are severable from the original intellectual property right which is licensed, it would be restrictive of competition

---

[44] [1972] CMLR D45.

if licensees were not allowed to remain free to use their own improvements during and after the term of the original licence, apart from their application to the licensed product or process. The licensee must also have a right to license its own severable improvements to others during this period although the licensor is entitled to contractual protection from disclosure of its protected know-how to third parties. Thus far the provisos in Article 2(1)(4) probably define the basis of clearance of grant back provisions. In *Delta Chemie*,[45] the Commission cleared this type of clause under Article 85(1). What is less clear under Article 85(1) is the position once the contract expires.

8.3.2.3 *Severable Improvements After the Expiry of the Contract*

Once the contract expires, the licensee will usually be bound by a post-term ban on using the licensor's technology. If nothing is provided in the contract, the ownership of severable improvements passes to the licensee. The Commission has carefully guarded the right of the licensee to retain its own severable improvements at the termination of the contract in its individual decisions. Thus in *Delta Chemie*,[46] it required the parties to amend the know-how licence so that upon the expiration of the original licence, the licensor could not continue to exploit the licensee's improvements. In *Rich Products/Jus Rol*,[47] the Commission commented favourably upon the fact that the licensor's rights to the licensee's improvements as well as the licensee's rights to use the original know-how ended at the expiry of the main licence agreement.[48]

If the licensor wishes to use the licensee's severable improvements after the original licence expires, it is not enough to extract a contractual right without an appropriate quid pro quo. One possibility under Article 85(1) is to lift the post-term ban on use of the original licensed product or process and provide a mutual obligation to continue to grant back improvements. This will allow the licensee to continue to use the original know-how and continue to exploit its own improvements, as well as any of those of the licensor. For example, in *Boussois/Interpane*,[49] the Commission cleared an obligation on the licensee to communicate its improvements to the licensor for indefinite use because the licensor had accepted a reciprocal obligation to communicate its improvements to the licensee as well as extending a right to use such improvements indefinitely. The Commission could see that under the arrangement there was no danger that the licensee would be unable to use the unseverable know-how at the expiry of the licence leaving the licensor free to use it in

---

[45] Op. cit. n. 12 above.
[47] [1988] 4 CMLR 527.
[49] [1988] 4 CMLR 124.

[46] Op. cit. n. 12 above.
[48] Ibid. at para. 36.

conjunction with its own original know-how. The decision suggested that the Commission's main concern was that the licensee who had developed improvements in the know-how should not be prevented, by a post-term ban on the use of the original know-how, from exploiting its own improvements. However, the decision also indicated that the Commission was concerned to preserve a right of access to both parties to the original know-how and improvements as long as the contract continued.

It is much less clear that Article 85(1) would allow the licensor to use the contract to obtain a competitive advantage over the licensee in the form of an option to continue to use the licensee's severable know-how after the expiry of the contract in return for royalties only. This type of arrangement might be acceptable in respect of non-severable improvements (see below) but would place the licensee at a competitive disadvantage in respect of severable improvements, unless the licensee has ceased manufacturing the technology itself. Moreover, the whitelist in the Technology Transfer Regulation has omitted any reference to the licensor's right to retain an option to examine the licensee's improvements before deciding whether or not to pay royalties for their use. This was contained in the Know-how Regulation and subjected to telling criticism.[50]

Further, if the licensor insists upon the right to sub-license severable improvements without approval this might be unacceptable under Article 85(1). For example, in *Kabel/Luchaire*, the licensor added, to a clause requiring the licensee to grant back improvements on a non-exclusive basis, another provision reserving a right to sub-license those improvements to others. The Commission expressed reservations about the sub-licensing clause because of its chilling effect on Luchaire's incentive to innovate and the way it would undermine its control over its own innovation, though in the particular case it decided that the agreement did not substantially affect competition. Finally, if the licensor insists upon a right to limit the licensee's right to sub-license its own severable improvements, other than a contractual protection of confidentiality, this might be contrary to Article 85(1).

In *Boussois/Interpane*, in clearing a non-exclusive reciprocal improvements provision, the Commission noted that the licence to use improvements was coextensive with the licence to use the original know-how and that there was no danger that Boussois would be prevented from using either the original know-how or any of its non-severable improvements.

---

[50] See e.g. Frazer's criticism of the option given to the licensor in the Know-how Regulation to examine the licensee's improvements before deciding whether or not to pay appropriate royalties for their use: 'Vorsprung durch Technik: The Commission's Policy on Know-how Agreements' [1989] *Oxford Yearbook of Euro. Law* 1 at p. 18.

Such clauses may be exemptible. In the know-how block exemption, the licensee's right to license its own improvements could be limited in the contract by an obligation requiring the licensee to obtain prior approval from the licensor (Article 2(1)(4)) as well as an obligation not to disclose the licensor's know-how while still secret. Although such approval could not be withheld unreasonably, the additional requirement created a restraint on the freedom of the licensee to engage in independent licensing.[51]

Under the new Technology Transfer Regulation, know-how and patents are treated with a clear concern for the autonomy of the parties in relation to their own improvements (Recital 20). The right of the licensor to use the licensee's severable improvements must be non-exclusive allowing the licensee the freedom to exploit its own improvements or license them to third parties as long as the licensor's know-how which is still secret is not disclosed. The grant back by the licensee must be accompanied by a reciprocal obligation on the licensor to divulge and allow use of its improvements to the licensee which can either be exclusive or non-exclusive. The whitelist is silent on the issue of allowing a provision which would give the licensor prior approval over the licensing of its own severable improvements. This does not preclude the possibility that such a provision would be exemptible, since it was viewed as not restrictive of competition under the know-how block exemption and it could be viewed as merely an extension of the original right of control. Nevertheless, its omission from the whitelist in the current block exemption could make it prudent to notify such a clause to the opposition procedure.

The whitelist is also silent on the issue of post-term rights although there is a general principle of reciprocality imposed by Recital 20. If the contract stipulates non-exclusive cross-licensing of the licensee's improvements together with the licensor's improvements with or without the original licensed intellectual property, the arrangement would be an optimum one from the competition point of view. It would not be caught by Article 85(1).

Moreover, in Article 8(3) it is possible for the initial duration of an exclusive licensing agreement to be automatically prolonged by the inclusion of new improvements, whether patented or not, communicated by the licensor. However, this is conditional upon the licensee having a right to refuse such improvements or each party having the right to terminate the agreement at the end of the original term or at least every three years thereafter (see Recital 14).

The whitelist is silent about the possibility that the licensor can reserve

---

[51] Frazer, *Oxford Yearbook of Euro. Law* 1 at p. 18.

for itself the right to continue exploiting the licensed technology in the licensee's severable improvements simply by paying royalties and without prolonging the original licence. Whilst this is not explicitly prohibited by Article 85(1), in the know-how block exemption, it was found to be not restrictive of competition only in the case of non-severable improvements. Again the prudent may prefer to make use of the opposition procedure when inserting such a clause, unless the licensee has abandoned any interest in continuing to exploit the relevant technology.

However, where the licensee's improvements are non-severable, the licensor would have an interest in controlling sub-licensing of the original licensed intellectual property right and ensuring protection of the secrecy of the know-how. In such cases, the licensee would not be able to sub-license the original intellectual property without the consent of the licensor, and a provision requiring the licensee to grant an exclusive licence of all non-severable improvements could be viewed as not caught by Article 85(1).[52] Similarly, the freedom of the licensor to license or sub-license the non-severable improvements of the licensee would be restricted in the territories in which the licensee enjoys an exclusive licence.[53] The Commission's approach to the reciprocality of grant back clauses under Article 85 has differed in cases where the improvements are severable and where they are non-severable.

An obligation placed upon the licensee to assign severable improvements to the licensor is blacklisted in Article 3(9) but no mention is made of a provision requiring an exclusive licence during the course of the contract. This indicates that an exclusive licence could be referred to the opposition procedure under the Technology Transfer Regulation.

8.3.2.4 *Non-severable Improvements*

The obligation placed upon the licensee to communicate and grant a licence to use non-severable improvements to the licensor during the term of the contract has long been viewed as compatible with Article 85(1) as long as it is non-exclusive and accompanied by a reciprocal obligation upon the licensor to divulge information about and grant a licence in respect of improvements and new applications. In *Boussois/Interpane*,[54] the Commission cleared an improvements clause because of its reciprocal and non-exclusive nature. It noted that there was no danger that Boussois would be prevented from using either the original know-how or the improvements made by it which were non-severable. Built into the arrangement was a clear limit to the right of the licensee to license its own improvements because of the licensor's control

---

[52] See *Merck/Merieux* [1994].
[54] Op. cit. n. 49 above.

[53] J. Venit op. cit. n. 32 at p. 596.

over the sub-licensing of the technology in the original licence. Moreover, the licensor had the protection of the licensee's obligation not to disclose the licensor's know-how to third parties.

In the Know-how Regulation the entitlement of the licensor to require the licensee to communicate and grant a licence to the licensor of any improvements or new applications of the licensed technology was whitelisted only on the condition that the licence was non-exclusive and the licensor agreed to disclose and grant a licence of its own improvements to the licensee during the term of the contract. It was difficult for the whitelist to extend this even-handed approach into the period after the contract expired because of the obstacles created by a post-term ban on the licensee using the original know-how in the case of non-severable improvements. At one stage in *Delta Chemie*,[55] the Commission cleared an obligation on the licensee to license its improvements to the licensor only after the parties had agreed that the licensor would not use the licensee's non-severable improvements after the expiry of the contract, thus preserving reciprocal rights in the original licence and paving the way for a negotiation of a bilateral arrangement for use of the complementary intellectual property rights at the end of the original contract.

Further, in the Know-how Regulation there was an attempt to preserve parity by requiring the licensor's right to use the licensee's non-severable improvements beyond the date when the licensee's right to use the licensor's know-how comes to an end. However, that parity was broken by the proviso that the licensor could require the licensee to give the licensor the option to continue to use the licensee's improvements after that date, if at the same time he relinquishes the post-term ban or instead chooses to pay appropriate royalties for their use. This placed the licensee in the unenviable position of having to accept royalties instead of a cross-licensing arrangement for improvements as part of the price of agreeing to the original licence. This seemed to be a step back from the parity requirement insisted on by the Commission in *Delta Chemie*.

8.3.2.5 *Grant Backs of Non-Severable Improvements under the New Block Exemption*

Under the new technology transfer block exemption, the Commission has indicated that in the case of non-severable improvements the licensor may, without offending Article 85(1), insist on an exclusive licence of the licensee's non-severable improvements during the period of the contract as long as the licensor is also bound to grant a licence of his own improvements to the licensee. This recognizes the reality of the licensor's

---

[55] Op. cit. n. 12 above.

control over any sub-licensing or disclosure of the secret technology in the original licence.

This marks a retreat from apparent parity of the Know-how Regulation which whitelisted only a non-exclusive licence of the licensee's non-severable improvements. However, the new block exemption allows an exclusive licence only for the duration of the contract and upon the condition that the licensor reciprocates (Article 2(1)(4)). The Regulation blacklists an obligation upon the licensee to assign in whole or in part to the licensor rights to improvements in new applications of the licensed technology. This applies to non-severable as well as severable improvements. If the licensor insists upon a post-term exclusive licence with royalties it must include a right to terminate to be exemptible. Otherwise, it would amount to an assignment allowing the licensor in effect to appropriate the licensee's improvements.

At the end of the agreement, the technology transfer block exemption applies a more even-handed approach to grant backs of the licensee's improvements. The whitelist is silent on the licensor's right to the licensee's improvements after the expiry of the agreement. The licensor's post-term use ban could be traded for a continued use of the licensee's improvements as was whitelisted in the know-how block exemption. Similarly, the licensor could attempt to insert a right to use the licensee's improvements after the expiry of the contract in exchange for the payment of royalties. Neither quid pro quo is explicitly whitelisted and therefore a non-symmetrical arrangement might have to be submitted to the opposition procedure to be safe. Where the arrangement is reciprocal, the reasoning of the Commission in *DDD/Delta Chemie*[56] suggests that it would not be caught by Article 85(1).

The more limited whitelist in the Technology Transfer Regulation therefore could have the effect of inhibiting the power of the licensor to extinguish the possibilities of the licensee emerging as a potential competitor since the royalty option combined with rights of prior approval over licensing by the licensee of its own improvements in the former Know-how Regulation could be criticized for having had just that effect.[57]

The opportunity for the licensee to license its improvements to other licensees acts as an incentive to continued competition in the field as well as a wider diffusion of higher levels of technology. It offers realistic recognition of the potential horizontal relationship that is inherent in the original vertical relationship.

This policy is reinforced in the blacklist which provides that the exemption does not apply to an agreement in which the licensee is

---

[56] Op. cit. n. 12 above. [57] See e.g. *Merck/Merieux* [1994].

obliged to assign in whole or in part to the licensor rights to improvements to or new applications of the licensed technology (Article (3)(6)).

8.3.2.6 *The Use of Improvements to Extend the Contractual Relationship*

The second issue in the regulation of improvement provisions under the block exemption is the concern to avoid an arrangement whereby a series of improvements are used to obtain extra periods of territorial protection under the block exemption. As Recital 14 puts it:

> parties are free to extend the term of their agreements in order to exploit any subsequent improvement and to provide for the payment of additional royalties. However, in such cases, further periods of territorial protection may be allowed only starting from the date of licensing of the secret improvements in the Community and by individual decision. Where the research for improvements results in innovations which are distinct from the licensed technology the parties may conclude a new agreement benefiting from an exemption under this Regulation. [See Articles 3(7) and 8(3).]

The Regulation thus introduces a crucial distinction between innovations distinct from the licensed technology and improvements to it. The former qualify for a new period of territorial exclusivity under Article 1 of the block exemption. The latter may not extend the period of territorial protection (Article 3(7)) without individual exemption. The lack of clarity in this distinction drawn by the Regulation will create pressure on the parties to apply for individual exemption to avoid legal uncertainty. The application of this distinction by national courts would be unpredictable. The Commission should offer clearer guidance.

8.4 FIELD OF USE PROVISIONS

Field of use provisions in technology licences between parties in a vertical relationship are generally procompetitive. They can help the licensors to exploit their own invention in those fields which are thought to be technically and commercially advantageous and pass on to other firms the possibility of exploitation in the untouched fields. They ensure that each licensee has an incentive to promote technical developments within its own field by providing the protection of exclusivity within each field as well as reinforcing other procompetitive restraints which result in increased efficiencies. They increase the number of licensees exploiting the innovation and in these respects promote diffusion of technology. The only risk from the point of view of competition policy is that the field of use provision could operate as a form of customer allocation arrangement between competitors. The art for competition authorities is to devise a mode of regulation which distinguishes between the two.

After a belated start, EC competition law has moved into such a position. In principle, insofar as the field of use provisions apply to products or processes covered by the patent or know-how regulations, they are regarded as not caught by Article 85(1) because they come within the scope of the intellectual property right. This was recognized by the Commission in respect of patents once it had given up an earlier more restrictive view that such provisions were only justified when the licensor was unable to operate in the particular technical field. In the original patent licensing block exemption, the Commission whitelisted 'an obligation on the licensee to restrict his exploitation of the licensed invention to one or more technical fields of application covered by the licensed patent'. The block exemption dealt with horizontal risks by blacklisting 'customer sharing' arrangements.[58] In the case of know-how, the Commission once again hesitated before recognizing that similar arguments applied. At one stage, in its working paper on the know-how group exemption, it suggested that field of use provisions in know-how agreements should be caught by Article 85(1) because of their restrictions on licensees.

However in *Delta Chemie*[59] and *Jus-Rol*[60] the Commission cleared field of use provisions under Article 85(1). In *Delta Chemie* it was on the grounds that it was the legitimate right of the licensor to dispose freely of his know-how and to limit its use by third parties. In both cases the Commission accepted that the combination of exclusivity and field of use would oblige the licensee to focus its production and sales efforts and concentrate on improving the quality of the products manufactured and the quantity produced.[61] Moreover, in *Jus Rol*, the Commission appeared to approve of the idea of slicing products into separate product markets with separate licensees.

When the Know-how Regulation was enacted, it provided that the licensor could place an obligation on the licensee to restrict his exploitation of the licensed technology not only to one or more technical fields of application covered by the licensed technology but also to one or more product markets. Again, if one party was restricted within the same technological field of use as to the customers he could serve, in particular by being prohibited from supplying certain classes of user, employing certain forms of distribution, or with the aim of sharing customers, using certain types of packaging, the use of field of use provisions was blacklisted (Article 3(6)).

Under the Technology Transfer Regulation, the treatment of field of use provisions draws a clearer distinction between provisions depending

---

[58] See Art. 3(7) of the Patent Licensing Regulation. [59] Op. cit. n. 12 above.
[60] Op. cit. n. 47 above. [61] At paras. 40–1.

upon whether they are vertical agreements or agreements between competitors. Thus, Article 2(1)(8) whitelists an obligation on the licensee to restrict his exploitation of the licensed technology to one or more technical fields of application or one or more product markets because, as Recital 22 states, 'the licensee is entitled to transfer the technology only for a limited purpose'.

On the other hand, customer allocation clauses within the same field of use or product market in agreements where the parties are competitors for the contract products will render the agreement ineligible for the block exemption (Article 3(4)).

If the parties are not competitors such restraints can be referred to the opposition procedure (Recital 23). Moreover, Article 3(4) does not apply to the special case of second sourcing, i.e. an agreement where the restriction grants a patent or know-how license in order to provide a single customer with a second source of supply.

8.5 THE REGULATION OF ROYALTIES

From a competition point of view, it is now accepted by the Commission and the Court that, for the most part, Article 85(1) should have little application to the bargain struck over royalty payments as long as it has been freely negotiated between the parties.[62] As the Commission puts it in the new Technology Transfer Regulation:

As a rule, parties do not need to be protected against the foreseeable consequences of an agreement freely entered into and they should therefore be free to choose the appropriate means of financing the technology transfer and sharing between them the risks of such use. [Recital 21.]

However the parties are not left entirely free of regulation of royalty arrangements in licensing agreements under Article 85. There are competition concerns with bargains which in some way go beyond the pure exchange of royalty for the licensed product in terms of (a) duration and (b) the base for calculating royalties; in both cases, the concern is that the licensor might exceed its entitlement under the scope of the IPR grant.

8.5.1 Duration

The freedom to spread royalty payments for the use of the technology over a period extending beyond the duration of the licensed patents or after the licensed know-how has entered the public domain was initially

---

[62] Art. 86 offers protection to cases of unfair pricing by undertakings in a dominant position.

viewed with suspicion under Article 85(1). An obligation to continue paying royalties after the intellectual property right protection expired was viewed as burdening the licensee with extra costs without any intellectual property right justification. Competitors would be in a position to make the product or use the process freely and could sell at a lower price. It also appeared to be a form of leveraging of the patent beyond its original scope.

This was particularly the case where the agreement contained a unilateral imposition of the extension. For example, in *AOIP/Beyrard*,[63] a licensing agreement for patented electrical devices, the French inventor Beyrard had insisted on a clause which allowed for an extension of the term by including new patents or improvements with a continuing obligation to pay royalties on expired patents during the extension period even if the new patents were not being used. The Commission found that the clause fell within Article 85(1) particularly because AOIP had no right to terminate at the end of the original term and Beyrard had a unilateral right to extend it.

If an agreement provides that there is a right for either party to terminate the agreement, then there is greater assurance that the period for calculating the royalties is part of the original bargain struck in respect of the original intellectual property package.

The significance of the issue of freedom to terminate was emphasized by the Court of Justice in *K Ottung* v. *Klee & Weilbach*[64] in which the licensee stopped paying royalties on expired patents without terminating the agreement according to its terms. The Court held that a clause providing for royalty payments after the expiry of the patent was caught by Article 85(1) if the licensee could not terminate the contract on reasonable notice or if it operates to seriously weaken his competitive position. Presumably therefore such a clause with a right to terminate could be compatible with Article 85(1) if it is combined with a right of the licensee to terminate on giving reasonable notice. In the original patent licensing block exemption, any agreement containing a clause extending the agreement for subsequent patents could not qualify for the exemption unless each party had the right to terminate once the original patents had expired (Article 3(2)).

Even assuming a right to terminate, however, there is still a residual concern for royalties on expired patents which could reduce the parties' freedom of contract in respect of method of paying royalties. In the case of licensed patents, under the new technology transfer block exemption, the agreement may contain an obligation on the licensee to continue paying the royalties over a period going beyond the duration of the

---

[63] [1976] 1 CMLR D14.　　　　[64] [1989] ECR 1177.

licensed patents but only if it is 'in order to facilitate payment' (Article 2(1)(7)(b)). In contrast, in the case of know-how, the parties are given the freedom to determine the nature of the obligation to continue paying royalties until the end of the agreement even if the know-how becomes publicly known (Article 2(1)(7)(a)). In *Boussois/Interpane*,[65] the Commission indicated that where payments have been agreed to continue after the know-how enters the public domain, because this method of payment represents the spread of a fixed sum rather than a royalty, it could be compatible with Article 85(1).

The language of the Technology Transfer Regulation in respect of know-how (Article 2(1)(7)) suggests that a form of turnover based royalty for know-how could be acceptable under Article 85(3). It is often the case that the licensee, having to undertake capital commitments on manufacturing and development facilities, is not in a position to or would prefer not to make a substantial upfront payment. Sometimes too, it may not be possible to establish the value of the patent or know-how to allow an agreed calculation of a fixed sum at the outset. In such cases, a royalty based on turnover which extends for the length of the contract even where the IPR has lost its protection offers a way out that appeals to both parties (see Recital 21).

8.5.2 The Base for Calculating Royalties

Connected with the regulation of the duration of royalty payments are the restrictions imposed by Article 85(1) on the base for calculating royalties in terms of the products used as the basis of calculation. In the original Patent Licensing Regulation, a clause which charged royalties on unpatented products, products not produced by a patented process or products produced by no longer secret know-how was blacklisted. In the know-how block exemption, clauses which charged royalties on goods not produced using the licensed technology or using it after it has been made public by the licensor in violation of the agreement were similarly proscribed.

In *Windsurfing*[66] the agreement provided a method of calculating royalties for the patented rig based on the net selling price of the entire sailboard (rig and board). The Commission held that this method contravened Article 85(1) because it regarded the net royalty clause as an attempt to prevent the separate sale of rigs to unlicensed third parties. The Court was more understanding of the practicalities in the case and held that once the method of calculation was adjusted to meet some of

---

65 [1988] 4 CMLR 124. See too *Rich Products/Jus Rol* [1988] 4 CMLR 527.
66 [1986] ECR 611.

the Commission's objections, so that the royalty rate for the separate sale of rigs was not lower than the rate under the old agreement, the royalty rate for the rigs based on the product as a whole did not violate Article 85(1). In respect of rigs, its object or effect was not restrictive of competition. Further, the Court indicated that the calculation of royalties for the patented part of a product based on the price of the product as a whole could be justified because it was impracticable to establish its value, either because the number of items manufactured or consumed was difficult to establish or if there was no separate demand for the patented product. On the other hand, the Court held that insofar as the calculation of royalties based on a 'bundling' of patented with unpatented products restricted the sale of the unprotected product, the board, it was not only caught by Article 85(1); it was not exemptible under Article 85(3).

In the technology transfer block exemption there is no specific reference to 'bundling' in the blacklist. Some hint that there continue to be competition concerns with the use of turnover based royalties, however, is indicated by the statement in Recital 21 that the setting of rates of royalty to achieve a blacklisted restriction renders the agreement ineligible for the block exemption.

8.6 NO-CHALLENGE CLAUSES

The desire of a licensor to insert a no-challenge clause in a licence is so strong that without such contractual protection many might be reluctant to license at all. The risk of a licensee using its intimate knowledge of the patent process acquired as a result of a patent licence to devalue the investment in the R&D for opportunistic reasons could deter a decision to license at all or at the very least restrict it to partners over which there were extra-contractual controls.[67] For many years, however, this factor was viewed as completely overshadowed by the issue of public policy, that the rules of competition law should not indirectly encourage the weakening of the integrity of the patenting process.[68] Thus in a number of cases, the Commission found that the presence of a no-challenge clause was a restriction of competition because it prevented the licensee from removing 'an obstacle to his freedom of action'.[69] In *Davidson Rubber*,[70] the Commission insisted upon the licensor removing the no-challenge clause as the price of granting the exemption. It felt that the

---

[67] See discussion by Korah (1996) at p. 184.

[68] See e.g *Vaessen/Moris* [1979] 1 CMLR 511 at paras. 34–5.

[69] Ibid. The one exception was *Raymond/Nagoya* but in that case the restriction on Nagoya was placed upon Nagoya's trade only in Asian markets.

[70] [1972] CMLR D52.

fact that the licensee was in the best position to detect a weakness in the validity of the IPR was a reason not to allow the licensor to restrain him.[71]

In the early IPR licensing block exemptions, the policy of protecting the licensee's right to challenge was continued. Thus in the patent licence block exemption, the use of a no-challenge restriction was blacklisted (Article 3(1)) and the licensor's entitlement to insist that the licensee act against infringers was made conditional upon the preservation of the licensee's right to challenge (Article 2(1)(8)). However, the patent licensing regulation introduced a right for the licensor to terminate the licence in the event of a challenge to the validity of the patent. A similar approach was taken in the Know-how Regulation to cases of challenge to the secrecy or the validity of the licensed technology.[72] It has been argued that this in effect 'permitted no challenge clauses since in all but the clearest cases, the licensee will not take the risk of mounting such a challenge'.[73] On the other hand, as has also been pointed out, the right to challenge has been misused by licensees seeking to avoid their contractual obligation to pay royalties or to have greater opportunity to use rival technology.[74]

In *Bayer and Henneke* v. *Sullhofer*,[75] the Court of Justice held on an Article 177 reference that before a no-challenge clause could be found to be contrary to Article 85(1), it must be looked at in its legal and economic context and that is a task for the national court. The Court rejected the Commission's argument that since the clause was part of a settlement of a litigation dispute over Bayer's challenge of Sullhofer's utility model and patent and Sullhofer's infringement claim, it could be viewed as an ancillary restraint to the compromise settlement. However, it gave two examples of cases where a no-challenge clause would not infringe Article 85(1): the first was a case where the no-challenge clause was in respect of a licence which was royalty free since it imposed no competitive disadvantage upon the licensee.[76] This has been criticized as focusing entirely on the position of the licensee and ignoring the fact that an invalid patent even if licensed free to one firm can still restrain competition *vis à vis* third parties.[77] The second was where substantial royalties were payable but the technology was outmoded. In cases where the technology was new and royalties were payable for its use, the national court would have to decide whether the agreement involved a significant lessening of competition based on the market position of the parties. The case is not helpful about the status of a compromise settlement of a challenge to the validity of an IPR which itself includes a no-challenge agreement.[78]

---

[71] See too *AOIP* v. *Beyrard* [1976] 1 CMLR D14.

[73] Frazer op. cit. n. 5. p. 18.

[75] [1988] ECR 5249.

[77] See OECD Report p. 89; Korah (1986) p. 185.

[78] See discussion, Korah (1986) pp. 184–6.

[72] See Arts. 3(4) and 2(1)(7).

[74] See Korah (1986) p. 183.

[76] At para. 17.

In the new Technology Transfer Regulation, the Commission has removed no-challenge clauses from the blacklist. Instead it provides that an obligation on the licensee not to contest the secrecy of the licensed know-how or challenge the validity of the licensor's patents licensed within the common market (Article 4(2)(b)) may be eligible for exemption, if it is notified to the Commission under the non-opposition procedure. If there is no opposition within four months, it is to be deemed exempt. In the new block exemption the licensor also retains the right to terminate the agreement in the event of a challenge to the secrecy or validity of the licensed technology. The availability of the opposition procedure for no-challenge clauses is a sign that the Commission is beginning to accept the argument that without the reassurance that a licensing arrangement and sharing of information will not itself jeopardize their investment in their original innovation, licensors have been deterred from using the licensing option.

Whether the Commission will apply similar reasoning to a clause in a licensing contract which requires the licensee to state that the patent is valid and the know-how is secret and valuable at the time the licence is signed is unclear. In *Moosehead/Whitbread*, the acknowledgement by Whitbread of Moosehead's title to the trade marks and the validity of the registration was referred to as amounting to a no-challenge clause (paragraph 15.4).[79]

8.7 EXCLUSIVE TERRITORIALITY, MINIMUM QUANTITIES, AND NON-COMPETITION CLAUSES

When the licensor agrees to an exclusive territorial licence to a licensee to manufacture and sell the licensed product, it must have an assurance that the licensee will actually work to produce a return. One form of assurance is a minimum royalty or minimum quantities clause in the agreement. A second would be a non-competition clause. Under Article 85, the former is whitelisted as indispensable whilst the latter is blacklisted. Let us look at each in turn.

8.7.1 Minimum Royalties and Minimum Quantities

For the licensor, one of the first priorities is to obtain an assurance of a return on the transfer of rights to manufacture and sell the licensed technology. From a competition point of view therefore, an obligation on a licensee to pay a minimum royalty, or to sell a minimum quantity, is not

---

[79] See discussion by Korah p. 186 n. 68.

normally caught by Article 85(1). It provides an indispensable condition for the licensor to take the risk of offering the licensee an exclusive licence. To this end, the new block exemption allows the licensor to place an obligation on the licensee to pay a minimum royalty or produce a minimum quantity of the licensed product or carry out a minimum number of operations exploiting the licensed technology (Article 2(1)(10)).

Yet, again, the use of this device is not entirely free of restrictive effects on competition. If the minimum royalty, or minimum quantity is set at too high a level, it could have an impact equivalent to a non-competition clause which is blacklisted.[80] This is particularly the case if it is accompanied by a clause providing that the licensee must use its best endeavours to manufacture and market the licensed product (Article 2(1)(17)) or a reservation of the right to terminate exclusivity and the right to access to improvements if the licensee enters into competition with the licensor during the period of the agreement in respect of competing products (Article 2(1)(18)). Nevertheless, this combination of minimum quantity, best endeavours, and right to terminate is normally exemptible in a vertical licensing relationship. It is only if such provisions occur in a licensing agreement between manufacturers who were competing at the time of the licence and prevent the licensee from using competing technologies, that the exemption can be withdrawn by the Commission (Article 7(4)).

Quantity or royalty minimum requirements are not viewed as caught by Article 85(1) as long as the royalty base does not extend beyond the licensed product. In *Windsurfing*,[81] the Court was prepared to tolerate a royalty based on a licensed rig combined with a non-licensed sailboard, but only because the net royalty for the two was the same as the royalty for the licensed product standing alone and it was difficult to calculate the value of the patented product alone. In cases where a base for calculating a royalty is wider than the licensed product and results in a higher net royalty than would otherwise be the case, then at the very least the agreement is caught by Article 85(1) and may not be exempted under Article 85(3).

Further, if the parties stipulate that the licensee is obliged to continue to pay royalties after the patent has expired or the know-how becomes public, this would be an offensive restriction on the competition of the licensee with other manufacturers of the formerly protected product. However, the block exemption allows the licensor to require the licensee to continue to pay royalties as agreed under the contract, for example, until the end of the agreement or the regular expiry of the patents, even where the intellectual property rights have declined in, or completely

---

[80] See next section.   [81] [1986] ECR 611.

lost their, value because the patents have prematurely lost their validity or the know-how has become publicly known other than by the action of the licensor (Article 2(1)(7)).

On the whole, therefore, the new block exemption continues the enlightened approach of its predecessors, particularly the Know-how Regulation, by allowing the parties to adjust the timing of payments for technology licences to reflect their own assessment of commercial risks. The opportunity to spread the royalty over a longer period reduces the need for a prohibitive upfront payment. The parties can be left to decide for themselves appropriate means of financing the technology transfer and sharing between them the risks of exploitation, including the premature loss of intellectual property protection. The Know-how Regulation provided that if the parties chose methods of calculating royalties which are neither directly nor indirectly related to the exploitation of the licensed technology this 'would render the agreement ineligible for the block exemption'. This clause which was blacklisted in the Know-how Regulation has been omitted from the blacklist in the new block exemption. Nevertheless, it might offer a line of attack for a disgruntled licensee.

8.7.2 Non-Competition Clauses

If an intellectual property rights licence between undertakings which are existing competitors includes a non-competition clause, it is often a clear restraint of competition and prohibited by Article 85(1). There may be exceptions under Article 85(1) because of the nature of the agreement. For example, a non-concentrative joint venture or an R&D joint venture or a specialization agreement may contain such clause and not be caught by Article 85(1) because of a block exemption or Commission Notice or by virtue of its non-appreciable impact on competition. However, absent special circumstances such a clause between competing manufacturers is regarded as a classic attribute of cartels and customer sharing arrangements.

In a vertical relationship, however, a non-competition clause may have certain procompetitive functions. The licensor to an exclusive licence requires an assurance that the licensed property will be commercially exploited and protection should the exclusive licensee be attracted to competing technology. A non-competition clause offers an assurance against both risks. Furthermore, in cases where the licensee uses the licensor's trade mark, it offers protection to the licensor (*Campari*).

There seem, however, to be two major concerns of competition policy with a non-competition obligation placed on the licensee in a vertical relationship. The first is the possibility that it will restrict the licensee in the development of commercial products from R&D in its own technology. The second is that while a non-competition clause is immensely reassuring to a licensor, it may not be indispensable given the availability of other clauses. Indispensability is part of the test in Article 85(3) but it also enters the test under Article 85(1) in the form of the ancillary restraints exception.

In the patent licensing and know-how regulations, concerns about R&D led to a blacklisting of non-competition clauses in respect of R&D, while allowing the licensor to impose best endeavours and minimum quantities obligations on the licensee. In the case of the Know-how Regulation, these rights of the licensor were reinforced by the addition of a right to terminate exclusivity and cease communicating improvements.

In the Technology Transfer Regulation, the Commission has chosen to retain the formula used in the Know-how Regulation. Article 3(2) black-lists a restriction on competition by the licensee in respect of research and development, production, use or distribution of competing products. At the same time, however, it whitelists a clause which requires the licensee to use its best endeavours to manufacture and market the licensed product (Article 2(1)(17)) and allows the licensor to reserve a right to terminate the exclusivity granted to the licensee and to stop licensing improvements to him when the licensee enters into competition with him in respect of R&D or production, use or distribution of products and the provision of services other than those licensed (Article 2(1)(18)). In addition the licensor can reserve a right to demand proof that the licensee is not being used for the production of products or the provision of services other than those licensed.

While there may be some reservations about the uncertainties of a best endeavours clause particularly in protecting the intensive exploitation of the trade mark, the possibility of revocation of exclusivity and the requirement of proof of non-competition can be major deterrents as long as the licensee remains interested in exploiting the licensed technology. Frazer has made a telling point that the combination does not protect the licensee sufficiently against a licensor determined to remove him as a potential competitor, i.e. as a potential developer of his own products.[82]

The policy of the blacklist in respect of non-competition clauses is to disallow any clause which would restrict the possibilities of either licensee or licensor independently competing with each other in respect of research and development, or the production, use or distribution of products resulting from such activity. At the same time, however, it provides that this is 'without prejudice to an obligation on the licensee to use his best endeavors to exploit the licensed technology' (Article 3(2)).

---

[82] See Frazer, op. cit. n. 50.

This is one of the least effective elements in the regulatory framework. The provision may have been fine-tuned to focus its restrictions more closely on independent R&D.[83] However, when one takes into account the possibility of a carefully calculated minimum quantities clause and the practical effects of a best endeavours clause, there is little need for a formal non-competition clause. This might be just as well since insofar as a licensing agreement is truly vertical, a non-competition clause is generally justified because, as Korah has rightly put it, 'few holders of valuable technology would grant an exclusive license if the licensee was entitled to sterilise the technology in his area and exploit rival technology'.[84] On the other hand, where the licensing agreement has a horizontal dimension, a best endeavours clause could be anticompetitive. At one point Korah suggested, with considerable logic on her side, that a better regulatory solution would have been to allow a best endeavours clause only if the agreement is vertical.[85] As if in response to this suggestion, Article 7 in the new block exemption specifically provides for the withdrawal of the block exemption in cases where 'the parties were already competing manufacturers before the grant of the license' and minimum quantity or best endeavours clauses 'have the effect of preventing the licensee from using competing technologies' (Article 7(4)).

---

[83] See Guttuso, op. cit., *supra* at p.19.

[84] Korah, 'The Preliminary Draft of New EC Group Exemption for Technology Licensing' [1994] 7 *EIPR* 263 at p. 266.

[85] Korah op. cit. *supra* at p. 266.

9

Conclusions

As mentioned the introduction of a new, unifying regulation for technology licensing, alongside the regulatory regimes for specialization agreements,[1] research and development agreements,[2] franchise agreements,[3] co-operative joint ventures,[4] and mergers,[5] offered the Commission an opportunity to make a substantial adjustment to traditional competition policy object-ives in the light of the pressing policy need of increasing the technological competitiveness of the EC in world trade.

A 1993 Commission White Paper, 'Growth, Competitiveness and Employment', had drawn attention to the fact that the competitive position of Europe *vis à vis* the USA and Japan had 'worsened as regards: employment; our share of market exports; R&D and innovation'.[6] It called for a new balance to be struck between competition and co-operation to allow EC firms to enter into strategic alliances to counterbalance the weight of US and Japanese competition. Moreover, a 1994 Commission Communication, also originating in DGIII, argued that there is 'a clear need to ensure expansion and take-up of R&D efforts' and 'to facilitate transfers of experience between businesses, particularly small businesses'[7] to ensure that the EC can compete at increasing levels of technology in world trade. As if in anticipation of resistance by DGIV, the White Paper warned that too strict an application of competition rules can place EC firms at a disadvantage on the world stage.

The logic of the White Paper and Communication suggested that a higher priority ought to be given to encouraging technology licensing because of the spur it provides to international competitiveness. Licensing increases incentives to innovation because the great majority of innovators are smaller firms, requiring an independent injection of risk capital, usually in return for an exclusive licence, to take the technology

[1] Reg. 417/85, amended by Reg. 151/93; see [1993] 4 CMLR 155.
[2] Reg. 418/85, as amended by Reg. 151/93; see [1993] 4 CMLR 163.
[3] Reg. 4087/88.
[4] See Commission's Notice on Co-operative Joint Ventures OJ [1993] C 43/2.
[5] See EC Merger Regulation, Council Regulation 4064/89, OJ [1990] L257/14.
[6] See European Commission's White Paper on Growth, Competitiveness, Employment. The Challenges and the Ways Forward into the 21st Century [1993] *Bulletin of the EC* Supp. 6/93 p. 9.
[7] See European Commission Communication, An Industrial Competitiveness Policy for the European Union, 14 Sept. 1994, III. A/JFM/DB/Com. EN 8 DOC.

from the stage of research and development to the next stages of manufacture and distribution. It also helps to raise levels of technology throughout the common market by promoting the transfer of technology between member states. In a situation where knowledge-based industries, such as aerospace, computers, communications equipment, drugs and medicines, scientific instruments, and electrical machinery constitute both a high and a dramatically increasing proportion of total manufacturing output, a policy to promote technology transfer would appear to command considerable support.

The Commission was never likely to respond to these economic arguments by adopting an overly permissive legal framework for IPR licensing. As it pointed out in the *XXVIth Report on Competition Policy* (1996), the best method to achieve competitiveness in international trade is to have a competitive internal market.[8] Nevertheless, the Commission began by stating that the purpose of the reform was 'to encourage the dissemination of technical knowledge in the Community and to promote the manufacture of technically sophisticated goods'.[9] In general, the block exemption accepts a presumption of procompetitiveness in technology licensing and attempts on the whole to translate it into the detail of the regulation of specific clauses. Indeed, it continues the process of progressive liberalization that began with the Patent Licensing Regulation in 1984,[10] while retaining provisions for the preservation of effective competition such as the withdrawal powers (Article 7), exclusions (Article 5), the blacklist (Article 3) and continued limits built into the whitelist (Article 2). However, its actual changes are on the whole restricted to marginal adjustments to the structure of regulation of the technology transfer process. They improve the substantive and procedural rules for those covered by the block exemption but do little to deal with the problems caused by the existence of a two-tiered structure.

In the block exemption itself, as we have seen there are five types of fine-tuning modifications introduced:

1. The time periods for territorial exclusivity have been increased in most cases, thus marginally increasing the incentives for investment in technology transfer—(Article 1);
2. The block exemption has lengthened the 'whitelist' adding to the categories of clauses which were either not caught by Article 85(1) or were exempt under Article 85(3)—(Article 2);

---

[8] At p. 5.   [9] Recital 3.
[10] See Whish, *Competition Law* (Butterworths, 3rd edn.) pp. 631–43; Frazer, 'Vorsprung durch Technik: The Commission's policy on Know-how Agreements' [1989] *Yearbook of Eur. Law* 1.

3. The blacklist has been retained as a list of *per se* prohibitions in technology licensing agreements, but reduced to a core of seven restraints—(Article 3);
4. The opposition procedure has been made more user-friendly—(Article 4);
5. The exclusions were defined to allow some room for manoeuvre for other types of intellectual property rights (IPRs) to be added to the mixed technology package—(Article 5).

There was some evidence, moreover, that the Commission had incorporated more of an assumption of verticality in its approach to licensing agreements. For example, the reduction in the range of blacklisted clauses showed a reduced suspicion of licences as a cover for an agreement between competitors. Moreover, the withdrawal power in Article 7 emphasizes that it is concerned with high market shares for horizontal licences only. In the new Regulation, the Commission has made some attempt to meet criticisms about the inflexibility of the earlier block exemptions. For example, it opened up the opposition procedure to a wider variety of clauses and has reduced its time limit to four months. The reduction in the blacklist allows a wider scope for the opposition procedure. It signals a greater willingness to accept that vertical licensing arrangements can be procompetitive even if they contain restrictions such as tie-ins or minimum quality specifications which are technically necessary for the satisfactory exploitation of the technology or respected by the licensor and other licensees.[11]

Nevertheless, the new block exemption continues to be inflexible in two important respects. First, it creates a divide between certain defined categories of IPR licensing agreement which can come within the block exemption and those which are left to the less user-friendly regulation regime of notification for individual exemption for legal certainty.

It appeared to loosen the requirements for other IPRs in a mixed IPR licence to be ancillary. Recital 6 sets out the policy of the block exemption to other IPRs in the following terms:

It is appropriate to extend the scope of this Regulation to pure or mixed agreements containing the licensing of intellectual property rights other than patents (in particular, trademarks, design rights,and copyright, especially software protection), when such additional licensing contributes to the achievement of the objects of the licensed technology and contains only ancillary provisions.

---

[11] Art. 2(1)(5).

Article 5(1)(4) provides that the regulation shall not apply to licensing agreements containing provisions relating to intellectual property rights other than patents which are not ancillary.[12]

Under the patent and know-how regulations, the concept of an ancillary provision relating to other IPRs was translated into a requirement that the other type of IPR must not be as important or more important to the agreement than the patent or know-how.[13] In the new Technology Transfer Regulation, the concept of ancillary restraint has been defined in rather different terms. Article 10(15) defines ancillary provisions as: 'provisions relating to the obligation of intellectual property rights other than patents which contain no obligations restrictive of competition other than those also attached to the licensed know how or patents and exempted under this Regulation'.

Under the Technology Transfer Regulation it appears that there might be a possibility for more mixed licences to qualify. As mentioned, however, the following tests must be met.

1. The provisions relating to other IPRs must be ancillary; i.e. any restrictions of competition attached to those rights must be also attached to the technology licence and exempted by the Regulation.
2. The additional IPRs must contribute to the objects of the licensed technology;

This means that some trade mark licences and copyright licences can be included in the new block exemption.[14] It has been argued that if the Commission had meant to change the policy of the block exemptions to a more inclusive one, it could have chosen a less indirect method of signalling a change of policy.[15] Yet, the Commission consciously chose to draft the definition of ancillarity in this way. Even so, there remain limits to the coverage of categories of IPR licences under the block exemption.

Secondly the new Regulation also retains the requirement that the parties apply the Articles of the block exemption to the clauses of the licensing agreement with a fine-tooth comb. If the parties miscalculate the requirements of the whitelist or blacklist and fail to use the opposition procedure, the block exemption will be non-applicable.[16]

---

[12] Art. 1(1) states that the block exemption can extend to licensing agreements containing provisions relating to intellectual property rights other than patents but only if they are 'ancillary'. See discussion at p. 88 above.

[13] e.g. in *Boussois/Interpane* and in *Moosehead*.

[14] See Korah's excellent analysis (1996) at pp. 118–20.

[15] See e.g. C. Kerse, 'Block Exemptions under Article 85(3): The Technology Transfer Regulation—Procedural Issues' [1996] *ECLR* 331.

[16] See *Delimitis* 1991 ECR I–935.

At one stage, the Commission contemplated a rule of 'partial severance' for those provisions in licensing agreements which were not acceptable under the block exemption but this form of flexibility was discarded.

The main problem with the Technology Transfer Regulation, therefore, is that it leaves intact a framework which has two types of adverse effects upon investment in technology licensing. The first is that it creates a sharp divide between agreements within the charmed circle of the block exemption and those without, whose parties must contemplate the choice of notification for individual exemption, with the likely prospect of a comfort letter, or self assessment of clearance or exemptibility. Thus, for any agreement which qualifies for the block exemption, the legal regime requires extremely careful treatment of the substantive rules, but offers the certainty of legal validity.[17] In contrast, for any agreement which does not fit under the block exemption, Article 85 requires either a careful analysis of contractual clauses, in the light of Commission practice and Court decisions, in order to obtain clearance, or the uncertainty of a notification for individual exemption. Both options entail disproportionate procedural costs which might deter investment in the licensing process.

Secondly, because of the wide differences between the two regulatory regimes, the parties may be deterred from choosing the best form economically for their licensing arrangement in their desire to obtain the security of the block exemption. In both respects the regulatory framework in the EC is open to the charge of placing a heavier regulatory burden upon the parties to licensing agreements than competitor systems such as the USA's system of guidelines, applying a single economic test of rule of reason for technology licensing.

The Commission made an abortive attempt to introduce one structural change partly because of the thinking underlying the US guidelines. Thus, in an early draft of the Technology Transfer Regulation it proposed a market shares test to IPR licensing agreements as a precondition for qualifying for the block exemption. It was concerned that dominant undertakings with exclusive licences 'might prevent access to the market of the technology by third parties and eliminate competition in respect of a substantial part of the products in question'.[18]

Initially, these market share tests were wide in scope, applying to all licensing agreements whether horizontal or vertical. In the penultimate version of the Regulation, however, the market share disqualifications

---

[17]   As to the relationship with national law see C. Kerse. [1996] *ECLR* 331.
[18]   Recital 11.

were limited to agreements between competing manufacturers. In the final version, they were taken out altogether.

The Commission's decision to introduce market share tests in the technology transfer block exemption was prompted by a mix of internal and external influences. Internally, the Commission's experience with the Merger Control Regulation and the formulation of the Guidelines for Co-operative Joint Ventures together with the *Tetrapak* case increased awareness of the possible market structure implications of agreements.[19] A market share test had been incorporated in the specialization and research and development block exemptions, and this perhaps was taken as evidence that the technique was not completely incompatible with a block exemption, even if the fact was that R&D and specialization agreements were predominantly horizontal and the experience, in particular with the R&D block exemption, was not the most successful of the Commission's regulatory attempts. Externally, the interest in oligopolistic structures was whetted by knowledge of the German law which creates a legal presumption of oligopoly when three companies have a combined share greater than 50 per cent.[20] The main external influence, however, appears to have been the Commission's awareness that in the US the Justice Department and the Federal Trade Commission were preparing new Antitrust Guidelines for the Licensing of Intellectual Property in which there was a greater awareness of concerns with market shares and intellectual property than the *laissez-faire* approach of the 1988 Guidelines.[21] Just as the 'Nine No-Nos' of US antitrust law in the early 1980s influenced the design of the Patent Licensing Regulation in 1984,[22] so too developments in US antitrust policy in the mid-1990s appears to have influenced the design of the Technology Transfer Regulation of 1995.

Unlike 1984, in 1995 the American influence was not confined to the issue of which types of restraints in licensing agreements were essentially anticompetitive and belonged on the blacklist. On this occasion, it was initially allowed to extend to the process of identification of high

[19] See S. Guttuso, 'Technology Transfer Agreements under EC Law' [1994] *Fordham Corp. Law Inst.* 227.

[20] S. 23a para. 2 GWB.

[21] Under the 1988 Guidelines for International Operations, 'the owner of intellectual property is entitled to enjoy whatever market power the property itself may confer' (p.22). In the early years of the Clinton administration there were several investigations by the Federal Trade Commission and the US Department of Justice of the licensing practices of large firms in the computer software industry. See e.g. Gotts and Bent, 'Comment' [1994] *EIPR* 245.

[22] See Johannes, 'Technology Transfer under EEC Law—Europe Between the Divergent Opinions of the Past and New Administration: A Comparative Law Approach' (1983) *Fordham Corp. Law Inst.* 65.

market shares and horizontal relationships as objects of potential antitrust concern and special regulatory treatment.

Yet there may have been a serious underestimation of the procedural differences between the two regulatory systems. For although the 1995 Guidelines in the US may have involved a tightening up of the regulatory model from a relatively *laissez-faire* framework in the 1980s, even in its new, heavier regulatory form, they constitute a lighter model of regulation with lower transaction costs for licensing agreements than that in the EC.

The basic reason for this is that, in the US, the majority of licensing agreements are analysed under the rule of reason. The antitrust authorities' recognition that licensing often has significant efficiency benefits, such as the integration of the licensed property with complementary factors of production,[23] and the general presumption of procompetitiveness of licensing has meant that a *per se* method of analysis is infrequently employed. Under the 1995 Guidelines, 'the Agencies general approach . . . under the rule of reason is to inquire whether the restraint is likely to have anticompetitive effects and, if so whether the restraint is reasonably necessary to achieve procompetitive benefits that outweigh those anticompetitive effects' (page 16). The key comparative point is that the rule of reason approach applies to situations of competing manufacturers with high market shares as well as to contractual restraints in vertical agreements.

9.1 THE US ANTITRUST GUIDELINES

As we have seen, under the Guidelines,[23a] the assessment of the economic effects of the agreement using a rule of reason analysis is a two step balancing test. First, there must be an examination to determine whether or not the restraint is likely to have anticompetitive effects. Secondly, if so, an assessment must be made whether the restraint is necessary to achieve procompetitive benefits that outweigh those anticompetitive effects.[24] Application of the rule of reason generally[25] requires a comprehensive inquiry into market conditions. However, even when the Guidelines identify situations in which the market structure could have anticompetitive consequences, i.e. 'when a licensing arrangement harms competition among entities that would have been actual or likely potential competitors in a relevant market in the absence of the license',[26] this is not

[23] See talk by Richard J. Gilbert, Deputy Assistant Attorney-General, Antitrust Division, US Department of Justice, to the ABA Section of Antitrust Law Spring Meeting, Washington DC.   [23a] Reproduced at Appendix III, below.
[24] Guidelines at p. 16.
[25] For the exceptions see Guidelines pp. 16–17.   [26] Guidelines at p. 7.

intended to replace the rule of reason approach but merely to identify when antitrust concerns arise in a licensing arrangement for the purpose of applying a rule of reason approach. Thus, even cross-licensing of IPRs involving horizontal competitors is dealt with by balancing the procompetitive with the anticompetitive effects of the arrangement.

Moreover, where the parties to a licensing arrangement would not have been actual or likely potential competitors in a relevant market in the absence of the licence, i.e. the relationship is vertical, the competition concern is limited to whether the licensing agreement includes restraints which harm competition with rivals and in such a case, the two steps of the rule of reason approach are applied solely to the restraint.[27]

If the Agencies conclude, upon an evaluation of the market factors ... that a restraint in a licensing arrangement is unlikely to have an anticompetitive effect, they will consider whether the restraint is reasonably necessary; the agencies will balance the procompetitive efficiencies and the anticompetitive effects to determine the probable net effect on competition in each relevant market.

The Agencies' comparison of anticompetitive harms and procompetitive efficiencies is necessarily a qualitative one. The risk of anticompetitive effects may be insignificant compared to the expected efficiencies, or vice versa. As the expected anticompetitive effects in a particular licensing arrangement increase, the Agencies will require evidence establishing a greater level of expected efficiencies.[28]

The Guidelines add that the test includes a determination of whether a restraint is reasonably necessary to achieve the procompetitive efficiencies, and whether the duration of the restraint is reasonably necessary to achieve them.[29]

The Guidelines then give a series of examples of how the principles of the rule of reason test may be applied to specific contractual restraints. In dealing with licensing agreements involving exclusivity, to take one example, the Guidelines in principle distinguish between exclusive licences and exclusive dealing. Generally, exclusive licences raise antitrust concerns only if the licensees themselves or the licensor and its licensees are in a horizontal relationship and the arrangement includes cross-licensing, grant backs or acquisitions.[30] Exclusive dealing, which arises when a licence precludes a licensee from access to competing technologies, is treated as a vertical restraint with a potential for anticompetitive effects but with the understanding that the restraint has the procompetitive effect of encouraging 'the licensee to develop and market the licensed technology or specialized applications of the technology'.[31] The Guidelines state:

---

[27] Guidelines s. 3.4 at p. 16.
[29] Id.
[31] Id.

[28] Guidelines s. 4.2 at p. 22.
[30] Guidelines s. 4.1.2.

The antitrust principles that apply to a licensor's grant of various forms of exclusivity to and among its licensees are similar to those that apply to comparable vertical restraints outside the licensing context, such as exclusive territories and exclusive dealing. However, the fact that intellectual property may in some cases be misappropriated more easily than other forms of property may justify the use of some restrictions that might be anticompetitive in other contexts.

The Guidelines then apply these principles to exclusive dealing in the following way:

In determining whether an exclusive dealing arrangement is likely to reduce competition in a relevant market, the agencies will take into account the extent to which the arrangement:

  (1) promotes the exploitation and development of the licensed technology, and (2) anti-competitively forecloses the exploitation and development of, or otherwise constrains competition among competing technologies.[32]

The likelihood that exclusive dealing may have anticompetitive effects is related, *inter alia*, to the degree of foreclosure in the relevant market, the duration of the exclusive dealing arrangement, and the other characteristics of the input and output markets, such as concentration, difficulty of entry, and the responsiveness of supply and demand to changes in price in the relevant markets. If the Agencies determine that a particular exclusive dealing arrangement may have an anticompetitive effect, they will evaluate the extent to which the restraint 'encourages licensees to develop and market the licensed technology . . ., increases licensors' incentives to develop or refine the licensed technology, or otherwise increases competition, and enhances output in a relevant market'.[33]

In other words, under the Department of Justice (DOJ) Guidelines, territorial exclusivity is allowed in respect of licensing, selling, manufacturing, distribution, and use of competing technologies as long as the anticompetitive elements are outweighed by the procompetitive elements such as incentives to innovation and technology diffusion. The issue is essentially one of economic balance.

This system of regulation in the USA thus requires the parties to make an assessment of the competitive effects of their licensing agreements in the light of the Guidelines. The skills required from legal advisers include the ability to assess the nature of the relationship between the parties, the conditions on the relevant market, and the purpose and economic effects of the restraints in the licensing agreement.

---

[32] Guidelines 5.4 at p. 28.   [33] Guidelines s. 5.4. at p. 28.

9.2 THE RELEVANCE OF THE US GUIDELINES FOR EC COMPETITION LAW

The application of the rule of reason analysis in the US has an important procedural advantage over individual exemption under the EC model. The rule of reason analysis can be applied by the legal adviser making use of legal and administrative precedent and market analysis without the need to notify for formal exemption. In marginal cases, there is the possibility of a 'quick look' procedure provided by the DOJ in which the parties can submit a description of the transaction and the relationship and market strength of the parties and receive a response from the agency that on the basis of the facts submitted there are no antitrust concerns.

By comparison, the opposition procedure in the EC Regulation, which allows a restriction to be deemed covered by the block exemption if the Commission has not opposed it within four months, is restricted in scope to non-blacklisted restrictions.

Finally, unlike the EC regulatory model, the 1995 Guidelines provide a substantial Antitrust 'safety zone' or 'safe harbour' for intellectual property licensing transactions where the licensor and licensees together account for no more than 20 per cent of each relevant market significantly affected by the restraint.[34] In such cases, the government authorities like the Federal Trade Commission (FTC) and the DOJ claim that they have no serious antitrust concerns about the licensing process and little interest in regulating the contents of such agreements. These agreements are presumed to be not anticompetitive without further inquiry, though they remain vulnerable to private antitrust actions. Only if a licensing agreement contains a 'facially anti-competitive' clause, i.e. one which is *per se* anti-competitive, such as a price fixing or market sharing restraint or agreements not to compete in terms of price or output, will the agreement be regarded as anticompetitive in character, without the need for elaborate market analysis.[35] Otherwise, the antitrust authorities will not challenge a restraint in the licensing agreement.

The legal regime in the 'safe harbour' in the US is quite different from that for parties with below 20 per cent market shares in the EC. As Guttuso has acknowledged: 'The Commission's approach differs from that under the Guidelines because the de minimis threshold at which the Commission accepts that the application of Article 85(1) can be precluded is 5% [now 10 per cent for vertical agreements]'.[36] In other

---

[34] 1995 Antitrust Guidelines for the Licensing of Intellectual Property, US Department of Justice and Federal Trade Commission, 4.3 pp. 22–3.

[35] See e.g. *NCAA* v. *Board of Regents of Univ. of Oklahoma*, 468 US 85, at 109 (1984).

[36] See Guttuso, op. cit., no. 19 *supra*. See discussion ch. 4.3.3 above.

words, for parties with market shares between the *de minimis* level and 20 per cent in the EC the rigours of Articles 1, 2, 3, and 7 are applicable. It is a fully regulated position rather than one subject to the relatively deregulated legal regime which exists in the US 'safe harbour'. The detailed provisions of the block exemption must be scrupulously followed. A deviation from the whitelist which is caught by Article 85(1) either requires resort to the opposition procedure or risks invalidation of the whole of the licensing agreement.

The comparison with the USA regulatory regime with its predominantly rule of reason approach and extremely limited use of *per se* restrictions left its mark on the Commission. They could see the relevance of a predominantly economic assessment of an agreement rather than a reliance solely on the form of restraints or category of agreement. They could see the significance of market structure at both ends of the concentration spectrum. They could see the relevance of the horizontal/vertical distinction as a filter. However, in reaching for a market shares test, the Commission attempted to bring in only one element of a package deal. It made the classical comparativist error of thinking that a good legal rule in one legal system could be transported into another legal system without reference to its context. The market shares test was part of a regulatory structure which was based on a rule of reason test. Under the EC block exemption system, this element was absent and instead the parties had a form based, relatively rigid system dividing IPR licences into the two main categories of potentially block exemptible and potentially non-block exemptible.

At the time, much of the opposition to the market shares test was based on the unsuitability of IPR licences to be capped by market shares because the market share at the start is nil and, if successful, it can reach to high levels quite quickly. Others criticized the inappropriateness of grafting a market share test onto a system which had as its main virtue a block exemption which was self-contained and offered legal certainty, albeit on the basis of formalistic criteria. Those features helped to make the regulatory structure work. The market share test was not simply an optional extra; it undermined the legal certainty of the block exemption. As we have seen, the Commission abandoned the market share test as a precondition to eligibility and inserted it as a basis for withdrawal under Article 7.

Nevertheless, this comparison indicates that the added transaction costs imposed upon technology licensing by parties unable to qualify for the new block exemption will be heavier than those imposed under the new DOJ and FTC Guidelines to licensors and licensees in a major trading block in technological competition with the EC.

The continued use of individual notification as a sifting mechanism may help to inform DGIV about the kinds of licensing agreements that are being made and may provide additional weaponry for DGIV in restricting cartels and market sharing. However, this will be at the cost of adding to the disincentives for licensees and licensors to engage in technology transfer within the EC. Some could decide to license manufacturing facilities outside the EC for export into the EC. Some could decide to ignore the exemption process altogether. Those who decide to proceed with notification and individual exemption will have to pay for the privilege.

In the Commission's current proposals for reform of vertical restraint regulation in the context of distribution agreements, a more comprehensive reform is suggested. In its Green Paper on Vertical Restraints in EC Competition Policy, the Commission offers three main options for change away from a form based system to a system of regulation which takes greater account of the economic effects of an agreement. Thus, the Green Paper proposes as one option for change a 'rebuttable presumption of compatibility with Article 85(1)' (the 'negative clearance presumption') for parties with less than for instance 20 per cent market share (Option IV(I)). Such a presumption would cover all vertical restraints except those relating to minimum resale prices, impediments to parallel trade or passive sales, or horizontal restraints (paragraph 295). This would require the parties to assess market shares, using guidelines prepared by the Commission to determine whether or not the share threshold has been reached. It would also require the parties to engage in a market analysis to assess whether any of the factors that could rebut the presumption is present in the context of the licensing agreement. The main factors which could rebut the negative clearance presumption are, market structures (for example, oligopoly), barriers to entry, and the degree of integration of the single market evaluated on the basis of indicators such as the price differential existing between member states and the level of market penetration in each member state of products imported from other member states, or the cumulative impact of parallel networks. The Commission has also resurrected as one option, the introduction of a market share limit of 40 per cent so that the block exemption would only apply where no single party to the agreement has a 40 per cent share of the relevant market in the contract territory (Option III). Above that threshold, there would be no protection against active sales from outside the territory or for exclusive dealing (paragraph 287). Finally, in Option II it also offers the option of wider and more flexible block exemptions, presumably to agreements between parties with market shares above 20 per cent and below 40 per cent: the block exemptions would cover not only the precise clauses listed, but also clauses which are similar or less restrictive; the inclusion of prohibited clauses might not deny the benefit of the exemption for the rest of the agreement (paragraph 283).

These options are not meant to be exhaustive. The Commission invites suggestions for alternatives. In its appearances before the Economic and Social Committee and other bodies, the Commission's representatives have made it plain that there is a strategic trade-off being sought. If it can introduce a filter for agreements made by parties with high market shares, Option III, it would be prepared to create flexibility below the 40 per cent level which goes considerably beyond the suggestions for widening and making more flexible the block exemptions in Option II. In other words, it would attempt to move a considerable way towards a rebuttable presumption of compatibility for vertical agreements under the 40 per cent market share level. This would help to adjust the regulatory regime to the changing pattern of distribution.

If the Green Paper should result in a reform with such a trade-off, it might appear to be appropriate to examine its relevance to the regulatory framework for intellectual property licensing agreements, because these are predominantly vertical agreements. The high stakes involved in the case of any attempt to introduce structural reform to the existing framework of regulation of licensing agreements should be borne in mind. There is little doubt that more should be done for those parties who do not have access to the block exemptions and do not have a position of near dominant market power. On the face of it, greater flexibility in the application of the requirements of a block exemption to such agreements has much to recommend it because of its reduction in regulatory costs to the parties to licensing agreements in the EU. Yet if the price of greater flexibility is a form of filtering mechanism which introduces undue legal uncertainty for the existing group of agreements within the block exemption system, the costs will be too high. For better or worse, the form based system has been one with which undertakings throughout the EU have been able to live. The goal of reform should be to lower the transaction costs for the licensing agreements outside the 'loop', not to raise them for those inside it.

The Commission must recognize that a test such as a market shares test, or even a more sophisticated test of market power, should be used merely as an indicator of a need for further scrutiny, as in the US system, rather than a precondition to legal validity. The legal consequences of a miscalculation of market share or market power by the parties should not be inordinate. The calculation of market power based on market shares is extremely difficult in the case of innovation and technology markets, as the US Guidelines illustrate by suggesting different methods of measurement depending upon whether the product is in a 'product', 'technology' or 'innovation' market. Although the Commission has made considerable efforts to clarify its methods of defining markets in its decisions, its Form A/B, and its Notices, and has recently released a new document offering guidance to the Definition of Markets, it cannot quite succeed in removing the discretionary element involved in its definition of markets. In the event, it would be wise not to insist on the factor of extensive market share or market power as the desideratum for a difference in legal status which has so much significance. It should give greater weight to the need for a method of monitoring licensing agreements which does not exact too heavy a cost of legal uncertainty in return for the satisfaction of regulatory concerns.

The bullet the Commission must bite is that if it wishes to graft on a system of closer scrutiny of high market share/market power agreements, it must offer an assurance of a reasonable time period for the results of such a process. The formula of the Merger Control Regulation is instructive here. If the Commission could devote the resources to a procedural mechanism with the time limits and legal outcome of, say, the non-opposition procedure, it could be introduced without disturbing the balance of the existing regulatory system. If it cannot face up to that precondition to any monitoring system which it uses to attempt to vet agreements prior to validity, it should content itself with a withdrawal power, despite the lack of convenience administratively. The Commission must recognize that the stakes involved in regulating technology transfer in the current conditions of global competition require it to be circumspect in striking the appropriate balance between inconvenience to the regulator and the burden of the regulatory system to the parties being regulated.

It has been suggested that there should be a fifth option of introducing a rule of reason to EC law for licensing agreements as well as vertical distribution agreements. The proponents of this view would be pleased to have more sophisticated reasoning applied to the assessment of intellectual property licensing agreements similar to the method used in the USA. This suggestion may well be a recipe for the long-term approach of EC competition law. However, in the short term, it will be difficult to move EC lawyers and their clients away from the culture of dependency on form based methods of regulation to one that requires a far greater awareness of the economic effects of licensing agreements. The lawyers in the larger practices and the larger clients can cope with the requirements of an economic assessment. It is less clear that away from Brussels, London, Paris, and Frankfurt, the small and medium sized law firms can provide that service. Nevertheless, it offers a possible blueprint for the future. As the influence of the integration objective wanes in the application of Article 85, the possibilities increase for a more economic assessment of the balance between competition costs and benefits under that Article.

PART III

Article 86 and Intellectual Property Rights

10

Introduction

The role of Article 86 in the system of EC competition law is to regulate undertakings which have been found to occupy dominant positions on particular markets, i.e. those firms with extensive market power, such as near monopolies. In common with Article 85, its aim is to prohibit the use of market power to damage effective competition in markets by preventing access to markets or driving out existing competition, as well as to fix prices at higher than competitive levels.[1]

Unlike Article 85, however, the method it uses is to concentrate on individual undertakings[2] which have acquired a dominant position in a particular market and closely regulate their conduct. As long as a firm is not dominant it is not touched by Article 86. Article 86 does not prohibit the legitimate acquisition of extensive market power by superior efficiency or innovativeness. Dominance itself is not unlawful. Once, however, an undertaking achieves a position of dominance it has a special responsibility 'not to allow its conduct to impair genuine undistorted competition on the common market'.[3]

The framework for the regulation of dominant undertakings under Article 86 is established by its prohibition of abusive conduct. Article 86 states:

Any abuse by one or more undertakings of a dominant position within the common market or in a substantial part of it shall be prohibited as incompatible with the common market . . .

Such abuse in particular may consist in:

(a) directly or indirectly imposing unfair purchase or selling prices or other unfair trading conditions;

---

[1] This means that both Arts. 85 and 86 can occasionally apply to the same agreement or practice, but they apply independently on their own terms. See e.g. *Hoffman La Roche* [1979] ECR 461; *Tetra Pak II* [1990] ECR II–309; *Italian Flat Glass* [1992] ECR II–1403. The Commission can choose to take action on one Article alone even when both may apply. See e.g. *IGR Stereo Television, Eleventh Report on Competition Policy*, point 63, *Fourteenth Report on Competition Policy*, point 76, discussed *infra*.

[2] This wording of Art. 86 makes it clear that the concept of dominance can include more than one undertaking, i.e, joint dominance. See e.g. *Nestle/Perrier* [1993] 4 CMLR M17. For a discussion of the complications raised by this point, see e.g. M. Schödermeir, 'Collective Dominance Revisited: An Analysis of the EC Commission's New Concept of Oligopoly Control [1990] *ECLR* 28. [3] *Michelin* v. *Commission* [1983] ECR 3461.

(b) limiting production, markets or technical development to the prejudice of consumers;

(c) applying dissimilar conditions to equivalent transactions with other trading parties, thereby placing them in a disadvantaged position;

(d) making the conclusion of contracts subject to acceptance by the other parties of supplementary obligations which, by their nature or according to commercial usage, have no connection with the subject of such contracts.

In its definition of abusive conduct, Article 86 havers between two different concepts of abuse. The first is the narrower economic concept of 'exploitive abuse', i.e. conduct which consists of using market power to extract supracompetitive gains from customers by unfairly high prices (Article 86(a)) and limiting supply to markets (Article 86(b)).

It also has been interpreted to include a second concept of abuse, predatory or 'anticompetitive abuse,' i.e. conduct attempting to evict or exclude competitors from markets. This is hinted at by the abuses set out in Article 86(c), discriminatory treatment, and Article 86(d), tie-ins, which refer to conduct which appears to be directed to customers but has the indirect effect of eliminating and deterring competitors.[4] The concern with the protection of competitors has been read into Article 86 as part of a wider view of its function in preventing distorted competition under Article 3(g). The Court has proceeded on the theory that the Treaty requires the competition authorities to preserve and maintain competitive structures in markets which have already been weakened by the presence of a dominant undertaking.[5] At the same time, however, the Court has acknowledged that since dominant undertakings can achieve a dominant position by virtue of greater efficiencies and innovativeness than competitors, they cannot be required to refrain from competing on the basis of legitimate competitive means even if such conduct has the effect of further weakening residual competition on a dominated market.[6]

Applying these principles, the Court has been willing to expand the list of abuses to include refusals to deal,[7] refusals to license,[8] predatory pricing,[9] and inappropriate acquisitions of competitors.[10] It has been prepared to protect individual customers who have become dependent upon dominant undertakings from unfair treatment.[11] It has also been

---

[4] See e.g. *Continental Can* v. *Commission* [1973] ECR 215 at para. 26.

[5] As the Court put it in *Continental Can*, at para. 24: 'if Article 3[g] provides for the institution of a system ensuring that competition in the Common Market is not distorted, then it requires a fortiori that competition must not be eliminated'. See discussion ch 13.

[6] *Hoffman La Roche* v. *Commission* [1979] ECR 461.

[7] *Commercial Solvents* v. *Commission* [1974] ECR 223.

[8] *RTE* v. *Commission* [1995] ECR I–743.

[9] *AKZO* v. *Commission* [1991] ECR I–3359.

[10] See e.g. *Continental Can* v. *Commission* [1973] ECR 215 para 24.

[11] See e.g. *United Brands* v. *Commission* [1978] ECR 207.

prepared to protect competitors in secondary markets where a dominant undertaking attempts to integrate vertically or already has been engaged in operations in two related markets. Thus, a dominant undertaking may now be required to supply or license products to competitors in secondary markets.[12] Moreover, its pricing and product packaging decisions, choice of customers, and exercise of intellectual property rights (IPRs) may be found to be unlawful because of their effect on existing competitors in secondary markets.[13]

To understand how this concept of regulation of market power applies to IPRs requires an appreciation of two steps: first, what types of exploitation of IPRs are likely to be regarded as prima facie abusive under the new expanded definition of abuse.[14] Secondly, to what extent does the normal exploitation of IPRs coincide with the concept of legitimate competitive means for a dominant undertaking, or is otherwise justified under Article 86.[15]

Before assessing how the widened concept of abuse applies to IPRs, however, it is necessary to examine the preconditions to the application of Article 86.[16]

In the first place, before an intellectual property right can be regulated by Article 86, its owner must be found to occupy a dominant position in a particular market, which is either the common market as a whole or a substantial part thereof. An exclusive right to exploit an IPR conferred by legislation does not automatically result in a finding of dominance. There must be a further finding that there are so few substitutes for the protected product or technology that the rightholder has the power in a relevant product market to enable it to prevent effective competition being maintained on that market.[17]

To assess dominance under Article 86, therefore, the first step is to determine the relevant product market upon which dominance is measured, and its geographic dimension. For intellectual property rightholders, this first step is particularly important. If the market is

---

[12] *RTE* v. *Commission* [1995] ECR I–743.

[13] See e.g. *Hilti* v. *Commission* [1994] ECR I–1439.

[14] See e.g. *Hoffman La Roche* [1979] ECR 461.   [15] See chs. 13–18.

[16] One precondition for the application of Art. 86 is that the abuse has an 'effect on trade between the Member States'. See *Hugin* v. *Commission* [1979] ECR 1869 for a rare case where a complaint under Art. 86 has been dismissed on this ground. This precondition has been discussed in connection with Art. 85 and the Commission's *de minimis* Notice. See ch. 4. A second precondition is that the dominant position must be held on a substantial part of the Common Market, if not the whole of it. This is a type of *de minimis* test requiring that the dominant position is held either in a member state or an important subdivision thereof such as a region, a city or even a port. The test is partly physical size but if the pattern and volume of production and consumption of the product is significant that can be enough. See e.g. *Suiker Line* v. *Commission* [1975] ECR 1663.

[17] *United Brands* v. *Commission*, Case 27/76 [1978] ECR 207 at 215.

defined in sufficiently narrow terms, it can limit the field of legitimate exploitation of an IPR. A narrowly defined market can produce the result that possession of an IPR can coincide with or contribute to a position of dominance on a market by reducing the possibilities of substitution. This then places the intellectual property rightowner into a regulated category under Article 86. Secondly, it can have the effect of making the exercise of exclusive IPRs in one 'market', which may have been perfectly acceptable as a lawful exploitation of a property right, unlawful in the second 'market' under Article 86 because it threatens the existence of competition on that 'market'[18] or because it goes beyond the scope of the IPR.[19] In other words the narrow definition of markets can have an effect on the treatment of IPRs in the test of dominance as well as abuse.

Under Article 86, the determination of whether or not a firm has a dominant position on that market depends in general on whether the firm can behave independently of other firms in the market in respect of pricing and other decisions. For intellectual property rightholders, however, it is important to recognize that there are different degrees of dominance with different legal consequences. There is, firstly, a general category of dominance which applies to undertakings in a powerful position in a market in which, however, some effective competition continues to exist. Secondly, there is a special category of dominance in a market, the extreme form of dominance—a *de facto* monopoly. If an IPR coincides with a monopoly, and that monopoly happens to be or become an essential infrastructure or essential facility, upon which other firms in related markets are dependent for their existence, competition law may place stricter limits upon the exercise of IPRs by requiring supply or access to essential inputs.

Since the whole structure of regulation by prohibition of abuse in Article 86 only applies if there is a finding of dominance upon a particular market, let us first examine the concepts of dominance (chapter 12) and relevant market (chapter 11) as they apply to IPRs before studying the concept of abuse and IPRs (chapters 13–18).

---

[18] See e.g. *RTE* v. *Commission* [1995] ECR I–743.
[19] See e.g. *Hilti* v. *Commission* [1994] ECR I–667.

11

The Relevant Market and Intellectual Property Rights

In principle, an assessment of dominance is meant to be a measure of the market power of a firm on a particular product market in a particular location. Hence before measuring dominance, it is first necessary to define the market. As the Court put it in *United Brands* v. *Commission*:[1]

The opportunities for competition under Article 86 of the Treaty must be considered having regard to the particular features of the product in question and with reference to a clearly defined geographic area in which it is marketed . . . for the effect of the economic power of the undertaking concerned to be evaluated.[2]

The Court made it clear that the determination of a 'relevant market' requires two separate steps: the identification of a market for a particular product and its geographic dimension.

11.1 THE RELEVANT PRODUCT MARKET

To identify a product market, one must start with an initial reference to a particular product, i.e. a good or service or group of related goods or services. There is an important distinction between a product market and a product. A product market is measured with initial reference to a single product but it is frequently wider than a single product. For any good or service there are substitutes and the analysis of competitive relationships between firms with respect to a product would normally require an assessment of the possible substitutes for that product taking into account its function, its suitability for satisfying user needs, and its price.

Hence, the traditional analysis of the relevant market by the Commission and the Court has tended to place great weight upon the exploration of competitive relationships in terms of the possible substitutes for the product on the demand side in particular but also on the supply side. As the ECJ put it in *Hoffman La Roche*:

---

[1] [1978] ECR 207.   [2] *United Brands* v. *Commission* [1978] ECR 207 at 287.

The concept of the relevant market in fact implies that there can be effective competition between the products which form part of it and this presupposes that there is a sufficient degree of interchangeability between all the products forming part of the same market insofar as a specific use of such products is concerned.[3]

If other goods exist which are substitutable from the point of view of users, they must be considered to be within the same product market. Moreover, if suppliers would be prepared to switch their production capacity to a new product, then they must be included in the measure of the supply side of the market. In theory, therefore the initial choice of product does not automatically define the relevant product market. Much still depends on the extent to which there are substitutes which are interchangeable in function with that product. Interchangeability can be tested by reference to the cross-elasticity of demand for a product. This is the response of demand to a small but significant increase in price such as 5 per cent. To what extent do users of the product switch to other products? If there was a higher than 5 per cent shift of demand to another product, that product would be included in the market. If there was a disproportionately lower switch in demand to other products, then the relevant market would have been established according to the Court's guidelines of inelastic need and limited interchangeability.[4]

To measure cross-elasticity in this way would require extensive econometric and statistical analysis but this the Commission is not always willing to resort to. Instead, the Commission has also tended to rely on a consideration of other types of evidence to determine which products are sufficiently similar to be regarded by users as reasonable substitutes for one another. The first step for the Commission is to select a product and analyse its characteristics and intended use to limit the field of investigation of possible substitutes.

The Commission then may look at the following types of evidence to determine whether two products are substitutes: substitution in the recent past; views of customers and competitors; consumer preferences; barriers to switching demand; different categories of customers. Throughout the case-law, there are examples of the Commission using the intended end use of the product as the starting-point for the definition of markets. In *United Brands*,[5] the Commission chose bananas as a separate market from fruit after receiving evidence of different patterns of use from different consumer groups. In *Hoffman La Roche*,[6] there were

---

³ [1978] ECR 1139.
⁴ See e.g. *Continental Can* v. *Commission* at para. 32. See too Commission's Guidelines on the Definition of the Relevant Market.   ⁵ [1978] ECR 215.
⁶ [1978] ECR 1139.

seven groups of vitamins, each with its own market. Vitamin C could be used for two purposes, 'bio-nutritive' and 'technical'. The Commission classified Vitamin C into two markets based on different use.

The tests of substitutability are largely demand side orientated taking into account consumer and user preferences. The Commission has tended to favour demand side tests partly because the exercise emphasizes product markets from the viewpoint of consumers and customers. It has been less regular in its consideration of supply side substitutability, such as the tendency of suppliers of other products (B, C, and D) to switch their resources to the production of good A in response to a rise in price in good A. It has tended to rely on supply side responses only when their effects are sufficiently immediate to be equivalent to demand side factors. On the other hand even if supply substitutability does not always figure in the Commission's determination of the issue of product market, it partly compensates by considering this factor at the later stage of assessing dominance.

At some point the possibility of substitution diminishes to the point where it becomes so limited that the product can be discounted as a source of real competition. The Court of Justice has defined that point where the products in the market 'are only to a limited extent interchangeable with other products'.[7] The precise cut-off point can be a matter of judgement, whether economic, administrative or judicial.

Although the Court has made much of the role of substitutability as the determinant of markets, for intellectual property rightholders the initial determination of the product or service upon which the market is based may be an even more important step.

11.1.1 Defining the Relevant Product

If a firm accused of an abuse of a dominant position is providing a simple product, then the initial determination of the 'relevant product' calls for little discretion on the part of the competition authorities. If the product is bananas, the initial product defines itself. The Commission or Court can move directly to the issue of interchangeability, i.e. testing whether the product forms part of a wider market. For example in *United Brands* v. *Commission*, the major issue in the test of relevant product market was whether the market for bananas could be viewed as part of a wider market for fruit in general or was a separate product market from other fruits. The Commission could test this issue by obtaining evidence relating to the characteristics of bananas from the viewpoint of consumers, for example the way they particularly satisfy the needs of the

---

[7] *Michelin* v. *Commission* [1983] ECR 282 at para. 37.

young, the elderly, and the infirm. The Court could support the Commission's decision, holding that bananas were 'only to a limited extent interchangeable with' other fruits and 'only exposed to their competition in a way that is hardly perceptible'. The initial selection of the product upon which the market analysis was to be based, itself, created no legal issue.[8]

When, however, the product is more technically complex, the selection of the initial product involves the exercise of greater discretion by the competition authorities. They can decide whether and to what extent to view the various sub-products or raw materials as components of an integrated product and to what extent to view each sub-product or raw material as a product in its own right. In the case of products such as consumables and spare parts, they can decide whether they are part of the product package presented by the firm to users and consumers or separate products creating separate markets. Furthermore, where a firm has integrated two different levels of economic activity within the same company, the Commission can decide whether these operations constitute an integrated operation offering one 'product' or are separate activities offering separate products on separate markets despite the corporate form of the operations.

From a commercial point of view, firms consider decisions such as the selection of product and product packaging to be the essence of their commercial judgement in marketing generally and in the exploitation of intellectual property rights (IPRs) in particular. Moreover, the organization of business operations is a matter of corporate strategy.

From the viewpoint of the competition authorities charged with protecting effective competition in markets, however, the choice of product market for the purpose of enforcing Article 86 is governed by considerations of regulatory policy. Even where a firm may be convinced that its product package or its business operation is an integrated whole, the Commission may choose a narrower definition of product in line with its regulatory priorities and thereby set the stage for a finding of narrow product market.

The significance of the step of selecting the initial product in defining markets for intellectual property rightholders can be illustrated by looking at the recent case of *Hilti* v. *Commission*.[9] Hilti was and is a firm that specializes in producing nail guns, cartridges, and nails as parts of a power activated fastening (PAF) system for the construction industry. Eurofix and Bauco, two independent manufacturers of Hilti compatible nails, complained to the Commission that Hilti were engaged in the practice of tying the sales of cartridges with requirements to buy nails and

---

[8] [1978] ECR 215.   [9] [1994] ECR I–669.

that this was having the effect of driving them out of the market. Hilti's response was to maintain that it had no dominant position in the relevant product market because that market was the market for PAF systems consisting of a combination of their nail guns, cartridge strips, and nails into an integrated product. This product competed with other types of fastening systems in the construction sector. The Commission, however, decided that Hilti compatible cartridge strips and Hilti compatible nails formed separate products and separate product markets. This finding then provided a springboard for the further finding that Hilti was dominant in the market for Hilti compatible cartridge strips. Prominent in this finding of dominance was the existence of a patent on the cartridges held by Hilti which allowed it legitimately to exclude competition. In addition, the strong economic position of Hilti in the nail gun market reinforced its dominance in the cartridge strip market.

In *Hilti*, moreover, the definition of market went beyond the issue of dominance and influenced the issue of abuse. Since there were separate markets for cartridge strips and nails, and only the cartridge strip was a patented product, the tie-in with the unpatented nails was caught by Article 86 as a case of attempted leveraging of the patent protection going beyond the scope of the patent. The Commission could characterize the commercial practices of Hilti in tying in sales of their patented product in the cartridge market to sales of non-patented nails as an abuse of its dominant position in the cartridge strip market. Furthermore, since Hilti's patents in the UK were subject to licences of right, the Commission could examine the level of royalties charged by Hilti to determine whether they were set so high as to constitute an indirect refusal to supply under Article 86. Both findings of abuse, as well as the finding of dominance, could only be sustained because of the prior definition of product markets.

The Court of First Instance supported this narrow view of the relevant product market stating that Hilti's argument that nail guns, cartridge strips, and nails 'should be regarded as forming an indivisible whole . . . is in practice tantamount to permitting producers of nail guns to exclude the use of consumables other than their own branded products in their tools'. The Court added that as far as Community competition law is concerned, 'any independent producer is quite free . . . to manufacture consumables intended for use in equipment manufactured by others, unless in so doing it infringes a patent or some other industrial or intellectual property right'.[10]

Once the Court had accepted that the market in nail guns had been designated as the relevant product, the finding of dominance was

---

[10] [1991] ECR II–1439 at para. 68.

assured by Hilti's high market share of between 70–80 per cent. The CFI also agreed with the Commission that the existence of a patent on cartridge strips strengthened Hilti's position in the market for Hilti-compatible consumables in general.[11]

On appeal, Advocate General Jacobs raised the point that if the PAF system competed with non-PAF systems in a wider market, which included both systems, Hilti would not be dominant. The ECJ, however, was not to be drawn on this substantive issue. The Court was reluctant to attack the determination of the relevant market decision which was a conclusion of law by the CFI, because it would in effect require the Court of Justice to reappraise the evidence before the CFI.[12] As an appellate court, the Court of Justice was willing only to investigate whether there was an error of law involved in the CFI's decision on the substitutability issue. As the Advocate General Jacobs pointed out, however, the Court would be bound to consider an argument that the CFI omitted to take relevant facts into consideration because this could amount to an error of law and a ground to annul the judgment.[13] Barring such an error, however, the Court is reluctant to intervene in the question of measuring substitutability of products in a particular case.

In the event, the discretion allowed to the Commission to define 'products' narrowly as the basis of product markets can predetermine the scope of the jurisdiction of Article 86. If the product selection allows the Commission to find that an undertaking is operating in two markets rather than one, it can lead to a finding of dominance in a secondary market, even where the firm may be engaged in robust competition in the primary market. Moreover, the definition of the product market can lead to the characterization of the conduct of the firm in exploiting its IPRs as an attempt to extend its dominance in one 'market' into related 'markets'. Since IPRs are regulated by Article 86 largely because of the characterization of markets, it is useful to look closely at the Commission's practice in this sphere as a separate step in the chain of steps leading to a finding of dominance.

A similar approach was taken by the Commission in *Tetra Pak II*, in which it found that there were four separate products and four separate product markets: aseptic carton machinery, aseptic cartons, non-aseptic carton machinery, and non-aseptic cartons. Tetra Pak had argued that the machinery and cartons were an integrated packaging system within

---

[11] [1991] ECR II–1439 at paras. 92 and 93.

[12] As the ECJ put it: 'It should be pointed out, before considering Hilti's pleas, that the Court of Justice has consistently held that . . . Article 51 of the Statute of the Court of Justice of the EEC an appeal may rely only on grounds relating to the infringement of rules of law to the exclusion of any appraisal of the facts.' [1994] ECR I–667 at para. 10.

[13] [1994] ECR I–667 at para. 28.

its own market. They also argued that separating machinery and cartons could give rise to health risks and to potential damage to reputation.

In this case the Commission was more forthcoming about its motivation. It stated that: 'Article 86 of the Treaty precludes the manufacturer of a complex product from hindering production by a third party of consumable products intended for use in its systems.'[14] Again, this approach of the Commission received support from the CFI which stated that: 'In the absence of general and binding standards or rules, any independent producer is quite free, as far as Community competition law is concerned, to manufacture consumables intended for use in equipment manufactured by others, unless in so doing it infringes a competitor's intellectual property right.'[15]

The implication of this statement is that unless a consumable itself is protected by the IPR, it is viewed as a separate product and cannot be bundled with another product which is protected by an IPR. The method used by the Commission to pursue this regulatory policy is to define each product as the base for a separate market.

11.1.2 Narrow Product Markets and Commission Practice

The technique of defining product markets narrowly in *Hilti* (and *Tetra Pak II*) could be traced back to the case of *Hugin*,[16] in which the cash register manufacturer ended a relationship with a distributor repairer, Lipton, and refused to supply him with spare parts once he was no longer part of Hugin's dealer network. In analysing the complaint under Article 86, the Court was prepared to find that there was a separate market for spare Hugin parts required by independent undertakings specializing in maintenance and repair of Hugin cash registers from the market for cash registers generally. This then led to a finding that Hugin was dominant in the 'market' for new spare parts for Hugin cash registers despite the robust degree of interbrand competition on the general cash register market.

The method of reasoning of the Commission and Court involved as a first step their acceptance of Hugin spare parts as separate products from new cash registers because of the existence of demand from independent undertakings specializing in the maintenance and repair of cash registers, the reconditioning and sale of used machines, and the rental of Hugin machines. In other words, in *Hugin*, the Court reasoned that a separate product market could be said to exist if there was a separate demand for the product.

---

[14] *Tetrapak* v. *Commission* [1994] ECR II–755 at para. 81.
[15] Ibid. at para. 83 affmd. ECJ [1997] 4 CMLR 602 at para 36.
[16] *Hugin* v. *Commission* [1979] ECR 1869.

Once the initial product could be defined as narrowly as new Hugin spare parts, they could then be found to be part of a single product 'market' because (i) they were not interchangeable with the spare parts for other cash registers, and (ii) they were not interchangeable with old Hugin spare parts, for the purpose required by independent undertakings in the maintenance market.[17]

One significance of this finding for intellectual property rightholders is that if the initial choice of product is defined by reference to demand, there is little room for arguments that product markets should be defined by conditions of supply such as product packaging. Similarly, it leaves little scope for strategies of exploitation of IPRs to override consumer or user preferences.

Thus in *Volvo* and *Maxicar*, the issue arose whether it was possible to designate a market for spare parts as separate from the market for new cars. The car firms had argued that the replacement parts could not be viewed as a separate market from new cars because they were part of a package deal offered to the customer. The relevant market was the market for new cars and/or maintenance and repair work.

Again, there was no doubt of the commercial logic to the car manufacturers' arguments. For as a result of keeping their car prices low in relation to costs in order to compete they have increasingly taken their profits in the after-sales maintenance market. In other words, from the point of view of commercial strategy, or considerations on the supply side of the market, the two separate stages of economic activity were viewed as a comprehensive package.

In the framework of competition policy, however, the issue of selection of initial product depends on the viewpoint of consumers and users. Thus Advocate General Mischo in the two spare part cases distinguished between the individual purchasers of cars who may be affected by the relationship between the price of spare parts and the new vehicle and those who are simply interested in repairs. The demand of the latter 'creates' a separate market:

The fact remains that the owner of a vehicle who, at a given moment decides to repair the bodywork of his vehicle rather than change model is obliged to purchase (either directly, if he repairs the car himself, or indirectly through a garage in the manufacturer's network or through an independent repairer) a body panel which is identical in shape to the original part. Consequently, for the owners of a vehicle of a particular make the relevant market is the market made up of the body panels sold by the manufacturer of the vehicle and of the components which, being copies, are capable of being substituted for them.[18]

---

[17] *Hugin* v. *Commission* [1979] ECR 1869 at paras. 7–8.
[18] [1988] ECR 6039 paras. 47–8 and [1988] ECR 6211 paras. 7–8.

On similar grounds the Advocate General also rejected the arguments that there was a spare parts market in general. In all such cases, the governing factor from the viewpoint of competition policy was whether there was a specific consumer demand for the product in question, i.e. the relevant spare parts, and whether *that* demand could be met by any other substitute products. The car makers' argument that some consumers might view the product mix as a package could not be sustained as the determinant of the relevant market if it could be shown that there were other consumers who had a need for separate spare parts either to repair cars themselves or to have their cars repaired by independent repairers.

One implication of this analysis is that the only effective defence against a Commission's initial designation of product in narrow terms is to show that it is too narrow from a demand point of view. For example in *Alsatel* v. *Novasam*,[19] the Commission had made the finding that the relevant product was the service of renting and maintaining telephone equipment. On appeal, the telephone company succeeded in convincing the Court that the relevant market was the market for telephone installations in general including telephones sold to the public. The Court's view was that since consumers would choose between buying the equipment or renting it with maintenance support, the relevant market had to be defined more widely to take account of the interchangeability.

The problem for an intellectual property rightholder who fails to widen the initial choice of product by the Commission, is that it can face a form of double jeopardy. The narrow definition of product in the first place can reduce the possibilities of substitutes to nil and this in turn can result in a product market so narrow as to amount to a single product market. The Court's decision in *Hugin* has been criticized because it failed to consider possible alternative sources of supply in the form of copies made by independent undertakings. Yet Advocate General Reischl found that there were significant barriers to entry for independent undertakings to manufacture Hugin spare parts. These barriers consisted of the existing doubts and threat of considerable penalties to such manufacture rather than the legal barriers of a design right. In the event a finding of a narrow market could be justified by the absence of substitutes.

Secondly, the finding of narrow product market can result in the IPRs so curtailing substitutes that the intellectual property rightowner is found to be dominant to the point of constituting a *de facto* monopoly.[20] In *Maxicar* v. *Renault* and *Volvo* v. *Veng*,[21] once it was accepted that the

---

[19] [1988] ECR 5987 at para. 17.
[20] See e.g. *RTE* v. *Commission* [1995] ECR I–743.
[21] [1988] ECR 6211.

relevant market could be defined by reference to the supply of goods or provision of services protected by an IPR, then ownership of the right itself would in practice have the effect of converting a narrowly defined product as the base for a market into a single product market.

We shall see in the next chapter that this in turn can also in practice make the holder dominant.[22] What is important to see at this stage is that whether or not an IPR has the effect of converting a narrowly defined product into a single product market is an important question of fact. A narrow product market does not automatically result in an IPR creating a position of dominance. The effect of an IPR in curtailing substitutes is dependent on whether there are substitute products capable of performing the same function as the relevant product. If, in a rare case, the product which is chosen as the base for the relevant market is dependent on a particular form to fulfil its function and the IPR precludes substitutes for that form, the IPR can effectively extinguish substitutes in that market and produce dominance. For example, in the case of *Volvo*, the product was a body panel protected by design rights. If the component in question had been, say, a distributor or alternator or any part which could have been made using another design, then the IPR would not have had the effect of narrowing the product market. As long as components performing the same function were available and they were 'interoperable' with Volvo cars, the existence of the design right would not have the effect of precluding substitutes from the product market. If, however, the function of the component is inseparable from its appearance, as in body panels, and the IPR gives an exclusive right to products with that appearance, the existence of the IPR can have the effect of narrowing down the product market to a single product market. This in turn sets the scene not only for a finding of dominance on that product market for the rightholder; it could also convert a position of dominance into a monopoly.

11.1.3 Dependence, 'Essential Facility', and Market Definition

The Commission's practice of narrowly defining markets is not directed specifically at the holders of IPRs. Its designation of spare parts and consumables as separate markets has been part of a wider tendency to

---

[22] For example, if the relevant market was reduced to the market for body parts which could fulfil the same function as those covered by the registered design right, it would extend to those which were identical in appearance to the latter. However, any part which is identical to the protected design, infringes it, since it is precisely the appearance of the part which is protected by the right. This means that the relevant market would consist solely of the manufacturer's parts and infringing parts, the manufacture and sale of which is prevented by the IPR.

regulate essential infrastructures which create dependency relationships in neighbouring markets. Its actions are in part prompted by the desire to exercise regulatory control over emerging markets in particular sectors. Thus as the Commission argued to the CFI in *Magill*,[23] it was determined to use Article 86 to supervise effective competition particularly in the computer software and telecommunications industries.

Moreover, the Commission's choice of relevant product market has on occasion been heavily influenced by the type of abuse that is alleged to have occurred. In *Hilti*,[24] the complaint came from the manufacturers of Hilti compatible nails complaining that Hilti was attempting to exclude them from the market. In *Tetra Pak*[25] the abuse alleged was that of extinguishing competition in the market for aseptic cartons and machinery by the acquisition of the exclusive rights to the technology. In *Magill*[26] the abuse was the control over the publication of advanced TV programme listings. In *Soda Ash*, the Commission was quite open about its approach. It stated that in determining 'the area of business in which conditions of competition and the market power of the allegedly dominant undertaking fall to be assessed ... account has to be taken of the nature of the abuse being alleged and of the particular manner in which competition is impaired in the case in question'.[27]

The Commission's desire to supervise markets and prohibit abuse is particularly strong where it can be shown that market in question consists of a natural monopoly which is an essential infrastructure for another related market. In such a case, the Commission sees its role as preventing the extinction of other competitors on that second market whether or not IPRs are involved. The desire to maintain effective competition on markets has led to the technique of narrow market definition as a jurisdictional method. The fact that the establishment of two markets as the basis for the regulation of 'essential facilities' may itself confuse jurisdictional issues with supervision issues does not appear to inhibit the Commission. Nor has it often been found to have exceeded its brief by the Court. In the event, it is useful to chart in greater detail how the Commission and the Court in cases other than *Hugin* have been influenced by the dependence upon essential facilities in their designation of the product market.

In the early case of *Commercial Solvents*,[28] the Court approved of the distinction drawn by the Commission between the raw materials market for nitropropane and aminobutanol and the final product market for the drug ethambutol, used in the treatment of tuberculosis. The raw materials

23 [1991] ECR II–485.
25 [1990] ECR II–309.
27 *ICI* v. *Solvay* OJ L 152/21 [1991] para. 42.

24 [1994] ECR I–667.
26 [1995] ECR I–743.
28 [1974] ECR 223.

were derived from the process of nitration of paraffin which at one stage had been protected by patents. In the ensuing years, Commercial Solvents had been able to protect its near monopoly position because of the capital costs of the manufacturing equipment and the lack of other commercially viable products which could be made from the raw materials. The Court accepted that the two markets were separate and that Commercial Solvents and its subsidiary ICI between them had a dominant position on the market for the raw materials.

This case signalled that the corporate form would not interfere with the Commission's designation of markets. Unlike Article 85, it was irrelevant that the undertaking had decided to vertically integrate from the raw material to the pharmaceutical product market. What counted was that there were two separate markets by virtue of the existence of demand on the pharmaceutical product market for the raw material. As it happened, Commercial Solvents also had a dominant position on the raw materials market because of its ownership of the production facilities for the raw materials which were indispensable for the downstream ethambutol market. However, it was a necessary condition of the finding of dominance that there were separate markets for the raw materials and the pharmaceutical product.

In *Télémarketing*,[29] a TV company in a relationship with an independent telemarketing firm attempted to vertically integrate into the lucrative market of TV advertising by ending its contractual relationship and setting up a subsidiary of its own in that field. When the advertising firm, Telemarketing, complained to the Commission, the Commission began its analysis under Article 86 by finding that there were two separate markets: the TV programme sending market and the TV advertising market. This led to a finding that the TV company was dominant in the TV programmes market and that it was abusing its dominance in that market to exclude a competitor from the secondary market.

The characterization of separate markets can be used as a method to identify dominance and regulate its effects in related markets. Thus, in the *IBM* case[30] in 1984, after receiving complaints from independent software companies about IBM's use of its information as a hardware provider to create advantageous marketing conditions for its own software providers, the Commission analysed the business operations of IBM's Systems 370 Central Processing Units and operating systems as falling into three separate markets. The Commission first isolated the market for mainframe computer systems of which IBM's Systems 370 Central Processing Unit was one product as a separate market. It then

---

[29] *Centre Belge d'Etudes de Marché—Télémarketing* [1985] ECR 3261.
[30] *IBM Personal Computer* EC Comm. Dec. 84/233 (1984).

designated (i) the market for main memory attached to IBM's System 370 CPU; and (ii) the market for software usable in IBM System 370, as two separate markets. The main factor in viewing the latter categories as separate markets was that once customers had chosen to buy and use IBM 370s, they could not readily switch to competitors in the mainframe market. By defining the market narrowly, the Commission placed itself in a position to allege in its statement of objections that IBM was dominant in the markets for the supply of (i) main memory and (ii) basic software for IBM 370 systems and had abused its dominant position by 'tying' memory and software to the purchase of its mainframe.

More recently, we can see this technique employed in the Microsoft case.[31] In June 1993, the Commission received a complaint from Novell that Microsoft's licensing practices were abusive under Article 86 because they foreclosed competitors from the market for PC operating systems software. In their investigation of the abuse, the Commission made the finding that the three layers of software which could be installed upon a PC constituted separate markets: disk operating systems (DOS); graphical user interfaces (GUI); and software applications, such as word processing, etc. Again, this then led to findings of dominance, i.e. *de facto* industry standard, on the DOS market, and tying and discrimination in its pricing, rebates, and licensing in the GUI and software applications markets.

This technique is not limited to the large-scale operation. It can also be applied to differentiate markets to regulate situations where the owner of a smaller scale infrastructure itself engages in the secondary market. In such a case, the definition of product and relevant product market can be stretched beyond traditional market categories into concepts such as essential inputs or facilities. In the *Decca Navigation Systems* case,[32] for example, the Commission was prepared to characterize the provision of navigation signals as a 'market' with a downstream 'market' consisting of Decca-compatible receivers.

We can also see it in the 'essential facilities' cases in which for example the underlying railway track infrastructure is viewed as a market separate from the market for operating rail services, an electricity grid is viewed as a market separate from the market for transmitting electricity, a port is viewed as a market separate from a ferry service. In such cases the characterization of markets appears to be prompted as much by the purpose of establishing dominance as by the requirement of establishing whether in fact more objectively the jurisdictional requirements of Article 86 have been met.

[31] *XXIVth Report on Competition Policy* (1994) Annex II at 364–5; see too *AT&T/NCR Merger* [1992] 4 CMLR M41; *Digital Kienzle* [1992] 4 CMLR M99.
[32] EC Comm. Dec. 89/113 [1989].

In *Magill*,[33] both the Court of First Instance and the Court of Justice, by implication if not explicitly, gave their approval of this practice. In that case, the Commission had divided the relevant product markets into three, each based upon a particular product: (i) the market for TV listings and (ii) the market for weekly TV guides, both of which were ancillary to (iii) the market for TV programmes. The Court of Justice upheld the finding that there was a market for weekly TV guides which was secondary and dependent upon the 'market' for information used to compile programme listings in which the TV companies had a *de facto* monopoly. Thus, a narrow and somewhat artificial view of product markets led to a finding of dominance in the TV listings market and a special responsibility for the TV guides market.

The finding of a separate market in TV listings information in *Magill* was a continuation of the pattern established in other cases involving IPRs in which the Court and the CFI have accepted the Commission's practice of using a narrow product definition as the basis of a narrow market definition in order to establish dominance and hence a platform to regulate essential infrastructures in various forms.[34] We shall look more closely at this development in the next chapters after examining the geographic dimension of the product market. To a large extent IPRs seem to be caught in the crossfire of a wider policy problem. The Commission's task-orientated definition of product market is part of its concern to be an effective enforcement authority giving it regulatory control over emerging markets in particular sectors such as information technology and telecommunications. Moreover, the Court appears to be willing to countenance this approach.

From the viewpoint of IPRs, this practice of the Commission requires careful scrutiny. For insofar as the Commission is able to establish narrow markets, it is able to place limits upon the scope for exploiting such rights. In *Volvo*,[35] the use of spare parts markets did not prevent full scope for exclusive exploitation in the spare parts market. In *Magill*, however, the Court accepted the point, hinted at in *Volvo*, that in the case of markets dependent upon another market in which an undertaking is dominant or owns an essential input or facility, the whole range of Article 86 rules relating to abuse are applicable to the exercise of IPRs.

The Court's decisions in *Magill* and *Hilti* suggest that the Commission's approach to narrow markets and vertical slicing can be acceptable from a competition point of view. The Court is prepared to back the Commission on its designation of product. There could still be

[33] Op. cit. nn. 23 and 26 *supra*.
[34] See e.g. *Hugin* v. *Commission* [1979] ECR 1869; *Hilti* v. *Commission* [1994] ECR I–1439; *Tetra Pak Intl.* v. *Commission* (*Tetra Pak II*) [1997] 4 CMLR 602.
[35] Op. cit. n. 21 *supra*.

an issue of whether a complex product can be designed to be so integrated that it cannot be unbundled by the Commission's definition of product. At all events, once the Commission takes a decision to define the product narrowly, the only barrier to a finding of dominance will be finding that there are other products which are substitutable.[36]

11.2 THE RELEVANT GEOGRAPHIC MARKET

A similar phenomenon can be seen in the definition of the relevant geographic market. In the general run of competition cases, as the Court pointed out in *United Brands* v. *Commission*,[37] the geographic market is determined by reference to the area in which the product is marketed where the conditions of competition are sufficiently homogeneous to allow an evaluation of the economic power of the undertaking concerned. As the Court put it in *United Brands*:

The conditions for the application of Article 86 to an undertaking in a dominant position presuppose the clear delineation of the substantial part of the common market in which it may be able to engage in abuses which hinder effective competition and this is an area where the objective conditions of competition applying to the product in question must be the same for all traders.[38]

In *United Brands*, a rough and ready consideration of transport costs resulted in the inclusion of six other member states, while the presence of specific regulations of imports and marketing arrangements in the UK, France, and Italy led to their exclusion from the relevant geographic market for bananas. In later cases, both economic factors such as transport costs and the location of production facilities and regulatory factors have figured prominently in the determination of the relevant geographic market.

From the viewpoint of IPRs, it is significant that the economic criteria used regularly in the assessment of relevant markets under the Merger Regulation are not always used as regularly under Article 86. Under the Merger Regulation, a more economic approach is taken to the assessment of the relevant geographic market, with the result that the degree of interpenetration of trade features in the assessment. In such cases, the geographic market has been drawn widely as consisting of Western

---

[36] In a new draft notice on the Definition of the Relevant Market the Commission indicates that it is prepared to place greater weight on economic factors in defining the relevant market. This may or may not produce a change which is relevant to IPRs. For an early general assessment see Bill Bishop, 'The Modernization of DGIV' [1997] *ECLR* 481.

[37] 1 CMLR 429 at paras. 10–11.

[38] [1978] ECR 287 at para. 44.

Europe[39] or the Community,[40] depending upon the actual trade flows or supply patterns.

Under Article 86, in contrast, the geographic market has often been chosen as the area in which a state monopoly is conferred, as in telecommunications, or an area in which a firm enjoys intellectual property protection, without the follow-up of an empirical analysis of interpenetration of trade. In part this is because the choice of the state as the relevant geographic area has been prompted more by regulatory than economic criteria. Thus in *British Telecom* and *Magill* the choice of national markets was dictated by the absolute monopoly conferred by legislation.

In some cases, the geographic area has been narrowed to the area in which the abuse has occurred. This could be seen in *Michelin*[41] in which the Netherlands was taken as the relevant market. This helps to support a finding of dominance and which in turn provides the basis of a finding of abuse by Michelin. However, the Commission's criterion for the determination of the geographic market was that the tyre manufacturers had chosen to organize themselves into national markets. Yet this ignored the possibilities of competing suppliers obtaining supplies outside the Netherlands either from passive or active sellers. In all such cases, the determination of the relevant geographic market looks less like an objective economic assessment of homogeneous market conditions and more an administrative device for underpinning findings of dominance and abuse.

Further examples of this tendency can be seen in the application of the test of whether the relevant geographical market is a substantial part of the common market. In some dependence and essential facility cases the choice of geographic market is so narrow that it can consist of a single port.[42] It is not at all clear that the Commission has the firm support of the Court on this issue. Although the Commission cites *Hugin* for support, more recent cases cast some doubt on the Court's willingness to accept the Commission's assessment of narrow markets which ignore competitive forces. In *Italian Flat Glass*,[43] for example, the Commission's assessment of Italy was rejected by the Court because the Commission had failed to examine the competitive effects of competing products from other countries. Even more significant for intellectual property

---

[39] See e.g. *Mannesman/Vallourec/Ilva* 1994 OJ L 102/15.

[40] See e.g. *Pilkington-Technint/SIV* OJ no. L 158, 25 June 1994.

[41] [1983] ECR 3461; see too *Solvay* v. *Commission; British Plasterboard and British Gypsum* v. *Commission* [1993] ECR II–389.

[42] See e.g *Merci Conventzionale Porto di Genova* [1991] ECR I–5889; *Corsica Ferries Italia SRL* v. *Corpo del Piloti del Porto di Genova* C18/93 7 May 1994.

[43] [1990] 4 CMLR 535 at para. 77.

rightholders was the case of *Tetra Pak II*[44] in which the Court of First Instance rejected the Commission's decision that significant price differences in different member states were relevant to a finding of the relevant geographic market.

In sum, if the definition of geographic markets underestimates substitutabilities, it can be used more readily as a springboard to a finding of dominance by the Commission.

[44] [1994] ECR II–755; see too [1997] 4 CMLR 662 ECJ.

12

The Concept of Dominance and Intellectual Property Rights

12.1 INTRODUCTION

Once the relevant market has been defined, the next step under Article 86 is to determine whether in fact the accused undertaking is in a dominant position on that market.

If dominance was measured according to purely economic criteria, the test would consist of the power to limit output in order to raise prices and to extract profits above the competitive level from that market. Under Article 86, however, the test of dominance has been traditionally defined by a legal assessment of prevention of effective competition and market independence. As the Court of Justice put it in *United Brands* v. *Commission*, a dominant position is:

a position of economic strength enjoyed by an undertaking which enables it to prevent effective competition being maintained on the relevant market by affording it the power to behave to an appreciable extent independently of its competitors, its customers and ultimately of its consumers.[1]

In *Hoffman La Roche*, the Court went on to indicate that the definition of dominance does not apply solely to monopolies:

Such a position does not preclude some competition, . . . but enables the undertaking which profits by it, if not to determine, at least to have an appreciable influence on the conditions under which that competition will develop, and in any case to act largely in disregard of it so long as such conduct does not operate to its detriment.[2]

It is equally the case, however, that dominance can extend to monopoly. In the *Hugin*[3] case for example, the cash register company was found not only to be dominant in the market for new Hugin spare parts; it was found to be the sole source of such products. In *Commercial Solvents*,[4] the dominant undertaking was found to have a world monopoly over the

---

[1] [1978] ECR 207 at para. 38; similar formulations were used in *Hoffman La Roche* v. *Commission* [1979] ECR 461 and *Michelin* v. *Commission* [1983] ECR 3461.

[2] [1979] ECR 461.　　　　　　　　　　　　　　　　[3] [1979] ECR 1869.

[4] [1974] ECR 223.

production facilities for raw materials. Finally, in *Magill*,[5] the TV companies were found to have *de facto* monopoly over the TV listings which were necessary for the production of TV guides. In all these cases, the more intense degree of dominance had an effect on the standards of conduct required under the test of abuse. For intellectual property rightholders, therefore, it is necessary to be aware not merely of the threshold definition of dominance but also the special category of natural monopoly or essential input.

12.2 DOMINANCE AND INTELLECTUAL PROPERTY RIGHTS

The Court has long reassured intellectual property rightholders that the ownership of an intellectual property right (IPR) does not amount to dominance. In *Deutsche Grammophon*, the Court stated that possession of an IPR did not automatically amount to a position of dominance:

The manufacturer of sound recordings who holds a right related to copyright does not occupy a dominant position within the meaning of Article 86 of the Treaty merely by exercising his exclusive rights to distribute the protected article. Article 86 further requires that the manufacturer should have the power to impede the maintenance of effective competition over a considerable part of the relevant market—in particular to the existence of any producers making similar products and to their position on the market.[6]

This indicates that exclusive IPRs are not equated with dominance. It gives recognition to the reality that exclusive rights are essentially negative rights; they do not automatically result in positive right to exploit a protected product. The actual possibilities of commercial exploitation depend upon the extent of demand and competition in the market for the protected product or process.

The Court's formulations have never precluded the possibility that the ownership and exercise of intellectual property can coincide with dominance. In *Télémarketing*, for example, the Court stated that: 'The fact that the absence of competition or its restriction on the relevant market is brought about or encouraged by provisions laid down by national law in no way precludes the application of Article 86.'[7] There are situations where the power to exclude the marketing of infringing goods can create a dominant position by impeding competition. Similarly, there are situations where the ownership of an IPR can be viewed under Article 86 as producing a *de facto* monopoly. Much depends upon the criteria used to establish when they will coincide with dominance or monopoly.

---

5 [1995] ECR I–743.   6 [1971] ECR 487 at para. 16.
7 [1985] ECR 3261 at para. 16.

The assessment of dominance by the Commission often begins with the market share of a firm. As the Court of Justice said in *Hoffman La Roche* v. *Commission*:[8]

although the importance of the market shares may vary from one market to another the view may legitimately be taken that very large shares are in themselves and save in exceptional circumstances, evidence of a dominant position. An undertaking which has a very large market share and holds it for some time by means of the volume of production and scale of the supply which it stands for . . . is by virtue of that share in a position of strength which makes it an unavoidable trading partner . . .

For example, in *Commercial Solvents* there was a finding of a 'world monopoly'.[9] In *Continental Can* market shares of 70–90 per cent[10] or in the *Sugar* case of 85–95 per cent[11] were clear cases of dominance. In the case of undertakings with IPRs, a sufficiently narrow definition of markets can produce a finding of similarly high market shares. In *Tetra Pak II*,[12] for example, Tetra Pak was found to have 92 per cent of the market for non-aseptic milk cartons.

Yet a high market share by itself is rarely sufficient to establish dominance. If used alone it offers only a static picture of relative shares at one point in time. Whether the size of the market share actually reflects market power in that market depends upon the state of actual competition faced by that undertaking in that market. Moreover, there needs to be a consideration of whether there is 'real' potential competition with access to the relevant product market.

One measure of the extent of actual competition on a market will be the market shares and strength of competitors. In *Michelin*, for example, the Court confirmed that the Commission was entitled to rely upon the fact that Michelin's share of the market for new replacement tyres for heavy vehicles of 57–65 per cent established dominance when the market shares of its main competitors were only 4–8 per cent.[13]

In contrast, in *Rhone Poulenc/SNIA*,[14] the Commission could find that the market share of the proposed joint venture of 53 per cent for nylon fibres would not impede competition on that market where another firm, Dupont—a powerful American multinational, had a market share of 20 per cent and the resources to compete fairly aggressively.

A second, behavioural indicator of dominance along with a high market share, is evidence of control over price. For example, in *AKZO* v.

---

8 Case 85/76 [1979] ECR 461.
9 *ICI and Commercial Solvents* v. *Commission* [1974] 1 ECR 223.
10 [1973] 1 ECR 215.   11 [1975] ECR 1663 at pp. 1973, 1977–8.
12 [1997] 4 CMLR 662.
13 [1983] ECR 3461 at para. 52.   14 OJ C 212/23 [1992].

Commission,[15] the ability of the undertaking to maintain its overall profit margins by regular price increases and increases in volume even in periods of general recession was a factor which led to a finding of dominance. Moreover, in *Hoffman La Roche* the Court indicated that, 'the fact that an undertaking is compelled by the pressure of its competitors' price reductions to lower its own prices is in general incompatible with that independent conduct which is the hallmark of a dominant position'.[16] This is not to say that price cuts during a time period, even if allied with market share reductions, are necessarily a defence to dominance. In *Hoffman La Roche* the Court found that the price cuts of vitamins varied with the volume of production and costs as opposed to being imposed by the pressure of competition.[17]

Even if there is little actual competition on the market, there still may be real potential competition which can convince an undertaking with a high market share to behave as if it was in a competitive market simply in order to discourage entry by other firms. Along with proof of the existence of real potential competitors outside the market and ready to move in,[18] the Commission will look to evidence of any existing barriers to entry which can reinforce a high market share and prevent access to the relevant market.

The barriers to entry encountered by a firm attempting to enter a market consist of the relevant resources of a firm with a high market share which are or can be used to raise the costs of or otherwise discourage potential competitors from taking the decision to invest in the market. These can include high expenditure on advertising. They can also apply to the extent to which a dominant firm has developed capital intensive operations raising the minimum level of investment needed to enter. If the capital equipment is highly specialized and would be difficult to sell off in the event of business failure, this tends to raise the ante even higher. A firm's high degree of vertical integration has also been viewed as giving firms a competitive advantage and thereby deterring entry.[19] In *United Brands*, for example, the extent to which the United Brands group extended into banana growing and shipping tended to reinforce its dominance on the upstream banana distribution market. Moreover, a firm's cushion of capital has been viewed as having the effect of deterring competitors.[20]

One resource commonly viewed by the competition authorities as reinforcing dominance has been the technological superiority of the firm

15 [1991] ECR I–3359.   16 [1979] ECR 461 at para. 71.
17 Ibid., para. 72.   18 See e.g. *Mannesman-Vallorec* OJ L102/15 [1994].
19 *United Brands* v. *Commission* Case 27/76 [1978] ECR 207.
20 *Continental Can* v. *Commission* [1973] ECR 215.

vis-à-vis its rivals. In *Hilti*,[21] the Commission identified a strong research and development function as a factor reinforcing its position of dominance. In *Tetra Pak I*,[22] technological superiority achieved through capital investment was a factor in dominance. In *Michelin*,[23] the Court stressed the lead established over competitors in matters of investment and research and the special extent of the range of its tyres. In the case of certain types of tyre, the Michelin group was the only supplier on the market. In *Hoffman La Roche*,[24] for example, there was a finding of technological superiority despite the fact that Roche's patents for the manufacture of vitamins had expired. Roche attempted to argue that the expiry of patent protection was a factor suggesting the absence of dominance. The Court, however, accepted the Commission's arguments that the extensive know-how of the company was a factor giving it a lead over its competitors and that exclusive rights preventing third parties from entering the market were not essential to a finding of technological advantage.

If technological supremacy is viewed as helping to establish dominance, it could be argued that EC competition law appears to be levying a penalty for R&D investment and high quality of product.[25] The Court's view, however, has been that a finding of dominance is not itself unlawful; it simply imposes a special responsibility on the dominant undertaking not to engage in prohibited conduct. Yet, as Whish has pointed out, this does not do justice to the point that the costs of defending Article 86 cases can be high.[26]

12.3 DOMINANCE, INTELLECTUAL PROPERTY RIGHTS, AND BARRIERS TO ENTRY

A similar issue arises in cases in which it has been held that the exclusivity created by protection of IPRs is an important barrier to entry, reinforcing dominance. In *Hilti*,[27] for example, the firm's cartridge strips were protected by patents in all member states apart from Greece and Germany and the firm claimed copyright protection in the UK and this was viewed as an important factor reinforcing dominance. (In *Tetra Pak I*[28] the acquisition of the exclusive patent licence was viewed as a barrier to entry because it prevented access to the technology by potential competitors.)

For rightholders the main risk of dominance occurs if the product

---

21 *Hilti* v. *Commission* [1994] ECR I–1439.   22 [1990] ECR II–309.
23 [1983] ECR 3461.   24 [1979] ECR 461.
25 This argument was made by the French Government in *Michelin* [1983] ECR 3461.
26 See R. Whish, *Competition Law* (3rd edn. 1993) at p. 268.
27 [1994] ECR I–1439.   28 [1990] ECR II–309.

market is defined in sufficiently narrow terms as to create a single product market. For then, the existence of an IPR could extinguish competition and thereby confirm the dominant position of the undertaking owning the right incorporated in the product.

We can see this in the case of *Hugin*[29] in which the Court of Justice was prepared to find that in the separate market for spare Hugin parts, Hugin was dominant because the independent maintenance firms specializing in maintenance and repair of Hugin cash registers could not find substitutes for supplies of Hugin spare parts. Implicit in that finding was that the IPR itself prevented their ability to compete in the maintenance market.

In the *Hugin* case, the finding that the IPRs were a barrier to entry and hence a factor reinforcing dominance went hand in hand with the finding that Hugin was the sole supplier of Hugin spare parts and that Lipton and others like Lipton were dependent upon the supply of such spare parts for their existence. The Court's finding that maintenance firms specializing in the repair of Hugin cash registers were dependent upon access to spare parts from Hugin in order to compete resulted in the finding of dominance.

In the later cases of *Volvo* v.*Veng*[30] and *CICRA & Maxicar* v. *Renault*,[31] moreover, the Advocate General alerted the Court to the point that when the relevant market is reduced to a product covered by an IPR, the fact that the IPR precludes substitutes itself ensured a finding of dominance. This suggests that the mere holding of the right could amount to dominance because the enforcement of the manufacturer's right makes it impossible for the consumer to obtain a substitute product. Friden too has picked up this point, commenting:

The crucial point here is the definition of the relevant market. If it can be defined with reference to the supply of products or the provision of services, subject to the right in question, then the right can in practice be said to make the holder dominant . . . such absence of substitutes logically implies dominance.[32]

Yet what is even more important a point is that in such a situation, the single product market can not only set the stage for dominance; it can set the stage for a finding of a *de facto* monopoly over an essential input or infrastructure. It is this category of dominance which contains the greatest threat of restriction of the exercise of IPRs by EC competition law.

The definition of this special category of dominance had its origins in the case of *Commercial Solvents*.[33] In that case, it will be recalled,

---

[29] *Hugin* v. *Commission* [1979] ECR 1869. [30] [1988] ECR 6211.
[31] [1988] ECR 6039.
[32] G. Friden, 'Recent Developments in EEC Intellectual Property Law: The Distinction between Existence and Exercise Revisited' (1989) *CML Rev.* 193 at p. 209.
[33] [1974] ECR 223.

Commercial Solvents was a multinational producer of the raw materials, nitropropane and aminobutanol, necessary for the production of the pharmaceutical product ethambutol. When Commercial Solvents decided to extend its operations from the raw materials market into the pharmaceutical market, it simultaneously stopped deliveries of the raw materials to its long-term customer in the pharmaceutical market, Zoya. The Commission found that the raw materials produced by Commercial Solvents by itself and through its subsidiary ICI were indispensable for the continued presence of Zoya on the upstream market for ethambutol. Without supplies from ICI, Zoya would be effectively eliminated from that market. There were no effective substitutes even though Commercial Solvents' patents had expired. Moreover, Zoya's manufacturing investments had made its production of ethambutol dependent upon supplies of raw materials from Commercial Solvents. The key to the ultimate decision by the Commission that Commercial Solvents had to resume supplies to Zoya was the finding that Commercial Solvents was not only dominant in the raw materials market: it had a monopoly and the existence of the monopoly made its refusal to sell to one of its principal users unlawful under Article 86.

If there had been an alternative supplier in competition with Commercial Solvents, the refusal to supply would not necessarily have constituted an abuse. As the Court stated, it would have required the presence of, on the raw material market, another raw material which could be substituted without difficulty for nitropropane or aminobutanol to invalidate a finding of dominance (paragraph 15).

Commercial Solvents had argued that another Italian company produced ethambutol from butaname and that there were other methods of producing the raw material nitropropane. The Commission found that these were not realistic alternatives. The company existed but the alternatives were of an experimental nature and had not been tested on an industrial scale. The development of the possibility involved considerable capital and considerable risk. It was not possible at present to have recourse to methods of manufacture on an industrial scale which made use of other raw materials (paragraph 16).

In *Hugin*,[34] as well, the Commission had found an extreme form of dominance. Hugin was the sole supplier of Hugin spare parts. Lipton would have been driven out of business if supplies from Hugin were not available.

In *Télémarketing*,[35] the decision of the TV company to end the commercial relationship with Telemarketing was found to be abusive in a situation where the TV company enjoyed a *de facto* monopoly over access to

---

[34] [1985] ECR 3261.   [35] [1985] ECR 3261.

telemarketing services. Anyone wishing to remain or enter the latter market was dependent upon access to the essential infrastructure of mention on the TV programme. In these cases, the existence of two markets and the monopoly over the infrastructure in the first market which was essential to the second market created the basis for a tight regulation of the commercial behaviour and freedom of contract in the second market.

The characterization of separate markets as a method of identifying dominance and regulating its spill-over effect in related markets is a technique the Commission has employed to regulate immensely powerful firms who seek to extend their power into contiguous markets. Thus, in the *IBM* case in 1984,[36] as we have seen, the Commission analysed the business operations of IBM's Systems 370 Central Processing Units and operating systems as falling into three separate markets: (i) the market for mainframe computer systems of which IBM's Systems 370 Central Processing Unit was one product; (ii) the market for main memory attached to IBM's System 370 CPU; and (iii) the market for software usable in IBM System 370, as two separate markets. The main factor in viewing the latter two categories as separate markets was that once customers had chosen to buy and use IBM 370s, they could not readily switch to competitors in the mainframe market. This then created a basis to regulate certain commercial activities of IBM, in particular memory and software bundling, and delays in supplying other manufacturers of memory and software with interface information, etc. These practices would have been perfectly lawful had IBM been non-dominant but because it was found to be dominant, they could be characterized as abusive conduct under Article 86. Hence by defining the market narrowly, the Commission placed itself in a position to allege in its statement of objections that IBM was dominant in the markets for the supply of (i) main memory and (ii) basic software for IBM 370 systems and had abused its dominant position by 'tying' memory and software to the purchase of its mainframe.[37]

More recently, we can see this technique employed in the Microsoft case.[38] In June 1993, the Commission received a complaint from Novell that Microsoft's licensing practices were abusive under Article 86 because they foreclosed competitors from the market for PC operating systems software. In their investigation of the abuse, the Commission made the finding that the three layers of software which could be installed upon a PC constituted separate markets: disk operating systems

---

[36] *IBM Corp.* v. *Commission* [1981] ECR 2639.

[37] See too *AT&T/NCR* [1992] 4 CMLR M41.

[38] Undertaking to the Commission 15 July 1994, *XXIVth Report on Competition Policy* (1994) 443–5.

(DOS); graphical user interfaces (GUI); and software applications, such as word processing, etc. Again, this then led to findings of dominance, i.e. *de facto* industry standard, on the DOS market, and tying and discrimination in its pricing, rebates, and licensing in the GUI and software applications markets.

This technique is not limited to the large-scale operation. It can also be applied to differentiate markets to regulate situations where the owner of a smaller scale infrastructure itself engages in the secondary market. In such a case, the definition of product and relevant product market can be stretched beyond traditional market categories into concepts such as essential inputs or facilities. In the *Decca Navigator Systems*[39] case, for example, the Commission was prepared to characterize the provision of navigation signals as a 'market' with a downstream 'market' consisting of Decca-compatible receivers. Decca's dominance in the navigation signals market gave it a special responsibility towards the operators in the downstream market for Decca-compatible receivers.

This idea was further developed by the Commission in a series of 'essential facility' cases. Thus in *Sea Containers* v. *Stena Sealink*,[40] a case in which Sea Containers attempting to introduce a high speed catamaran ferry service in the port of Holyhead for the Holyhead–Ireland route encountered resistance from Stena Sealink, the owner of the port facilities. Stena refused access to the new entrant because it was afraid of competition with its own traditional ferry service. The Commission found that Stena Sealink occupied a dominant position as port owner because it was the only British port serving the market for the provision of maritime transport services for cars and passengers on the 'central corridor' route between the United Kingdom and Ireland. It also found that there were no realistic substitutes for this facility. The Liverpool port was not substitutable for Holyhead because of the added length of the journey and the possibilities of Sea Containers building a second port for itself were not realistic economically or physically. In this case, the Commission referred for the first time to the special responsibilities of '[a]n undertaking which occupies a dominant position in the provision of an essential facility and itself uses that facility (i.e. a facility or infrastructure without access to which competitors cannot provide services to their customers)...[41] From the Commission's viewpoint, the definition of dominance now included a subcategory which could be defined in this way. It applied to physical facilities such as ports, railways, airline

---

[39] [1990] 4 CMLR 627.
[40] [1995] 1 CMLR 84.
[41] Para. 66. Such an undertaking may not refuse other companies access to that facility without objective justification or grant access to competitors on terms less favourable than those which it gives its own services without infringing Article 86.

computer systems, etc.[42] It also appeared to apply to intangible facilities or inputs such as IPRs?

The application of essential facility analysis to IPRs would appear to depend on whether the owner of the product incorporating the IPR had a natural monopoly as opposed to a more traditional dominant position. Much depends upon whether there were alternative methods of achieving the same commercial step.

The complication for IPR owners is that in some situations, the right itself can have the effect of creating a *de facto* monopoly. In such a case, Article 86 can be used as a basis to override the essential nature of the IPR, the right to exclude rivals at least in the second dependent market.[43] At that point competition law will not attempt to balance EC competition law with IPRs, it will subject them to an essential facility analysis.[44]

In such cases, the argument has been made that the possession of an IPR cannot be viewed as a barrier to entry reinforcing dominance because it is identical to the existence of the IPR. However, as early as 1975, in *GM/Continental*,[45] the Court held that a monopoly right granted by the state may give rise to a dominant position, at least when combined with the power to determine prices. In *Télémarketing*,[46] the Court reiterated that the fact that the 'absence of competition' was brought about by law did not prevent the application of Article 86 and a finding of dominance

In *Magill*, the Court of Justice did not appear to allow that concern to prevent the application of an essential facility type of analysis to a situation where as a result of narrow market definition the IPR contributed to 'a factual monopoly'. The Commission had decided that the TV broadcasting companies held a dominant position under Article 86 of the Treaty by virtue of their factual monopoly over their respective weekly listings which placed third parties interested in publishing a weekly TV guide 'in a position of economic dependence'. The Commission further found that by claiming copyright protection for their TV programme listings, the TV organizations strengthened their factual monopoly into a legal monopoly creating a situation where 'no competition from third parties is permitted to exist on the relevant markets'.

The Court of First Instance accepted the Commission's definition of the relevant product markets[47] and its finding that the copyright in the

---

[42] See John Temple Lang, 'Defining Legitimate Competition: Companies Duties to Supply Competitors, and Access to Essential Facilities' [1994] *Fordham Corp. Law Inst.* 245.
[43] See Venit and Kallaugher, 'Essential Facilities: A Comparative Approach' [1994] *Fordham Corp. Law Inst.* 315, at 337. [44] Ibid. at p. 337.
[45] [1976] ECR 1367. [46] [1985] ECR 3261.
[47] i.e., (i) the market for TV listings and (ii) the market for weekly TV guides, both of which were ancillary to (iii) the market for TV programmes. [1991] ECR II–485.

TV listings, together with the factual monopoly of the TV companies over their programme schedules, gave the TV companies a dominant position in the TV listings 'market' placing third parties such as Magill in a position of economic dependence. This in turn created a platform for a finding that Magill was an entrant in a market for TV guides, separate from, but related to, the market for TV listings in which the TV broadcasters owned a facility or infrastructure which was essential.

The Court of Justice showed a greater awareness of the sensitivities of intellectual property rightholders to the issue of dominance. It began by excluding the possibility that the finding of dominance could be based on the 'mere ownership of an intellectual property right'.[48] It then went on to make the point that the dominant position of the television companies was based on the *de facto* monopoly enjoyed by them by force of circumstances over the information used to compile listings for television programmes. As the only source of listings information for firms like Magill, the television companies were placed in a position to prevent effective competition on the market in weekly television magazines.[49]

Though the Court agreed with the CFI and the Commission's conclusion that the television companies occupied a dominant position, it chose not to make any reference to their finding that the dominant position of the television companies was reinforced by their legal monopoly based on copyright protection for the listings. The ECJ was concerned to underline that the existence of the IPR in this case was only incidental to the finding of dominance. It emphasized the point made in *Michelin* that the true test of market dominance was possession of economic strength in a market, i.e. the ability to behave independently of competitors and consumers,[50] a test which presupposes an economic analysis of market strength.

However, as we have seen, if 'mere ownership' of the IPR occurs in conjunction with a *de facto* monopoly on a market and that is sufficient to justify a finding of dominance, then we are not too far from a position where the existence of ownership alone can confer dominance. Of course, it could always be argued that the finding of dominance is not a finding of unlawful conduct and the only threat to the existence of an IPR by Article 86 was if mere existence could constitute an abuse of a dominant position. In the event, the crucial question will be where the dominant undertaking uses its IPR as an instrument in abusing its dominant position. The Court can of course always fall back to the position that dominance itself is not unlawful. It is only if the dominant firm abuses its position of dominance that there is an infringement of Article 86.

---

48 Para. 45. [1995] ECR I–743.   49 Para. 47.
50 *Michelin* v. *Commission* [1983] ECR 3461 para. 30.

However, this rather understates the difficulties for a firm of adjusting its commercial behaviour or an intellectual property rightholder of adjusting its preferred method of commercial exploitation to the specific groundrules provided by the law of abuse under Article 86.

Another way of viewing this approach is to acknowledge that it is a special definition of dominance, one which is based on a situation of dependence on an essential input or facility. While this special version of dominance and indispensability may have been foreshadowed in discussions in other Article 86 cases of the Court of Justice,[51] and apply more widely, its use in *Magill* strongly suggests that it can be applicable to the exercise of IPRs. In the event, it is an issue which must be taken into account by intellectual property rightholders in assessing the curbs imposed by EC competition law.[52]

[51] See e.g. comments by the AG in *Michelin* v. *Commission* [1985] CMLR 232 at pp. 297–9.

[52] Cf. the decision of the ECJ in *Tetra Pak. Rausing* v. *Commission* [1997] 4 CMLR 602.

13

The Concept of Abuse and Intellectual Property Rights

Once an undertaking owning an intellectual property right (IPR) achieves a position of dominance it has a special responsibility 'not to allow its conduct to impair genuine undistorted competition on the common market'. The Court has used its definition of abuse under Article 86 to place curbs on the exploitation of IPRs.[1] A dominant IPR owner, particularly one in an enhanced dominant position, can be restrained from acquiring other firms with competing technology.[2] It may be required to supply or license the protected products or processes to competitors in secondary markets.[3] Its pricing and product bundling decisions may be found to be unlawful because of their effect on existing competitors in secondary markets.[4]

These restrictions will only be applied in exceptional circumstances. The normal exercise of an IPR will not be an abuse. However, the application of the exceptional circumstances test to IPRs has proved to be a controversial process. Article 86 itself gives only examples of abuse. It states: 'Any abuse by one or more undertakings of a dominant position within the common market or in a substantial part of it shall be prohibited as incompatible with the common market . . .'. Such abuse in particular may consist in:

(a) directly or indirectly imposing unfair purchase or selling prices or other unfair trading conditions;

(b) limiting production, markets or technical development to the prejudice of consumers;

(c) applying dissimilar conditions to equivalent transactions with other trading parties, thereby placing them at a disadvantaged position;

(d) making the conclusion of contracts subject to acceptance by the other parties of supplementary obligations which, by their nature or according to commercial usage, have no connection with the subject of such contracts.

---

[1] *Michelin* [1983] ECR 3461.　　　　　　　　[2] *Tetra Pak I* [1990] ECR II–309.
[3] *RTE* v. *Commission* [1995] ECR I–743.
[4] *Tetra Pak Rausing* v. *Commission* [1997] 4 CMLR 602, *Hilti* v. *Commission* [1994] ECR I–667.

On first reading, these abuses suggest a concern to place limits on the capacity of a dominant firm to exploit its customers or consumers by extracting monopoly rents from them by such practices as excessive pricing, limiting markets, tie-ins, etc. For example, the first two abuses, (a) unfair pricing and (b) limiting production, suggest a conscious policy of limiting the damage caused to customers and consumers by excessive pricing. Insofar as that was the case, they were not likely to impinge upon the exercise of IPRs except in a marginal way. Competition law has long recognized that the pricing of IPRs included a reward element that could take it above price levels which would apply in a more normal competitive market.[5] Moreover, the Court has also accepted that the logic of the exclusive right allows its holder to eliminate competition from unauthorized manufacturers and sellers of the protected product.[6]

The problem for intellectual property rightholders is that Article 86 has been interpreted to apply more widely than merely prohibiting exploitive abuses; it is also aimed at 'structural' or 'anti-competitive' abuses directed against competitors, both in primary and related markets. These abuses include acquisitions,[7] predatory pricing,[8] and refusals to supply[9] and license,[10] none of which are explicitly mentioned in Article 86. The theory is that maintaining the levels of competition in markets, both primary and related markets, which have already been weakened by the presence of the dominant firm in a market operates indirectly to protect consumers[11] and ensures that, as Article 3 of the Treaty requires, competition in the common market is not distorted.[12]

To understand how this widened concept of Article 86 has virtually redrawn the borderline between EC competition law and IPRs requires us to trace two steps: (1) the development of a general rule of structural or anticompetitive abuse in primary and related markets; and (2) the way this wider interpretation of Article 86 has impinged upon the exploitation of IPRs.

13.1 THE EXPANSION OF THE CONCEPT OF ABUSE UNDER ARTICLE 86 FROM EXPLOITIVE TO ANTICOMPETITIVE CONDUCT

Although Article 86 may appear to be primarily concerned with exploitive abuses,[13] the Court of Justice has interpreted it to apply to

---

[5] *CICRA and Maxicar* [1988] ECR 6211 at para. 17.   [6] Ibid. at para. 15.
[7] *Tetra Pak I*, n. 2 *supra*.   [8] See *AKZO* v. *Commission* [1991] ECR I–3359.
[9] See n. 5 *supra*.   [10] See *RTE* v. *Commission*, n. 3 *supra*.
[11] *Continental Can* [1973] ECR 215 para. 24.   [12] Ibid. at para. 26.
[13] See Joliet, *Monopolization and Abuse of a Dominant Position: A Comparative Study of American and European Approaches to the Control of Economic Power* (The Hague, 1970). See too Temple Lang, 'Monopolisation and the Definition of Abuse of a Dominant Position under Article 86 EEC Treaty' [1970] 16 *CML Rev.* 345.

conduct causing damage to the competitive structure of markets already weakened by the presence of a dominant firm. In other words, it has been interpreted to protect competitors as well as consumers and customers. In *Michelin* v. *Commission*,[14] in one of the clearest statements of this wider approach as a general rule for Article 86,[15] the Court reaffirmed that:

Article 86 covers practices which are likely to affect the structure of a market where, as a direct result of the presence of the undertaking in question, competition is weakened and which through recourse to methods different from those governing normal competition in products or services based on traders' performance, has the effect of hindering the maintenance or development of the level of competition still existing in the market.[16]

This general rule of Article 86 contains two separate elements: first, conduct which is likely to weaken the structure of a market by restricting competition, i.e. driving out existing competitors or denying entry to new firms, will be prima facie abusive; secondly, if the methods used to achieve this effect are different from those which govern normal competition on the basis of traders' performance, it will be conclusively abusive.

13.1.1 Weakening Levels of Competition in Markets

The foundation of the wider interpretation of Article 86 was the early case of *Continental Can*,[17] in which the alleged abuse consisted solely of an acquisition of a competitor. The Court held that even though this was a purely structural change and the language of Article 86 presupposed abusive conduct, where the acquisition of a competitor by a dominant firm would virtually eliminate all competition in the market there was a distortion of the market which made it abusive. The Court stated that if the test of abuse was whether there was a distortion of the market, then *a fortiori* the elimination of competition was abusive.[18]

In two subsequent cases, the Court developed the point that conduct by an undertaking which damaged or attempted to damage residual levels of competition on a market, which fell short of the complete elimination of competition, could also be caught by Article 86. In *Commercial Solvents*,[19] an undertaking with a monopoly of an indispensable raw

---

[14] [1983] ECR 3461, at para. 70. See too *Hoffman La Roche* [1978] ECR 1139 and *AKZO* v. *Commission* [1991] ECR I–3359.

[15] See e.g. J. Venit and J. Kallaugher, 'Essential Facilities: A Comparative Law Approach' [1994] *Fordham Corp. Law Inst.* 315 at 328.

[16] [1983] ECR 3461 at para. 70.

[17] *Europemballage and Continental Can* v. *Commission* [1973] ECR 215.

[18] Ibid. at para. 24.   [19] [1974] ECR 223.

material was found to be abusive when it refused to continue to supply a long-standing customer because it wanted to eliminate that firm *as a competitor* in a market into which it had decided to enter. The Court affirmed the finding of abuse, stating that:

an undertaking being in a dominant position as regards the production of raw material and therefore able to control the supply to manufacturers of derivatives, cannot just because it decides to start manufacturing those derivatives (in competition with former customers) act in such a way as to eliminate competition which in the case in question, would amount to eliminating one of the principal manufacturers of ethambutol in the common market.[20]

In that case, the Court also indicated that the damage to competition could occur in *a market* other than the one in which the undertaking was dominant, where the dominant undertaking was using its dominant position to get a competitive advantage over a rival in that related market.

In *Hoffman LaRoche*,[21] the Court confirmed that less than complete forms of damage to competitive structures in markets could be abusive because of their exclusionary effect on competitors as well as their restrictive effects on customers. In that case, the use of fidelity rebates, exclusive supply contracts and tied sales to deny access to the market to competitors were held to be abusive.

Hoffman La Roche was the first case to grapple with the obvious question raised by the wider interpretation given to Article 86. If the test of abuse as market distortion consisted of whether the conduct of the firm damaged the remaining level of competition in the market, and damage short of an elimination of all independent competition could be regarded as abusive, then how could a dominant firm continue to function? For even organic growth through investment in R&D and increasing efficiencies in production and distribution could result in a further weakening of the competitive structure in that market. In effect, unless some exception for legitimate competition by dominant firms was built into Article 86, its prohibition of abuse would be so wide that it would call into question the lawfulness of the very existence of a dominant position. In *Hoffman La Roche*, the Court acknowledged this point by requiring that in addition to distorting the competitive structure of the market, the dominant firm's conduct must involve 'recourse to methods different from those which condition normal competition in products and services'. If the dominant firm engaged in 'normal competition', it was entitled to compete to the point of eliminating rivals and discouraging new entrants.[22]

[20] Ibid. at pp. 250–1. [21] [1979] ECR 461.
[22] Ibid at para. 91.

13.1.2 Methods of Normal Competition

The requirement that the dominant undertaking must have used methods differing from normal competition is technically a precondition for the finding of abuse and therefore part of the burden of proof for the Commission. In principle, as Kallaugher and Venit have pointed out, it should be distinguished from the test of 'business justification' on that ground:

Although there is clearly a relation between business justifications and performance based competition, the better view would probably be that the concepts are distinct. That is the burden is on the dominant firm to prove a business justification, while the burden of proving abuse, including proof that conduct is not performance related, should rest with the Commission (or the plaintiff in a private action).[23]

However, care must be taken to observe that the concept of 'normal' or legitimate competition by performance is a creature of competition policy concerns and does not merely reflect normal commercial practice. This point was graphically illustrated in *Continental Can*,[24] where the decision by a dominant firm to take over a competitor was found to be abusive because of its structural effects. In *Commercial Solvents*,[25] the decision to vertically integrate into a related market as a means of assuring a continued return on an expanding capital base was found to be abusive because of its exclusionary effect. In neither case did the fact that the means used were normal commercial practice preclude the finding of abuse. In the later cases of *Hilti*[26] and *Tetra Pak II*,[27] the dominant undertakings argued that their practice of product bundling was normal commercial usage. Again, neither Commission nor Court were prepared to accept commercial usage as an objective justification for a practice which had the likely effect of excluding existing competitors from and preventing entrants to the market.

On the other hand, the concept of legitimate competition by performance clearly extends to the use of internal economic efficiencies to grow and compete with other firms by passing on those economic efficiencies in the form of lower prices. For example, in *AKZO* v. *Commission*,[28] a case

---

[23] Op. cit. at p. 339. The authors add: 'This conclusion is supported by the fact that the objective justification defense appears to be based on a proportionality analysis (i.e., do the interests of the dominant firm justify the impact of its conduct on third parties and is there a less restrictive alternative for protecting those interests?) whereas the criterion of 'normal methods of competition based on performance' looks to a categorization of types of conduct without regard for the effect of that conduct in a particular case.'

[24] [1973] ECR 275.   [25] [1974] ECR 223.
[26] [1994] ECR I–667.   [27] [1997] 4 CMLR 662.
[28] [1991] ECR I–3359.

concerning alleged predatory pricing,[29] the Court held that charging prices which were lower than average total costs could be presumed to be anticompetitive, and pricing below average variable costs was *per se* anticompetitive.[30] The clear implication of these presumptions was that, as long as a dominant undertaking priced above average total cost, it could pass on its efficiencies in the form of low prices and legitimately compete with and weaken competitors remaining in the market without acting abusively.

Similarly, the development of a competitive edge through innovation is legitimate competition by performance which can be translated into practices which result in the elimination of competitors, either those who attempt to copy the protected product or those who are forced out of the market owing to the superior quality of the innovation in relation to their products. For example, in *Volvo*,[31] the Court acknowledged that the dominant manufacturer of spare parts could eliminate competition from other manufacturers of spare parts by using its design right.[32] However, the Court qualified that right in respect of the supplying of spare parts to secondary markets, such as maintenance markets.[33]

In contrast, the issue of self-defence under Article 86, is probably better characterized as an objective justification. As the Court of Justice said in *United Brands*:

... the fact that an undertaking is in a dominant position cannot disentitle it from protecting its own commercial interests if they are attacked, and that such an undertaking must be conceded the right to take such reasonable steps as it deems appropriate to protect its said interests.[34]

The self-defence of 'reasonable steps' incorporates an 'objective' measure of justification. It can apply to discriminatory pricing[35] as well as to predatory pricing.[36] Its scope, however, is limited to 'meeting competition' and not 'beating competition'. As the Commission indicated in *ECS v. AKZO*,[37] AKZO as a dominant undertaking could only offer or supply below a determined minimum price 'only in respect of a particular customer and only if it is necessary to do so in good faith to meet (but not to undercut) a lower price shown to be offered by a supplier ready

---

[29] See discussion ch. 18 below.

[30] If prices were lower than average variable costs, they could be presumed to be conduct designed to eliminate competition because of the sacrifice of any contribution to relevant fixed costs. If prices were fixed at levels above average variable costs but below average total costs they could still be found to be anticompetitive where they were part of a deliberate plan to eliminate a competitor.

[31] [1988] ECR 6211.   [32] Ibid. at para. 8.

[33] Ibid. at para. 9.   [34] [1978] ECR 207 at para.189.

[35] See discussion ch. 17.   [36] See *AKZO* v. *Commission* [1991] ECR I–3359.

[37] [1983] 3 CMLR 694.

and able to supply to that customer'.[38] This also implies that it is left to the dominant undertaking to verify the information about the pricing practices of its opposition.[39]

Under Article 86, the concepts of competition on the merits and objective justification apply to a dominant undertaking's relationships with customers. For example, in *Hoffman La Roche*,[40] the Court made it plain that if the dominant firm offered discounts to customers based on quantities ordered as opposed to 'loyalty rebates', that would be normal competition on the merits and objectively justified. Similarly, in *Hilti*[41] and *Tetra Pak II*,[42] the Court was prepared to accept in principle that issues of safety and hygiene and quality control were legitimate grounds for tie-ins[43] as long as these could be shown to be objectively justified.

Furthermore, Article 86 also incorporates a legitimate means test by applying a limiting principle of proportionality. The dominant undertaking may act as efficiently as it wishes in its attempts to gain profits and improve its market position but only by employing methods which are necessary to pursue its legitimate aims, i.e. methods which limit competition no more than is necessary. In *United Brands*,[44] the Court declared that a prohibition imposed by a dominant undertaking upon the resale of green bananas by its customers was abusive because its effects went beyond the object to be attained. In *Hoffman La Roche* there was an indirect reference to the proportionality concept when the Court held that the exclusive purchasing agreements concluded with customers could only be admissible subject to the conditions of Article 85(3).[45] In *BRT* v. *SABAM and Fonier*[46] the Court held that conditions imposed by a copyright-management association in contracts intended to protect members' rights were abusive because they encroached more severely on members' freedom to exercise their copyrights than was necessary to protect its rights. Implicit in this decision was a view that measures requiring members to assign their present and future rights on a global basis could be justified by a test of necessity or indispensability. In *GEMA*,[47] the

---

[38] [1983] 3 CMLR 694 at para. 36 of the legal assessment and Art. 4 of the Interim Decision. This may create difficulties of verification for the dominant undertaking, but the principle must be respected. See discussion ch. 17.

[39] See U. Springer, 'Meeting competition: Justification of Price Discrimination under EC and US Antitrust Law' [1997] *ECLR* 251 at 254.   [40] [1978] ECR 1139.

[41] [1994] ECR I–667.   [42] [1997] ECR.

[43] See discussion ch. 15.   [44] [1978] ECR 207 at p. 293.

[45] At para. 120.

[46] [1974] ECR 313 at 316. See too *Ministère Public* v. *Tournier* [1989] ECR 2565 in which the Court decided that proportionality was the test for ascertaining whether the royalties charged by the French copyright-management agency SACEM were abusive because it insisted that licensees took the whole of its repertoire rather than just the works they were interested in.

[47] [1979] ECR 3173.

Court held that the decisive factors in assessing a Collecting Society's rules in the light of the competition rules were (i) the indispensability test, i.e. whether they exceed the limits absolutely necessary for effective protection; and (ii) the equity test, i.e. whether they would limit the individual copyright holders' freedom to dispose of his work no more than necessary.

In the case of a refusal to supply, there are special reasons why a justification test is necessary. Kallaugher and Venit suggest the following:

> It could be argued . . . that there is a legitimate presumption that a dominant firm will supply any customer that is willing and able to pay the purchase price for its goods and services. Thus in the special case of refusals to supply, a burden could be put on the dominant firms to rebut the presumption by showing that it had a good reason for refusal.[48]

For example in *Commercial Solvents*,[49] the decision to refuse to supply Zoya was not compelled by necessity; ICI had sufficient capacity to supply itself and Zoya. Moreover, in *United Brands*, the Court indicated that a proportionality principle was a constituent element of the necessity test. It found that the decision to discontinue deliveries to its distributor for selling competing bananas and taking part in its competitor's advertising campaign was a disproportionately severe sanction, implying that a less severe sanction related to the action of the distributor may have been justified.

Further, it could be possible to argue for example that there was no space capacity. In *British Plasterboard*,[50] the Court was prepared to accept that a sudden shortage of oil supplies justified a refusal to supply a former customer since it would have meant that existing customers could not have been accommodated. Finally, a legitimate basis for justification for refusing to supply is that the creditworthiness of the buyer was questionable.[51]

13.2 THE EXPANDED CONCEPT OF ABUSE AND RESTRICTIONS ON INTELLECTUAL PROPERTY RIGHTS

This wider concept of abuse under Article 86 raises important issues in the context of IPRs. For example, how can it be reconciled with the entitlement to eliminate competition which is an inherent part of the grant of the exclusivity of an IPR? Further, to what extent does the concept of

---

[48] Op. cit. n. 15 *supra*, at p. 329.
[49] [1974] ECR 223. See too *Centre Belge d'Etudes de Marche Télémarketing* v. *CLT* [1985] ECR 3261 in which it was held to be abusive to exclude firms other than its subsidiary from the telemarketing market because there was no objective necessity for such exclusion.
[50] See *BPB Industries and British Gypsum* v. *Commission* [1993] ECR II–389.
[51] See e.g. *United Brands* v. *Commission* [1978] ECR 207.

normal exploitation of IPRs constitute competition on the merits or an objective justification?

The answers to these questions appear to be shaped by the Court's and Commission's definition of markets. In principle, the exclusive exploitation of an IPR is acceptable in the market for a specific product which incorporates it. Attempts to extend the method of exclusive exploitation into neighbouring markets or related products could be caught by Article 86, either as a specific abuse such as a tie-in or as a refusal to supply or license in cases where the dominant position precludes alternative sources of supply. In other words, exclusive exploitation could be legitimate competition on the merits in the primary market but could become abusive in a secondary, dependent market in certain exceptional circumstances.

Where an IPR owner enjoys a quasi-monopoly in a product market, and the exploitation of the IPR is used in conjunction with a practice designed to foreclose new competitors or drive out existing competitors in secondary markets, the Court is prepared to restrict the exercise of an IPR if it is contrary to the requirements of Article 86. As the lawyers for the TV companies in *Magill* discovered, the fact that the exercise of IPRs was within the scope of national law by itself offered no defence to complaints of anticompetitive abuse.[52] In effect, the Commission, with the support of the Court, is entitled to draw the borderline between IPRs and competition law in its definition of abuse with reference to its definitions of relevant product markets.

Before looking at the enforcement of the specific abuses under Article 86 and the way the concern of the Court to protect competition levels in secondary markets has impinged on the exploitation of IPRs, let us examine a case where the widened general concept of abuse impinges on the conduct of a dominant IPR owner in its primary market.

13.2.1 Structural Abuse and Intellectual Property Rights in the Primary Market

In the primary market in which an undertaking is dominant, the main effect of Article 86 is to regulate exploitive abuses, such as excessive pricing,[53] predatory pricing,[54] tie-ins,[55] and discriminatory pricing.[56] *Continental Can*, however, raised an issue whether, within a relevant market, the acquisition of an IPR by a dominant undertaking might be abusive. The internal development of innovation was clearly competition by performance entitling the rightholder to exclude potential competitors

---

[52] [1995] ECR I–743.   [53] See ch. 16.   [54] See ch. 18.
[55] See ch. 15.   [56] See ch. 17.

from the market. Could an acquisition of relevant technology be viewed differently? In *Tetra Pak I*[57] the Court and Commission gave their answer. Tetra Pak had a 91.8 per cent share of the market for the supply of machines for sterilizing and filling aseptic cartons, as well as the cartons themselves. Elopak, a licensee of Liquipak, were attempting to develop a product to compete in the aseptic market making use of Liquipak's exclusive patent licence from BTG. On the threshold of development, Tetra Pak acquired the entire Liquipak group of companies putting at an end the entry of the Elopak/Liquipak product. Elopak complained to the Commission and when the Commission commenced infringement proceedings, Tetra Pak relinquished the exclusive licence, agreeing to keep it on a non-exclusive basis. The Commission continued with the proceedings finding that Tetra Pak had behaved abusively in acquiring the exclusive licence by buying the Liquipak group because it strengthened its monopoly and frustrated the attempts of potential competitors from entering the field.

In *Tetra Pak I*,[58] Advocate General Kirschner was of the view that under Article 86 the normal exploitation of originated rights should be distinguished from acquisition through purchase:

I do not consider that the principles which the Court of Justice has developed in regard to the original acquisition of industrial property rights, can be transposed directly upon the derived acquisition of an exclusive license. Where a patent or registered design is obtained by its originator, the undertaking is protecting its own development work from imitation by third parties. An undertaking occupying a dominant position may also protect itself in that way, even when in so doing, as in the *Maxicar* case, it drives out from the market undertakings whose business previously consisted in imitating the products in question.

In contrast, the acquirer of a patent license procures for himself the development work carried out by others. That is legitimate, but it distinguishes his legal position from that of the original proprietor of the protective right. It is to the latter that the exclusive entitlement belongs and it is intended to allow him to obtain the reward for his creative effort.[59]

These differences persuaded the Advocate General to recommend that 'the special position which the proprietor of an industrial property right enjoys in the context of Article 86' should not be extended to the licensee:[60]

The fact that an inventor occupying a dominant position on the market may exclude third parties from exploiting his own invention without his conduct constituting an abuse does not signify that undertakings occupying a dominant position may, by acquiring an exclusive license, invariably exclude their potential competitors from using the research findings made by third parties.[61]

---

[57] [1990] ECR II–309.   [58] Ibid. at p. 364.   [59] Ibid. at p. 364.
[60] Id.   [61] Ibid. at p. 365.

The Advocate General also made the case that not only was the acquisition of the exclusive right not protected by the existence of the IPR, it was disproportionate conduct and therefore an infringement under Article 86 because a non-exclusive licence would have allowed Tetra Pak to use the protected product for its own improvements and would not have had adverse effects on competitors and new entrants. The acquisition of the exclusive licence not only extinguished the threat of potential competition from Liquipak, it removed the possibility that any other potential competitors could use the alternative sterilization process to get access to the market.

The Court of First Instance held that the mere fact that an undertaking in a dominant position acquires an exclusive licence does not *per se* constitute abuse within the meaning of Article 86. For the purpose of applying Article 86, the circumstances surrounding the acquisition and, in particular, its effects on the structure of competition in the relevant market must be taken into account.[62]

It agreed with the Commission that it was not the acquisition as such that was abusive. It was the acquisition given the position of Tetra Pak on the market. The exclusivity of the licence strengthened Tetra Pak's already very considerable dominance. It also had the effect of preventing or considerably delaying the entry of a competitor into a market in which very little, if any, competition is found because access to the 'use of the process protected by the BTG license was alone capable of giving an undertaking the means of competing effectively with Tetra Pak in the field of aseptic packaging of milk'.[63] In the light of those circumstances, the acquisition of the exclusive licence was abusive.

13.2.2 Specific Abuses, Second Markets and Intellectual Property Rights

As we have seen, as long as the exclusive exploitation remains in the primary market for a protected product, Article 86 is not unduly restrictive of IPR exploitation. Discrimination (c) and tie-ins (d) can apply to exploitive abuses in the primary market even to IPRs; but the latter would probably limit only tie-ins consisting of a combination of a protected product with unprotected products.

Once, however, the exclusive exploitation of IPRs extends into a second market, particularly a dependent market, or to a second product unprotected by the right, the balance between lawful exploitation and the exclusion of competitors can be struck at less favourable levels for intellectual property rightholders because of the application of the structural

---

[62] [1990] ECR II–309 at para. 23.   [63] Id.

rule of abuse. Under Article 86, the policy of maintaining effective competition in secondary markets can in exceptional circumstances trump the policy of encouraging the process of innovation through reward to inventors.

The specific abuses listed in Article 86 have been adapted to a two market situation to protect against attempts to foreclose competition in both markets. For example, in Article 86(c) and (d)—applying discriminatory conditions to customers and tying arrangements—we have examples of exclusionary action against rivals. At first sight, these specific prohibitions appear to be concerned with protecting customers rather than competitors. Yet whilst the conduct is directed at a different level of economic activity, its underlying motivation is to exclude competitors from the primary market. As the Court put it in *Continental Can*:

As may be further seen from letters (c) and (d) of Article 86, the provision is not only aimed at practices which may cause damage to consumers directly, but also at those which are detrimental to them through their impact on the effective competition structure as mentioned in Article 3(f) of the Treaty . . .[64]

Refusal to supply offers an example of abuse which can arise under either main head. If the second market is not being supplied by a good or service wanted by consumers or users, a refusal to supply can be classified under Article 86(b), as in *Commercial Solvents* or *Magill*. On the other hand, if the issue is that the dominant firm has a subsidiary in the secondary market, the refusal to supply may be abusive because of its discriminatory effect. For example in *Commercial Solvents*, the Advocate General made the point that if paragraph (c) of Article 86 makes discrimination between trading parties an abuse, then it 'must, a fortiori, be an abuse for a dominant undertaking to place another trading party at a disadvantage by refusing to supply to him a raw material which the dominant undertaking supplies to others in an equivalent position'.[65]

13.2.3 The Concept of Related Markets under Article 86

For Article 86 to apply to conduct in a second market, i.e. one other than the dominated market, there must be a link between the two markets. The general rule is that conduct must be such as to threaten the level of residual competition in a market where, as a result of the presence of that dominant undertaking, competition is already weakened. This presupposes that there is a sufficient link between the dominant position and the residual levels of competition in the second market. The way the

---

[64] [1973] ECR 275 at para. 26. [65] [1974] ECR 223 at p. 270.

Community Courts and the Commission have defined the nature of associative links between markets under Article 86 has varied widely, depending on the nature of the abuse.

In one line of cases starting with *Commercial Solvents*,[66] the relationship between markets has been vertical, with the dominant undertaking controlling supply to a downstream market by virtue of dominance or monopoly in the upstream market. In such cases, the Community Courts and the Commission have held that the undertaking which was dominant in the upstream market, could not without objective justification use its market power in that market to reserve to itself an operation in the downstream market. In those cases, since the dominance in the primary market was clearly the source of the power to control the downstream market, a sufficient nexus was established between dominance and the second market.

In a second line of cases, the link between the two markets was vertical but the dominant undertaking acted in the secondary market to reinforce its dominant position in the primary market. For example, in *BPB Industries and British Gypsum* v. *Commission*,[67] an undertaking, dominant in the market of manufacturing plasterboard, used a system of loyalty rebates in the secondary market to discriminate against distributors using the plasterboard of foreign manufacturers. The Court held that the basis for the association between the two markets was the fact that the dominant undertaking was dealing with customers who were operating simultaneously in the two markets. This placed BPB and British Gypsum in a position to use their market power in the dominated market to cross-subsidize pricing in the second market. The CFI held that because this discriminatory treatment was used to strengthen the dominant position in the primary market, it could be viewed as abusive conduct despite the fact that it occurred on a secondary market. Similarly, in *AKZO* v. *Commission*,[68] a case of predatory pricing, the giant chemical firm was dominant in the market for organic peroxide used for plastics, but was found to have acted abusively in the flour preservative market to preserve its position in the plastics market. At this point in time, there was an assumption that there had to be a nexus between the market in which there was a dominant position and the market in which the abuse was committed. Commentators thought that there was no authority for the application of Article 86 to actions committed by a dominant undertaking on a secondary market for the purpose of strengthening its position on that

---

[66] See e.g. *Commercial Solvents* [1974] ECR 223; see too *Télémarketing, CBEM* v. *CLT and IPB* [1985] ECR 3261. See discussion ch. 14.

[67] [1993] ECR II–389.   [68] [1991] ECR I–3359.

secondary market.[69] Yet this was to underestimate the scope of the associative links which the Court was prepared to take into account under Article 86. In *Tetra Pak II*,[70] the Court was prepared to apply Article 86 to an abuse committed by a dominant undertaking on a market upon which the undertaking was not dominant and where the conduct and the effects of that abuse were concentrated on that secondary market.

The Court acknowledged 'that the application of Article 86 presupposes a link between the dominant position and the alleged abusive conduct, which is normally not present where conduct on a market distinct from the dominant market produces effects on that distinct market'. It went on to add, however, that: 'In the case of distinct, but associated, markets, as in the present case, application of Article 86 to conduct found on that associated, non-dominated market and having effects on that associated market can ... be justified by special circumstances.'[71]

In *Tetra Pak II*, the Court found that Article 86 could apply to the particular facts of the case, 'given that the quasi monopoly enjoyed by Tetra Pak on [one] market and its leading position on the [other] market placed it in a position comparable to that of holding a dominant position on the markets in question as a whole' (paragraph 31).

The Court of Justice drew attention to the detailed findings of associative links between the two markets:

The fact that the various materials involved are used for packaging the same basic liquid products shows that Tetra Pak's customers in one sector are also potential customers in the other. ... It is also relevant to note that Tetra Pak and its most important competitor, PKL, were present on all four markets. Given its almost complete domination of the aseptic markets, Tetra Pak could also count on a favoured status on the non-aseptic markets. Thanks to its position on the former markets, it could concentrate its efforts on the latter by acting independently of the other economic operators on those markets.[72]

The Court added that these circumstances, 'taken together and not separately', justified a finding that Tetra Pak enjoyed freedom of operation *vis-à-vis* other economic operators which made a finding of dominance on the second market unnecessary.

Consequently, in an assessment of the constraints placed by the definition of abuse on the legitimate exercise of IPRs, it is necessary to take into account the market context as well as the type of abuse. The designation

---

[69] See e.g. Alison Jones, 'Distinguishing Predatory Prices from Competitive Ones' [1995] *EIPR* 252 at 255.

[70] *Tetra Pak Int'l.* v. *Commission* [1997] 4 CMLR 662, Case C–333/94P, 14 Nov. 1996.

[71] Ibid. para. 27.   [72] Ibid. at para. 29.

of markets is highly relevant to the existence of abuse as well as the existence of dominance. In the next five chapters, we shall look at five main heads of specific abuse largely in terms of their relevance as limits on the exercise of IPRs:

1. Refusals to supply (chapter 14)
2. Tie-ins (chapter 15)
3. Excessive pricing (chapter 16)
4. Discriminatory pricing (chapter 17)
5. Predatory pricing (chapter 18).

14

Refusals to Supply and Intellectual Property Rights

14.1 REFUSALS TO SUPPLY: THE COURT AND COMMISSION

From an early stage, the Court of Justice was prepared to give strong support to the Commission's policy of treating a refusal by a dominant firm to supply existing, dependent customers as an abuse of a dominant position. In *Commercial Solvents*,[1] a manufacturer of a raw material for ethambutol, a pharmaceutical product useful in treating tuberculosis, decided to vertically integrate into the downstream, ethambutol market. In consequence, it stopped supplying its long-standing customer, Zoya, who was dependent upon it for commercial survival as a producer of the drug. The Court of Justice held that the dominant firm's plans to begin producing ethambutol itself did not justify its refusal to continue to supply the raw material to its long-standing customer, even though it would now be a competitor, when the refusal would eliminate the competitor, who was one of the principal manufacturers of ethambutol, from the market. The abuse was an extreme form of discrimination under 86(c). The Court further confirmed the Commission's order to Commercial Solvents to resume supply as a legitimate exercise of its powers under Regulation 17.

The Court was particularly concerned about the dominant undertaking's use of its market power in the dominated market to acquire power for itself in the downstream market. The abuse consisted of refusing to supply an existing customer 'with the object of reserving such raw material for manufacturing its own derivatives'.[2] The Court also observed that Commercial Solvents had the capacity to continue meeting the needs of Zoya as well as its own new subsidiary and hence had no objective justification for the refusal. In effect, the special responsibility of a dominant firm under Article 86 could be used in such circumstances to curb its freedom of contract and place limits on its business strategy to vertically integrate.

The reasoning of the Court of Justice in *Commercial Solvents* was later applied in *Télémarketing*.[3] Telemarketing was a phone-in marketing

---

[1] [1974] ECR 223.   [2] Ibid. at pp. 250–1.
[3] Case 311/84 [1985] ECR 3261.

company providing phone lines and telephone operators to deal with responses to television advertisements. After working with Tele-marketing for several years, the TV broadcasting company decided to enter the field itself and stopped supplying services to Telemarketing by the device of withholding advertising time from advertisers who did not make use of the telemarketing services of its own associated phone-in marketing company. The Court held that such a refusal was abusive where, without objective necessity, a firm in a dominant position on a particular market reserves to itself 'an ancillary activity which might be carried out by another undertaking as part of its activities on a neigh-bouring but separate market, with the possibility of eliminating all competition from such undertaking.'[4]

These cases made it clear that, where a dominant undertaking's refusal to supply drives an existing customer/competitor out of business on an ancillary market, it would be viewed as acting abusively under Article 86.[5] What was less clear were the responsibilities of a dominant undertaking to a new entrant to such a market. Nor was it clear from these cases whether and to what extent the obligation of a dominant undertaking not to refuse supply of a product could be extended to a refusal to license where the dominant undertaking held a copyright or other intellectual property right (IPR) entitling the firm to exclusive exploitation.

At one point, the Commission was prepared to accept that 'a dominant undertaking should not have to subsidize its competitors', but this was in circumstances where the customer of a dominant firm reorganized itself to promote a competing brand.[6] By the time of the *IBM*[7] case, however, it had begun to formulate a view that in certain circumstances a firm in a dominant position had a positive obligation both to allow new competi-tion to enter, as well as to ensure that existing competition is not lessened in, the market in which the firm is dominant as well as in related markets.

In *Boosey & Hawkes*,[8] it stated:

A course of conduct adopted by a dominant undertaking with a view to excluding a competitor from the market by means other than legitimate competition on the merits may constitute an infringement of Article 86. The injury to competition would be aggravated where the stated purpose of the action is indirectly to prevent the entry into the market of a potential competitor to the dominant producer. A dominant undertaking may always take reasonable steps to protect its commercial interests, but such measures must be fair and proportional to the threat.

---

    4 Case 311/84 [1985] ECR 3261.
    5 See e.g. R. Subbiotto, 'The Right to Deal with Whom One Pleases under EEC Competition Law' [1992] *ECLR* 234.
    6 *BBI/Boosey & Hawkes* OJ [1987] L286/36, [1971] CMLR D35.
    7 *IBM* v. *Commission* [1981] ECR 2639; see too [1984] 3 CMLR 147.
    8 Op. cit. n. 6.

In effect, the Commission had placed itself in the position of arbiter of the legitimacy of the grounds on which a dominant undertaking refrained from supplying existing competitors and new entrants. In *Volvo UK v. Veng AB*,[9] a case referred to the Court of Justice by a national court for a preliminary ruling under Article 177, Veng argued that Volvo's refusal to license him to supply spare parts for Volvo motor cars was an abuse of its dominant position. Volvo had used its design right to stop Veng from importing cheaper copies of Volvo front wings. The Court of Justice refused to overturn the injunction Volvo obtained under national law stating quite emphatically that:

the right of a proprietor of a protected design to prevent third parties from manufacturing and selling or importing, without its consent, products incorporating the design constitutes the very subject matter of its exclusive rights. It follows that an obligation imposed upon the proprietor of a protected design to grant to third parties, even in return for a reasonable royalty, a license for the supply of a product incorporating the design would lead to the proprietor being deprived of the substance of its exclusive right.

It went on to add that, 'a refusal to grant such a license cannot itself constitute an abuse of a dominant position'.[10]

The Court also applied its decision in *Keurkoop v. Nancy Kean Gifts* to Article 86. It stated that, 'in the absence of Community harmonization of intellectual property law, the determination of the conditions and procedures under which protection of designs is granted is a matter of national rules'.[11]

If it had stopped there it would have been extremely helpful to intellectual property rightholders. However, it went on to state that the exercise of exclusive rights by the proprietor of a registered design in respect of car body panels may be prohibited as abusive conduct under Article 86 in three types of cases:

1. if the intellectual property rightholder 'arbitrarily' refuses to deliver spare parts to independent repairers;
2. if it fixes prices for spare parts at an unfair or excessively high level;
3. if it decides no longer to produce spare parts for a particular model though many cars of that model are still in use.[12]

These three examples in *Volvo* of additional circumstances going beyond legitimate exercise of IPRs under Article 86 were not meant to be exhaustive. For they all related to the examples of conduct specifically prohibited under Article 86(a)–(d). For example, the second exception in *Volvo* is specifically caught by the prohibition in Article 86(a) on excessive

---

9 [1988] ECR 6211.   10 Ibid., para. 8.
11 Ibid., para. 8.   12 Ibid. at para. 9.

pricing. The first and third exceptions in *Volvo* are caught by Article 86(b) which prohibits limits on production, markets or technical development to the prejudice of the consumer.

Moreover, they contained a basis for a deduction that a refusal to license an IPR could in certain circumstances be abusive under Article 86. It is true that in all three examples the offence could be remedied by a simple order to supply. In the first two examples the conduct complained of has little reference to the IPR; they are simple refusals to supply the goods under Article 86(b) or the charge of unfair prices under Article 86(a) which could be remedied without affecting the specific subject-matter of the IPR. In the third case, however, if the rightholder has refused to supply, and also refuses to license, such behaviour would be abusive under Article 86, and ultimately susceptible to a remedy of compulsory licence.

Similarly, dominant undertakings which exploit their IPRs by a process of discriminatory licensing or by demanding unreasonably high royalties would be acting abusively under Article 86 despite exercising rights allowed under national law. For example, in the two *GEMA* cases[13] the German national performing rights society collecting royalties on behalf of composers, authors, and music publishers was held to have abused its dominant position in Germany by discriminating against independent importers of sound recordings and sound reproduction machinery in favour of German producers. Moreover, in *Tournier*,[14] *Lucazeau*,[15] and *Basset*[16] the Court of Justice held that the French copyright-management agency practice of charging unreasonably high royalties for the public performance of recorded musical works by importers of sound recordings from other member states amounted to an abuse of its dominant position under Article 86. In such cases the exercise of exclusive rights granted under national law by, for example, imposing royalties for reproduction or use or refusing to grant licences could be curbed by Article 86.

Whether these actions were within or without the specific subject-matter of copyright is a nice, but not necessarily relevant, question, since the specific subject-matter is not identical to the bundle of rights provided by national law; those are curbed *inter alia* by the principle of exhaustion.[17] At all events, it was clear from *Volvo* that the exercise of the

---

[13] [1971] ECR 791; 1979 [ECR] 3173.

[14] *Ministère Public* v. *Tournier* Cases 110/88, 241/88, 242/88 [1989] ECR 2521.

[15] Case 395/87 *Lucazeau* v. *SACEM* [1989] ECR 2811.

[16] Case 402/85 [1987] ECR 1747.

[17] For a discussion of the specific subject-matter concept under Art. 36, see Marenco and Banks, 'Intellectual Property and the Community Rules on Free Movement: Discrimination Unearthed' [1990] 15 *EL Rev.* 224; F.-K. Beier, 'Industrial Property and the Free Movement of Goods in the Internal Market' [1990] *IIC* 131.

bundle of rights provided by national law is curbed by Article 86 in certain circumstances.

The balance established by the Court of Justice in *Volvo* between the values of Article 86 and national intellectual property laws left unclear the precise circumstances in which compulsory licensing could arise under Article 86. Nor did the case offer clear guidance on the issue of how a dominant position by a holder of an IPR in one market affects its behaviour in a related or downstream market, since the facts of that case related solely to an attempt to enter the primary market protected by the IPR.

14.2 FROM REFUSAL TO SUPPLY TO REFUSAL TO LICENSE:
THE COMMISSION DECISIONS

The extension of Article 86 obligations not to refuse to supply into obligations not to refuse to license created little conceptual difficulty for the Commission. As long as the firm in a dominant position engaged in exclusionary behaviour in secondary markets, it mattered little that the dominance was associated with an IPR. The fact that intellectual property laws confer exclusive rights of exploitation upon proprietors for a limited period of time in the interests of encouraging innovation and creativity was accepted by the Commission. They also understood that without the exclusive rights to exploit the innovation or creation there would be insufficient financial reward for the innovator because others could copy the innovation and sell it more cheaply.

The Commission's main concern, however, was to regulate the conduct of a firm which occupied a dominant position amounting to an essential infrastructure which gives it control over a downstream market for the supply of compatible products. The fact that such a position is created or reinforced by an IPR, could not preclude the application of Article 86. If the dominant firm prevents potential competitors from entering markets, or uses methods intended to drive out existing firms from markets in which the proprietor firm was itself operating, this was an offence under EC competition law whatever the logic of intellectual property law.

In the *IBM* case in 1984 the Commission had taken the position that IBM had acted abusively under Article 86 by unnecessarily 'tying' two software products to its mainframe computer product. By refusing to supply the software for use with non-IBM mainframe computers IBM was thought to have wrongfully created a disadvantage for its competitors selling non-IBM mainframe computers. By delaying disclosure of interface information on new IBM products while taking orders for them, IBM had, the Commission asserted, created an artificial advantage for itself and denied its competitors an opportunity to adapt their products to the new IBM products.[18] The Commission accepted IBM's undertakings particularly in relation to interface information and memory binding.

In *Decca Navigation Systems*,[19] the owner of a marine navigation system claimed copyright on the frequency charts supplied with receivers. When firms entered the market with compatible receivers, Decca brought an infringement action and gave licences containing market sharing provisions in order to settle the litigation, a use of copyright found abusive by the Commission under Article 86. Decca also deliberately changed the signals transmitted by its navigation equipment so that the non-Decca receivers could not enjoy proper reception. It required two months for them to modify their software to receive the changed Decca signals. The Commission found that in this respect too Decca's behaviour was an abuse of a dominant position, because it denied users of non-Decca receivers in the receivers 'market' proper access to Decca's navigation signals. It held that the dominance of Decca in the market for the provision of navigation signals, together with the fact that the Decca signals were essential for all receivers, created a positive duty for Decca to give access in the receiver market.

Further, in *IGR Stereo-Television*,[20] the Commission dealt with a case involving IGR, a firm owned by all the TV manufacturers in Germany, which was also the proprietor of the patents for stereo receivers needed to equip German TV sets for stereo TV reception. IGR granted patent licences to its members, but planned to license non-members at a later date and subject to quantity limits. The patent rights were used to stop Salora, a Finnish company, from supplying stereo TV sets to German mail order firms since a patent licence for the stereo receivers was essential in order for a firm to enter the German Stereo TV market. After the Commission began proceedings against IGR, it agreed to license immediately and without a quantity limit. Though the case involved an unlawful agreement under Article 85, the Commission also viewed IGR as a firm in a dominant position, abusing its market power by refusing to supply Salora. The Commission did not consider that the patent rights, which were the foundation for the dominant position, could justify the refusal to supply or the imposition of restrictions on supplies to outsiders. If necessary, the Commission would have been prepared to order compulsory licences under Articles 85 or 86. In the event, after the Commission had begun proceedings against IGR, the latter agreed to license Salora immediately and without limit.

18　See n. 7 op. cit. *supra.*　　　　　　　　　　　　19　[1990] 4 CMLR 627.
20　EC Commission, *XIth Competition Policy Report* (1982) p. 63.

14.2.1 New Entrants and Commission Decisions

The Commission's views on the extension of the duty not to refuse to supply new entrants as well as existing customers were further developed in two airline cases. In *London European/Sabena*,[21] Sabena, which was dominant in Belgium in the market for computer reservation services (CRS), refused access to its CRS to London European because they were entering the London–Brussels route and undercutting Sabena's fare rates. The refusal effectively prevented London European from operating that route. When London European complained to the Commission, it applied the reasoning of *Commercial Solvents* and treated Sabena's conduct as an abusive refusal for competitive reasons to supply an essential service. It observed that there was little competition on the route in question and that Sabena had sufficient CRS capacity.

In *British Midland/Aer Lingus*,[22] Aer Lingus decided to end its 'interlining agreement' with British Midland, i.e. its arrangement to issue tickets reciprocally on behalf of the other airline, once British Midland began to compete on the Dublin–London route. The Commission decided that the potential loss of revenue that Aer Lingus might suffer from the new entrant's competition did not justify the refusal to interline and the handicap it would impose on the new entrant in the form of higher start up costs.

The Commission said:

Refusing to interline is not normal competition on the merits ... the argument that interlining would result in a loss of revenue would not of itself make the refusal legitimate. Both a refusal to grant new interline facilities and the withdrawal of existing interline facilities may, depending on the circumstances, hinder the maintenance of competition.

In both cases, it was not clear that the denial of access to the new entrants threatened their survival as opposed to merely creating a competitive disadvantage. In *Aer Lingus*, the Commission summed up the issue in the following way:

Whether a duty to interline arises depends on the effects on competition of the refusal to interline; it would exist in particular when the refusal or withdrawal of interline facilities by a dominant airline is objectively likely to have a significant impact on the other airline's ability to start a new service or sustain an existing service on account of its effects on the other airline's costs and revenue in respect of the service in question, and when the dominant airline cannot give any objective commercial reason for its refusal (such as concerns about creditworthiness) other than its wish to avoid helping this particular competitor.[23]

---

[21] [1989] 4 CMLR 881. [22] [1993] CMLR 596.
[23] Ibid.

At this point, the Commission was applying a test which differed from an essential facility test similar to *Commercial Solvents* and *IBM* in two important respects. First, it imposed an obligation to interline without first investigating whether the interlining service was indispensable and incapable of duplication. Secondly, the Commission did not appear to be concerned with the issue whether Aer Lingus, the airline with the dominant CRS, was also dominant in the airlines market.

It might be more helpful to characterize *Aer Lingus, Boosey & Hawkes,* and *United Brands* as cases of 'dependence' rather than 'essential facilities'. They were all cases of retaliation by dominant firms against customers who either entered into, or joined with competitors to enter into, competition with their 'supplier'. In such a situation Article 86 can apply even if the degree of dominance is such that there are some alternative sources of supply and the legal test is one of objective justification and proportionality for the dominant undertaking's use of the sanction of refusal to supply as a punishment. It would be wrong in principle, however, for the Commission to adopt a test for essential facility which falls short of both indispensability and non-duplicability. To impose the obligations on an essential facility which the Commission has envisaged presupposes a strict test on both counts: that the facility is an indispensable input; and TINA applies, i.e. there is no alternative source of supply.

14.2.2 The Commission's 'Essential Facility' Doctrine

In its refusal to deal cases in general, the Commission had begun to formulate a view, based it claimed on the reasoning of the Court of Justice in *Commercial Solvents* and *Télémarketing,* that the preservation of effective competition required dominant companies which owned 'essential facilities' to offer access to competitors as well as customers on a non-discriminatory basis. One of the first cases where the doctrine was mentioned explicitly was *Sea Containers* v. *Stena Sealink.*[24] In this case, Sea Containers, wishing to introduce a high-speed catamaran ferry service from Holyhead to Ireland, asked Stena Sealink, the owner of the port facilities, to provide access to its new ferry service. Stena Sealink declined because of the competition that would create to its ferry service on the same route. The Commission stated that an undertaking which:

occupies a dominant position in the provision of an essential facility and itself uses that facility (i.e. a facility or infrastructure without access to which competitors cannot provide services to their customers) and which refuses other companies access to that facility without objective justification or grants access to competitors only on terms less favourable than those which it gives to its own services, infringes Article 86 if the other conditions for applying that Article are met.[25]

²⁴ [1995] 5 CMLR 84.   ²⁵ Ibid., para. 66.

The Commission found that Stena Sealink's rejection of Sea Containers' application was not consistent with the obligations of an undertaking which enjoys a dominant position in relation to an essential facility nor conduct which would have been expected from an independent port authority. The Commission's conclusion was that by denying access to its competitor on non-discriminatory terms, Stena Sealink had abused its dominant position as the harbour authority for Holyhead. The Commission had little doubt that the principle of access to essential facilities applied to new entrants in the relevant market, particularly where, as in this case, it was offering a new service. Abuse could be defined in terms of a dominant firm hindering the development of growth in competition in a market as well as the maintenance of the degree of existing competition in that market. Again, as if to pre-empt a claim of objective justification for refusing access, the Commission indicated that the capacity of the harbour was such that an additional competitor could be accommodated without undue inconvenience.[26]

The Commission justified its development of the essential facilities doctrine by reference to the decisions of the Court of Justice in *Commercial Solvents* and *Télémarketing*. However, in two important respects *Stena Sealink* and its successors differ from those cases. First, the Commission's decision in *Stena Sealink* appears to suggest that where a firm controls an essential facility it is under a stricter duty not to discriminate, stemming from its dual role both as administrator of an infrastructure and an operator on a market utilizing that infrastructure. For example, in the *Port of Rødby*[27] decision, the Commission indicated that even if the existing facilities at the port were fully utilized and could not accommodate additional sailings, it would be desirable to introduce competition by providing access to the new entrant. Secondly, there may be additional procedural obligations on firms that control an essential facility. In *Stena Sealink*, for example, the fact that Stena Sealink had failed to negotiate and consult with its customers as an independent operator contributed to the finding of abuse.[28]

At all events, by the time of the *Magill* case, the Commission viewed its mission under Article 86 to require dominant firms owning essential facilities or infrastructure in a market to make such facilities available, on a non-discriminatory basis, to enable competitors to compete in the same or related markets. As John Temple Lang described it:

---

[26] See too the Commission's decision, *Europort AIS* v. *Denmark* [1993] CMLR 457 (re access to facilities of Port of Rødby); see further *Irish Continental Group* v. *CCI Morlaix* [1995] 5 CMLR 177.   [27] Ibid.

[28] See J. Venit and J. Kallaugher, 'Essential Facilities—A Comparative Law Approach' [1994] *Fordham Corp. Law Inst.* 315.

In Europe, important sections of industry are being deregulated or at least liber-
alised by the European Union. These measures would be of little value if the
companies concerned, most of which are dominant in their own areas, were free
to integrate forward and to discriminate in favour of their own downstream
operations.

Regulated or state-owned companies often own facilities that are essential for
all or most of their downstream competitors. The essential facilities principle is,
in effect, the follow-up of Article 90 of the EEC Treaty.[29]

This development in EC competition policy enforcement applied to a
wide range of commercial activities: airlines, harbour facilities, railways,
telecommunications, and energy. It was not directed solely at IPRs.
However, if ownership of an intellectual property amounted to, or was
associated with, an essential facility, and unlicensed competitors could
not gain entrance to the market, then in the Commission's view, compulsory licensing of IPRs could be an appropriate remedy.[30]

14.3 MAGILL

14.3.1 *Magill* and the Commission

In *Magill* the three TV broadcasting companies in Ireland, RTE, BBC, and
ITP, refused to license the information contained in their programme listings for publication in a new weekly comprehensive TV guide. The TV
programme listings were no more than information created as a by-
product of programming decisions as to channel, date, and time of
programme. Each TV company had a factual monopoly over this information because they were its only source. Although there was no particular artistic merit in the material, the TV companies were able
successfully to maintain in the Irish and English courts that they held a
copyright in the TV listings. They would not have succeeded with such a
claim in any other member state of the EU.

The TV companies insisted that they were entitled under their copyright to reserve the right to publish weekly TV listings in their own
single channel weekly guides. However, they made certain concessions
to the newspapers. The newspapers could publish the listings for all six
channels twenty-four hours ahead for weekdays or forty-eight hours
ahead for weekends, and the weekend newspapers could publish high-
lights of the weeks viewing on all six channels. These concessions were
carefully calibrated to ensure, however, that viewers in the area could

---

[29] John Temple Lang, 'Defining Legitimate Competition: Companies' Duties to Supply
Competitors, and Access to Essential Services' [1994] *Fordham Corp. Law Inst.* 245 at p. 281.
[30] See e.g. Temple Lang *op. cit.*

only obtain comprehensive information about the coming weekly programmes on the six TV channels by buying three separate magazines.

When Magill TV Guides Ltd. began to publish a weekly comprehensive guide to all radio and TV programmes, the three publishers obtained an injunction from the Irish High Court to prevent its publication on the ground that it constituted an unlicensed reproduction of literary works in which they had copyright. The Irish High Court held that the TV broadcasters were entitled to copyright protection for their programme listings under Irish copyright law.

In the meantime, Magill had complained to the European Commission that the publishers in refusing to license were abusing their dominant position in violation of Article 86 of the EC Treaty. The Commission decided that this refusal was an abuse of a dominant position under Article 86 because it prevented the introduction of a new product—the comprehensive TV guide—for which there was a significant consumer demand. Rejecting the argument that the conduct could be justified as protection of copyright, the Commission stated that the right was being used by the TV companies 'as an instrument of abuse in a manner that falls outside the scope of the specific subject matter of that intellectual property right'. It further decided to order the broadcasters to end the abuse by permitting third parties on request, and on a non-discriminatory basis, to publish its weekly listings, since that was the only way that the infringement could be ended.

The Commission further held that the conduct of the TV companies was abusive because by using their dominant position to prevent the introduction to the market of a new product, the comprehensive weekly TV guide, and retaining the derivative market for weekly guides for themselves, they were 'limiting production or markets to the prejudice of consumers' which was a prohibited abuse under Article 86(b).

Underlying the Commission's position in the *Magill* case were two concerns. The first was the worry that if the ECJ's decision in *Volvo*[31] allowed exclusive rights to enjoy immunity from Article 86, it meant that copyright could be used as an instrument of abuse with impunity.[32] The second concern of the Commission was that it thought that the TV companies' copyright in the TV listings was an essential facility for the TV guide market and that they were using it to stop a company introducing a

[31] Case 238/87 [1988] ECR 6211. This case was accompanied by *CICRA* v. *Renault*, Case 53/87 [1988] ECR 6039.

[32] Indeed, in its position as an enforcer of competition policy the Commission even raised objections to the validity of the copyright in TV listings saying that they contained only factual information and were a mere by-product of the TV companies' broadcasting activities, requiring no creative effort. This of course ignored the Court of Justice's commitment to the principle of non-interference with the right of member states to determine the grant of IPRs.

new and improved product for consumers in that market. The Commission's view was that in cases where a firm has a dominant market position consisting of an essential facility or infrastructure for another market, there may be a duty to supply competitors as well as to provide access to such facilities on a non-discriminatory basis, particularly in telecommunications, energy transmission, transport, and information technology.[33]

14.3.2 The Judgment of the Court of First Instance in *Magill*

In the appeal to the Court of First Instance by the TV companies, the Court confirmed the Commission's decision on the most important issues. It held that the BBC, ITV, and RTE held dominant positions in the markets for TV listings and TV guides by virtue of their factual monopoly over the information upon which the programmes were based and their legal monopoly owing to the copyright protection. It also held that in such circumstances the refusal of the TV companies to license Magill was an abuse under Article 86. Finally it held that the appropriate remedy was that the TV companies license the listings to Magill for a reasonable royalty.

On the issue of abuse, the Court of First Instance began by suggesting that there must be a reconciliation between the legitimate exercise of IPRs and the 'improper exercise thereof likely to ... pervert the rules governing competition within the Community', and that the exercise of such rights must be restricted as far as necessary to achieve that reconciliation because the primacy of Community law, particularly as regards principles as fundamental as those of the free movement of goods and freedom of competition, prevails over any use of a rule of national intellectual property law in a manner contrary to those principles.[34]

The Court accepted that in principle the protection of the specific subject-matter of copyright entitles the copyright holder to reserve the exclusive right to reproduce the protected work and that the exercise of that exclusive right in itself is not an abuse. However, it made the point that if, in a particular case, the right is exercised in such a way as to pursue an aim manifestly contrary to Article 86, and in particular if it involves evidence of abusive conduct, then the exclusive right cannot be so exercised. The CFI went on to hold that in this case the copyright monopoly enjoyed by the TV companies in the TV listings had been used improperly to prevent the emergence of a new product—the comprehensive weekly

---

[33] See S. Anderman, 'Copyright, Compulsory Licenses and EC Competition Policy' [1995] *Oxford Yearbook of Media Law and Entertainment.*
[34] Para 71 [1991] ECR II–485.

TV guide—for which there was considerable potential consumer demand, and to exclude a competitor in a related market, the market for TV guides.[35] Although the CFI used its own definition of essential function to define the protected core of copyright,[36] it relied on the judgment of the Court of Justice in *Volvo* to justify its decision in *Magill*. It held that, as the Commission had pointed out, the publishers' refusal to authorize on request and on a non-discriminatory basis any third party to publish their programme listings was comparable to an arbitrary refusal by a car manufacturer to supply spare parts, produced in the course of its main activity as a manufacturer of car bodies, to an independent repairer competing in the related market of car maintenance and repair.[37] The Court also thought that the third example in *Volvo* was similar to the TV broadcasters' suppression of the emergence of a comprehensive weekly TV guide because it failed to take consumer demand into account.[38]

14.3.3 The Advocate General's Opinion in *Magill*

RTE and ITP, but not BBC, appealed to the Court of Justice. They were supported by Industrial Property Organization, a US based organization in the IT field.

On appeal, Advocate General Gulman recommended that the Court of Justice should set aside the judgments of the Court of First Instance and annul the decision of the Commission. He began by recalling that 'the aim of copyright is precisely to give the proprietor the possibility of restricting competition and that possibility must also be afforded to a dominant undertaking'.[39] He accepted that Article 86 could apply to regulate and restrict the exercise of an IPR which falls within the specific subject-matter but in such a case, there must be 'such special circumstances in connection with a refusal to license that it can no longer be regarded as a refusal to license in itself'.[40]

His view was that the fact that the refusal to license resulted in the frustration of a new product—the comprehensive TV guide—was not a special circumstance where the new product competed with that of the copyright holder because the right to refuse a licence must be regarded

---

[35] Para 70.

[36] It introduced the concept of 'essential function' of copyright as the method to determine whether the exercise of rights falling within the 'specific subject-matter' is caught by Art. 86. It said that in cases where the copyright was exercised in a manner 'manifestly contrary to the objectives of Article 86 . . . the copyright is no longer exercised in a manner which corresponds to its essential function . . . which is to protect the moral rights in the work and ensure a reward for creative effort while respecting the aims of Article 86'.

[37] See para. 74.

[38] See para. 74.

[39] [1995] ECR I–743 at para 63.

[40] Para. 40.

as necessary to provide a reward for its creative effort, even if its product was inferior to that of its competitors. He said it would only be abusive to refuse to license if the new product did not compete with a product of the copyright holder. Nor did he think that the fact that the product was on a derivative market was a special circumstance justifying the application of Article 86, since it was normal for copyright holders to exploit derivative markets. The Advocate General asserted that:

the contrary is true, in my view, if copyright is used in order to prevent the emergence of a product which is produced by means of the work protected by the copyright and which competes with the products produced by the copyright owner himself. Even if that product is newer and better, the interests of consumers should not in such circumstances justify interference in the specific subject matter of the copyright where the product is one that largely meets the same needs of consumers as the protected product, the interests of the copyright owner carry great weight. Even if the market is limited to the prejudice of consumers, the right to refuse licenses in that situation must be regarded as necessary in order to guarantee the copyright owner the reward for his creative effort.[41]

This distinction raises the difficulty that what is or is not a competing product is not itself wholly unambiguous. Moreover, it ignores the difference between reward based on inventive value and that based on the exercise of market power.

14.3.4 The Judgment of the Court of Justice in *Magill*

The Court of Justice was not persuaded by the Advocate General's version of special circumstances and upheld the decision of the CFI and the Commission on the finding of abuse and the entitlement of the Commission to award a remedy of compulsory licence for a violation of Article 86.

On the issue of abuse, the Court began by emphasizing that it was wrong to presuppose that all forms of exercise of copyright which are legitimate under national law can never be reviewed under Article 86.[42] It reiterated that in the absence of Community harmonization, the determination of the conditions and procedures for granting protection of an IPR are a matter for national rules. It also admitted that the exclusive right of reproduction is part of the author's rights, so a refusal to grant a licence, even by a firm in a dominant position, cannot in itself constitute abuse of a dominant position.[43] Nevertheless, it insisted that in exceptional circumstances, the exercise of such an exclusive right by a proprietor may amount to abusive conduct.[44]

---

[41] [1995] ECR I–743 at para 40.   [42] Ibid., para. 48.
[43] Ibid., para. 49.   [44] Ibid., para. 50.

The Court was prepared to uphold the CFI's finding that 'exceptional circumstances' made the refusal of the TV companies to license the TV listings to Magill abusive conduct on the basis of three circumstances in particular. The first circumstance was that there was no actual or potential substitute for a weekly guide offering comprehensive listings of the programmes for the week ahead, a product for which there was a strong potential consumer demand. This meant that the television companies' refusal to provide basic listings information, for which they were the only source, by relying on their copyright prevented the emergence of a new product, one moreover which they themselves did not offer. The result gave viewers no choice but to buy weekly guides from the three TV companies and was an abuse under Article 86(b), i.e. 'limiting production, markets or technical development to the prejudice of the consumer'.[45] Secondly, the Court found that there was no objective justification for the refusal of the TV companies to license Magill, either in the activity of television broadcasting or in that of publishing television magazines. The implication here is that in the face of a violation of Article 86(b), the mere possession of the IPR is not an objective justification for exclusionary conduct. There must be evidence of some other objective justifying factor such as poor creditworthiness, safety, etc.

The third circumstance was that the TV companies reserved to themselves the secondary market for weekly television guides by excluding all competition on that market, since they denied access to the basic information which was indispensable to the publication of such a guide. Effectively, they used a *de facto* monopoly position on one market, consisting of an essential input or facility, to maintain a monopoly on a secondary, dependent market. This was an abuse of the type prohibited in *Commercial Solvents* v. *Commission*. By approving the holding of the CFI on this point, the Court of Justice has effectively endorsed the basis of the 'essential facilities' doctrine promoted by the Commission, albeit under certain conditions. One precondition was that the facility in the first market was not merely dominant; it was a *de facto* monopoly. Secondly, it must be an indispensable input to the secondary market. There was no alternative source of supply. Thirdly, the direct result of the refusal to make that essential facility available was to maintain a monopoly for the firm on the second market.

Yet the Court's judgment could also be read as suggesting that the abuse consisted of the suppression of a new product in that secondary market, one which the dominant firm was not itself offering, rather than the prevention of all competition for a product it was already offering to the market. This would suggest that the first and the third findings made by the Court may be cumulative rather than separate preconditions and

[45] Ibid., para. 54.

that, as a result, the scope of the decision was fairly circumscribed. Evidence for this interpretation is suggested in paragraph 57 where the Court concludes that in 'the light of all those circumstances the Court of First Instance did not err in law in holding that the appellants' conduct was an abuse of a dominant position within the meaning of Article 86 of the Treaty'.

However, it is also possible to argue that the combination of circumstances in *Magill* presented a stronger case than was necessary upon which to base a finding of abuse. The fact that there was a new product with a proven demand which was not offered by the rightholder was the strongest possible case for insisting upon compulsory supply and by necessity compulsory licence in this case. In another case, where the essential facility owner actually provides the product to a second market, it would be effectively reserving the second market to itself if it did not supply or license competitors in the second market. It might be viewed as discriminatory treatment favouring its own subsidiary. In *Volvo* the IPR owner was entitled to insist on exclusive use of the IPR right, but that was in the market in which the rightholder was dominant. It is difficult to see how the *Volvo* case can prevent a judgment that the use of essential information to underpin a monopoly in a second market is unlawful under Article 86. In the event, it seems quite clear that the logic of the essential facility cases must now be taken on board in monitoring the use of IPRs.[46]

Finally, the Court confirmed that the Commission had the power under Article 3 of Regulation 17 to impose compulsory licensing of an IPR conferred by the member states. The basis for the Court's decision was that the Commission was entitled under Article 3 to require the TV companies to provide the information in order to ensure that its decision was effective. Again the facts of *Magill* were unusual. The imposition of a duty to license, subject to the condition of reasonable royalties, was the only way to bring the infringement to an end.[47] The reason for this was that a simple order to supply the information would not be adequate to allow Magill to publish the information. For that a licence was required. In other cases, it might be enough to order supply on reasonable terms since the principle of proportionality would preclude a compulsory licence remedy in all but the unavoidable cases.

[46] See Anderman, 'Copyright, Compulsory Licenses and EC Competition Policy' [1995] *Oxford Yearbook of Media and Entertainment Law* (OUP). See now *Tierce Ladbroke SA* v. *Commission* Case T–504/93 12 June 1997 (CFI): 'The refusal to supply the applicant could not fall within the prohibition laid down by Article 86 unless it concerned a product or service which was *either* essential *or* was a new product whose introduction might be prevented, despite specific, constant and regular potential demand on the part of customers' (para. 131; emphasis added).   [47] Paras. 90–1.

14.3.5 Some Implications of *Magill*

The immediate consequence of the *Magill* decision is that the Court's endorsement of *Commercial Solvents* will encourage the Commission to continue to apply its essential facilities analysis in cases in which such facilities are shored up or reinforced by the exclusivity of an IPR. Knowledge of this will encourage competitors in their negotiations with rightholders, their complaints to the Commission, and possibly their litigation in member state courts.

Intellectual property lawyers may be tempted, in an effort to question the overriding force of Article 86 over IPRs, to look for arguments to give a more restrictive reading to the decision: the unusual facts; the non-creative nature of the copyright material;[48] the element of discrimination between licensees; or even that the copyright in the programme listings was based on the statutory monopoly of RTE as a broadcasting authority.[49] That temptation should be stoutly resisted. The Court of Justice made it plain that the case was not about differences in the grant of IPRs by member states.[50] More importantly, the reference to *Commercial Solvents* placed the decision in the mainstream of the developing law of 'essential facilities'. There is little doubt that the decision in *Magill* means that Article 86 reaches more widely into the realm of the exercise of IPRs.

The way to give a restrictive reading to the *Magill* decision is to subject its preconditions to a careful examination. One issue is whether or not the Court held that a finding of 'exceptional circumstances' required both that the IPRs had to be linked to essential inputs for secondary markets and that a new product had to be introduced in that market for which there was significant demand which was not met by the rightholder. The Court hints at this when it states in paragraph 57 that in 'the light of all those circumstances, the Court of First Instance did not err in law in holding that the appellant's conduct was an abuse of a dominant position under Article 86 of the Treaty'. If that proves to be the case, Article 86 will apply in a much narrower range of circumstances. If, on the other hand, these circumstances can apply individually, its impact will be felt far more widely. It is possible to read *Magill* as consisting of two separate rules. The first is the new product rule, in paragraphs 53–4; the second is the essential facility rule in paragraph 56.

[48] The CFI hinted at this point, but the ECJ's reiteration of the principle in *Keurkoop* v. *Nancy Kean Gifts* suggested that there was no force in this argument.

[49] See D. Goyder, *EC Competition Law* (2nd edn., 1993) p. 368.

[50] See para. 49: 'in the absence of Community standardization or harmonization of laws, determinination of the conditions and procedures for granting protection of an IPR is a matter for national rules . . .'.

The 'new product' rule suggests that one test of exceptional circumstances is that if an IPR owner owns an indispensable raw material for a new product with clear consumer demand and (a) that raw material is a *de facto* monopoly, i.e. there are no existing or potential substitutes for it, (b) it uses it without objective justification to prevent the emergence of that new product, (c) which it does not offer itself, then the refusal to supply or license the raw material could be an abuse of a dominant position. The interest protected by this abuse is apparently consumer demand.

In such a case, the limiting conditions are (a), (b), and (c) cumulatively. For example if, as has been suggested,[51] a firm owns a unique biotechnology invention which it uses to cure clinical obesity but refrains from offering it as a general slimming drug, can another firm use this first holding of *Magill* as a springboard for compulsory access? It may be argued that the decision to limit the technical field of application is part of the company's commercial strategy of exploitation, but the logic of competition law suggests that the better argument is that one of the three conditions are not met, i.e. either there are substitutes for the raw material or there are safety reasons for not releasing it for general consumption as a slimming pill.

Similarly, if the second test of *Magill*, the 'essential facility' test, is to offer a separate test of abuse, there must be a showing of (a) a firm who owns an indispensable raw material for a secondary market; (b) a *de facto* monopoly; (c) the effect of the refusal is to enable the IPR holder to reserve for itself that secondary market by excluding all competition on it. Inevitably, there will be difficulties in establishing how these guidelines apply to specific fields such as computer software, telecommunications, and other media industries, in which copyright is conferred on information as opposed to artistic or literary work. How does one identify secondary markets which require licensing to competitors at different stages of product development?[52] How can one distinguish between improvements and completely new products? Again, the answers will depend upon an understanding of the logic of competition law as it applies to the particular field.

For example, in the field of IT law, in cases of products which are industry standards, particularly software operating systems, the principles applied in the *IBM* case in the 1980s and the *Microsoft* case in the 1990s are likely to be applied to rights of access to information about interfaces to other secondary products such as software applications,

---

[51] See Susan Singleton, *Legal Times*, 2 May 1995.

[52] See *Tetra Pak II*, discussed in V. Korah, 'The Paucity of Economic Analysis in the EEC Decisions on Competition'—Tetra Pak II [1994] *Current Legal Problems* 148.

peripherals, and hardware. The effect of the *Magill* decision will be to reinforce the interoperability obligations under the EC Computer Program Directive,[53] particularly where the essential facility owner is itself operating in the second market.

In addition, where a dominant firm owning an indispensable industry standard decides at some point to vertically integrate into a secondary market, there will be an obligation towards other firms already working in that market on the basis of licences, and there may be an obligation to license new entrants with competing products. The principles of *Commercial Solvents*, as affirmed in *Magill*, will apply to place limits upon the dominant firm's use of its licensing power to foreclose or exclude competitors from such secondary markets.

What remains unclear after the decision, however, is when a product will be viewed as an essential input or facility for another product or market as opposed to being simply part of another product. Take, for example, a firm with a hardware product which has a major share of a market. As part of its product package it provides an application in the form of diagnostic software for maintenance purposes which is then used exclusively by its own maintenance contractors. Are the diagnostic software and the hardware to be viewed as integral parts of the same 'product'? Or, is the diagnostic software to be viewed as a separate product constituting an essential input for the maintenance 'market' for the hardware? If the latter is the case, would the undertaking be required to license it to competing third party maintenance companies even where it offers maintenance contracts along with the sale of its hardware package?

Of course, if it had already allowed third party maintenance firms to enter the market and license its diagnostic software and then suddenly stopped licensing in order to vertically integrate into the maintenance market, that would probably be caught by Article 86 under the reasoning in *Commercial Solvents*. If, however, it has all along viewed its investment in the diagnostic software as part of its programme to exploit the value of its innovative hardware and insists on retaining exclusive rights to use it in the secondary market, will that be viewed as a normal exercise of IPRs?[54]

The obvious difference with the facts of *Magill* is that consumers are in fact being supplied by the IPR holder with the product. The charge

---

[53] Vinje has argued moreover that the provision in the EC Software Directive's (91/250) Recital 27, that Art. 86 may still apply 'if a dominant supplier refuses to make information available which is necessary for interoperability', could apply to strengthen the hands of competitors' rights under Art. 6 where access to interface information is not complete as a result of reverse engineering or decompilation. See T. Vinje, 'Comment: The Final Word on Magill' [1995] 6 *EIPR* 297 at 302.

[54] It cannot be viewed as a tie-in under Art. 86(d). It does not require customers to use it as a condition of buying the hardware; it simply makes it available exclusively with its own maintenance service.

cannot be levied under Article 86(b). To win, the third party maintenance companies will have to succeed with two arguments. First, they must show that the diagnostic software is both indispensable to their entry into the maintenance market for that product and that there are no substitutes, i.e. that the diagnostic software is itself an 'essential' input for the maintenance market requiring the firm to license it even to competitors. Secondly, they will have to show that the hardware company is discriminating between its own company in the maintenance market and the new entrant, with a view to excluding all competition. In such a case, they would succeed if a court would be prepared to find that the second test of *Magill* can be applied independently of the first. This interpretation of the case should not be altogether excluded.[55] These issues of abuse which arise in the post-product market can arise at different stages of production prior to the final product phase in cases of novel software as well as to other industries such as telecommunications, as the Commission has already acknowledged.[56]

If the guidelines to conduct after *Magill* may be unclear on this point, the case is clear that the principles from which they must be derived require a deep understanding of Article 86. Two lines of guidance are provided by the decision. First, if an intellectual property rightholder has a dominant position by virtue of the IPR, its exercise of the IPR is limited by the prohibitions in Article 86 (a), (c) and (d) as well as (b).[57] Secondly, if the intellectual property rightholder has a dominant position in the form of an essential facility it will have certain positive duties towards competitors which may be inconsistent with the full exclusive exploitation of the IPR in a downstream market. These principles will not normally impinge on the exercise of the exclusivity of IPRs in primary markets and even secondary markets, but there will be cases of dependence and exclusionary refusals to supply or license which will be found to be abusive under Article 86 and thereby place constraints on the exclusive exploitation of IPRs, particularly in secondary markets.

14.4 THE PRICING OF COMPULSORY LICENSING

A further implication of *Magill's* acceptance of the prospect of compulsory licence and compulsory access to markets is that it raises the issue of

---

[55] See e.g. *Tierce Ladbroke SA* v. *Commission* op. cit. n. 46.

[56] See Vinje, n. 53 above at p. 303.

[57] For example, following the third exception in *Volvo* there may be an obligation under Art. 86 to continue to produce spares to allow maintenance of an outdated technical product even if the dominant undertaking would like to shift all consumer demand to a new upgraded product.

how the required access is to be priced. In *Magill* the Court approved the Commission's decision to order a licence on terms which were 'reasonable' and 'non-discriminatory', but it gave little indication how these concepts were to be defined. This standard appears to be used by the Commission more generally in its regulation of access in the telecommunications sphere.[58]

Broadly, it is necessary to distinguish between the issue of excessive pricing under Article 86(a) and the formula of reasonable and non-discriminatory pricing in the case of compulsory access or licence under Article 86(b). In the case of Article 86(a), it is necessary to avoid pricing which is so extremely high, and can be shown to be so, that it is outside the range of permissible pricing even in a free market context. At its most extreme, it could be set so high as to amount in practice to a refusal to supply or trade. The important point is that Article 86(a) is not meant to put the courts or Commission in the position of being an industrial regulator. It presupposes a wide range of 'fair' prices and is meant to step in only in the extreme case when a price is set which no fair dominant undertaking would set. That room for high pricing includes considerable space for a dominant undertaking with an IPR to obtain an extensive reward for innovation.

In contrast, to set fee levels under the formula of reasonable and non-discriminatory pricing of compulsory access in a two market situation, where those markets are vertically integrated, requires the courts and Commission to attempt to approximate a regulator's task. In the *Magill* case itself the issue was eventually referred to a Copyright Tribunal set up under the Broadcasting Act 1992 to determine fees in cases of disputes between the parties. In other cases, there will be a need for regulatory principles to be applied to determine the issue of 'reasonable' royalties.

The starting-point in most cases is that the essential facility owner, whether or not an IPR is involved, is often engaged in some capacity in the downstream market. The first element in a reasonableness test of pricing in the second market must be to separate the proprietor of the essential infrastructure from the downstream operation in any calculation of its costs so as to ensure that there are no hidden cross-subsidies or discrimination. Insofar as there are two or more organizations under common ownership or control, there are bound to be shared costs and some method must be devised to ensure that these common costs are properly allocated to the relevant operation.[59] This will require a method

---

[58] See e.g. the Commission's Guidelines on the Application of EEC Competition Rules in the Telecommunications Sector, 91/C 233/02 [1991] OJ C233/2.

[59] Economists might prefer to use concepts such as incremental and stand-alone costs.

of regulating the internal 'transfer pricing' of the two organizations. It might help if two separate sets of books are kept, but there may be a need for a system of imputing costs to ensure that even separate books accurately reflect the division of costs between the two operations.

At the same time, it must be recognized that compulsory access allows in effect a sharing of an asset, whether the asset is material such as a gas line, port or railway track or telephone line, or an IPR embedded in a product or process, such as a digital transmitter or software. In either case, therefore, some compensation must be given for the costs to the owner of creating and maintaining the shared asset.

In the intellectual property licensing context, it is worth recalling the words of Advocate General Mischo in *Maxicar*, that 'the proprietor of protective rights may lawfully call for a return on the amounts he has invested in order to perfect the protected design'.[60]

This suggests that a reasonable fee would be set at a higher level than the access costs and the incremental costs of adding the compulsory licensee. The fee must include provision for an additional element to compensate for the costs of originating and maintaining the infrastructure. In the context of compulsory licensing, a licensing fee set too low could have the effect of allowing compulsory access to create an institutionalized form of 'free riding'. This would act as an even greater deterrent to investment in innovation than the fact of a compulsory licence itself.

On the other hand, the terms of a compulsory licence are not meant to compensate an IPR owner for the full appropriation value of the right in the second market. An important reason for regulating the exercise of the essential infrastructure in a downstream market is to ensure that price levels approximate those of a market with workable competition rather than monopoly. If one allowed monopoly prices in both markets, this would defeat the object of the exercise. Moreover, in the licensing context, there may be a case for taking into account the reward to the manufacturer of an upstream product in the calculation of a reasonable return in a downstream market. For example, in *Maxicar*, Advocate General Mischo made the point that, when fixing the price of bodywork components sold as spare parts, due account should be taken of the fact that the manufacturers have already recovered part of the expenditure on perfecting the protected design.[61] It would be wrong in principle to adopt a standard based on compensation for loss of profits based on sales of licensed products[62] since this would approximate monopoly

---

[60] [1988] ECR 6039 at para. 17.   [61] Ibid. at paras. 17 and 63.

[62] This is the usual measure of damages for patent infringement which presupposes a return based on enforcement of the IPR 'monopoly' return. See e.g. *Catnic Components Ltd. and another* v. *Hill & Smith Ltd.* [1983] FSR 512 (Ch. Patents Ct.).

conditions for the intellectual property rightholder in the downstream market.

What basis can be used to calculate a reasonable royalty in such cases? In principle the approach must be cost based with an element added on to compensate for a proportionate return on investment. A short cut could be available where the proprietor of the essential infrastructure has already set a royalty in the downstream market. This would represent its view of the part of the investment costs which should be returned along with the payment for the extra costs of the licensing process. Although this figure would have to be adjusted to take into account the state of competition on the licensee market, it represents a potential benchmark.

There is still the major problem of assessing the appropriate return either to compare with the existing royalty or where there is no existing royalty set. The Court or Commission has to construct a basis for approximating a reasonable royalty in a workably competitive market. In the telecoms sector, an issue has arisen over whether the loss of market caused by the undertakings who have received compulsory access should be added to the 'reasonable return' to an essential infrastructure holder. In *Telecom Corporation of New Zealand* v. *Clear Communication Ltd.*,[63] the Privy council appeared to have been persuaded that the application of the 'Baumol-Willig rule' or 'efficient component pricing rule' could allow the inclusion of opportunity costs (i.e. lost profit) as the basis of calculating a fair return to the monopoly provider of telecoms infrastructure when interconnecting other network operators.

The basis of the Baumol-Willig rule is the claim that the efficient component pricing rule is a necessary condition for efficiency and competitive neutrality in the provision of access to essential facilities. Only the efficient component pricing rule gives neither the owner nor its rivals a competitive advantage aside from any derived from superior efficiency. It is a test of discrimination that a reasonable price can be calculated in a perfectly contestable market to include opportunity costs, the sacrifice of profit entailed in supplying access to the essential facility to another firm instead of carrying out the operation itself.

In the New Zealand Telecoms case, the issue raised was the application of the Baumol-Willig rule of parity pricing under section 36 of the New Zealand Commerce Act which *inter alia* prohibits the use of a dominant position to (b) prevent or deter any person from engaging in competitive conduct on that or any other market.

The High Court held that the application of the Baumol-Willig rule as the basis of New Zealand Telecoms pricing was not a breach of section 36

---

[63] [1995] 1 NZLR 385.

because despite the risks of monopoly rents initially it was a method which was likely to improve efficient competition rather than prevent or deter it.

The New Zealand Court of Appeal was more concerned about the risks of following the Baumol-Willig rule under section 36. Gault J was deeply sceptical about the inclusion of opportunity costs in the price demanded by a firm controlling an essential service in a perfectly contestable market. If that meant that the price charged could include monopoly rents for the firm in the dependent market, he doubted the validity of the model. He could 'not accept that the objects of the Commerce Act are served by a method of pricing that secures the profits of a firm in a dominant position'. Cooke J agreed with Gault but added that if the principle in Baumol-Willig was to set a price which made the supplier indifferent as to whether the other components of the final product are provided by itself or others, then the principle was anticompetitive because it would 'amount to allowing a new entry into a market on condition only that the competitor indemnify the monopolist against any loss of custom'.

The Privy Council, in a judgment delivered by Lord Browne-Wilkinson, held that the terms for interconnection set by Telecom did not contravene Article 36 of the the New Zealand Commerce Act. With the pricing based on the Baumol-Willig rule, Telecom could not be shown to have used its dominant position, as was required of the New Zealand Act, for the purpose of preventing or deterring competition from the competing service operator.

Underlying the Privy Council's decision, however, was its acceptance of the finding that section 36 did not have as its purpose the elimination of monopoly profits obtained by the dominant market position as such. This was the target of the price control provisions of Part IV of the Act and not section 36. In effect, as long as the pricing was comparable between the different service operators, including Telecom's subsidiary, the Privy Council accepted that it was not contrary to section 36; it accepted Baumol's evidence that the efficient component pricing rule was not designed to decide if there were monopoly rents in the original pricing of the dominant market position, but only if the pricing was unfair as between existing service operators.

Insofar as the efficient component pricing rule is aimed at non-discriminatory competition and does not preclude monopoly rents, it appears to be only partly relevant for the purposes of assessing the level of reasonable terms for compulsory access under Article 86(b) and analogous regulatory legislation. As we have seen, the purpose of the reasonableness test is to attempt to create charges in a related market which are both non-discriminatory and set at a reasonable level when that market is dependent upon an essential facility. This requires a method of assessing prices which is cost based but includes a return for the investment in the asset which is compulsorily 'shared'.

A more relevant model from the telecoms field is offered by the new Guidelines issued by OFTEL in the UK on The Regulation of Conditional Access for Digital Television Services.[64] These Guidelines offer a discussion of the pricing issues raised by the obligation to offer technical conditional access services on a fair, reasonable, and non-discriminatory basis. The Guidelines distinguish between a fair and reasonable element and a non-discriminatory element. The latter is primarily concerned with the comparison of prices offered to different organizations for the same or similar services. Fair and reasonable prices are primarily concerned with the relationship between prices and the costs involved in providing the services. The starting-point for the Guidelines is that the costs of each service should be calculated separately on an incremental basis. Consequently, any specific cost associated with technical conditional access services which is identifiable, measurable, and attributable to the activities of specific broadcasters must form the base for the price of or charges for the provision of services to those broadcasters.

In addition, where there are common costs not directly attributable to any individual set of activities, it suggests several methods of allocation, all subject to the requirement that the provider of common services must choose a method which is independent of any interests as a broadcaster (downstream operator).

It is in its treatment of fixed costs that the Guidelines suggest a useful method of calculating reasonable prices. It proposes that account should be taken of the position *ex ante* when the investment was made in the shared service. The Guidelines state:

A related issue is the impact the uncertainty of demand for conditional access services has on the actual costs of provision of units of conditional access service. Many of the costs of setting up the infrastructure ... might be fixed irrespective of the use that is subsequently made of those services. ... Variations in the level of demand are likely to have a significant impact on the unit costs. OFTEL considers that it would be appropriate to take into account the risk that predictions of demand may turn out to be wrong (in either direction). [A72]

Its treatment of the costs of capital takes a similar *ex ante* approach. In assessing the fairness or otherwise of the pricing of services, OFTEL will need to take into account the cost of capital 'and' the possibility that any

---

[64] These are contained in Statement issued by the Director-General in Mar. 1997.

investment may fail to make a return at all. It also uses a methodology for evaluating the appropriate cost of capital (A79).[65]

The Guidelines also make allowance for the timing of the recovery of costs including front loading and variability. OFTEL uses a calculation of 'net present value' which takes into account the prices charged over the project period (A 73–5). Finally, there is a check on input costs to ensure that these are not excessive. The method used is to give particular attention to the allocation of common costs between related companies and the licensee as well as the transfer prices of inputs from associated companies (A76). In cases of monopoly suppliers, for example because it is the only supplier with an IPR, then an external evaluation is made (A77).

---

[65] The appropriate cost of capital would be calculated with reference to e.g. the risk-free rate of return; the level of systemic risk incurred by investors in the conditional access business, the returns available from comparable investments; the debt-equity ratio. See para. A79.

15

Tie-ins and Intellectual Property Rights

A tie-in is a commercial practice of bundling two or more products into an integrated product so that a buyer must buy other products in order to obtain the one it wants. It is defined in Article 86(d) as 'making the conclusion of contracts subject to acceptance by the other parties of supplementary obligations which, by their nature or according to commercial usage, have no connection with the subject of such contracts'.[1] In the Article 86 context it is abusive because it excludes competitors as well as limits the freedom of choice of customers. Insofar as it applies to exclusionary methods, the abuse has been defined quite widely. It overlaps conceptually with the abuse of refusing to supply and discrimination.

The tie-in as an exclusionary tactic was present in the *Commercial Solvents* and *Télémarketing* cases. In both cases, the decision of the dominant undertaking to enter a related market was accompanied by a practice which tied the service in the second market to the indispensable service or good in the primary market. In the Commission's settlement with IBM in 1984, Article 86(d) was used as part of the regulatory framework which resulted in IBM agreeing to discontinue its practice of 'bundling' its main memory function with the sale of its System 370 Central Processing Units, by including the price of its main memory function in the price of its CPU and refusing to supply the CPU separately.[2]

In the subsequent case of *Hilti*,[3] the Commission responded to a complaint by Eurofix-Bauco that Hilti was tying the sale of its cartridge strips to sale of its nails. The Commission found that Hilti was reinforcing the tie-in by a practice of charging excessively high royalties to deter independent nail manufacturers from obtaining licences of right in the cartridge strips. The Commission found that these and other practices were abusive because they prevented or limited the entry of independent producers into those markets, and levied a fine of six million ECUs.

---

[1] The conclusion of such a contractual obligation is also viewed as a restriction of competition under Art. 85(1)(c) and is applicable to the terms of patent licences.
[2] There was also an issue of implicit tying of software by IBM's practice of refusing to disclose interface information. See Refusal to Supply, ch. 14 *supra*. See D. Goyder, *EC Competition Law* (2nd edn.) pp. 364–5; see too Microsoft Undertaking to the EC Commission. op cit p. 175.   [3] *Hilti* v. *Commission* [1994] ECR I–667.

Hilti appealed to the Court of First Instance on the grounds that the cartridge strip, nails, and gun were an integrated product, a power activated fastening system, and that they were not separate product markets. The CFI rejected Hilti's arguments and upheld the Commission's view that there were three separate markets and that Hilti was dominant on the cartridge market. It accepted the existence of independent nail manufacturers as evidence of a separate market and went on to state that, 'in the absence of general and binding standards and rules, any independent producer is quite free, as far as Community competition law is concerned, to manufacture consumables intended for use in equipment manufactured by others, unless in doing so it infringes a patent or some other industrial or intellectual property right' (paragraph 68). The fact that Hilti had a patent on the cartridge strip and not on the nails was regarded as the major consideration in the finding that attempts to exclude others from the Hilti-compatible nail market were abusive. Effectively Article 86(d) was to be used to prevent Hilti from extending the scope of its exclusive exploitation rights beyond the patented product to unpatented products.

The definition of relevant product markets appeared to reinforce that decision because it separated the patented and the unpatented goods into separate markets. It also provided the foundation for the finding of dominance. In principle, Article 86(d) could still apply to attempts to bundle patented and unpatented goods in the same product market unless such a tie-in was objectively necessary or had 'a connection with the subject of such contracts'.

In *Hilti*, the dominant firm's argument that safety considerations objectively necessitated the bundling was given short shrift by the CFI. It stated that considerations of product safety which were enforced by other laws and public bodies could not override Community rules on competition. It was 'clearly not the task of an undertaking in a dominant position to take steps on its own initiative to eliminate products which, rightly or wrongly, it regards as dangerous or at least inferior in quality to its own products' (paragraphs 118–19).

In *Tetra Pak II*,[4] the Commission found that the practice of tying the sale of machines for the sterilization and filling of aseptic liquid food cartons to the purchase of the cartons, the maintenance of the machines, and the purchase of spare parts was abusive in a situation where it was part of a deliberate strategy of excluding existing competitors in the carton manufacturing market, maintenance and spare parts markets. The company gave undertakings to the Commission that it would no longer

---

[4] *Tetra Pak* v. *Commission* [1997] CMLR 602.

tie spare parts and maintenance services to the sale of the machines. However, it chose to contest the Commission's findings that the tie-in between the machines and the cartons was abusive. Its appeals to the CFI and later to the Court of Justice were based on the ground that there was a natural link between the two products and that their integration was in accordance with commercial usage and Article 86(d) presupposed no link between the additional services and the subject-matter of the contracts (paragraph 34 ECJ).

The CFI rejected the argument that commercial usage supported the conclusion that the machinery for packaging a product was indivisible from its cartons in a situation where 'for a considerable time there have been independent manufacturers who specialize in the manufacture of non-aseptic cartons designed for use in machines manufactured by other concerns, and who do not manufacture machinery themselves' (paragraph 82 CFI). Its judgment did not rule out the legitimacy of the defence as such but only its application to the facts of *Tetra Pak*.

In respect of the aseptic carton market, the CFI found that 'any independent producer is quite free, as far as Community competition law is concerned, to manufacture consumables intended for use in equipment managed by others, unless in so doing it infringes a competitor's intellectual property right' (paragraph 83). This reiterated the Court's view that the fact that an intellectual property right protected a particular product was a necessary condition for an entitlement to exclusive rights of manufacture and sale. If sales of a protected product—the machines—were tied to sales of an unprotected product—the cartons—there would be an abuse because of the exclusionary and exploitive effects unless there could be an objective justification.

The CFI also rejected the second ground for the company's appeal, that there was an objective justification for their linkage based on concern with the hygiene standards of other producers. It noted, paragraph 138, that it was not for Tetra Pak to impose measures on its own initiative on the basis of technical considerations, product liability, protection of public health or its own reputation. The CFI concluded that Tetra Pak was not alone in being able to manufacture cartons for its machines. On appeal, the Court of Justice endorsed the judgment of the CFI on these issues. However, it insisted on a residual regulatory role for Article 86(d) and tied sales even where there was evidence of a natural link between the two products or where tied sales were in accordance with commercial usage: 'such sales may still constitute abuse within the meaning of Article 86 unless they are objectively justified' (paragraph 37 ECJ).

16

Excessive Pricing and Intellectual Property Rights

16.1 INTRODUCTION

Under Article 86(a), a dominant firm is prohibited 'directly or indirectly imposing unfair purchase or selling prices or other unfair trading conditions.' From an early stage, the Court of Justice has held that in principle, a particularly high price, unjustified by any objective criteria, may be an abuse of a dominant position.[1] The Court at one stage described the abuse as attempting to reap trading benefits which are higher than an undertaking would have reaped if there had been normal and sufficiently effective competition in the market.[2]

At first glance, this appears to call into question the entitlement of an intellectual property rightholder to a just reward for originating the intellectual property right (IPR) because of the effect on competition of the exclusive right. As economists have often pointed out, the ability to charge higher than competitive prices for a protected product, and to restrict competition, is 'the very essence of patents'.[3] The regulation of the pricing of IPRs therefore places Article 86(a) right at the heart of the patent-antitrust interface.

The Court of Justice has accepted that there is considerable room for a high return on IPRs based on the amounts which rightholders have invested in order to perfect the protected right.[4] It has never said, however, that under Article 86 rightholders in a dominant position can recoup the full value to which they would be entitled if the commercial exploitation of the IPR were regulated solely under national law. How in practice can the requirement of a fair price and a lawful return under Article 86(a) be reconciled with the concept of just reward under IPRs? To answer this requires three steps. First, we must look at how Article 86(a) has been interpreted generally. Second, we shall examine how that

---

[1] See *Sirena* v. *Eda* [1971] ECR 3169.

[2] *United Brands* v. *Commission* [1978] ECR 207 at para. 249.

[3] See e.g. F. Machlup, 'An Economic Review of the Patent System, Study of the Committee on Patents, Trademarks and Copyright', Senate Judiciary Committee, US 85th Congress, Study no. 15, Washington, DC 1958 at p.12.

[4] *Parke Davis* v. *Probel* [1968] ECR 55.

interpretation applies to IPRs. In the course of this second step we shall look at how Article 86(a) applies differently depending on whether the pricing of the IPR occurs in a single market or in two related markets.

16.2 ARTICLE 86(A) GENERALLY

In *General Motors*, the Court gave an initial definition of abusive pricing under Article 86(a) by stating that when a charge for inspecting vehicles imported by parallel importers from other member states was 'excessive in relation to the economic value of the service provided', it could constitute an abuse.[5] *British Leyland* v. *Commission*,[6] decided a year later, offered a good example of how Article 86(a) can result in a finding of excessive charges. In that case, British Leyland had sole authority under British law to issue certificates of conformity for traders of left-hand drive Metros wanting access to the British market. After a period of charging a single fee of £25 for both right- and left-hand drive vehicles, it raised its fee for left-hand vehicles to £150. The Court found that British Leyland had abused its dominant position in respect of the supply of certificates of conformity by refusing to approve certificates and by charging excessive fees.

British Leyland illustrates two important points about Article 86(a): first, the charge of excessive prices may be proved by evidence of the dominant undertaking's own previous pricing conduct, particularly when the discrepancy is so great. Secondly, excessive pricing under Article 86(a) could be abusive because of its exclusionary effects, where it is linked to a policy of discouraging competitors by refusing to approve.

In *United Brands* v. *Commission*,[7] the Court restated the definition of Article 86(a) in *General Motors*, amending it only slightly to, 'charging a price which is excessive because it had no reasonable relation to the economic value of the product supplied'.[8] It also emphasized the importance of making this assessment on the basis of an analysis of production costs. The method to be used to make an objective determination of whether the sales price exceeded the economic value of a product was to compare sales prices with production costs to determine the profit margin. If that difference appeared excessive, the next step was to decide 'whether a price has been imposed which is unfair itself . . .'. Alternatively, a test of unfairness could consist of a comparison of product prices with the selling

---

[5] *General Motors Continental* v. *Commission* [1976] ECR 1367 at 1379.
[6] [1986] ECR 3263.   [7] [1978] ECR 207.
[8] Ibid. at p.301.

prices of 'competing products'.[9] It could also include a comparison of its own costs in a different market, although this meant that careful consideration had to be given to the cost structures and other conditions in the local markets which could influence profit margins.[10]

While in *United Brands*, the Court overturned the Commission's finding of excessive prices based on the comparative prices test, it did not reject the comparative price method as such. It merely insisted that if a comparison of prices was to be used, it should be based on adequate evidence that the lower prices actually covered costs.[11] To the extent that the Court accepted the need for price comparisons as supplementary tests to an analysis of the price/cost on its own, it acknowledged the problems the Commission faced in implementing Article 86(a) by looking solely at the cost structure and price levels of any one firm. The Court recognized that there were difficulties entailed in:

working out production costs which may sometimes include a discretionary apportionment of interest costs and general expenditure and which may vary significantly according to the size of the undertaking, its object, the complex nature of its set up, its territorial area of operations, whether it manufactures one of several products, the number of its subsidiaries and their relationship with each other.[12]

Yet it may have underestimated the complications inherent in a cost based assessment of 'economic value'.[13]

In *SACEM II*,[14] an Article 177 reference from the French Court ten years later, the complications of such an assessment were made clearer. The Court of Justice found that the royalties charged by the French copyright-management society were abusive under Article 86. On this occasion, the

---

⁹ [1978] ECR 207, p. 301.

¹⁰ Siragusa points out that these factors are also relevant to the analysis of discriminatory pricing under Art. 86(a). See M. Siragusa, 'The application of Article 86 to the Pricing Policies of Dominant Companies: Discriminatory and Unfair Prices' (1979) 16 *CMLRev.* 179, at 188.

¹¹ Op. cit. n. 7. In *United Brands*, the Commission had found that United Brands had charged excessive prices based on a comparison of the price in Ireland with that in other countries. This was the 'comparative cost' method borrowed from German jurisprudence. The Commission had found that the price in Belgium was 80% higher than in Ireland and ordered United Brands to reduce its prices wherever they were higher than the Irish baseline. The Court of Justice rejected the Commission's finding of excessive prices because of the failure of the Commission to refute United Brands' contention that the Irish price was making a loss and therefore constituted a false base.

¹² [1978] ECR 207 at 302.

¹³ Siragusa has pointed out, 'the cost of production is not necessarily a sure indication of the economic value of the product' (op. cit. n. 10 at p. 187). On the other hand, economic value could be the Court's shorthand for a price which reflects the market clearing price on a workably competitive market, in which case it could according to economic microtheory be closely cost related.

¹⁴ *Ministère Public* v. *Tournier* and *Lucazeau* v. *SACEM* [1991] 4 CMLR 248.

Court introduced a more sophisticated version of the test of excessive pricing by indicating that where there was a cost based justification for a particular price, there must be some indication that the costs were not themselves inflated by the inefficiencies of the dominant firm. Again, this test makes a valid conceptual point but it also creates doubts about its practical application. One doubt concerns the capability of the Commission or Courts to evaluate evidence that the dominant firm was acting inefficiently and pricing inequitably.

The contrast with US practice under the Sherman Act is instructive here. Under US antitrust law, it is recognized that the regulation of pricing is so demanding an exercise that it requires the establishment of a specific regulatory commission.[15] In interpreting Article 86(a) to involve hands-on regulation of excessive pricing[16] the Court may have underestimated the handicap of not having dedicated regulatory institutions to carry out the type of sophisticated analysis of prices and costs which is needed in most cases to substantiate a charge of excessive prices.

Secondly, it is implicit in the evaluation of efficiency in an assessment of excessive pricing that the Commission and Court must define the legitimate rewards to firms whose growth has come about through greater efficiency and reduced production costs. If the gap between costs and prices is used as the yardstick, there is the possibility that the more efficient firms could be penalized by the regulatory standard. One problem here is that the test appears to make little allowance for the way the dominant position was acquired.[17] If a firm achieves dominance through efficiencies and maintains that dominance through continued internally generated efficiencies, it could nevertheless be penalized for its pricing decisions as excessive and exploitive. One would expect the defence of legitimate competition by performance to apply to such a position should it ever arise in practice.[18]

Analogous problems arise where the dominance of the undertaking has arisen as a result of innovation protected by IPRs. To what extent in principle does the concept of competition by performance apply to the just reward for IPR exploitation?

---

[15] As Fox has described it 'American law rests on the principle that price should be controlled by the free market unless Congress has in effect determined that the market cannot work and has established a regulatory commission.' E. Fox, 'Monopolization and Dominance in the United States and the European Community: Efficiency, Opportunity, and Fairness' (1986) 61 *Notre Dame L Rev.* 981 at 993.

[16] EC law rejects the concept of US antitrust policy which holds that if a firm attains monopoly on its competitive merits and prices at monopoly levels, the high price itself will invite new entry and market forces would gradually wear away the monopoly power. See T. Kauper, 'Article 86, Excessive Prices and Refusals to Deal, Vol. 59 *Antitrust Law Journal* 441 [1991]. [17] Ibid. at 449.

[18] See discussion ch. 13.

The difficulties of measuring unfair pricing in general under Article 86(a) are intensified when an assessment must be made of a fair return to innovators exploiting their IPRs under Article 86(a). In *Parke Davis*, the Court held that a higher sale price for a patented product as compared with that of an unpatented product . . . does not necessarily constitute an abuse.[19] This indicated that in principle the concept of a higher than competitive return being a fair return where intellectual property is concerned is partly based on an acceptance of the costs of innovation, including the need to reward the individual firm for its investment in research and development.[20] As the Court noted in *Maxicar*, the higher price for components sold by the manufacturer as compared to those sold by the independent producers 'does not necessarily constitute an abuse, since the proprietor of protective rights in respect of an ornamental design may lawfully call for a return on the amounts which he has invested in order to perfect the protected design'.[21]

This case also gave some indication that the principle of a return on amounts invested does not necessarily embody a narrow cost-plus approach. In *Maxicar*, Advocate General Mischo stated that 'the inventor is entitled to recover not only his production costs in the strict sense and a reasonable profit margin but also his research and development expenditure'.[22] Moreover, as Korah has pointed out, 'the concept of costs can be reconciled with providing incentives to investment provided that factors for the risk of failure and delay in obtaining a return are included in the costs that can be recovered before prices are considered unreasonable'.[23]

Furthermore, the principle of return on amounts invested allows some flexibility in assessing a fair return for different types of IPRs. For example, R&D costs are particularly applicable to IPRs such as design rights and patents and perhaps informational copyright.[24] In the case of other rights such as trade marks, the costs can include the expense involved in promotion, advertising, and systems of quality control.[25] There is room to develop a separate type of calculation under Article 86(a) depending upon the particular character of the IPR.

---

[19] [1968] ECR 55 at p. 73. [20] Ibid. at p. 90.
[21] [1988] ECR 6039 para. 17. [22] Ibid.
[23] V. Korah 'No Duty to License Independent Repairers to Make Spare Parts: The Renault, Volvo and Bayer Henneke Cases' (1988) *EIPR* 381 at 383.
[24] See e.g. I. Govaere, *The Use and Abuse of Intellectual Property Rights in EC Law* (London, Sweet & Maxwell, 1996) ch. 2.
[25] See G. Tritton, *Intellectual Property in Europe* (Sweet & Maxwell, 1995).

Nevertheless, the concept of fair pricing as based on a fair return on costs under Article 86(a) does not give full recognition to the reward function of the grant of the IPR. Even though the Court has recognized that charging a higher than competitive price is legitimate competition by performance, this does not go so far as to allow rightholders to appropriate the full value of their IPR as that value is conceived under national law. The argument for a high return on products or processes protected by IPRs is that the return is not simply a reward to the individual inventor; it is also designed to act as an incentive for other inventors or originators to invest in innovation. Machlup has described this as the monopoly-profit-incentive theory of patent protection, emphasizing its incentive for innovation.[26] It also includes an element to compensate for the failures of other efforts at commercial exploitation.[27]

From an intellectual property point of view, this incentive function of 'just reward' results in a figure which is established by what consumers and customers are willing to pay for the added value the IPR confers on a product compared with another product which does not incorporate that right, in other words what the market will bear. As Friden has pointed out:

It represents not the possibility to charge reasonable prices and obtain reasonable profits but rather the possibility, for the holder of an exclusive right, to charge whatever the market will pay, one of the main justifications being the need to give the innovator an incentive to bear the risk of innovation which he might refuse to do if only promised a reasonable profit.[28]

Moreover, economists have made the point that the methodological difficulties of measuring what is a reasonable or unreasonable reward are so great that it is best left to a regulation of the duration of the period of the grant of the exclusive right.

Machlup has suggested that:

Since it is the very essence of patents to restrict competition and permit output to be kept below, and price above, competitive levels, it is difficult to conceive economic criteria by which one could judge whether output is less than reasonably 'practicable' and price is 'unreasonably high'.[29]

Nevertheless, the Court has not been willing to stretch the logic of Article 86(a) to entitle the rightholder to charge what the market can bear during the period of the patent or design right. The reason for this is that

---

[26] See discussion by Govaere, op. cit. n. 24 at p. 19.

[27] See e.g. V. Korah, *EC Competition Law and Practice* (5th edn.) at p. 99.

[28] G. Friden, 'Recent developments in EEC Intellectual Property Law: The Distinction Between Existence and Exercise Revisited' [1989] 26 *CMLRev*. 193 at 211.

[29] See Machlup, op. cit. n. 3 at p. 12.

Article 86(a) requires a differentiation between dominant and non-dominant undertakings, including undertakings whose position coincides with, or is reinforced by, ownership of an IPR. In case of non-dominant firms they can charge what the market will bear. However, those in a dominant position are entitled only to fair return, not an excessive one.[30] EC competition law appears to take the position that the 'just reward' for the exclusive right is not the standard to be applied to the rightholder with the market power of dominance. Although competition law accepts that an exclusive right is not automatically a dominant position, it can require a modification of the exploitive possibilities of a rightholder when in a dominant position.

It can be argued that where the right owner is merely seeking to appropriate the full value of its intellectual property, i.e. by charging prices as high as the market can afford, this is no more than the economic corollary of the 'existence' of the right, i.e. the grant under national laws of the exclusive rights of exploitation, and should not *per se* amount to an abuse of a dominant position. Nevertheless, that misinterprets the role of Article 86(a) as a safeguard against exploitive pricing.

Korah reminds us of this because while she criticizes the cost-plus approach, drawing attention to its failure to allow sufficient room for the IPR concept that the person financing innovation should be able to obtain the prices that the market will bear, she also acknowledges 'it is difficult to criticise the Court for condemning excessive prices given the wording of Article 86(a)'.[31]

The implication of the above analysis is that Article 86(a) could potentially impose a limit on the pricing of IPRs. In practice, however, this is not likely to affect intellectual property rightholders unless their conduct is both egregious and can easily be demonstrated to be excessive in the light of their own previous conduct.[32] Moreover, there is considerable room for IPR owners to price at high levels to obtain a return on their intellectual property investment. As the Advocate General expressed it in *Maxicar*, 'the proprietor of protective rights . . . may lawfully call for a return on the amounts which he has invested in order to perfect the protected design'.[33] Furthermore, prices charged by a rightholder which are considerably higher than those charged by competing independents are not necessarily abusive because of this right of return.

---

[30] See e.g. *Sirena* v. *Eda*: 'A higher price for a trademarked product does not *per se* constitute sufficient proof of abuse but it may nevertheless become so, in view of its size, if it does not seem objectively justified.' [1971] ECR 3169 at para. 17.

[31] V. Korah, *EC Competition Law and Practice* (Sweet & Maxwell, 5th edn., 1994) at p. 98. This sentence was deleted from the 6th edition.

[32] See e.g. *British Leyland*, op. cit. n. 8 *supra*.

[33] [1988] ECR 6039 at para. 17.

16.4 DUAL MARKETS, INTELLECTUAL PROPERTY RIGHTS, AND UNFAIR PRICING

Yet it is important to recognize that this analysis of Article 86(a) is limited to the situation where the effects of the high pricing are purely exploitive. If the effects of the high pricing are exclusionary of competitors, then there may be a conflict between a just reward for the IPR and the need to prevent a weakening of competition on a secondary market. In *Maxicar*, the Court referred to the fixing of prices at an unfair level as an alternative abuse to refusing to supply spare parts to an independent repairer.[34] Insofar as a high price has the effect of excluding demand in a secondary market, it could be abusive on that ground.

Moreover, in analysing the fairness of prices in a secondary market like spare parts, the reward can be reduced because of the consideration that part had been recouped on the sale of the original manufactured product. In *Maxicar*, the Advocate General stated in the case of 'bodywork components sold as spare parts the problem displays an unusual aspect in so far as part of that expenditure has probably already been recovered from the sale of new cars. It is therefore necessary, when fixing the prices of spare parts, to take due account of that factor.'[35]

In practice, the issue of high pricing in the two market context is likely to be governed by the rules applicable to the obligations to set a reasonable price when an IPR holder has been ordered to license (see chapter 14). Insofar as commentators consider the regulation of the pricing of IPRs to be 'unworkable',[36] they quite legitimately describe the methodological difficulties facing courts and indeed the Commission dealing with a complaint under Article 86(a). Nevertheless, that does not mean that rightholders can price freely as if Article 86(a) does not exist. That sub-article must be taken into account in pricing decisions along with the limits on discriminatory pricing imposed by Article 86(c) and predatory pricing (see next chapters).

[34] [1988] ECR 6039 at para. 16.
[35] [1988] ECR 6039 at para. 63.
[36] See e.g. Govaere, op. cit. at p. 260.

17

Discriminatory Pricing and Intellectual Property Rights

Discriminatory pricing is prohibited by Article 86(c) which defines it as 'applying dissimilar conditions to equivalent transactions with other trading parties thereby placing them at a competitive disadvantage'.

Yet the case-law indicates that this prohibition regulates a wide variety of pricing practices. It can extend to price differentiation which has the effect of excluding competitors from markets, such as predatory pricing and loyalty rebates,[1] as well as pricing practices which cause injury directly to customers and consumers.[2] It can apply to differential pricing in separate product markets and in separate geographic markets. If Article 86(c) is viewed as a basis for regulation, two main issues arise: (i) what is meant by 'equivalent transactions'? and (ii) what types of justifications can be offered for differential pricing?

17.1 THE CONCEPT OF EQUIVALENT TRANSACTIONS

In principle, price differences are only discriminatory under Article 86(c) if they can be shown to apply to 'equivalent transactions'. This implies that the products themselves must either be identical[3] or substitutable.[4] The concept of 'transaction', however, is wider than the good or service on its own; it includes other conditions of sale such as terms of payment and delivery.[5] For example, in *United Brands*, the Court found that the price differences were discriminatory in a situation where the bananas were sold to the different distributor ripeners under the same conditions of sale, terms of payment, and costs of unloading.[6] Had any of those factors varied from distributor to distributor, that would have raised

---

[1] This is sometimes referred to as primary line injury.
[2] This is referred to as secondary line injury.
[3] See e.g. the bananas in *United Brands* v. *Commission* [1978] ECR 207.
[4] See e.g. *HOV SVZ/MCN* [1994] OJ L104/34.
[5] For example, in *United Brands* the bananas were sold to the ripener distributors on the same conditions of sale and terms of payment (para. 235). Had these conditions varied, they may have made the transactions non-equivalent.
[6] [1978] ECR 207 at para. 225.

questions about the equivalence of transactions.[7] The concept of equivalence also raises questions about different prices when the product is sold in different product markets or in different geographic markets. Before looking at these two complications, let us first examine how Article 86(c) applies to discounting practices in the single market situation.

17.2 DISCRIMINATORY DISCOUNTS AND REBATES IN A SINGLE MARKET

The Commission and the Court have long viewed certain discounting strategies of dominant firms as abusive because they were motivated by exclusionary aims towards competitors. Thus in *Hoffman La Roche*,[8] a case in which a dominant pharmaceutical manufacturer offered discounts for its vitamins in the form of 'fidelity rebates', i.e. an extra discount applied to the quantities ordered conditional upon the customer obtaining from the one manufacturer all or most of its requirements, the Court held that the discount was abusive under Article 86 as an indirect method of binding a customer to an exclusive relationship. The Court was concerned with the business strategy of Hoffman La Roche in using discounting as a method of supplementing the more formal exclusive agreements it had reached with some of its customers. It even viewed the dominant firm's use of an 'English clause' not so much as a method of competition but as a method of finding out about rivals pricing policies and underpricing them. The 'English clause' encouraged customers to inform Hoffman La Roche of any competitors offering lower prices. It provided that if Hoffman La Roche would not match the competitor's price, the customer would be free to obtain supplies from the competitor without forfeiting its loyalty rebate. The Court held the clause to be *per se* abusive. The machinery of the English clause was not viewed as an aid to meeting competition but as a device to allow the dominant supplier 'to decide whether by adjusting its prices, it will permit competition'.[9]

This concern of the Court and Commission with exclusionary motives of dominant firms was a regular feature of later cases. In *British Plasterboard*,[10] the Commission found loyalty rebates based on exclusive requirements agreements abusive because they went beyond normal methods of competition. In *Michelin*,[11] the Court found the more subtle conduct of rebates based on sales targets abusive because of their exclusionary purpose. Further, in *Soda Ash*,[12] the Commission held that the

---

7 See U. Springer, '*Borden* and *United Brands* Revisited' [1997] *ECLR* 42 at 44.
8 [1979] ECR 461.   9 [1979] ECR 461 at para. 107.
10 [1995] ECR I–865; [1997] 4 CMLR 238.   11 [1983] ECR 3461.
12 [1991] OJ L152/21 at 33; L152/40 at 50.

technique of 'top slice' discounts was abusive. In all these cases, the use of discounts which varied from rates which applied to quantities of individual products ordered were seized upon as evidence of abusive exclusionary activity directed against competitors (primary line injury).

The price differences in such cases had the added element of abuse that they placed customers at a disadvantage in relation to other customers (secondary line injury). For example, in *Hoffman La Roche*[13] an added discount in the form of a rebate was paid to customers for all vitamins ordered across the whole range of vitamin products rather than on the basis of the order for each vitamin. The Court held that the use of aggregated rebates was a bundling exercise which unlawfully restricted competition between Roche and its competitors because it deprived Roche's customers of their freedom to choose their source of supply. The Court added that this conduct was also unlawful discrimination against its customers because different prices were offered to different customers for an identical product depending upon whether they agreed to avoid placing orders with other competitors.[14]

In all these cases, the seller was offering identical goods for different prices to customers without any objective justification. The Court's view was that the only conceivable commercial return to the dominant undertaking in exchange for the loyalty or fidelity discounts was the unlawful one of driving competitors out of the market.

17.2.1 Non-Equivalent Transactions: Different Quantities

From an early stage the Court was prepared to acknowledge that discounts were not abusive if they differed according to different quantities ordered. There was no need to show elaborate proof of being cost related by being related to lorry load, etc. as long as such discounts were open to all customers on the same basis, i.e. the same percentage discount for the same quantities of the product ordered. In *Hoffman La Roche*, for example, the Court indicated that quantity discounts exclusively linked to the volume of purchases fixed objectively and open to all customers were lawful.[15] In *Hilti*,[16] the Commission made the point that it was the fact that Hilti's customers bought in equivalent quantities that made the different treatment abusive. In *Tetra Pak II*, the CFI indicated that quantity discounts might be the sole objective justification for differential pricing.[17]

---

13 [1979] ECR 461.   14 Ibid.

15 In one case where the Commission has found that a dominant firm has adopted a pricing policy which is discriminatory, it has made an order that any further discounts offered by the firm must reflect actual cost savings. The decision was later annulled on procedural grounds. See *Soda Ash-Solvay et Cie* v. *Commission* [1995] ECR II–1775.

16 [1994] 4 CMLR 16.   17 [1994] ECR II–755.

There is of course an element of discrimination in quantity rebates, i.e. they discriminate against small firms with small orders. However, the conduct of the dominant firm can probably be justified by the language of Article 86(c) which allows different conditions to be offered for non-equivalent transactions.

17.2.2 The Effects of the Discriminatory Practice

Article 86(c) prohibits discriminatory pricing only if it has the effect of placing trading parties at a competitive disadvantage. It would have been possible to give this element of Article 86(c) an economic interpretation. However, it has been given a more formalistic interpretation. The exploration of competitive effect in *Hoffman La Roche*, for example, was limited to a supposition that the difference in rates of rebate caused damage to those customers who received less favourable rates. In *United Brands*, the differences in prices as such had no competitive effect on competition between the distributor ripeners. They were only potential competitors because the ripening clauses prevented arbitrage between them. It was enough to state that the differential pricing had an effect on the potential freedom of action of customers rather than the actual effect on competitors.

The cases on rebates and discounts suggest that the conditions of Article 86(a) have been applied highly legalistically. The emphasis has been placed on differences in price, other terms of the contract, and the method of performance of the contract as such rather than the economic effects of the price differential.[18] It has been claimed, with some justice, that the rules are applied rather rigidly and are not easy to reconcile with the commercial realities of companies' pricing policies.[19]

17.3 SEPARATE MARKETS AND PRICE DISCRIMINATION

In cases of intermarket discrimination, as opposed to intramarket discrimination, Article 86(c) has been more realistically applied. In principle, where a similar product is put to different uses in separate product markets, a dominant undertaking can differentiate its price for the same product in the two markets. The fact of different use could operate as an objective factor distinguishing one transaction from another, allowing an

---

[18] See e.g. L. Zanon, 'Price Discrimination under Article 86 of the EEC Treaty: A Comment on the UBC Case' (1982) 31 *ICLQ* 36; W. Bishop, 'Price Discrimination under Article 86: Political Economy in the European Court' [1981] *MLR* 282.

[19] See e.g. M. Waelbroeck, 'Price Discrimination and Rebate Policies under EU Competition Law' [1995] *Fordham Corp. Law Inst.* 147 at 148.

undertaking in a dominant position to take into account in its pricing practices the different market conditions on different product markets, assuming the markets are separate. At least to this extent, Article 86(c) allows a commercial pricing strategy which extracts from each separate market what that market will bear. In *Tetra Pak II*,[20] the CFI appeared to endorse this proposition when it suggested that for the purpose of determining a case of price discrimination, each relevant market had to be assessed separately. This suggests that there is no general policy of equalizing prices across markets under Article 86(c).[21]

In cases, however, where the price differentiation occurs on two markets which are 'linked',[22] either because one is 'downstream'[23] or 'neighbouring',[24] the price differences may be abusive because they are part of a two market commercial strategy by a dominant undertaking which has an exclusionary aim or effect in one of those markets. For example, in the case *BPB and British Gypsum* v. *Commission*,[25] where there was an associative link between the two markets, with customers operating on both markets, profits made in one market and used to subsidize pricing on the second market, particularly with the purpose of preserving dominance upon the separate market, could be viewed as abusive even if the conduct is concentrated on the market other than the one in which the undertaking is dominant.

17.3.1 Intellectual Property Rights and Separate Markets

In cases where the dominant firm enjoys the protection of an IPR, the IPR owner can by defining the field of technical application of a protected product, create separate markets in which the product can be offered on different terms. For example, the commercial licensing strategy of an IPR owner can include licensing the same patent for different fields of use and charging different rates of royalty. This is recognized as non-discriminatory under Article 85 in the technology transfer block exemption[26] and it would be non-abusive under Article 86(c) as long as the different treatment applied to non-equivalent transactions.

However, the rules of Article 86(c) in relation to separate markets continue to apply. The issue is essentially one of establishing non-equivalence rather than a justification for the use of the IPR. Consequently, as long as the markets are separate, Article 86(c) will not interfere with a differentiated exploitation policy in each market. If, however, there are

---

[20] Op. cit. n. 17 *supra* at para. 162 *et seq.*
[21] See e.g. U. Springer, '*Borden* and *United Brands* Revisited' [1997] 1 *ECLR* 42 at 45.
[22] See e.g. *BPB Industries* [1995] ECR I–865; see too *Tetra Pak II* n. 17 *supra.*
[23] See e.g. *Hilti* v. *Commission* op. cit. n. 16 *supra.*   [24] Op. cit. n. 17 *supra.*
[25] Op. cit., n. 22.   [26] See Part II *supra.*

associative links established between different product markets, the prohibition in Article 86(c) can apply to intermarket price differentials.

For example, in the case of *Tetra Pak II*,[27] the CFI held that the practice of Tetra Pak of offering widely varying discounts to customers for their aseptic and non-aseptic milk carton machines, i.e. from 20–40 per cent and in some cases from 50–60 per cent higher discounts in the non-aseptic market in which Tetra Pak was not dominant, was itself discriminatory pricing under Article 86(c). Tetra Pak had argued that if one looked at the pricing of the overall package of machines with cartons, a 50 per cent difference in the discount for machines would produce a considerably narrower discount, i.e about 4 per cent, for the package of products as a whole, presumably because of correspondingly higher prices for cartons. However, the Court agreed with the Commission that it was correct to look solely at the pricing of the machines, as such, since users must be perfectly free to use cartons from other manufacturers on Tetra Pak machines.

The CFI added that, 'discounts on cartons should be granted solely according to the quantity of each order, and orders for different types of carton should not be aggregated for that purpose'. The CFI was decidedly unsympathetic to the argument that Tetra Pak could treat its packaging system as integrated and indivisible as a justification for its abusive differential pricing. Similarly, all arguments about technical considerations, product liability, protection of public health and public reputation were not accepted as objective justifications for differential pricing. They could not outweigh the point that the products were separate and it was not up to the dominant undertaking to 'take steps on its own initiative to eliminate products which rightly or wrongly it regards as dangerous or inferior in quality to its own products' (para. 138). The Court added that reliability and hygiene 'could be ensured by disclosing to users of Tetra Pak machines all the technical specifications concerning the cartons to be used on those systems, without the applicant's intellectual property rights being thereby prejudiced' (para. 139).

It is clear that the IPR holder must take into account the legal ground rules for defining separate product markets in assessing whether or not a pricing practice is abusive. This is particularly true when the IPR holder has been designated as an 'essential facility'. In such cases, the test laid down by Article 86(c) can be expected to be even more stringent particularly on the issue of justification.

Another possible objective basis for different rates of royalty or licence fees is differing frequency of use. For example, in *Coditel* v. *Cine Vog*,[28] the copyright holder was able to limit the number of acts of exploitation

---

[27] Op. cit. n. 17 *supra*. Upheld by ECJ. [28] [1982] ECR 3381.

of the right which was offered to third parties and charged amounts which varied with the frequency of use. In these respects, the treatment of IPRs under Article 86(c) gives recognition to the discretion given to IPR holders under national legislation. When an IPR owner divides up an IPR, each component is viewed as a different product entitling the owner to apply dissimilar conditions. This entitlement to slice IPRs is subject to restraints when an attempt is made to package services and charge for the package rather than the individual product. For example, in its Guidelines on the Application of EEC Competition Rules in the Telecommunications Sector, the Commission has ruled that a telecommunications operator may not charge an additional price for the supply of a leased line based on the use made by the lessee of that line, but can base such charges only upon differences in costs directly entailed to the telecommunications operator.[29] Although the Commission acknowledges that the value of the use of the leased circuit may be different depending upon the profitability of the service supplied on the circuit, a dominant undertaking cannot, consistent with Article 86(c), use this difference as a basis for a difference in price. Waelbroeck suggests that if the supplier owns an IPR covering the use of the product the situation will be different because the IPR owner will be entitled to charge a fee based on the acts of utilization.[30] However, there may be a distinction to be drawn between fields of use and usage under Article 86(c). The former are separate markets coinciding with the use of the IPR and reinforcing it. An essential facility owner may not be able to justify charges based on usage simply because an IPR is involved if the effect in a particular market is discriminatory. There would have to be a closer link between the IPR leased and a performance right.

The discretion given to an IPR owner to divide and price separately under Article 86(c) does not extend to attempts to bundle and tie separate products. In certain circumstances, the offer of different conditions for similar components can be an offence under Article 86(c). For example, in *Hilti* v. *Commission*,[31] the dominant firm's use of selective pricing policies included two types of discrimination. It gave particularly favourable discounts to targeted customers of competitors who were prepared to switch to Hilti. This was abusive conduct towards competitors. Secondly, it reduced discounts to Hilti customers who bought Hilti cartridge strips without Hilti nails, thus effectively charging higher prices to those customers who bought nails from competitors. This conduct was held to be discriminatory to customers. Since the source of the latter abuse was Hilti's commercial strategy of attempting to 'bundle'

---

29 OJ C233/2 6 Sept. 1991 paras. 95–7.
30 See M.Waelbroeck, op. cit. n. 19 at p. 157.   31 [1994] ECR I–667.

its cartridge strips sales with its nail sales, it suggested that Article 86(c) set limits to the commercial pricing strategies of dominant firms which were based on product packages.

17.4 GEOGRAPHIC PRICE DISCRIMINATION

A further constraint on pricing decisions by IPR owners is the way the case-law applies Article 86(c) to the commercial practice of pricing differently in different geographic markets. Where a dominant firm, whether in possession of an IPR or not, attempts to maximize returns by charging different prices in different geographic markets, that can be prohibited as an exercise in market partitioning. The Commission, with the support of the Court, has read into Article 86(c) the objective of preventing private companies in their pricing decisions reintroducing 'the barriers which the single market has abolished'.[32]

In *United Brands*,[33] the Commission and the Court were confronted by a pattern in which identical bananas packed in identical boxes were sold free on rail at either Rotterdam or Bremerhaven at widely differing prices depending upon which one of six countries was their country of destination. Although the Court announced at the outset that 'the responsibility for establishing a single banana market did not lie with the applicant', it added that United Brands might only charge 'what the market can bear provided that it complies with the rules for the regulation and coordination of the market laid down by the Treaty'.[34] In the end, the Court concluded that a rigid partitioning of the market was created at price levels which were artificially different placing certain distributor ripeners at a comparative disadvantage, thus 'distorting' competition.[35] What was slightly curious about this judgment was its failure to acknowledge that the main cause of partitioning was not the different prices but the 'green banana' clause which prevented distributors from parallel importing from low to high price countries. In principle, different prices in different member states as such should not be abusive since interstate trade can help to level the differences. On the other hand, obstacles to parallel trading would create market partitioning. It would have been possible for the Court to strike down the green banana clause and leave pricing to find its own level. However, the Court decided effectively to treat the clause and the differential pricing as two independent infringements.[36]

---

[32] See *XXIst Report on Competition Policy* [1991] at point 43.　　　[33] [1978] ECR 207.
[34] Ibid. at p. 227.　　　[35] Ibid. at p. 298.
[36] See e.g. M. Siragusa, 'The Application of Article 86 to the Pricing Policies of Dominant Companies: Discriminatory and Unfair Prices' (1979) 16 *CMLRev*. 179.

The Court accepted that differences in costs such as transport, tax, customs duties, wages, conditions of marketing, and density of competition could result in differences in retail prices. But it held that United Brands should only take such factors into account to 'a limited extent' since it sells the same product in the same place to distributors who alone bear the risks of the consumers market. In fact, United Brands priced on its view of the expected market price in each market about four days before the ship was unloaded, taking into account the effect on demand of weather, strikes, currency fluctuations, etc. The Court claimed that this direct pricing by the producer to the consumer left out the stage of the market consisting of the exchange between producer and distributor and thereby adversely affected the mechanisms of the market.[37] According to the Court, 'the interplay of supply and demand should, owing to its nature', only be taken into account at the stage where the supplier sells to the consumer.[38] The distortion to competition consisted of the producer operating a centralized system of pricing which effectively took away from the local distributors their opportunity to maximize monopoly profits in the local market.

In principle the judgment of the Court in *United Brands* implied that there could be a defence of 'meeting competition' at least at local levels. This defence would apply to dominant undertakings to enable them to defend themselves against lower pricing by competitors. The Court had no objection to the pricing by each of the distributors being different, as indeed it would have no objection to the pricing of different licensees or subsidiaries of an IPR owner being different, as long as the different prices reflected differences in the risks attached to different market conditions. The abuse in *United Brands* consisted of the extension of market power by United Brands, the dominant producer, into the distribution market in the way that they did it.

The decision in *United Brands*[39] should not be read to suggest that dominant IPR owners cannot price differently in different geographic markets within the EC and be lawful under Article 86(c). Much depends on the basis for the price differences. For example in *Tetra Pak II*,[40] the Commission found that Tetra Pak had been charging different prices to customers in different member states for non-aseptic milk cartons and milk packaging machines. It was prepared to accept that price differences could be justified where they resulted solely from the specific local market conditions as long as they did not involve discriminatory discounts. However, the Commission found that the price differences were not based on objectively justifiable economic differences but

---

[37] [1978] ECR at p. 230.
[39] [1978] ECR at paras. 208 and 233.
[38] Ibid. at p. 229.
[40] [1994] ECR II–755.

instead were evidence of a market partitioning policy which could be artificially maintained by Tetra Pak.[41] It therefore ordered Tetra Pak to refrain from discriminatory pricing and discounting. The Commission ordered Tetra Pak to ensure that any differences between the prices charged for its products in the various member states must result solely from the specific local market conditions. It also required that any customer within the Community shall be supplied by any Tetra Pak subsidiary it chooses and at the price it practices.

The issue of price discrimination has also arisen in a number of collecting society cases. Insofar as the national society prices at different levels simply because the licensee comes from a different member state, it will be unlawful. For example, in *GEMA*,[42] the Commission found that the rules of the German Performing Rights Society violated Article 86 *inter alia* by requiring higher royalties on records imported or reimported from other member states, discriminating against the nationals of other member states.[43] The Commission required GEMA to apply the same licence fee for domestic and imported records even though the latter required more expensive controls. Nationality as such could not justify price differences where all other aspects of the transaction are equivalent. What, however, is the position where there are differences in the national IPR legislation which result in differences in treatment based on nationality?

In *Basset* v. *SACEM*,[44] for example, the French collecting society levied a fee from Basset which consisted of a performance royalty for playing music in discothèques and a supplementary fee which applied regardless of whether or not such a fee was levied by the collecting society in the member state from which the import had come. The Court of Justice held that since the French licensing fee, including the supplementary fee, did not vary depending upon the origin of the product, it could be viewed as the normal exploitation of the copyright and did not in principle constitute an abuse of Article 86(c).[45] The fact that the price differences were due to the different legislation of the member states[46] meant that the situation was not comparable to *United Brands* because that case was concerned with the dominant undertaking's exploitation of different market conditions.

The Court's willingness to accept differences in national legislation as a justified basis for differences in pricing rests in part on its acceptance of the fact that in the case of IPRs legislation, it would not be realistic to

---

[41] Ibid. at para. 1154. [42] [1971] CMLR D 35.
[43] See too *GVL* v. *Commission* [1983] ECR 483 where a German collecting society refused to make management agreements with artists who were not German residents.
[44] [1987] 3 CMLR 173. [45] Nor was it contrary to Arts. 30 or 36.
[46] Op. cit. at para. 18.

force private bodies to take pricing decisions which compensate for differences in national conditions for IPR protection. In the event, differences in national legislation can justify differences in prices even where the effect is to treat some customers more favourably than others on the basis of their nationality.[47]

The Court's insistence in *United Brands* that the degree of involvement of the dominant firm in the local consumer market was the key to the availability of the 'meeting competition' defence of justification for differences in prices is not altogether defensible in purely economic terms.[48] However, the basis for the Court's concern was more a concept of appropriateness of conduct by a dominant undertaking. If a dominant IPR owner licensed a product to licensees in different national territories or invested in subsidiaries in different national territories, that would not preclude the respective licensees or subsidiaries meeting the competitive conditions of competition locally. The gravamen of the abuse in *United Brands* was that the producer asserted the defence that it was responding to local competition in its pricing when it did not 'bear the risks of the consumers market'. The Court thought that Article 86 required that the 'interplay of supply and demand should only be applied to each stage where it is really manifest'.[49]

It is not altogether the case, therefore, that Article 86(c) requires standard pricing throughout the common market. If it did so, it would of course artificially require higher prices in certain countries than would otherwise be the case if the producer could price at levels adjusted to local conditions. However, the Commission's rules allow for price differentiation as long as it reflects local conditions and as long as the operator in the local market bears the risk and reaps the benefit of those local conditions. Nevertheless, the Commission and the Court's approach to geographic price discrimination under Article 86(c) could be improved if they took greater account of whether or not a differential pricing practice is accompanied by measures to prevent parallel imports.[50]

17.5 ARTICLE 86(C) AS A REGULATORY FRAMEWORK FOR AN ESSENTIAL FACILITY

Where a dominant undertaking is an essential facility for a downstream market, Article 86(c) applies to prevent discrimination on any of the

---

[47] See U. Springer, '*Borden* and *United Brands* Revisited' [1997] *ECLR* 42 at 51.

[48] See e.g. M. Siragusa, 'The Application of Article 86 to the Pricing Policy of Dominant Companies: Discriminatory and Unfair Prices' [1979] 16 *CMLRev*. 179.

[49] [1978] ECR 207 at para. 228. See Springer, op. cit. at p. 253.

[50] See e.g. M. Waelbroeck, 'Price Discrimination and Rebate Policies under EU Competition Law' [1995] *Fordham Corp. Law Inst*. 147 at 154.

terms which it offers to operators in that market where such discrimination would restrict competition. The discrimination could take the form of imposing different conditions upon different operators, whether of price or other conditions of access, without any difference in cost, technical factors or differences in intensity of use or operation in different sub-markets.[51] The application of dissimilar conditions to equivalent transactions is unlawful discrimination because it could discourage entry or expansion of the competitor on the downstream market.

Article 86(c) also applies where an essential facility owner offers the same price and other conditions to competitors or customers for different types of 'transactions'. For example if a dominant firm in an upstream market cross-subsidizes its downstream subsidiary by funding its operations by capital remunerated substantially below the market rate or provides activities, premises, equipment, experts, and/or services with a remuneration substantially below the market rate, this will be regarded as a cross-subsidization of costs which would make identical tariffs discriminatory.[52] A dominant undertaking operating an essential facility will need to use accounting methods which make its allocations of cost transparent to avoid suspicion of hidden cross-subsidization.[53]

[51] See e.g. Notice on the Application of the Competition Rules To Access Agreements in the Telecommunications Sector.

[52] See e.g. an analysis of cross-subsidization as discrimination in the Commission's Guidelines on the application of the Competition Rules in the Telecommunications Sector, OJ No. C 233/2 6 Sept. 91 at paras. 102–4.   [53] Ibid. at paras. 105–6.

18

Predatory Pricing

Article 86 has been applied by the Commission with the approval of the Community Courts to cases of predatory pricing. The abuse consists of pricing below cost with an intention to eliminate competitors. Insofar as Article 86 is used to regulate predatory pricing because of its exclusionary effects, courts must be careful not to prevent firms from competing on the basis of performance. If firms have achieved a dominant position by virtue of efficiency and innovation, they must be allowed to pass on the benefits to consumers even if that damages competitors.

In *AKZO* v. *Commission*,[1] the Court of Justice indicated that there were two basic methods of analysis to determine whether or not an undertaking has practised predatory pricing. The first is that pricing below average variable costs is *per se* abusive in the sense that no proof of intent is necessary. For 'in such a case, there is no conceivable economic purpose other than the elimination of a competitor, since each item produced and sold entails a loss for the undertaking. The second method is that pricing products 'below average total costs but above average variable costs is only to be considered abusive if an intention to eliminate can be shown. In *AKZO*, the Commission found that AKZO had offered products to ECS's customers at unreasonably low prices with a view to damaging ECS's chances of survival. The dominant company had sought out the customers of ECS offering to supply at prices below costs and below the prices it charged its own customers. AKZO's low pricing was below average total costs but above average variable cost but its clearly expressed intent combined with its targeting of ECS customers was sufficient to prove predatory pricing under Article 86.

In *Tetra Pak II*, the Commission found that the pricing by Tetra Pak of non-aseptic cartons in Italy was considerably below average variable costs from 1976 to 1981 though it showed no proof of intention to eliminate competitors. This finding was supported by the CFI's own examination of the facts.[2] In 1982, the Commission found that prices for the cartons were between average variable costs and average total costs and CFI made it a point to find evidence of intent to eliminate a competitor.[3]

---

[1] [1993] 5 CMLR 215.   [2] At para. 150.
[3] At para. 151. The same reasoning was applied by the CFI to sales of aseptic machines in the UK from 1981 to 1984 (paras. 189–91).

Tetra Pak argued that there was inadequate proof of predatory pricing because the Commission had not shown that Tetra Pak had a realistic prospect of recouping its losses once it had eliminated the competitor in question. Underlying this argument was the model of predation occurring in two stages: the dominant undertaking first prices below costs attempting to drive out a competitor and then in a subsequent stage attempts to recoup its losses by charging at supra-competitive prices. Tetra Pak, relying on the theories of US economists and the decision of the US Supreme Court in *Brook Group*,[4] maintained that where there was no prospect of recoupment that could be evidence on non-predatory intent. The CFI held that, 'it is not necessary to demonstrate specifically that the undertaking in question had a reasonable prospect of recouping losses'.[5] On appeal, the Court of Justice agreed, stating:

it would not be appropriate in the circumstances of the case to require in addition proof that Tetra Pak had a realistic prospect of recouping its losses. It must be possible to penalise predatory pricing whenever there is a risk that competitors will be eliminated. The Court of first Instance found . . . that there was such a risk in this case. The aim pursued, which is to maintain undistorted competition, rules out waiting until such a strategy leads to the elimination of competitors.[6]

The Court also reaffirmed that the precepts of the *AKZO* test provided the correct basis to assess whether a pricing practice was predatory or came within the scope of competition on the basis of quality [paras 147–9]. The Court added that the period during which prices are applied as part of a plan to damage a competitor is a factor to be taken into account [para 149].

These cases suggest that ownership of an IPR confers no special position under Article 86 should a product incorporating an IPR be sold at below cost. Such conduct is governed in the usual way by the case-law of the Court interpreting Article 86.

---

[4] *Brook Group Ltd.* v. *Brown and Williamson Tobacco Group* 405 US 209 (1993).
[5] At para. 150.   [6] At para. 44.

19

Conclusions

The role of Article 86 in the regulation of technological intellectual property rights (IPRs) presents particular difficulties to IPR owners because in the name of preserving effective competition, it places limits on the capacity of IPR owners to obtain a full appropriation of the reward for their invention. The policy argument has been that the EC competition rules go too far. By encroaching on the lawful prerogatives of IPR owners, they undermine the system of rewards built into IPR legislation and thereby threaten levels of investment and innovation in the European economy. Yet there are at least four distinct reasons why it is by no means clear that this is the case.

19.1 THE EXCEPTIONAL CIRCUMSTANCES TEST AND NORMAL EXPLOITATION

In the first place, it is important to remember that the competition rules limit the exploitation of IPRs only in exceptional circumstances owing to two significant balancing mechanisms incorporated within them. First, EC competition law is careful to assess whether or not the possession of an IPR coincides with market power approaching monopoly. There is no presumption that the grant of an exclusive right confers an economic monopoly. As long as there are substitutes for the protected product or process, the effects of Article 86 upon IPRs can be minimal. In that sense, Article 86 leaves considerable room for the normal exploitation of IPRs.

Moreover, the Court's definition of abuse recognizes that the efficiency and innovation which assisted in the acquisition of dominance continues to be a legitimate form of competition even by a dominant firm. Thus, as the Court pointed out in *Volvo*,[1] the exclusive exploitation of an IPR is acceptable in a primary market for which the product is protected as a reward for invention and an incentive to innovation. An IPR owner can use the Courts to obtain an injunction to prevent competitors entering that market.

The limits imposed by the Courts mainly occur when an IPR coincides with real market power because the owner enjoys a form of dominance

---

[1] [1988] ECR 6211.

which amounts to a *de facto* monopoly. In such a situation, IPRs are not regarded as a special case. They are treated as all other physical assets which are 'essential facilities'. The IPR owners must trade with down-stream operators even if they themselves operate in a secondary market. They cannot discriminate between their own operator and a competitor on the derivative market by tying or integrating their product or service in the secondary market with their IPR in the primary market.

In the eyes of competition law, in such a situation, IPRs are viewed as analogous to tangible property rights. In such a case, as with any asset which is a monopoly, they are subject to regulation.

. . . the owner of IP rights in one of a number of rival widget-making technologies should be free to maximise its own exploitation of that technology just as the owner of one of a number of competing widget-making factories would be. Conversely, if there is some impediment to competition between alternative widget-making technologies (perhaps because one firm has bought up a cluster of IP rights that somehow blocks the ability of new rivals to develop alternatives), that IP owner must expect its rights to be curtailed by competition law intervention, just as would apply to a manufacturer who had bought up all the physical property rights to rival widget-making factories (thus enjoying a widget-making monopoly).[2]

In other words, the fact that there may be a general presumption that IPRs are not as such essential facilities does not preclude the possibility that 'they may be an essential facility where there is some serious impediment to the way competition between IPR owners works'.[3]

19.2 THE EFFECT OF THE COMPETITION RULES UPON INCENTIVES

Secondly, it is by no means certain that the application of essential facilities reasoning to IPRs inevitably results in a weakening of the incentive to invest in R&D.[4] This is partly because in striking this particular

---

[2] See D. Ridyard, 'Essential Facilities and the Obligation to Supply Competitors' [1996] *ECLR* 438, at 445.   [3] Id.

[4] The argument by IPR owners that the restrictions of the competition rules will devalue an IPR to the point where it is no longer worthwhile investing in the R&D ignores important empirical evidence. Compulsory licensing does not necessarily reduce levels of investment in R&D, (see e.g. F. M. Scherer, *Innovation and Growth*, at p. 216); it may only induce firms to switch out of IPRs like patents and into secret know-how for protection (pp. 207–8). Whether there will be a switch to secret know-how or that it will result in a reduction in diffusion because of the added difficulties of negotiating know-how agreements is unclear.

It is also the case that the choice of IPR is often dictated by factors other than the competition rules. Empirical evidence shows that many firms prefer to use secret know-how protection rather than patent protection where they have access to non-patent barriers to entry such as advantages of being first in the field, difficulties of imitation, exclusive distri-

balance, the competition rules do not necessarily reduce the reward. Control over exclusive exploitation in secondary markets is different in its effect on return and incentives from control over exploitation in primary markets. Insofar as the secondary market is a by-product of the first inventive activity, a reward/incentive has already been obtained in the first market. Moreover, regulation in the second market by its nature ensures a return from exploitation in that market. It requires that in cases of monopoly, access must be shared based on a reasonable return to the IPR owner for sharing the essential facility. In cases where access is compulsory, as for example in telecommunications, demand for such access may be sufficiently stimulated to produce a higher return than if the asset were individually exploited.

19.3 APPROPRIATION OF VALUE AND MARKET POWER

Thirdly, the limits established by EC competition law do not necessarily prevent the full appropriation of value. They are addressed to the prevention of undue leveraging of market power.

A case has sometimes been made that IPR legislation already incorporates its own form of self-regulation which balances access to markets with reward for invention. Thus, as Machlup puts it: 'Striking the correct balance between access and incentives is the central problem in copyright law.'[5] Govaere adds a more comprehensive case for self-regulation:

No additional restraints on intellectual property owners need to be introduced in order to safeguard competition; it suffices to reinforce the restrictions inherent in the different types of intellectual property rights. Take for instance, patent and copyright protection. Patent protection confers exclusivity on a new product or process and may under exceptional circumstances lead to a monopoly position in the marketplace. As a counterbalance, stringent conditions for protectability are imposed, the exclusive right is limited in time to 20 years and the invention is duly publicised. Furthermore, the possibility of imposing compulsory licenses, as well as the conditions under which they can be imposed, is already provided for under national laws. Conversely, copyright does not confer a monopoly on ideas or facts, but merely offers protection against the unauthorised reproduction of the original manner in which an idea is expressed.[6]

---

bution arrangements, and strong brand advertising (see e.g. T. Scherer, *Industrial Market Structure and Economic Performance* (2nd edn., 1980) 444–7). On the other hand, patent protection is the IPR of choice for smaller firms, independent inventors, and firms in particular sectors such as pharmaceuticals (Taylor and Silberstone, *The Economic Impact of the Patent System* (Cambridge, 1973).

[5] F. Machlup, 'An Economic Review of the Patent System, Study of the Committee on Patents, Trademarks and Copyright', Senate Judiciary Committee, US 85th Congress, Study no. 15, Washington, DC 1958 at p. 12.   [6] I. Govaere at p. 305.

Yet it seems to be overly optimistic to expect that IPR legislation by itself can regulate the exercise of IPRs so comprehensively that it meets the objectives of public policy generally and competition policy in particular in relation to markets. The offer of an exclusive right to an undertaking or individual for a fixed period of time by IPR legislation is granted irrespective of the market power of the owner or the quality of the innovation, assuming that minimum standards of qualification are met. It entails no careful assessment of the balance between the social benefits of the reward and the social costs of the exclusive right in the case of any individual IPR. It provides, for the most part, a standard period of exclusivity for all IPRs which qualify. Suggestions that it would be more rational from an economic policy perspective to recognize this point by regulating IPRs by varying the length of protection depending on the balance between social benefit and social cost[7] have been acknowledged to be impractical. For pragmatic reasons, IPR legislation adopts a single period of time for exclusivity for all who meet the minimum requirements for validity.

The thinking underlying the grant of a fixed period of exclusivity is that market forces should determine the return to the inventor during that period. The reason for this is that it is difficult to place a value on an invention and it would not be appropriate to leave to a state agency the task of providing a reward based on industrial policy considerations.

However, the assumptions of IPR legislation that inventors are entitled to appropriate 'what the market can bear' presuppose that there is actually a market to regulate the return to the IPR owner. The theory is that there should be an appropriation of the value related to the invention, not the rewards of market power unrelated to the invention. Even under the assumptions of the IPR legislation, the return extracted can be excessive.

Whilst IPR legislation cannot be expected to assume the responsibilities of competition law to ensure that market forces actually operate in any one market, it can regulate the scope of IPR protection to protect access to markets and innovation. IPR legislation such as patent laws build in certain safeguards to the scope of the exclusivity granted. Thus, a patent is granted only to a 'single invention' and a compulsory licence is available in cases where a licence or cross-licence is arbitrarily refused or the patent is not used. In the development of IPR legislation within the EC, moreover, there are signs that the issue of interoperability is modifying the contours of the grant of exclusivity. Possibly because the process of innovation is more complex today in an era of high technology, care is taken to ensure that the scope of intellectual property exclusivity does not

---

[7] See e.g. Kaplow, *The Patent Antitrust Intersection: An Appraisal*, at pp. 1823–9.

extend to the access elements of an invention. Access information is sometimes required to be made available to competitors making related products, as if there is acceptance of a modern imperative that there must be certain safeguards for diffusion.

The concept of interoperability contained within the Computer Program Directive offers a good example of this policy. The presence of section 5 (protection of interfaces) indicates that access protocols and interfaces are regarded as not within the legitimate scope for exclusivity. Section 6 (permissibility of reverse analysis) suggests a concern to ensure that the innovation can be used as a platform for further innovation even during the period of exclusivity. Whether this policy offers an example of competition policy incorporated into intellectual property law or an acceptance of the principle of interoperability within IPR law itself is a debatable issue. What is undoubtedly the case is that interoperability has become an important issue on the overall agenda of legal and economic policy.

19.4 BALANCING ACCESS TO MARKETS AND EXCLUSIVITY

Finally, the need to balance access to markets with exclusivity is part of a wider balance that must be struck by economic policy in promoting innovation. The view of EC competition law, that IPRs must not be able to leverage monopoly market power beyond the scope of the primary market for the protected product or process, is based on a mixture of the old and new assumptions about monopoly behaviour. The old assumption is that by preventing monopolies spreading to secondary markets and by keeping such markets open to access, such markets obtain the rewards of effective competition, i.e. innovative, allocative, and productive efficiency, and minimize exploitive abuse. This is reinforced by the more modern view that because technology markets are changing in nature in the wake of global competition for higher technologies, such as information technology, and the privatization of dominant undertakings using IPRs, such as in telecommunications, EC competition policy must regulate monopolies and insist on the sharing of access to, or interoperability with, essential infrastructures for public policy reasons. There may be reservations about the use of this concept in 'aftermarkets' for spare parts and consumables, where the degree of competition in upstream markets can limit the effects of dominance or monopoly in downstream markets.[8] Moreover, there are concerns that the concept of essential facilities is not

---

[8] See e.g. *Pelican* v. *Kyocera, Competition Policy Newsletter,* Vol. 1 No. 6. Cf. *Eastman Kodak Co.* v. *Image Technical Services Inc.* 112 Sup. Ct. Rep. 2072 [1992].

always limited to genuine monopolies.[9] However, if properly applied, this doctrine is justified by public policy considerations which include the promotion of innovation, albeit with a new emphasis.

The traditional model of technological IPR legislation, such as patents, consists of the right of exclusion for a fixed period of time, during which the inventor has the right of exclusive exploitation to obtain a reward for itself. This also acts as an incentive to others to innovate. The entitlement to charge 'what the market will bear' for the invention is viewed as part of the monopoly/reward/incentive paradigm.

During the period of protection, information about the invention is publicly disclosed but there are limits to what can be used without a licence. It is only at the end of the prescribed period that the information becomes freely available. During the protected period, therefore, diffusion can be tightly controlled by the inventor's decision to self-exploit, license or sell, and the contractual limits which can be imposed on improvements made by those undertakings using the process or product. There is a possibility of compulsory licences, but only in marginal situations.

Whilst the traditional model of innovation based on strong IPR protection continues to command support from the economists,[10] there is an awareness that some impetus to the diffusion of innovation may be lost during the protected period because of the grant of exclusivity. Other contemporary models of invention/diffusion based on narrower IPR rights and a pattern of co-operation between inventors offer an instructive comparison. For example, Japan's experience with narrow patent protection, strong competition policy, and a culture of cross-licensing of improvements suggests an alternative model for innovation which provides more intensified diffusion during the protected period.[11] The point is not that the Japanese model is necessarily better. Rather, it is that the issue of adequate diffusion is still an issue for economic policy to explore in this era of intense competitiveness in world trade. There is little certainty that the existing EC model based on strong IPR is the best assurance of optimum diffusion of innovation. The economic literature seems to provide no clear conclusions.[12]

In sum, the case against competition policy as a force reducing innovation because of its actions as the ultimate guarantor of markets is at best not proven. If anything, a case has been made that competition law and intellectual property law are converging in their aims of ensuring an optimum balance between access to markets and protection of invention.

[9] See J. Kallaugher and J. Venit, 'Essential Facilities: A Comparative Law Approach [1994] *Fordham Corp. Law Inst.* 315 at 344.
[10] See e.g. J. Ordover, 'A Patent System for Both Diffusion and Exclusion', *Journal of Economic Perspectives* [1991] Vol. 5 No. 1, 43. [11] Ibid. at p. 51.
[12] Ibid.

Appendices

Appendix I

Excerpts from the Treaty establishing the European Community[1]

PART ONE—PRINCIPLES

Article 2

The Community shall have as its task, by establishing a common market and an economic and monetary union and by implementing the common policies or activities referred to in articles 3 and 3a, to promote throughout the Community a harmonious and balanced development of economic activities, sustainable and non-inflationary growth respecting the environment, a high degree of convergence of economic employment, a high level of employment and of social protection, the raising of the standard of living and quality of life, and economic and social cohesion and solidarity among Member States.

Article 3

For the purposes set out in Article 2, the activities of the Community shall include, as provided in this Treaty and in accordance with the timetable set out therein:

(a) the elimination, as between Member States, of customs duties and of quantitative restrictions on the import and export of goods, and of all other measures having equivalent effect;
(b) a common commercial policy;
(c) an internal market characterised by the abolition, as between Member States, of obstacles to the free movement of goods, persons, services and capital;
(d) measures concerning the entry and movement of persons in the internal market as provided for in Article 100(c);
(e) a common policy in the sphere of agriculture and fisheries;
(f) the adoption of a common policy in the sphere of transport;
(g) the institution of a system ensuring that competition in the internal market is not distorted;
(h) the approximation of the laws of Member States to the extent required for the proper functioning of the common market;
    . . .

---

[1] The additions and deletions made by the Maastricht Treaty have been incorporated, but not the renumbering proposed by the Amsterdam Treaty.

(l)   the strengthening of the competitiveness of Community industry;
(m) the promotion of research and technological development;

. . .

Article 5

Member States shall take all appropriate measures, whether general or particular, to ensure fulfilment of the obligations arising out of this Treaty or resulting from action taken by the institutions of the Community. They shall facilitate the achievement of the Community's tasks.

They shall obstain from any measure which could jeopardise the attainment of the objectives of this Treaty.

PART THREE—COMMUNITY POLICIES

Article 30

Quantitative restrictions on imports and all measures having equivalent effect shall, without prejudice to the following provisions, be prohibited between Member States.

Article 36

The provisions of Articles 30–36 shall not preclude prohibitions or restrictions on imports, exports or goods in transit justified on grounds of public morality, public policy or public security; the protection of health and life of humans, animals or plants; the protection of national treasures possessing artistic, historic or archaeological value; or the protection of industrial and commercial property. Such prohibitions or restrictions shall not, however, constitute a means of arbitrary discrimination or a disguised restriction on trade between Member States.

Article 85

1. The following shall be prohibited as incompatible with the common market: all agreements between undertakings, decisions by associations of undertakings and concerted practices which may affect trade between Member States and which have as their object or effect the prevention, restriction or distortion of competition within the common market, and in particular those which:

(a) directly or indirectly fix purchase or selling prices or any other trading conditions;
(b) limit or control production, markets, technical development, or investment;
(c) share markets or sources of supply;
(d) apply dissimilar conditions to equivalent transactions with other trading parties, thereby placing them at a competitive disadvantage;

(e) make the conclusion of contracts subject to acceptance by the other parties of supplementary obligations which, by their nature or according to commercial usage, have no connection with the subject of such contracts.

2. Any agreements or decisions prohibited pursuant to this Article shall be automatically void.

3. The provisions of paragraph 1 may, however, be declared inapplicable in the case of:

—any agreement or category of agreements between undertakings;
—any decision or category of decisions by associations of undertakings;
—any concerted practice or category of concerted practices;

which contributes to improving the production or distribution of goods or to promoting technical or economic progress, while allowing consumers a fair share of the resulting benefit, and which does not:

(a) impose on the undertakings concerned restrictions which are not indispensable to the attainment of these objectives;
(b) afford such undertakings the possibility of eliminating competition in respect of a substantial part of the products in question.

Article 86

Any abuse by one or more undertakings of a dominant position within the common market or in a substantial part of it shall be prohibited as incompatible with the common market in so far as it may affect trade between Member States. Such abuse may, in particular, consist in:

(a) directly or indirectly imposing unfair purchase or selling prices or other unfair trading conditions;
(b) limiting production, markets or technical development to the prejudice of consumers;
(c) applying dissimilar conditions to equivalent transactions with other trading parties, thereby placing them at a competitive disadvantage;
(d) making the conclusion of contracts subject to acceptance by the other parties of supplementary obligations which, by their nature or according to commercial usage, have no connection with the subject of such contracts.

PART SIX—GENERAL AND FINAL PROVISIONS

Article 222

This Treaty shall in no way prejudice the rules of Member States governing the system of property ownership.

Appendix II

Commission Regulation (EC) No. 240/96

of 31 January 1996

on the application of Article 85 (3) of the Treaty to certain categories of
technology transfer agreements

(Text with EEA relevance)

THE COMMISSION OF THE EUROPEAN COMMUNITIES,

Having regard to the Treaty establishing the European Community,

Having regard to Council Regulation No 19/65/EEC of 2 March 1965 on the
application of Article 85 (3) of the Treaty to certain categories of agreements and
concerted practices[1], as last amended by the Act of Accession of Austria, Finland
and Sweden, and in particular Article 1 thereof,

Having published a draft of this Regulation[2],

After consulting the Advisory Committee on Restrictive Practices and Dominant
Positions,

Whereas:

(1) Regulation No 19/65/EEC empowers the Commission to apply Article 85
(3) of the Treaty by regulation to certain categories of agreements and
concerted practices falling within the scope of Article 85 (1) which include
restrictions imposed in relation to the acquisition or use of industrial property rights—in particular of patents, utility models, designs or trademarks—
or to the rights arising out of contracts for assignment of, or the right to use,
a method of manufacture of knowledge relating to use or to the application
of industrial processes.

(2) The Commission has made use of this power by adopting Regulation (EEC)
No 2349/84 of 23 July 1984 on the application of Article 85 (3) of the Treaty
to certain categories of patent licensing agreements[3], as last amended by
Regulation (EC) No 2131/95[4], and Regulation (EEC) No 556/89 of 30
November 1988 on the application of Article 85 (3) of the Treaty to certain
categories of know-how licensing agreements[5], as last amended by the Act
of Accession of Austria, Finland and Sweden.

(3) These two block exemptions ought to be combined into a single regulation
covering technology transfer agreements, and the rules governing patent
licensing agreements and agreements for the licensing of know-how ought

---

[1] OJ No 36, 6. 3. 1965, p. 553/65.   [2] OJ No C 178, 30. 6. 1994, p. 3.
[3] OJ No L 219, 16. 8. 1984, p. 15.   [4] OJ No L 214, 8. 9. 1995, p. 6.
[5] OJ No L 61, 4. 3. 1989, p. 1.

to be harmonized and simplified as far as possible, in order to encourage the dissemination of technical knowledge in the Community and to promote the manufacture of technically more sophisticated products. In those circumstances Regulation (EEC) No 556/89 should be repealed.

(4) This Regulation should apply to the licensing of Member States' own patents, Community patents[6] and European patents[7] ('pure' patent licensing agreements). It should also apply to agreements for the licensing of non-patented technical information such as descriptions of manufacturing processes, recipes, formulae, designs or drawings, commonly termed 'know-how' ('pure' know-how licensing agreements), and to combined patent and know-how licensing agreements ('mixed' agreements), which are playing an increasingly important role in the transfer of technology. For the purposes of this Regulation, a number of terms are defined in Article 10.

(5) Patent or know-how licensing agreements are agreements whereby one undertaking which holds a patent or know-how ('the licensor') permits another undertaking ('the licensee') to exploit the patent thereby licensed, or communicates the know-how to it, in particular for purposes of manufacture, use or putting on the market. In the light of experience acquired so far, it is possible to define a category of licensing agreements covering all or part of the common market which are capable of falling within the scope of Article 85 (1) but which can normally be regarded as satisfying the conditions laid down in Article 85 (3), where patents are necessary for the achievement of the objects of the licensed technology by a mixed agreement or where know-how—whether it is ancillary to patents or independent of them—is secret, substantial and identified in any appropriate form. These criteria are intended only to ensure that the licensing of the know-how or the grant of the patent licence justifies a block exemption of obligations restricting competition. This is without prejudice to the right of the parties to include in the contract provisions regarding other obligations, such as the obligation to pay royalties, even if the block exemption no longer applies.

(6) It is appropriate to extend the scope of this Regulation to pure or mixed agreements containing the licensing of intellectual property rights other than patents (in particular, trademarks, design rights and copyright, especially software protection), when such additional licensing contributes to the achievement of the objects of the licensed technology and contains only ancillary provisions.

(7) Where such pure or mixed licensing agreements contain not only obligations relating to territories within the common market but also obligations relating to non-member countries, the presence of the latter does not prevent this Regulation from applying to the obligations relating to territories within the common market. Where licensing agreements for non-member countries or for territories which extend beyond the frontiers of the

---

[6] Convention for the European patent for the common market (Community Patent Convention) on 15 December 1975, OJ No L 17, 26. 1. 1976, p. 1.

[7] Convention on the grant of European patents (European Patent Convention) of 5 October 1973.

Community have effects within the common market which may fall within the scope of Article 85 (1), such agreements should be covered by this Regulation to the same extent as would agreements for territories within the common market.

(8) The objective being to facilitate the dissemination of technology and the improvement of manufacturing processes, this Regulation should apply only where the licensee himself manufactures the licensed products or has them manufactured for his account, or where the licensed product is a service, provides the service himself or has the service provided for his account, irrespective of whether or not the licensee is also entitled to use confidential information provided by the licensor for the promotion and sale of the licensed product. The scope of this Regulation should therefore exclude agreements solely for the purpose of sale. Also to be excluded from the scope of this Regulation are agreements relating to marketing know-how communicated in the context of franchising arrangements and certain licensing agreements entered into in connection with arrangements such as joint ventures or patent pools and other arrangements in which a licence is granted in exchange for other licences not related to improvements to or new applications of the licensed technology. Such agreements pose different problems which cannot at present be dealt with in a single regulation (Article 5).

(9) Given the similarity between sale and exclusive licensing, and the danger that the requirements of this Regulation might be evaded by presenting as assignments what are in fact exclusive licences restrictive of competition, this Regulation should apply to agreements concerning the assignment and acquisition of patents or know-how where the risk associated with exploitation remains with the assignor. It should also apply to licensing agreements in which the licensor is not the holder of the patent or know-how but is authorized by the holder to grant the licence (as in the case of sublicences) and to licensing agreements in which the parties' rights or obligations are assumed by connected undertakings (Article 6).

(10) Exclusive licensing agreements, i.e. agreements in which the licensor undertakes not to exploit the licensed technology in the licensed territory himself or to grant further licences there, may not be in themselves incompatible with Article 85 (1) where they are concerned with the introduction and protection of a new technology in the licensed territory, by reason of the scale of the research which has been undertaken, of the increase in the level of competition, in particular inter-brand competition, and of the competitiveness of the undertakings concerned resulting from the dissemination of innovation within the Community. In so far as agreements of this kind fall, in other circumstances, within the scope of Article 85 (1), it is appropriate to include them in Article 1 in order that they may also benefit from the exemption.

(11) The exemption of export bans on the licensor and on the licensees does not prejudice any developments in the case law of the Court of Justice in relation to such agreements, notably with respect to Articles 30 to 36 and Article 85 (1). This is also the case, in particular, regarding the prohibition on the

licensee from selling the licensed product in territories granted to other licensees (passive competition).

(12) The obligations listed in Article 1 generally contribute to improving the production of goods and to promoting technical progress. They make the holders of patents or know-how more willing to grant licences and licensees more inclined to undertake the investment required to manufacture, use and put on the market a new product or to use a new process. Such obligations may be permitted under this Regulation in respect of territories where the licensed product is protected by patents as long as these remain in force.

(13) Since the point at which the know-how ceases to be secret can be difficult to determine, it is appropriate, in respect of territories where the licensed technology comprises know-how only, to limit such obligations to a fixed number of years. Moreover, in order to provide sufficient periods of protection, it is appropriate to take as the starting-point for such periods the date on which the product is first put on the market in the Community by a licensee.

(14) Exemption under Article 85 (3) of longer periods of territorial protection for know-how agreements, in particular in order to protect expensive and risky investment or where the parties were not competitors at the date of the grant of the licence, can be granted only by individual decision. On the other hand, parties are free to extend the term of their agreements in order to exploit any subsequent improvement and to provide for the payment of additional royalties. However, in such cases, further periods of territorial protection may be allowed only starting from the date of licensing of the secret improvements in the Community, and by individual decision. Where the research for improvements results in innovations which are distinct from the licensed technology the parties may conclude a new agreement benefiting from an exemption under this Regulation.

(15) Provision should also be made for exemption of an obligation on the licensee not to put the product on the market in the territories of other licensees, the permitted period for such an obligation (this obligation would ban not just active competition but passive competition too) should, however, be limited to a few years from the date on which the licensed product is first put on the market in the Community by a licensee, irrespective of whether the licensed technology comprises know-how, patents or both in the territories concerned.

(16) The exemption of territorial protection should apply for the whole duration of the periods thus permitted, as long as the patents remain in force or the know-how remains secret and substantial. The parties to a mixed patent and know-how licensing agreement must be able to take advantage in a particular territory of the period of protection conferred by a patent or by the know-how, whichever is the longer.

(17) The obligations listed in Article 1 also generally fulfil the other conditions for the application of Article 85 (3). Consumers will, as a rule, be allowed a fair share of the benefit resulting from the improvement in the supply of goods on the market. To safeguard this effect, however, it is right to exclude from the application of Article 1 cases where the parties agree to refuse to

meet demand from users or resellers within their respective territories who would resell for export, or to take other steps to impede parallel imports. The obligations referred to above thus only impose restrictions which are indispensable to the attainment of their objectives.

(18) It is desirable to list in this Regulation a number of obligations that are commonly found in licensing agreements but are normally not restrictive of competition, and to provide that in the event that because of the particular economic or legal circumstances they should fall within Article 85 (1), they too will be covered by the exemption. This list, in Article 2, is not exhaustive.

(19) This Regulation must also specify what restrictions or provisions may not be included in licensing agreements if these are to benefit from the block exemption. The restrictions listed in Article 3 may fall under the prohibition of Article 85 (1), but in their case there can be no general presumption that, although they relate to the transfer of technology, they will lead to the positive effects required by Article 85 (3), as would be necessary for the granting of a block exemption. Such restrictions can be declared exempt only by an individual decision, taking account of the market position of the undertakings concerned and the degree of concentration on the relevant market.

(20) The obligations on the licensee to cease using the licensed technology after the termination of the agreement (Article 2 (1) (3)) and to make improvements available to the licensor (Article 2 (1) (4)) do not generally restrict competition. The post-term use ban may be regarded as a normal feature of licensing, as otherwise the licensor would be forced to transfer his know-how or patents in perpetuity. Undertakings by the licensee to grant back to the licensor a licence for improvements to the licensed know-how and/or patents are generally not restrictive of competition if the licensee is entitled by the contract to share in future experience and inventions made by the licensor. On the other hand, a restrictive effect on competition arises where the agreement obliges the licensee to assign to the licensor rights to improvements of the originally licensed technology that he himself has brought about (Article 3 (6)).

(21) The list of clauses which do not prevent exemption also includes an obligation on the licensee to keep paying royalties until the end of the agreement independently of whether or not the licensed know-how has entered into the public domain through the action of third parties or of the licensee himself (Article 2 (1) (7)). Moreover, the parties must be free, in order to facilitate payment, to spread the royalty payments for the use of the licensed technology over a period extending beyond the duration of the licensed patents, in particular by setting lower royalty rates. As a rule, parties do not need to be protected against the foreseeable financial consequences of an agreement freely entered into, and they should therefore be free to choose the appropriate means of financing the technology transfer and sharing between them the risks of such use. However, the setting of rates of royalty so as to achieve one of the restrictions listed in Article 3 renders the agreement ineligible for the block exemption.

(22) An obligation on the licensee to restrict his exploitation of the licensed

technology to one or more technical fields of application ('fields of use') or to one or more product markets is not caught by Article 85 (1) either, since the licensor is entitled to transfer the technology only for a limited purpose (Article 2 (1) (8)).

(23) Clauses whereby the parties allocate customers within the same technological field of use or the same product market, either by an actual prohibition on supplying certain classes of customer or through an obligation with an equivalent effect, would also render the agreement ineligible for the block exemption where the parties are competitors for the contract products (Article 3 (4)). Such restrictions between undertakings which are not competitors remain subject to the opposition procedure. Article 3 does not apply to cases where the patent or know-how licence is granted in order to provide a single customer with a second source of supply. In such a case, a prohibition on the second licensee from supplying persons other than the customer concerned is an essential condition for the grant of a second licence, since the purpose of the transaction is not to create an independent supplier in the market. The same applies to limitations on the quantities the licensee may supply to the customer concerned (Article 2 (1) (13)).

(24) Besides the clauses already mentioned, the list of restrictions which render the block exemption inapplicable also includes restrictions regarding the selling prices of the licensed product or the quantities to be manufactured or sold, since they seriously limit the extent to which the licensee can exploit the licensed technology and since quantity restrictions particularly may have the same effect as export bans (Article 3 (1) and (5)). This does not apply where a licence is granted for use of the technology in specific production facilities and where both a specific technology is communicated for the setting-up, operation and maintenance of these facilities and the licensee is allowed to increase the capacity of the facilities or to set up further facilities for its own use on normal commercial terms. On the other hand, the licensee may lawfully be prevented from using the transferred technology to set up facilities for third parties, since the purpose of the agreement is not to permit the licensee to give other producers access to the licensor's technology while it remains secret or protected by patent (Article 2 (1) (12)).

(25) Agreements which are not automatically covered by the exemption because they contain provisions that are not expressly exempted by this Regulation and not expressly excluded from exemption, including those listed in Article 4 (2), may, in certain circumstances, nonetheless be presumed to be eligible for application of the block exemption. It will be possible for the Commission rapidly to establish whether this is the case on the basis of the information undertakings are obliged to provide under Commission Regulation (EC) No 3385/94[8]. The Commission may waive the requirement to supply specific information required in form A/B but which it does not deem necessary. The Commission will generally be content with communication of the text of the agreement and with an estimate, based on directly

[8] OJ No L 377, 31. 12. 1994, p. 28.

available data, of the market structure and of the licensee's market share. Such agreements should therefore be deemed to be covered by the exemption provided for in this Regulation where they are notified to the Commission and the Commission does not oppose the application of the exemption within a specified period of time.

(26) Where agreements exempted under this Regulation nevertheless have effects incompatible with Article 85 (3), the Commission may withdraw the block exemption, in particular where the licensed products are not faced with real competition in the licensed territory (Article 7). This could also be the case where the licensee has a strong position on the market. In assessing the competition the Commission will pay special attention to cases where the licensee has more than 40% of the whole market for the licensed products and of all the products or services which customers consider interchangeable or substitutable on account of their characteristics, prices and intended use.

(27) Agreements which come within the terms of Articles 1 and 2 and which have neither the object nor the effect of restricting competition in any other way need no longer be notified. Nevertheless, undertakings will still have the right to apply in individual cases for negative clearance or for exemption under Article 85 (3) in accordance with Council Regulation No 17[9], as last amended by the Act of Accession of Austria, Finland and Sweden. They can in particular notify agreements obliging the licensor not to grant other licences in the territory, where the licensee's market share exceeds or is likely to exceed 40%,

HAS ADOPTED THIS REGULATION:

Article 1

1. Pursuant to Article 85 (3) of the Treaty and subject to the conditions set out below, it is hereby declared that Article 85 (1) of the Treaty shall not apply to pure patent licensing or know-how licensing agreements and to mixed patent and know-how licensing agreements, including those agreements containing ancillary provisions relating to intellectual property rights other than patents, to which only two undertakings are party and which include one or more of the following obligations:

(1) an obligation on the licensor not to license other undertakings to exploit the licensed technology in the licensed territory;
(2) an obligation on the licensor not to exploit the licensed technology in the licensed territory himself;
(3) an obligation on the licensee not to exploit the licensed technology in the territory of the licensor within the common market;
(4) an obligation on the licensee not to manufacture or use the licensed product, or use the licensed process, in territories within the common market which are licensed to other licensees;

[9] OJ No 13, 21. 2. 1962, p. 204/62.

(5) an obligation on the licensee not to pursue an active policy of putting the licensed product on the market in the territories within the common market which are licensed to other licensees, and in particular not to engage in advertising specifically aimed at those territories or to establish any branch or maintain a distribution depot there;

(6) an obligation on the licensee not to put the licensed product on the market in the territories licensed to other licensees within the common market in response to unsolicited orders;

(7) an obligation on the licensee to use only the licensor's trademark or get up to distinguish the licensed product during the term of the agreement, provided that the licensee is not prevented from identifying himself as the manufacturer of the licensed products;

(8) an obligation on the licensee to limit his production of the licensed product to the quantities he requires in manufacturing his own products and to sell the licensed product only as an integral part of or a replacement part for his own products or otherwise in connection with the sale of his own products, provided that such quantities are freely determined by the licensee.

2. Where the agreement is a pure patent licensing agreement, the exemption of the obligations referred to in paragraph 1 is granted only to the extent that and for as long as the licensed product is protected by parallel patents, in the territories respectively of the licensee (points (1), (2), (7) and (8)), the licensor (point (3)) and other licensees (points (4) and (5)). The exemption of the obligation referred to in point (6) of paragraph 1 is granted for a period not exceeding five years from the date when the licensed product is first put on the market within the common market by one of the licensees, to the extent that and for as long as, in these territories, this product is protected by parallel patents.

3. Where the agreement is a pure know-how licensing agreement, the period for which the exemption of the obligations referred to in points (1) to (5) of paragraph 1 is granted may not exceed ten years from the date when the licensed product is first put on the market within the common market by one of the licensees.

The exemption of the obligation referred to in point (6) of paragraph 1 is granted for a period not exceeding five years from the date when the licensed product is first put on the market within the common market by one of the licensees.

The obligations referred to in points (7) and (8) of paragraph 1 are exempted during the lifetime of the agreement for as long as the know-how remains secret and substantial.

However, the exemption in paragraph 1 shall apply only where the parties have identified in any appropriate form the initial know-how and any subsequent improvements to it which become available to one party and are communicated to the other party pursuant to the terms of the agreement and to the purpose thereof, and only for as long as the know-how remains secret and substantial.

4. Where the agreement is a mixed patent and know-how licensing agreement, the exemption of the obligations referred to in points (1) to (5) of paragraph 1 shall apply in Member States in which the licensed technology is protected by necessary patents for as long as the licensed product is protected in those

Member States by such patents if the duration of such protection exceeds the periods specified in paragraph 3.

The duration of the exemption provided in point (6) of paragraph 1 may not exceed the five-year period provided for in paragraphs 2 and 3.

However, such agreements qualify for the exemption referred to in paragraph 1 only for as long as the patents remain in force or to the extent that the know-how is identified and for as long as it remains secret and substantial whichever period is the longer.

5. The exemption provided for in paragraph 1 shall also apply where in a particular agreement the parties undertake obligations of the types referred to in that paragraph but with a more limited scope than is permitted by that paragraph.

Article 2

1. Article 1 shall apply notwithstanding the presence in particular of any of the following clauses, which are generally not restrictive of competition:

(1) an obligation on the licensee not to divulge the know-how communicated by the licensor; the licensee may be held to this obligation after the agreement has expired;

(2) an obligation on the licensee not to grant sublicences or assign the licence;

(3) an obligation on the licensee not to exploit the licensed know-how or patents after termination of the agreement in so far and as long as the know-how is still secret or the patents are still in force;

(4) an obligation on the licensee to grant to the licensor a licence in respect of his own improvements to or his new applications of the licensed technology, provided:

— that, in the case of severable improvements, such a licence is not exclusive, so that the licensee is free to use his own improvements or to license them to third parties, in so far as that does not involve disclosure of the know-how communicated by the licensor that is still secret,

— and that the licensor undertakes to grant an exclusive or non-exclusive licence of his own improvements to the licensee;

(5) an obligation on the licensee to observe minimum quality specifications, including technical specifications for the licensed product or to procure goods or services from the licensor or from an undertaking designated by the licensor, in so far as these quality specifications, products or services are necessary for:

(a) a technically proper exploitation of the licensed technology; or

(b) ensuring that the product of the licensee conforms to the minimum quality specifications that are applicable to the licensor and other licensees;

and to allow the licensor to carry out related checks;

(6) obligations:

(a) to inform the licensor of misappropriation of the know-how or of infringements of the licensed patents; or

(b) to take or to assist the licensor in taking legal action against such misappropriation or infringements;

(7) an obligation on the licensee to continue paying the royalties;

(a) until the end of the agreement in the amounts, for the periods and according to the methods freely determined by the parties, in the event of the know-how becoming publicly known other than by action of the licensor, without prejudice to the payment of any additional damages in the event of the know-how becoming publicly known by the action of the licensee in breach of the agreement;

(b) over a period going beyond the duration of the licensed patents, in order to facilitate payment;

(8) an obligation on the licensee to restrict his exploitation of the licensed technology to one or more technical fields of application covered by the licensed technology or to one or more product markets;

(9) an obligation on the licensee to pay a minimum royalty or to produce a minimum quantity of the licensed product or to carry out a minimum number of operations exploiting the licensed technology;

(10) an obligation on the licensor to grant the licensee any more favourable terms that the licensor may grant to another undertaking after the agreement is entered into;

(11) an obligation on the licensee to mark the licensed product with an indication of the licensor's name or of the licensed patent;

(12) an obligation on the licensee not to use the licensor's technology to construct facilities for third parties; this is without prejudice to the right of the licensee to increase the capacity of his facilities or to set up additional facilities for his own use on normal commercial terms, including the payment of additional royalties;

(13) an obligation on the licensee to supply only a limited quantity of the licensed product to a particular customer, where the license was granted so that the customer might have a second source of supply inside the licensed territory; this provision shall also apply where the customer is the licensee, and the licence which was granted in order to provide a second source of supply provides that the customer is himself to manufacture the licensed products or to have them manufactured by a subcontractor;

(14) a reservation by the licensor of the right to exercise the rights conferred by a patent to oppose the exploitation of the technology by the licensee outside the licensed territory;

(15) a reservation by the licensor of the right to terminate the agreement if the licensee contests the secret or substantial nature of the licensed know-how or challenges the validity of licensed patents within the common market belonging to the licensor or undertakings connected with him;

(16) a reservation by the licensor of the right to terminate the licence agreement of a patent if the licensee raises the claim that such a patent is not necessary;

(17) an obligation on the licensee to use his best endeavours to manufacture and market the licensed product;

(18) a reservation by the licensor of the right to terminate the exclusivity granted to the licensee and to stop licensing improvements to him when the licensee enters into competition within the common market with the licensor, with undertakings connected with the licensor or with other undertakings in respect of research and development, production, use or distribution of competing products, and to require the licensee to prove that the licensed know-how is not being used for the production of products and the provision of services other than those licensed.

2. In the event that, because of particular circumstances, the clauses referred to in paragraph 1 fall within the scope of Article 85 (1), they shall also be exempted even if they are not accompanied by any of the obligations exempted by Article 1.

3. The exemption in paragraph 2 shall also apply where an agreement contains clauses of the types referred to in paragraph 1 but with a more limited scope than is permitted by that paragraph.

Article 3

Article 1 and Article 2 (2) shall not apply where:

(1) one party is restricted in the determination of prices, components of prices or discounts for the licensed products;

(2) one party is restricted from competing within the common market with the other party, with undertakings connected with the other party or with other undertakings in respect of research and development, production, use or distribution of competing products without prejudice to the provisions of Article 2 (1) (17) and (18);

(3) one or both of the parties are required without any objectively justified reason:

    (a) to refuse to meet orders from users or resellers in their respective territories who would market products in other territories within the common market;

    (b) to make it difficult for users or resellers to obtain the products from other resellers within the common market, and in particular to exercise intellectual property rights or take measures so as to prevent users or resellers from obtaining outside, or from putting on the market in the licensed territory products which have been lawfully put on the market within the common market by the licensor or with his consent;

    or do so as a result of a concerted practice between them;

(4) the parties were already competing manufacturers before the grant of the licence and one of them is restricted, within the same technical field of use or within the same product market, as to the customers he may serve, in particular

by being prohibited from supplying certain classes of users, employing certain forms of distribution or, with the aim of sharing customers, using certain types of packaging for the products, save as provided in Article 1 (1) (7) and Article 2 (1) (13);

(5) the quantity of the licensed products one party may manufacture or sell or the number of operations exploiting the licensed technology he may carry out are subject to limitations, save as provided in Article (1) (8) and Article 2 (1) (13);

(6) the licensee is obliged to assign in whole or in part to the licensor rights to improvements to or new applications of the licensed technology;

(7) the licensor is required, albeit in separate agreements or through automatic prolongation of the initial duration of the agreement by the inclusion of any new improvements, for a period exceeding that referred to in Article 1 (2) and (3) not to license other undertakings to exploit the licensed technology in the licensed territory, or a party is required for a period exceeding that referred to in Article 1 (2) and (3) or Article 1 (4) not to exploit the licensed technology in the territory of the other party or of other licensees.

Article 4

1. The exemption provided for in Articles 1 and 2 shall also apply to agreements containing obligations restrictive of competition which are not covered by those Articles and do not fall within the scope of Article 3, on condition that the agreements in question are notified to the Commission in accordance with the provisions of Articles 1, 2 and 3 of Regulation EC No 3385/94 and that the Commission does not oppose such exemption within a period of four months.

2. Paragraph 1 shall apply, in particular, where:

(a) the licensee is obliged at the time the agreement is entered into to accept quality specifications or further licences or to procure goods or services which are not necessary for a technically satisfactory exploitation of the licensed technology or for ensuring that the production of the licensee conforms to the quality standards that are respected by the licensor and other licensees;

(b) the licensee is prohibited from contesting the secrecy or the substantiality of the licensed know-how or from challenging the validity of patents licensed within the common market belonging to the licensor or undertakings connected with him.

3. The period of four months referred to in paragraph 1 shall run from the date on which the notification takes effect in accordance with Article 4 of Regulation (EC) No 3385/94.

4. The benefit of paragraphs 1 and 2 may be claimed for agreements notified before the entry into force of this Regulation by submitting a communication to the Commission referring expressly to this Article and to the notification. Paragraph 3 shall apply *mutatis mutandis*.

5. The Commission may oppose the exemption within a period of four months.

It shall oppose exemption if it receives a request to do so from a Member State within two months of the transmission to the Member State of the notification referred to in paragraph 1 or of the communication referred to in paragraph 4. This request must be justified on the basis of considerations relating to the competition rules of the Treaty.

6. The Commission may withdraw the opposition to the exemption at any time. However, where the opposition was raised at the request of a Member State and this request is maintained, it may be withdrawn only after consultation of the Advisory Committee on Restrictive Practices and Dominant Positions.

7. If the opposition is withdrawn because the undertakings concerned have shown that the conditions of Article 85 (3) are satisfied, the exemption shall apply from the date of notification.

8. If the opposition is withdrawn because the undertakings concerned have amended the agreement so that the conditions of Article 85 (3) are satisfied, the exemption shall apply from the date on which the amendments take effect.

9. If the Commission opposes exemption and the opposition is not withdrawn, the effects of the notification shall be governed by the provisions of Regulation No 17.

Article 5

1. This Regulation shall not apply to:

(1) agreements between members of a patent or know-how pool which relate to the pooled technologies;

(2) licensing agreements between competing undertakings which hold interests in a joint venture, or between one of them and the joint venture, if the licensing agreements relate to the activities of the joint venture;

(3) agreements under which one party grants the other a patent and/or know-how license and in exchange the other party, albeit in separate agreements or through connected undertakings, grants the first party a patent, trademark or know-how licence or exclusive sales rights, where the parties are competitors in relation to the products covered by those agreements;

(4) licensing agreements containing provisions relating to intellectual property rights other than patents which are not ancillary;

(5) agreements entered into solely for the purpose of sale.

2. This Regulation shall nevertheless apply:

(1) to agreements to which paragraph 1 (2) applies, under which a parent undertaking grants the joint venture a patent or know-how licence, provided that the licensed products and the other goods and services of the participating undertakings which are considered by users to be interchangeable or substitutable in view of their characteristics, price and intended use represent:

— in case of a licence limited to production, not more then 20%, and
— in case of a licence covering production and distribution, not more than 10%;

of the market for the licensed products and all interchangeable or substitutable goods and services;

(2) to agreements to which paragraph 1 (1) applies and to reciprocal licences within the meaning of paragraph 1 (3), provided the parties are not subject to any territorial restriction within the common market with regard to the manufacture, use or putting on the market of the licensed products or to the use of the licensed or pooled technologies.

3. This Regulation shall continue to apply where, for two consecutive financial years, the market shares in paragraph 2 (1) are not exceeded by more than one-tenth; where that limit is exceeded, this Regulation shall continue to apply for a period of six months from the end of the year in which the limit was exceeded.

Article 6

This Regulation shall also apply to:

(1) agreements where the licensor is not the holder of the know-how or the patentee, but is authorized by the holder or the patentee to grant a licence;
(2) assignments of know-how, patents or both where the risk associated with exploitation remains with the assignor, in particular where the sum payable in consideration of the assignment is dependent on the turnover obtained by the assignee in respect of products made using the know-how or the patents, the quantity of such products manufactured or the number of operations carried out employing the know-how or the patents;
(3) licensing agreements in which the rights or obligations of the licensor or the licensee are assumed by undertakings connected with them.

Article 7

The Commission may withdraw the benefit of this Regulation, pursuant to Article 7 of Regulation No 19/65/EEC, where it finds in a particular case that an agreement exempted by this Regulation nevertheless has certain effects which are incompatible with the conditions laid down in Article 85 (3) of the Treaty, and in particular where:

(1) the effect of the agreement is to prevent the licensed products from being exposed to effective competition in the licensed territory from identical goods or services or from goods or services considered by users as interchangeable or substitutable in view of their characteristics, price and intended use, which may in particular occur where the licensee's market share exceeds 40%;
(2) without prejudice to Article 1 (1) (6), the licensee refuses, without any objectively justified reason, to meet unsolicited orders from users or resellers in the territory of other licensees;
(3) the parties:

  (a) without any objectively justified reason, refuse to meet orders from users or resellers in their respective territories who would market the products in other territories within the common market; or

(b) make it difficult for users or resellers to obtain the products from other resellers within the common market, and in particular where they exercise intellectual property rights or take measures so as to prevent resellers or users from obtaining outside, or from putting on the market in the licensed territory products which have been lawfully put on the market within the common market by the licensor or with his consent;

(4) the parties were competing manufacturers at the date of the grant of the licence and obligations on the licensee to produce a minimum quantity or to use his best endeavours as referred to in Article 2 (1), (9) and (17) respectively have the effect of preventing the licensee from using competing technologies.

Article 8

1. For purposes of this Regulation:

(a) patent applications;
(b) utility models;
(c) applications for registration of utility models;
(d) topographies of semiconductor products;
(e) *certificats d'utilité* and *certificats d'addition* under French law;
(f) applications for *certificats d'utilité* and *certificats d'addition* under French law;
(g) supplementary protection certificates for medicinal products or other products for which such supplementary protection certificates may be obtained;
(h) plant breeder's certificates,

shall be deemed to be patents.

2. This Regulation shall also apply to agreements relating to the exploitation of an invention if an application within the meaning of paragraph 1 is made in respect of the invention for a licensed territory after the date when the agreements were entered into but within the time-limits set by the national law or the international convention to be applied.

3. This Regulation shall furthermore apply to pure patent or know-how licensing agreements or to mixed agreements whose initial duration is automatically prolonged by the inclusion of any new improvements, whether patented or not, communicated by the licensor, provided that the licensee has the right to refuse such improvements or each party has the right to terminate the agreement at the expiry of the initial term of an agreement and at least every three years thereafter.

Article 9

1. Information acquired pursuant to Article 4 shall be used only for the purposes of this Regulation.

2. The Commission and the authorities of the Member States, their officials and other servants shall not disclose information acquired by them pursuant to this Regulation of the kind covered by the obligation of professional secrecy.

3. The provisions of paragraphs 1 and 2 shall not prevent publication of general information or surveys which do not contain information relating to particular undertakings or associations of undertakings.

Article 10

For purpose of this Regulation:

(1) 'know-how' means a body of technical information that is secret, substantial and identified in any appropriate form;

(2) 'secret' means that the know-how package as a body or in the precise configuration and assembly of its components is not generally known or easily accessible, so that part of its value consists in the lead which the licensee gains when it is communicated to him; it is not limited to the narrow sense that each individual component of the know-how should be totally unknown or unobtainable outside the licensor's business;

(3) 'substantial' means that the know-how includes information which must be useful, i.e. can reasonably be expected at the date of conclusion of the agreement to be capable of improving the competitive position of the licensee, for example by helping him to enter a new market or giving him an advantage in competition with other manufacturers or providers of services who do not have access to the licensed secret know-how or other comparable secret know-how;

(4) 'identified' means that the know-how is described or recorded in such a manner as to make it possible to verify that it satisfies the criteria of secrecy and substantially and to ensure that the licensee is not unduly restricted in his exploitation of his own technology, to be identified the know-how can either be set out in the licence agreement or in a separate document or recorded in any other appropriate form at the latest when the know-how is transferred or shortly thereafter, provided that the separate document or other record can be made available if the need arises;

(5) 'necessary patents' are patents where a licence under the patent is necessary for the putting into effect of the licensed technology in so far as, in the absence of such a license, the realization of this licensed technology would not be possible or would be possible only to a lesser extent or in more difficult or costly conditions. Such patents must therefore be of technical, legal or economic interest to the licensee;

(6) 'licensing agreement' means pure patent licensing agreements and pure know-how licensing agreements as well as mixed patent and know-how licensing agreements;

(7) 'licensed technology' means the initial manufacturing know-how or the necessary product and process patents, or both, existing at the time the first licensing agreement is concluded, and improvements subsequently made to the know-how or patents, irrespective of whether and to what extent they are exploited by the parties or by other licensees;

(8) 'the licensed products' are goods or services the production or provision of which requires the use of the licensed technology;

(9) 'the licensee's market share' means the proportion which the licensed products and other goods or services provided by the licensee, which are considered by users to be interchangeable or substitutable for the licensed products in view of their characteristics, price and intended use, represent the entire market for the licensed products and all other interchangeable or substitutable goods and services in the common market or a substantial part of it;

(10) 'exploitation' refers to any use of the licensed technology in particular in the production, active or passive sales in a territory even if not coupled with manufacture in that territory, or leasing of the licensed products;

(11) 'the licensed territory' is the territory covering all or at least part of the common market where the licensee is entitled to exploit the licensed technology;

(12) 'territory of the licensor' means territories in which the licensor has not granted any licences for patents and/or know-how covered by the licensing agreement;

(13) 'parallel patents' means patents which, in spite of the divergences which remain in the absence of any unification of national rules concerning industrial property, protect the same invention in various Member States;

(14) 'connected undertakings' means:

    (a)   undertakings in which a party to the agreement, directly or indirectly:

        — owns more than half the capital or business assets, or
        — has the power to exercise more than half the voting rights, or
        — has the power to appoint more than half the members of the supervisory board, board of directors or bodies legally representing the undertaking, or
        — has the right to manage the affairs of the undertaking;

    (b)   undertakings which, directly or indirectly, have in or over a party to the agreement the rights or powers listed in (a);

    (c)   undertakings in which an undertaking referred to in (b), directly or indirectly, has the rights or powers listed in (a);

    (d)   undertakings in which the parties to the agreement or undertakings connected with them jointly have the rights or powers listed in (a): such jointly controlled undertakings are considered to be connected with each of the parties to the agreement;

(15) 'ancillary provisions' are provisions relating to the exploitation of intellectual property rights other than patents, which contain no obligations restrictive of competition other than those also attached to the licensed know-how or patents and exempted under this Regulation;

(16) 'obligation' means both contractual obligation and a concerted practice;

(17) 'competing manufacturers' or manufactures of 'competing products' means manufacturers who sell products which, in view of their characteristics, price and intended use, are considered by users to be interchangeable or substitutable for the licensed products.

Article 11

1. Regulation (EEC) No 556/89 is hereby repealed with effect from 1 April 1996.
2. Regulation (EEC) No 2349/84 shall continue to apply until 31 March 1996.
3. The prohibition in Article 85 (1) of the Treaty shall not apply to agreements in force on 31 March 1996 which fulfil the exemption requirements laid down by Regulation (EEC) No 2349/84 or (EEC) No 556/89.

Article 12

1. The Commission shall undertake regular assessments of the application of this Regulation, and in particular of the opposition procedure provided for in Article 4.
2. The Commission shall draw up a report on the operation of this Regulation before the end of the fourth year following its entry into force and shall, on that basis, assess whether any adaptation of the Regulation is desirable.

Article 13

This Regulation shall enter into force on 1 April 1996.
It shall apply until 31 March 2006.
Article 11 (2) of this Regulation shall, however, enter into force on 1 January 1996.

This Regulation shall be binding in its entirety and directly applicable in all Member States.
Done at Brussels, 31 January 1996.

For the Commission
Karel VAN MIERT
Member of the Commission

Appendix III

Antitrust Guidelines for the Licensing of Intellectual Property

April 6, 1995

Issued by the
U.S. Department of Justice*
and the
Federal Trade Commission

1. Intellectual property protection and the antitrust laws
2. General principles
    2.1 Standard antitrust analysis applies to intellectual property
    2.2 Intellectual property and market power
    2.3 Procompetitive benefits of licensing
3. Antitrust concerns and modes of analysis
    3.1 Nature of the concerns
    3.2 Markets affected by licensing arrangements
        3.2.1 Goods markets
        3.2.2 Technology markets
        3.2.3 Research and development: Innovation markets
    3.3 Horizontal and vertical relationships
    3.4 Framework for evaluating licensing restrains
4. General principles concerning the Agencies' evaluation of licensing arrangements under the rule of reason
    4.1 Analysis of anticompetitive effects
        4.1.1 Market structure, coordination, and foreclosure
        4.1.2 Licensing arrangements involving exclusivity
    4.2 Efficiencies and justifications
    4.3 Antitrust 'safety zone'
5. Application of general principles
    5.1 Horizontal restraints
    5.2 Resale price maintenance
    5.3 Tying arrangements
    5.4 Exclusive dealing
    5.5 Cross-licensing and pooling arrangements

---

* These Guidelines supersede section 3.6 in Part I, 'Intellectual Property Licensing Arrangements,' and cases 6, 10, and 12 in Part II of the U.S. Department of Justice 1988 Antitrust Enforcement Guidelines for International Operations.

5.6 Grantbacks
5.7 Acquisition of intellectual property rights
6. Enforcement of invalid intellectual property rights

1. INTELLECTUAL PROPERTY PROTECTION AND THE ANTITRUST LAWS

1.0 These Guidelines state the antitrust enforcement policy of the U.S. Department of Justice and the Federal Trade Commission (individually, 'the Agency', and collectively, 'the Agencies') with respect to the licensing of intellectual property protected by patent, copyright, and trade secret law, and of know-how.[1] By stating their general policy, the Agencies hope to assist those who need to predict whether the Agencies will challenge a practice as anticompetitive. However, these Guidelines cannot remove judgment and discretion in antitrust law enforcement. Moreover, the standards set forth in these Guidelines must be applied in unforeseeable circumstances. Each case will be evaluated in light of its own facts, and these Guidelines will be applied reasonably and flexibly.[2]

In the United States, patents confer rights to exclude others from making, using, or selling in the United States the invention claimed by the patent for a period of seventeen years from the date of issue.[3] To gain patent protection, an invention (which may be a product, process, machine, or composition of matter) must be novel, nonobvious, and useful. Copyright protection applies to original works of authorship embodied in a tangible medium of expression.[4] A copyright protects only the expression, not the underlying ideas.[5] Unlike a patent, which protects an invention not only from copying but also from independent creation, a copyright does not preclude others from independently creating similar expression. Trade

---

[1] These Guidelines do not cover the antitrust treatment of trademarks. Although the same general antitrust principles that apply to other forms of intellectual property apply to trademarks as well, these Guidelines deal with technology transfer and innovation-related issues that typically arise with respect to patents, copyrights, trade secrets, and know-how agreements, rather than with product-differentiation issues that typically arise with respect to trademarks.

[2] As is the case with all guidelines, users should rely on qualified counsel to assist them in evaluating the antitrust risk associated with any contemplated transaction or activity. No set of guidelines can possibly indicate how the Agencies will assess the particular facts of every case. Parties who wish to know the Agencies' specific enforcement intentions with respect to any particular transaction should consider seeking a Department of Justice business review letter pursuant to 28 C.F.R. § 50.6 or a Federal Trade Commission Advisory Opinion pursuant to 16 C.F.R. §§ 1.1–1.4.

[3] *See* 35 U.S.C. § 154 (1988). Section 532(a) of the Uruguay Round Agreements Act, Pub. L. No. 103–465, 108 Stat. 4809, 4983 (1994) would change the length of patent protection to a term beginning on the date at which the patent issues and ending twenty years from the date on which the application for the patent was filed.

[4] *See* 17 U.S.C. § 102 (1988 & Supp. V 1993). Copyright protection lasts for the author's life plus 50 years, or 75 years from first publication (or 100 years from creation, whichever expires first) for works made for hire. *See* 17 U.S.C. § 302 (1988). The principles stated in these Guidelines also apply to protection of mask works fixed in a semiconductor chip product (*see* 17 U.S.C. § 901 *et seq.* (1988)), which is analogous to copyright protection for works of authorship.   [5] *See* 17 U.S.C. § 102(b) (1988).

secret protection applies to information whose economic value depends on its not being generally known.[6] Trade secret protection is conditioned upon efforts to maintain secrecy and has no fixed term. As with copyright protection, trade secret protection does not preclude independent creation by others.

The intellectual property laws and the antitrust laws share the common purpose of promoting innovation and enhancing consumer welfare.[7] The intellectual property laws provide incentives for innovation and its dissemination and commercialization by establishing enforceable property rights for the creators of new and useful products, more efficient processes, and original works of expression. In the absence of intellectual property rights, imitators could more rapidly exploit the efforts of innovators and investors without compensation. Rapid imitation would reduce the commercial value of innovation and erode incentives to invest, ultimately to the detriment of consumers. The antitrust laws promote innovation and consumer welfare by prohibiting certain actions that may harm competition with respect to either existing or new ways of serving consumers.

2. GENERAL PRINCIPLES

2.0 These Guidelines embody three general principles: (a) for the purpose of antitrust analysis, the Agencies regard intellectual property as being essentially comparable to any other form of property; (b) the Agencies do not presume that intellectual property creates market power in the antitrust context; and (c) the Agencies recognize that intellectual property licensing allows firms to combine complementary factors of production and is generally procompetitive.

2.1 Standard antitrust analysis applies to intellectual property

The Agencies apply the same general antitrust principles to conduct involving intellectual property that they apply to conduct involving any other form of tangible or intangible property. That is not to say that intellectual property is in all respects the same as any other form of property. Intellectual property has important characteristics, such as ease of misappropriation, that distinguish it from many other forms of property. These characteristics can be taken into account by standard antitrust analysis, however, and do not require the application of fundamentally different principles.[8]

---

[6] Trade secret protection derives from state law. *See generally Kewanee Oil Co.* v. *Bicron Corp.*, 416 U.S. 470 (1974).

[7] '[T]he aims and objectives of patent and antitrust laws may seem, at first glance, wholly at odds. However, the two bodies of law are actually complementary, as both are aimed at encouraging innovation, industry and competition.' *Atari Games Corp.* v. *Nintendo of America, Inc.*, 897 F.2d 1572, 1576 (Fed. Cir. 1990).

[8] As with other forms of property, the power to exclude others from the use of intellectual property may vary substantially, depending on the nature of the property and its status under federal or state law. The greater or lesser legal power of an owner to exclude others is also taken into account by standard antitrust analysis.

Although there are clear and important differences in the purpose, extent, and duration of protection provided under the intellectual property regimes of patent, copyright, and trade secret, the governing antitrust principles are the same. Antitrust analysis takes differences among these forms of intellectual property into account in evaluating the specific market circumstances in which transactions occur, just as it does with other particular market circumstances.

Intellectual property law bestows on the owners of intellectual property certain rights to exclude others. These rights help the owners to profit from the use of their property. An intellectual property owner's rights to exclude are similar to the rights enjoyed by owners of other forms of private property. As with other forms of private property, certain types of conduct with respect to intellectual property may have anticompetitive effects against which the antitrust laws can and do protect. Intellectual property is thus neither particularly free from scrutiny under the antitrust laws, nor particularly suspect under them.

The Agencies recognize that the licensing of intellectual property is often international. The principles of antitrust analysis described in these Guidelines apply equally to domestic and international licensing arrangements. However, as described in the 1995 Department of Justice and Federal Trade Commission Antitrust Enforcement Guidelines for International Operations, considerations particular to international operations, such as jurisdiction and comity, may affect enforcement decisions when the arrangement is in an international context.

2.2 Intellectual property and market power

Market power is the ability profitably to maintain prices above, or output below, competitive levels for a significant period of time.[9] The Agencies will not presume that a patent, copyright, or trade secret necessarily confers market power upon its owner. Although the intellectual property right confers the power to exclude with respect to the *specific* product, process, or work in question, there will often be sufficient actual or potential close substitutes for such product, process, or work to prevent the exercise of market power.[10] If a patent

[9] Market power can be exercised in other economic dimensions, such as quality, service and the development of new or improved goods and processes. It is assumed in this definition that all competitive dimensions are held constant except the ones in which market power is being exercised; that a seller is able to charge higher prices for a higher-quality product does not alone indicate market power. The definition in the text is stated in terms of a seller with market power. A buyer could also exercise market power (e.g., by maintaining the price below the competitive level, thereby depressing output).

[10] The Agencies note that the law is unclear on this issue. *Compare Jefferson Parish Hospital District No. 2* v. *Hyde*, 466 U.S. 2, 16 (1984) (expressing the view in dictum that if a product is protected by a patent, 'it is fair to presume that the inability to buy the product elsewhere gives the seller market power') *with id.* at 37 n. 7 (O'Connor, J., concurring) ('[A] patent holder has no market power in any relevant sense if there are close substitutes for the patented product.'). *Compare also Abbot Laboratories* v. *Brennan*, 952 F.2d 1346, 1354–55 (Fed. Cir. 1991) (no presumption of market power from intellectual property right), *cert. denied*, 112 S. Ct. 2993 (1992) *with Digidyne Corp.* v. *Data General Corp.*, 734 F.2d 1336, 1341–42 (9th Cir. 1984) (requisite economic power is presumed from copyright), *cert. denied*, 473 U.S. 908 (1985).

or other form of intellectual property does confer market power, that market power does not by itself offend the antitrust laws. As with any other tangible or intangible asset that enables its owner to obtain significant supracompetitive profits, market power (or even a monopoly) that is solely 'a consequence of a superior product, business acumen, or historic accident' does not violate the antitrust laws.[11] Nor does such market power impose on the intellectual property owner an obligation to license the use of that property to others. As in other antitrust contexts, however, market power could be illegally acquired or maintained, or, even if lawfully acquired and maintained, would be relevant to the ability of an intellectual property owner to harm competition through unreasonable conduct in connection with such property.

2.3 Procompetitive benefits of licensing

Intellectual property typically is one component among many in a production process and derives value from its combination with complementary factors. Complementary factors of production include manufacturing and distribution facilities, workforces, and other items of intellectual property. The owner of intellectual property has to arrange for its combination with other necessary factors to realize its commercial value. Often, the owner finds it most efficient to contract with others for these factors, to sell rights to the intellectual property, or to enter into a joint venture arrangement for its development, rather than supply these complementary factors itself.

Licensing, cross-licensing, or otherwise transferring intellectual property (hereafter 'licensing') can facilitate integration of the licensed property with complementary factors of production. This integration can lead to more efficient exploitation of the intellectual property, benefiting consumers through the reduction of costs and the introduction of new products. Such arrangements increase the value of intellectual property to consumers and to the developers of the technology. By potentially increasing the expected returns from intellectual property, licensing also can increase the incentive for its creation and thus promote greater investment in research and development.

Sometimes the use of one item of intellectual property requires access to another. An item of intellectual property 'blocks' another when the second cannot be practiced without using the first. For example, an improvement on a patented machine can be blocked by the patent on the machine. Licensing may promote the coordinated development of technologies that are in a blocking relationship.

Field-of-use, territorial, and other limitations on intellectual property licenses may serve procompetitive ends by allowing the licensor to exploit its property as efficiently and effectively as possible. These various forms of exclusivity can be used to give a licensee an incentive to invest in the commercialization and distribution of products embodying the licensed intellectual property and to develop

---

[11] *United States* v. *Grinnell Corp.*, 384 U.S. 563, 571 (1966); *see also United States* v. *Aluminum Co. of America*, 148 F.2d 416, 430 (2d Cir. 1945) (Sherman Act is not violated by the attainment of market power solely through 'superior skill, foresight and industry').

additional applications for the licensed property. The restrictions may do so, for example, by protecting the licensee against free-riding on the licensee's investments by other licensees or by the licensor. They may also increase the licensor's incentive to license, for example, by protecting the licensor from competition in the licensor's own technology in a market niche that it prefers to keep to itself. These benefits of licensing restrictions apply to patent, copyright, and trade secret licenses, and to know-how agreements.

Example 1[12]

Situation: ComputerCo develops a new, copyrighted software program for inventory management. The program has wide application in the health field. ComputerCo licenses the program in an arrangement that imposes both field of use and territorial limitations. Some of ComputerCo's licenses permit use only in hospitals; others permit use only in group medical practices. ComputerCo charges different royalties for the different uses. All of ComputerCo's licenses permit use only in specified portions of the United States and in specified foreign countries.[13] The licenses contain no provisions that would prevent or discourage licensees from developing, using, or selling any other program, or from competing in any other good or service other than in the use of the licensed program. None of the licensees are actual or likely potential competitors of ComputerCo in the sale of inventory management programs.

Discussion: The key competitive issue raised by the licensing arrangement is whether it harms competition among entities that would have been actual or likely potential competitors in the absence of the arrangement. Such harm could occur if, for example, the licenses anticompetitively foreclose access to competing technologies (in this case, most likely competing computer programs), prevent licensees from developing their own competing technologies (again, in this case, most likely computer programs), or facilitate market allocation or price-fixing for any product or service supplied by the licensees. (*See* section 3.1.) If the license agreements contained such provisions, the Agency evaluating the arrangement would analyze its likely competitive effects as described in parts 3–5 of these Guidelines. In this hypothetical, there are no such provisions and thus the arrangement is merely a subdivision of the licensor's intellectual property among different fields of use and territories. The licensing arrangement does not appear likely to harm competition among entities that would have been actual or likely potential competitors if ComputerCo had chosen not to license the software program. The Agency therefore would be unlikely to object to this arrangement. Based on these facts, the result of the antitrust analysis would be the same whether the technology was protected by patent, copyright, or trade secret. The Agency's conclusion as to likely competitive effects could differ if, for example, the license barred licensees from using any other inventory management progam.

---

[12] The examples in these Guidelines are hypothetical and do not represent judgments about, or analysis of, any actual market circumstances of the named industries.

[13] These Guidelines do not address the possible application of the antitrust laws of other countries to restraints such as territorial restrictions in international licensing arrangements.

3. ANTITRUST CONCERNS AND MODES OF ANALYSIS

3.1 Nature of the concerns

While intellectual property licensing arrangements are typically welfare-enhancing and procompetitive, antitrust concerns may nonetheless arise. For example, a licensing arrangement could include restraints that adversely affect competition in goods markets by dividing the markets among firms that would have competed using different technologies. *See, e.g.,* Example 7. An arrangement that effectively merges the research and development activities of two of only a few entities that could plausibly engage in research and development in the relevant field might harm competition for development of new goods and services. *See* section 3.2.3. An acquisition of intellectual property may lessen competition in a relevant antitrust market. *See* section 5.7. The Agencies will focus on the actual effects of an arrangement, not on its formal terms.

The Agencies will not require the owner of intellectual property to create competition in its own technology. However, antitrust concerns may arise when a licensing arrangement harms competition among entities that would have been actual or likely potential competitors[14] in a relevant market in the absence of the license (entities in a 'horizontal relationship'). A restraint in a licensing arrangement may harm such competition, for example, if it facilitates market division or price-fixing. In addition, license restrictions with respect to one market may harm such competition in another market by anticompetitively foreclosing access to, or significantly raising the price of, an important input,[15] or by facilitating coordination to increase price or reduce output. When it appears that such competition may be adversely affected, the Agencies will follow the analysis set forth below. *See generally* sections 3.4 and 4.2.

3.2 Markets affected by licensing arrangements

Licensing arrangements raise concerns under the antitrust laws if they are likely to affect adversely the prices, quantities, qualities, or varieties of goods and services[16] either currently or potentially available. The competitive effects of licensing arrangements often can be adequately assessed within the relevant markets for the goods affected by the arrangements. In such instances, the Agencies will delineate and analyze only goods markets. In other cases, however, the analysis may require the delineation of markets for technology or markets for research and development (innovation markets).

---

[14] A firm will be treated as a likely potential competitor if there is evidence that entry by that firm is reasonably probable in the absence of the licensing arrangement.

[15] As used herein, 'input' includes outlets for distribution and sales, as well as factors of production. *See, e.g.,* sections 4.1.1 and 5.3–5.5 for further discussion of conditions under which foreclosing access to, or raising the price of, an input may harm competition in a relevant market.

[16] Hereinafter, the term 'goods' also includes services.

3.2.1 Goods markets

A number of different goods markets may be relevant to evaluating the effects of a licensing arrangement. A restraint in a licensing arrangement may have competitive effects in markets for final or intermediate goods made using the intellectual property, or it may have effects upstream, in markets for goods that are used as inputs, along with the intellectual property, to the production of other goods. In general, for goods markets affected by a licensing arrangement, the Agencies will approach the delineation of relevant market and the measurement of market share in the intellectual property area as in section 1 of the U.S. Department of Justice and Federal Trade Commission Horizontal Merger Guidelines.[17]

3.2.2 Technology markets

Technology markets consist of the intellectual property that is licensed (the 'licensed technology') and its close substitutes—that is, the technologies or goods that are close enough substitutes significantly to constrain the exercise of market power with respect to the intellectual property that is licensed.[18] When rights to intellectual property are marketed separately from the products in which they are used,[19] the Agencies may rely on technology markets to analyze the competitive effects of a licensing arrangement.

Example 2

Situation: Firms Alpha and Beta independently develop different patented process technologies to manufacture the same off-patent drug for the treatment of a particular disease. Before the firms use their technologies internally or license them to third parties, they announce plans jointly to manufacture the drug, and to assign their manufacturing processes to the new manufacturing venture. Many firms are capable of using and have the incentive to use the licensed technologies to manufacture and distribute the drug; thus, the market for drug manufacturing and distribution is competitive. One of the Agencies is evaluating the likely competitive effects of the planned venture.

Discussion: The Agency would analyze the competitive effects of the proposed

---

[17] U.S. Department of Justice and Federal Trade Commission, Horizontal Merger Guidelines (April 2, 1992) (hereafter '1992 Horizontal Merger Guidelines'). As stated in section 1.41 of the 1992 Horizontal Merger Guidelines, market shares for goods markets 'can be expressed either in dollar terms through measurement of sales, shipments, or production, or in physical terms through measurement of sales, shipments, production, capacity or reserves.'

[18] For example, the owner of a process for producing a particular good may be constrained in its conduct with respect to that process not only by other processes for making that good, but also by other goods that compete with the downstream good and by the processes used to produce those other goods.

[19] Intellectual property is often licensed, sold, or transferred as an integral part of a marketed good. An example is a patented product marketed with an implied license permitting its use. In such circumstances, there is no need for a separate analysis of technology markets to capture relevant competitive effects.

joint venture by first defining the relevant markets in which competition may be affected and then evaluating the likely competitive effects of the joint venture in the identified markets. (*See* Example 4 for a discussion of the Agencies' approach to joint venture analysis.) In this example, the structural effect of the joint venture in the relevant goods market for the manufacture and distribution of the drug is unlikely to be significant, because many firms in addition to the joint venture compete in that market. The joint venture might, however, increase the prices of the drug produced using Alpha's or Beta's technology by reducing competition in the relevant market for technology to manufacture the drug.

The Agency would delineate a technology market in which to evaluate likely competitive effects of the proposed joint venture. The Agency would identify other technologies that can be used to make the drug with levels of effectiveness and cost per dose comparable to that of the technologies owned by Alpha and Beta. In addition, the Agency would consider the extent to which competition from other drugs that are substitutes for the drug produced using Alpha's or Beta's technology would limit the ability of a hypothetical monopolist that owned both Alpha's and Beta's technology to raise its price.

To identify a technology's close substitutes and thus to delineate the relevant technology market, the Agencies will, if the data permit, identify the smallest group of technologies and goods over which a hypothetical monopolist of those technologies and goods likely would exercise market power—for example, by imposing a small but significant and nontransitory price increase.[20] The Agencies recognize that technology often is licensed in ways that are not readily quantifiable in monetary terms.[21] In such circumstances, the Agencies will delineate the relevant market by identifying other technologies and goods which buyers would substitute at a cost comparable to that of using the licensed technology.

In assessing the competitive significance of current and likely potential participants in a technology market, the Agencies will take into account all relevant evidence. When market share data are available and accurately reflect the competitive significance of market participants, the Agencies will include market share data in this assessment. The Agencies also will seek evidence of buyers' and market participants' assessments of the competitive significance of technology market participants. Such evidence is particularly important when market share data are unavailable, or do not accurately represent the competitive significance of market participants. When market share data or other indicia of market power are not available, and it appears that competing technologies are comparably efficient,[22] the Agencies will assign each technology the same market share. For new technologies, the Agencies generally will use the best available information to

---

[20] This is conceptually analogous to the analytical approach to goods markets under the 1992 Horizontal Merger Guidelines. *Cf.* § 1.11. Of course, market power also can be exercised in other dimensions, such as quality, and these dimensions also may be relevant to the definition and analysis of technology markets.

[21] For example, technology may be licensed royalty-free in exchange for the right to use other technology, or it may be licensed as part of a package license.

[22] The Agencies will regard two technologies as 'comparably efficient' if they can be used to produce close substitutes at comparable costs.

estimate market acceptance over a two-year period, beginning with commercial introduction.

3.2.3 *Research and development: Innovation markets*

If a licensing arrangement may adversely affect competition to develop new or improved goods or processes, the Agencies will analyze such an impact either as a separate competitive effect in relevant goods or technology markets, or as a competitive effect in a separate innovation market. A licensing arrangement may have competitive effects on innovation that cannot be adequately addressed through the analysis of goods or technology markets. For example, the arrangement may affect the development of goods that do not yet exist.[23] Alternatively, the arrangement may affect the development of new or improved goods or processes in geographic markets where there is no actual or likely potential competition in the relevant goods.[24]

An innovation market consists of the research and development directed to particular new or improved goods or processes, and the close substitutes for that research and development. The close substitutes are research and development efforts, technologies, and goods[25] that significantly constrain the exercise of market power with respect to the relevant research and development, for example by limiting the ability and incentive of a hypothetical monopolist to retard the pace of research and development. The Agencies will delineate an innovation market only when the capabilities to engage in the relevant research and development can be associated with specialized assets or characteristics of specific firms.

In assessing the competitive significance of current and likely potential participants in an innovation market, the Agencies will take into account all relevant evidence. When market share data are available and accurately reflect the competitive significance of market participants, the Agencies will include market share data in this assessment. The Agencies also will seek evidence of buyers' and market participants' assessments of the competitive significance of innovation market participants. Such evidence is particularly important when market share data are unavailable or do not accurately represent the competitive significance of market participants. The Agencies may base the market shares of participants in an innovation market on their shares of identifiable assets or characteristics upon which innovation depends, on shares of research and development expenditures, or on shares of a related product. When entities have comparable capabilities and

---

[23] *E.g., Sensormatic*, FTC Inv. No. 941–0126, 60 Fed. Reg. 5428 (accepted for comment Dec. 28, 1994); *Wright Medical Technology, Inc.*, FTC Inv. No. 951–0015, 60 Fed. Reg. 460 (accepted for comment Dec. 8, 1994); *American Home Products*, FTC Inv. No. 941–0116, 59 Fed. Reg. 60,807 (accepted for comment Nov. 28, 1994); *Roche Holdings Ltd.*, 113 F.T.C. 1086 (1990); *United States* v. *Automobile Mfrs. Ass'n*, 307 F. Supp. 617 (C.D. Cal. 1969), *appeal dismissed sub nom. City of New York* v. *United States*, 397 U.S. 248 (1970), *modified sub nom. United States* v. *Motor Vehicles Mfrs. Ass'n.* 1982–83 Trade Cas. (CCH) ¶ 65,088 (C.D. Cal. 1982).

[24] *See* Complaint, *United States* v. *General Motors Corp.*, Civ. No. 93–530 (D. Del., filed Nov. 16, 1993).

[25] For example, the licensor of research and development may be constrained in its conduct not only by competing research and development efforts but also by other existing goods that would compete with the goods under development.

incentives to pursue research and development that is a close substitute for the research and development activities of the parties to a licensing arrangement, the Agencies may assign equal market shares to such entities.

Example 3

Situation: Two companies that specialize in advanced metallurgy agree to cross-license future patents relating to the development of a new component for aircraft jet turbines. Innovation in the development of the component requires the capability to work with very high tensile strength materials for jet turbines. Aspects of the licensing arrangement raise the possibility that competition in research and development of this and related components will be lessened. One of the Agencies is considering whether to define an innovation market in which to evaluate the competitive effects of the arrangement.

Discussion: If the firms that have the capability and incentive to work with very high tensile strength materials for jet turbines can be reasonably identified, the Agency will consider defining a relevant innovation market for development of the new component. If the number of firms with the required capability and incentive to engage in research and development of very high tensile strength materials for aircraft jet turbines is small, the Agency may employ the concept of an innovation market to analyze the likely competitive effects of the arrangement in that market, or as an aid in analyzing competitive effects in technology or goods markets. The Agency would perform its analysis as described in parts 3–5.

If the number of firms with the required capability and incentive is large (either because there are a large number of such firms in the jet turbine industry, or because there are many firms in other industries with the required capability and incentive), then the Agency will conclude that the innovation market is competitive. Under these circumstances, it is unlikely that any single firm or plausible aggregation of firms could acquire a large enough share of the assets necessary for innovation to have an adverse impact on competition.

If the Agency cannot reasonably identify the firms with the required capability and incentive, it will not attempt to define an innovation market.

Example 4

Situation: Three of the largest producers of a plastic used in disposable bottles plan to engage in joint research and development to produce a new type of plastic that is rapidly biodegradable. The joint venture will grant to its partners (but to no one else) licenses to all patent rights and use of know-how. One of the Agencies is evaluating the likely competitive effects of the proposed joint venture.

Discussion: The Agency would analyze the proposed research and development joint venture using an analysis similar to that applied to other joint ventures.[26]

---

[26] *See, e.g.*, U.S. Department of Justice and Federal Trade Commission, Statements of Enforcement Policy and Analytical Principles Relating to Health Care and Antitrust 20–23, 37–40, 72–74 (September 27, 1994). This type of transaction may qualify for treatment under the National Cooperative Research and Production Act of 1993, 15 U.S.C.A §§ 4301–05.

The Agency would begin by defining the relevant markets in which to analyze the joint venture's likely competitive effects. In this case, a relevant market is an innovation market—research and development for biodegradable (and other environmentally friendly) containers. The Agency would seek to identify any other entities that would be actual or likely potential competitors with the joint venture in that relevant market. This would include those firms that have the capability and incentive to undertake research and development closely substitutable for the research and development proposed to be undertaken by the joint venture, taking into account such firms' existing technologies and technologies under development, R&D facilities, and other relevant assets and business circumstances. Firms possessing such capabilities and incentives would be included in the research and development market even if they are not competitors in relevant markets for related goods, such as the plastics currently produced by the joint ventures, although competitors in existing goods markets may often also compete in related innovation markets.

Having defined a relevant innovation market, the Agency would assess whether the joint venture is likely to have anticompetitive effects in that market. A starting point in this analysis is the degree of concentration in the relevant market and the market shares of the parties to the joint venture. If, in addition to the parties to the joint venture (taken collectively), there are at least four other independently controlled entities that possess comparable capabilities and incentives to undertake research and development of biodegradable plastics, or other products that would be close substitutes for such new plastics, the joint venture ordinarily would be unlikely to adversely affect competition in the relevant innovation market (*cf.* section 4.3). If there are fewer than four other independently controlled entities with similar capabilities and incentives, the Agency would consider whether the joint venture would give the parties to the joint venture an incentive and ability collectively to reduce investment in, or otherwise to retard the pace or scope of, research and development efforts. If the joint venture creates a significant risk of anticompetitive effects in the innovation market, the Agency would proceed to consider efficiency justifications for the venture, such as the potential for combining complementary R&D assets in such a way as to make successful innovation more likely, or to bring it about sooner, or to achieve cost reductions in research and development.

The Agency would also assess the likelihood that the joint venture would adversely affect competition in other relevant markets, including markets for products produced by the parties to the joint venture. The risk of such adverse competitive effects would be increased to the extent that, for example, the joint venture facilitates the exchange among the parties of competitively sensitive information relating to goods markets in which the parties currently compete or facilitates the coordination of competitive activities in such markets. The Agency would examine whether the joint venture imposes collateral restraints that might significantly restrict competition among the joint venturers in goods markets, and would examine whether such collateral restraints were reasonably necessary to achieve any efficiencies that are likely to be attained by the venture.

3.3 Horizontal and vertical relationships

As with other property transfers, antitrust analysis of intellectual property licensing arrangements examines whether the relationship among the parties to the arrangement is primarily horizontal or vertical in nature, or whether it has substantial aspects of both. A licensing arrangement has a vertical component when it affects activities that are in a complementary relationship, as is typically the case in a licensing arrangement. For example, the licensor's primary line of business may be in research and development, and the licensees, as manufacturers, may be buying the rights to use technology developed by the licensor. Alternatively, the licensor may be a component manufacturer owning intellectual property rights in a product that the licensee manufactures by combining the component with other inputs, or the licensor may manufacture the product, and the licensees may operate primarily in distribution and marketing.

In addition to this vertical component, the licensor and its licensees may also have a horizontal relationship. For analytical purposes, the Agencies ordinarily will treat a relationship between a licensor and its licensees, or between licensees, as horizontal when they would have been actual or likely potential competitors in a relevant market in the absence of the license.

The existence of a horizontal relationship between a licensor and its licensees does not, in itself, indicate that the arrangement is anticompetitive. Identification of such relationships is merely an aid in determining whether there may be anti-competitive effects arising from a licensing arrangement. Such a relationship need not give rise to an anticompetitive effect, nor does a purely vertical relationship assure that there are no anticompetitive effects.

The following examples illustrate different competitive relationships among a licensor and its licensees.

Example 5

Situation: AgCo, a manufacturer of farm equipment, develops a new, patented emission control technology for its tractor engines and licenses it to FarmCo, another farm equipment manufacturer. AgCo's emission control technology is far superior to the technology currently owned and used by FarmCo, so much so that FarmCo's technology does not significantly constrain the prices that AgCo could charge for its technology. AgCo's emission control patent has a broad scope. It is likely that any improved emissions control technology that FarmCo could develop in the foreseeable future would infringe AgCo's patent.

Discussion: Because FarmCo's emission control technology does not significantly constrain AgCo's competitive conduct with respect to its emission control technology, AgCo's and FarmCo's emission control technologies are not close substitutes for each other. FarmCo is a consumer of AgCo's technology and is not an actual competitor of AgCo in the relevant market for superior emission control technology of the kind licensed by AgCo. Furthermore, FarmCo is not a likely potential competitor of AgCo in the relevant market because, even if FarmCo could develop an improved emission control technology, it is likely that it would infringe AgCo's patent. This means that the relationship between AgCo and FarmCo with regard to the supply and use of emissions control technology is vertical. Assuming that AgCo and FarmCo are actual or likely potential competitors in sales of farm equipment products, their relationship is horizontal in the relevant markets for farm equipment.

Example 6

Situation: FarmCo develops a new valve technology for its engines and enters into a cross-licensing arrangement with AgCo, whereby AgCo licenses its emission control technology to FarmCo and FarmCo licenses its valve technology to AgCo. AgCo already owns an alternative valve technology that can be used to achieve engine performance similar to that using FarmCo's valve technology and at a comparable cost to consumers. Before adopting FarmCo's technology, AgCo was using its own valve technology in its production of engines and was licensing (and continues to license) that technology for use by others. As in Example 5, FarmCo does not own or control an emission control technology that is a close substitute for the technology licensed from AgCo. Furthermore, as in Example 5, FarmCo is not likely to develop an improved emission control technology that would be a close substitute for AgCo's technology, because of AgCo's blocking patent.

Discussion: FarmCo is a consumer and not a competitor of AgCo's emission control technology. As in Example 5, their relationship is vertical with regard to this technology. The relationship between AgCo and FarmCo in the relevant market that includes engine valve technology is vertical in part and horizontal in part. It is vertical in part because AgCo and FarmCo stand in a complementary relationship, in which AgCo is a consumer of a technology supplied by FarmCo. However, the relationship between AgCo and FarmCo in the relevant market that includes engine valve technology is also horizontal in part, because FarmCo and AgCo are actual competitors in the licensing of valve technology that can be used to achieve similar engine performance at a comparable cost. Whether the firms license their valve technologies to others is not important for the conclusion that the firms have a horizontal relationship in this relevant market. Even if AgCo's use of its valve technology were solely captive to its own production, the fact that the two valve technologies are substitutable at comparable cost means that the two firms have a horizontal relationship.

As in Example 5, the relationship between AgCo and FarmCo is horizontal in the relevant markets for farm equipment.

3.4 Framework for evaluating licensing restraints

In the vast majority of cases, restraints in intellectual property licensing arrangements are evaluated under the rule of reason. The Agencies' general approach in analyzing a licensing restraint under the rule of reason is to inquire whether the restraint is likely to have anticompetitive effects and, if so, whether the restraint is reasonably necessary to achieve procompetitive benefits that outweigh those anticompetitive effects. *See Federal Trade Commission* v. *Indiana Federation of Dentists*, 476

U.S. 447 (1986); *NCAA* v. *Board of Regents of the University of Oklahoma*, 468 U.S. 85 (1984); *Broadcast Music, Inc.* v. *Columbia Broadcasting System, Inc.*, 441 U.S. 1 (1979); Phillip E. Areeda, *Antitrust Law* § 1502 (1986). *See also* part 4.

In some cases, however, the courts conclude that a restraint's 'nature and necessary effect are so plainly anticompetitive' that it should be treated as unlawful per se, without an elaborate inquiry into the restraint's likely competitive effect. *Federal Trade Commission* v. *Superior Court Trial Lawyers Association*, 493 U.S. 411, 433 (1990); *National Society of Professional Engineers* v. *United States*, 435 U.S. 679, 692 (1978). Among the restraints that have been held per se unlawful are naked price-fixing, output restraints, and market division among horizontal competitors, as well as certain group boycotts and resale price maintenance.

To determine whether a particular restraint in a licensing arrangement is given per se or rule of reason treatment, the Agencies will assess whether the restraint in question can be expected to contribute to an efficiency-enhancing integration of economic activity. *See Broadcast Music*, 441 U.S. at 16–24. In general, licensing arrangements promote such integration because they facilitate the combination of the licensor's intellectual property with complementary factors of production owned by the licensee. A restraint in a licensing arrangement may further such integration by, for example, aligning the incentives of the licensor and the licensees to promote the development and marketing of the licensed technology, or by substantially reducing transactions costs. If there is no efficiency-enhancing integration of economic activity and if the type of restraint is one that has been accorded per se treatment, the Agencies will challenge the restraint under the per se rule. Otherwise, the Agencies will apply a rule of reason analysis.

Application of the rule of reason generally requires a comprehensive inquiry into market conditions. (*See* sections 4.1–4.3.) However, that inquiry may be truncated in certain circumstances. If the Agencies conclude that a restraint has no likely anticompetitive effects, they will treat it as reasonable, without an elaborate analysis of market power or the justifications for the restraint. Similarly, if a restraint facially appears to be of a kind that would always or almost always tend to reduce output or increase prices,[27] and the restraint is not reasonably related to efficiencies, the Agencies will likely challenge the restraint without an elaborate analysis of particular industry circumstances.[28] *See Indiana Federation of Dentists*, 476 U.S. at 459–60; *NCAA*, 468 U.S. at 109.

Example 7

Situation: Gamma, which manufactures Product X using its patented process, offers a license for its process technology to every other manufacturer of Product

---

[27] Details about the Federal Trade Commission's approach are set forth in *Massachusetts Board of Registration in Optometry*, 110 F.T.C. 549, 604 (1988). In applying its truncated rule of reason inquiry, the FTC uses the analytical category of 'inherently suspect' restraints to denote facially anticompetitive restraints that would always or almost always tend to decrease output or increase prices, but that may be relatively unfamiliar or may not fit neatly into traditional per se categories.

[28] Under the FTC's *Mass. Board* approach, asserted efficiency justifications for inherently suspect restraints are examined to determine whether they are plausible and, if so, whether they are valid in the context of the market at issue. *Mass. Board*, 110 F.T.C. at 604.

X, each of which competes world-wide with Gamma in the manufacture and sale of X. The process technology does not represent an economic improvement over the available existing technologies. Indeed, although most manufacturers accept licenses from Gamma, none of the licensees actually uses the licensed technology. The licenses provide that each manufacturer has an exclusive right to sell Product X manufactured using the licensed technology in a designated geographic area and that no manufacturer may sell Product X, however manufactured, outside the designated territory.

Discussion: The manufacturers of Product X are in a horizontal relationship in the goods market for Product X. Any manufacturers of Product X that control technologies that are substitutable at comparable cost of Gamma's process are also horizontal competitors of Gamma in the relevant technology market. The licensees of Gamma's process technology are technically in a vertical relationship, although that is not significant in this example because they do not actually use Gamma's technology.

The licensing arrangement restricts competition in the relevant goods market among manufacturers of Product X by requiring each manufacturer to limit its sales to an exclusive territory. Thus, competition among entities that would be actual competitors in the absence of the licensing arrangement is restricted. Based on the facts set forth above, the licensing arrangement does not involve a useful transfer of technology, and thus it is unlikely that the restraint on sales outside the designated territories contributes to an efficiency-enhancing integration of economic activity. Consequently, the evaluating Agency would be likely to challenge the arrangement under the per se rule as a horizontal territorial market allocation scheme and to view the intellectual property aspects of the arrangement as a sham intended to cloak its true nature.

If the licensing arrangement could be expected to contribute to an efficiency-enhancing integration of economic activity, as might be the case if the licensed technology were an advance over existing processes and used by the licensees, the Agency would analyze the arrangement under the rule of reason applying the analytical framework described in this section.

In this example, the competitive implications do not generally depend on whether the licensed technology is protected by patent, is a trade secret or other know-how, or is a computer program protected by copyright; nor do the competitive implications generally depend on whether the allocation of markets is territorial, as in this example, or functional, based on fields of use.

4. GENERAL PRINCIPLES CONCERNING THE AGENCIES' EVALUATION OF LICENSING ARRANGEMENTS UNDER THE RULE OF REASON

4.1 Analysis of anticompetitive effects

The existence of anticompetitive effects resulting from a restraint in a licensing arrangement will be evaluated on the basis of the analysis described in this section.

4.1.1 *Market structure, coordination, and foreclosure*

When a licensing arrangement affects parties in a horizontal relationship, a restraint in that arrangement may increase the risk of coordinated pricing, output restrictions, or the acquisition or maintenance of market power. Harm to competition also may occur if the arrangement poses a significant risk of retarding or restricting the development of new or improved goods or processes. The potential for competitive harm depends in part on the degree of concentration in, the difficulty of entry into, and the responsiveness of supply and demand to changes in price in the relevant markets. *Cf.* 1992 Horizontal Merger Guidelines §§ 1.5, 3.

When the licensor and licensees are in a vertical relationship, the Agencies will analyze whether the licensing arrangement may harm competition among entities in a horizontal relationship at either the level of the licensor or the licensees, or possibly in another relevant market. Harm to competition from a restraint may occur if it anticompetitively forecloses access to, or increases competitors' costs of obtaining, important inputs, or facilitates coordination to raise price or restrict output. The risk of anticompetitively foreclosing access or increasing competitors' costs is related to the proportion of the markets affected by the licensing restraint; other characteristics of the relevant markets, such as concentration, difficulty of entry, and the responsiveness of supply and demand to changes in price in the relevant markets; and the duration of the restraint. A licensing arrangement does not foreclose competition merely because some or all of the potential licensees is an industry choose to use the licensed technology to the exclusion of other technologies. Exclusive use may be an efficient consequence of the licensed technology having the lowest cost or highest value.

Harm to competition from a restraint in a vertical licensing arrangement also may occur if a licensing restraint facilitates coordination among entities in a horizontal relationship to raise prices or reduce output in a relevant market. For example, if owners of competing technologies impose similar restraints on their licensees, the licensors may find it easier to coordinate their pricing. Similarly, licensees that are competitors may find it easier to coordinate their pricing if they are subject to common restraints in licenses with a common licensor or competing licensors. The risk of anticompetitive coordination is increased when the relevant markets are concentrated and difficult to enter. The use of similar restraints may be common and procompetitive in an industry, however, because they contribute to efficient exploitation of the licensed property.

4.2.1 *Licensing arrangements involving exclusivity*

A licensing arrangement may involve exclusivity in two distinct respects. First, the licensor may grant one or more *exclusive licenses*, which restrict the right of the licensor to license others and possibly also to use the technology itself. Generally, an exclusive license may raise antitrust concerns only if the licensees themselves, or the licensor and its licensees, are in a horizontal relationship. Examples of arrangements involving exclusive licensing that may give rise to antitrust concerns include cross-licensing by parties collectively possessing market power (*see* section 5.5), grantbacks (*see* section 5.6), and acquisitions of intellectual property rights (*see* section 5.7).

A non-exclusive license of intellectual property that does not contain any restraints on the competitive conduct of the licensor or the licensee generally does not present antitrust concerns even if the parties to the license are in a horizontal relationship, because the non-exclusive license normally does not diminish competition that would occur in its absence.

A second form of exclusivity, *exclusive dealing*, arises when a license prevents or restrains the licensee from licensing, selling, distributing, or using competing technologies. *See* section 5.4. Exclusivity may be achieved by an explicit exclusive dealing term in the license or by other provisions such as compensation terms or other economic incentives. Such restraints may anticompetitively foreclose access to, or increase competitors' costs of obtaining, important inputs, or facilitate coordination to raise price or reduce output, but they also may have procompetitive effects. For example, a licensing arrangement that prevents the licensee from dealing in other technologies may encourage the licensee to develop and market the licensed technology or specialized applications of that technology. *See, e.g.,* Example 8. The Agencies will take into account such procompetitive effects in evaluating the reasonableness of the arrangement. *See* section 4.2.

The antitrust principles that apply to a licensor's grant of various forms of exclusivity to and among its licensees are similar to those that apply to comparable vertical restraints outside the licensing context, such as exclusive territories and exclusive dealing. However, the fact that intellectual property may in some cases be misappropriated more easily than other forms of property may justify the use of some restrictions that might be anticompetitive in other contexts.

As noted earlier, the Agencies will focus on the actual practice and its effects, not on the formal terms of the arrangement. A license denominated as non-exclusive (either in the sense of exclusive licensing or in the sense of exclusive dealing) may nonetheless give rise to the same concerns posed by formal exclusivity. A non-exclusive license may have the effect of exclusive licensing if it is structured so that the licensor is unlikely to license others or to practice the technology itself. A license that does not explicitly require exclusive dealing may have the effect of exclusive dealing if it is structured to increase significantly a licensee's cost when it uses competing technologies. However, a licensing arrangement will not automatically raise these concerns merely because a party chooses to deal with a single licensee or licensor, or confines his activity to a single field of use or location, or because only a single licensee has chosen to take a license.

Example 8

Situation: NewCo, the inventor and manufacturer of a new flat panel display technology, lacking the capability to bring a flat panel display product to market, grants BigCo an exclusive license to sell a product embodying NewCo's technology. BigCo does not currently sell, and is not developing (or likely to develop), a product that would compete with the product embodying the new technology and does not control rights to another display technology. Several firms offer competing displays, BigCo accounts for only a small proportion of the outlets for distribution of display products, and entry into the manufacture and distribution of display products is relatively easy. Demand for the new technology is uncertain and successful market penetration will require considerable promotional effort. The license contains an exclusive dealing restriction preventing BigCo from selling products that compete with the product embodying the licensed technology. *Discussion*: This example illustrates both types of exclusivity in a licensing arrangement. The license is exclusive in that it restricts the right of the licensor to grant other licenses. In addition, the license has an exclusive dealing component in that it restricts the licensee from selling competing products.

The inventor of the display technology and its licensee are in a vertical relationship and are not actual or likely potential competitors in the manufacture or sale of display products or in the sale or development of technology. Hence, the grant of an exclusive license does not affect competition between the licensor and the licensee. The exclusive license may promote competition in the manufacturing and sale of display products by encouraging BigCo to develop and promote the new product in the face of uncertain demand by rewarding BigCo for its efforts if they lead to large sales. Although the license bars the licensee from selling competing products, this exclusive dealing aspect is unlikely in this example to harm competition by anticompetitively foreclosing access, raising competitors' costs of inputs, or facilitating anticompetitive pricing because the relevant product market is unconcentrated, the exclusive dealing restraint affects only a small proportion of the outlets for distribution of display products, and entry is easy. On these facts, the evaluating Agency would be unlikely to challenge the arrangement.

4.2 Efficiencies and justifications

If the Agencies conclude, upon an evaluation of the market factors described in section 4.1, that a restraint in a licensing arrangement is unlikely to have an anticompetitive effect, they will not challenge the restraint. If the Agencies conclude that the restraint has, or is likely to have, an anticompetitive effect, they will consider whether the restraint is reasonably necessary to achieve procompetitive efficiencies. If the restraint is reasonably necessary, the Agencies will balance the procompetitive efficiencies and the anticompetitive effects to determine the probable net effect on competition in each relevant market.

The Agencies' comparison of anticompetitive harms and procompetitive efficiencies is necessarily a qualitative one. The risk of anticompetitive effects in a particular case may be insignificant compared to the expected efficiencies, or vice versa. As the expected anticompetitive effects in a particular licensing arrangement increase, the Agencies will require evidence establishing a greater level of expected efficiencies.

The existence of practical and significantly less restrictive alternatives is relevant to a determination of whether a restraint is reasonably necessary. If it is clear that the parties could have achieved similar efficiencies by means that are significantly less restrictive, then the Agencies will not give weight to the parties' efficiency claim. In making this assessment, however, the Agencies will not engage in a search for a theoretically least restrictive alternative that is not realistic in the practical prospective business situation faced by the parties.

When a restraint has, or is likely to have, an anticompetitive effect, the duration of that restraint can be an important factor in determining whether it is reasonably necessary to achieve the putative procompetitive efficiency. The effective duration of a restraint may depend on a number of factors, including the option of the affected party to terminate the arrangement unilaterally and the presence of contract terms (e.g. unpaid balances on minimum purchase commitments) that encourage the licensee to renew a license arrangement. Consistent with their approach to less restrictive alternative analysis generally, the Agencies will not attempt to draw fine distinctions regarding duration; rather, their focus will be on situations in which the duration clearly exceeds the period needed to achieve the procompetitive efficiency.

The evaluation of procompetitive efficiencies, of the reasonable necessity of a restraint to achieve them, and of the duration of the restraint, may depend on the market context. A restraint that may be justified by the needs of a new entrant, for example, may not have a procompetitive efficiency justification in different market circumstances. *Cf. United States* v. *Jerrold Electronics Corp.*, 187 F. Supp. 545 (E.D. Pa. 1960), *aff'd per curiam*, 365 U.S. 567 (1961).

4.3 Antitrust 'safety zone'

Because licensing arrangements often promote innovation and enhance competition, the Agencies believe that an antitrust 'safety zone' is useful in order to provide some degree of certainty and thus to encourage such activity.[29] Absent extraordinary circumstances, the Agencies will not challenge a restraint in an intellectual property licensing arrangement if (1) the restraint is not facially anticompetitive[30] and (2) the licensor and its licensees collectively account for no more than twenty percent of each relevant market significantly affected by the restraint. This 'safety zone' does not apply to those transfers of intellectual property rights to which a merger analysis is applied. *See* section 5.7.

Whether a restraint falls within the safety zone will be determined by reference only to goods markets unless the analysis of goods markets alone would inadequately address the effects of the licensing arrangement on competition among technologies or in research and development.

If an examination of the effects on competition among technologies or in research and development is required, and if market share data are unavailable or do not accurately represent competitive significance, the following safety zone criteria will apply. Absent extraordinary circumstances, the Agencies will not challenge a restraint in an intellectual property licensing arrangement that may affect competition in a technology market if (1) the restraint is not facially anticompetitive and (2) there are four or more independently controlled technologies in addition to the technologies controlled by the parties to the licensing arrangement that

---

[29] The antitrust 'safety zone' does not apply to restraints that are not in a licensing arrangement, or to restraints that are in a licensing arrangement but are unrelated to the use of the licensed intellectual property.

[30] 'Facially anticompetitive' refers to restraints that normally warrant per se treatment, as well as other restraints of a kind that would always or almost always trend to reduce output or increase prices. *See* section 3.4.

may be substitutable for the licensed technology at a comparable cost to the user. Absent extraordinary circumstances, the Agencies will not challenge a restraint in an intellectual property licensing arrangement that may affect competition in an innovation market if (1) the restraint is not facially anticompetitive and (2) four or more independently controlled entities in addition to the parties to the licensing arrangement possess the required specialized assets or characteristics and the incentive to engage in research and development that is a close substitute of the research and development activities of the parties to the licensing agreement.[31]

The Agencies emphasize that licensing arrangements are not anticompetitive merely because they do not fall within the scope of the safety zone. Indeed, it is likely that the great majority of licenses falling outside the safety zone are lawful and procompetitive. The safety zone is designed to provide owners of intellectual property with a degree of certainty in those situations in which anticompetitive effects are so unlikely that the arrangements may be presumed not to be anticompetitive without an inquiry into particular industry circumstances. It is not intended to suggest that parties should conform to the safety zone or to discourage parties falling outside the safety zone from adopting restrictions in their license arrangements that are reasonably necessary to achieve an efficiency-enhancing integration of economic activity. The Agencies will analyze arrangements falling outside the safety zone based on the considerations outlined in parts 3–5.

The status of a licensing arrangement with respect to the safety zone may change over time. A determination by the Agencies that a restraint in a licensing arrangement qualifies for inclusion in the safety zone is based on the factual circumstances prevailing at the time of the conduct at issue.[32]

5. APPLICATION OF GENERAL PRINCIPLES

5.0 This section illustrates the application of the general principles discussed above to particular licensing restraints and to arrangements that involve the cross-licensing, pooling, or acquisition of intellectual property. The restraints and arrangements identified are typical of those that are likely to receive antitrust scrutiny; however, they are not intended as an exhaustive list of practices that could raise competitive concerns.

5.1 Horizontal restraints

The existence of a restraint in a licensing arrangement that affects parties in a horizontal relationship (a 'horizontal restraint') does not necessarily cause the

---

[31] This is consistent with congressional intent in enacting the National Cooperative Research Act. *See* H.R. Conf. Rpt. No. 1044, 98th Cong., 2d Sess., 10, *reprinted in* 1984 U.S.C.C.A.N. 3105, 3134–35.

[32] The conduct at issue may be the transaction giving rise to the restraint or the subsequent implementation of the restraint.

arrangement to be anticompetitive. As in the case of joint ventures among horizontal competitors, licensing arrangements among such competitors may promote rather than hinder competition if they result in integrative efficiencies. Such efficiencies may arise, for example, from the realization of economies of scale and the integration of complementary research and development, production, and marketing capabilities.

Following the general principles outlined in section 3.4, horizontal restraints often will be evaluated under the rule of reason. In some circumstances, however, that analysis may be truncated; additionally, some restraints may merit per se treatment, including price fixing, allocation of markets or customers, agreements to reduce output, and certain group boycotts.

Example 9

Situation: Two of the leading manufacturers of the consumer electronic product hold patents that cover alternative circuit designs for the product. The manufacturers assign their patents to a separate corporation wholly owned by the two firms. That corporation licenses the right to use the circuit designs to other consumer product manufacturers and establishes the license royalties. None of the patents is blocking; that is, each of the patents can be used without infringing a patent owned by the other firm. The different circuit designs are substitutable in that each permits the manufacture at comparable cost to consumers of products that consumers consider to be interchangeable. One of the Agencies is analyzing the licensing arrangement.

Discussion: In this example, the manufacturers are horizontal competitors in the goods market for the consumer product and in the related technology markets. The competitive issue with regard to a joint assignment of patent rights is whether the assignment has an adverse impact on competition in technology and goods markets that is not outweighed by procompetitive efficiencies, such as benefits in the use or dissemination of the technology. Each of the patent owners has a right to exclude others from using its patent. That right does not extend, however, to the agreement to assign rights jointly. To the extent that the patent rights cover technologies that are close substitutes, the joint determination of royalties likely would result in higher royalties and higher goods prices than would result if the owners licensed or used their technologies independently. In the absence of evidence establishing efficiency-enhancing integration from the joint assignment of patent rights, the Agency may conclude that the joint marketing of competing patent rights constitutes horizontal price fixing and could be challenged as a per se unlawful horizontal restraint of trade. If the joint marketing arrangement results in an efficiency-enhancing integration, the Agency would evaluate the arrangement under the rule of reason. However, the Agency may conclude that the anticompetitive effects are sufficiently apparent, and the claimed integrative efficiencies are sufficiently weak or not reasonably related to the restraints, to warrant challenge of the arrangement without an elaborate analysis of particular industry circumstances (*see* section 3.4).

5.2 Resale price maintenance

Resale price maintenance is illegal when 'commodities have passed into the channels of trade and are owned by dealers.' *Dr. Miles Medical Co.* v. *John D. Park & Sons Co.*, 220 U.S. 373, 408 (1911). It has been held per se illegal for a licensor of an intellectual property right in a product to fix a licensee's *resale* price of that product. *United States* v. *Univis Lens Co.*, 316 U.S. 241 (1942); *Ethyl Gasoline Corp.* v. *United States*, 309 U.S. 436 (1940).[33] Consistent with the principles set forth in section 3.4, the Agencies will enforce the per se rule against resale price maintenance in the intellectual property context.

5.3 Tying arrangements

A 'tying' or 'tie-in' or 'tied sale' arrangement has been defined as 'an agreement by a part to sell one product . . . on the condition that the buyer also purchases a different (or tied) product, or at least agrees that he will not purchase that [tied] product from any other supplier.' *Eastman Kodak Co.* v. *Image Technical Services, Inc.*, 112 S. Ct. 2072, 2079 (1992). Conditioning the ability of a licensee to licence one or more items of intellectual property on the licensee's purchase of another item of intellectual property or a good or a service has been held in some cases to constitute illegal tying.[34] Although tying arrangements may result in anticompetitive effects, such arrangements can also result in significant efficiencies and procompetitive benefits. In the exercise of their prosecutorial discretion, the Agencies will consider both the anticompetitive effects and the efficiencies attributable to a tie-in. The Agencies would be likely to challenge a tying arrangement if: (1) the seller has market power in the tying product,[35] (2) the arrangement has an adverse effect on competition in the relevant market for the tied product, and (3) efficiency justifications for the arrangement do not outweigh the anticompetitive effects.[36] The Agencies will not presume that a

[33] But *cf. United States* v. *General Electric Co.*, 272 U.S. 476 (1926) (holding that an owner of a product patent may condition a license to manufacture the product on the fixing of the *first* sale price of the patented product). Subsequent lower court decisions have distinguished the *GE* decision in various contexts. *See, e.g., Royal Indus.* v. *St. Regis Paper Co.*, 420 F.2d 449, 452 (9th Cir. 1969) (observing that *GE* involved a restriction by a patentee who also manufactured the patented product and leaving open the question whether a nonmanufacturing patentee may fix the price of the patented product); *Newburgh Moire Co.* v. *Superior Moire Co.*, 237 F.2d 283, 293–94 (3rd Cir. 1956) (grant of multiple licenses each containing price restrictions does not come within the GE doctrine); *Cummer-Graham Co.* v. *Straight Side Basket Corp.*, 142 F.2d 646, 647 (5th Cir.) (owner of an intellectual property right in a process to manufacture an unpatented product may not fix the sale price of that product), *cert. denied*, 323 U.S. 726 (1944); *Barber-Colman Co.* v. *National Tool Co.*, 136 F.2d 339 343–44 (6th Cir. 1943) (same).

[34] *See, e.g., United States* v. *Paramount Pictures, Inc.*, 334 U.S. 131, 156–58 (1948) (copyrights); *International Salt Co.* v. *United States*, 332 U.S. 392 (1947) (patent and related product).

[35] *Cf.* 35 U.S.C. § 271(d) (1988 & Supp. V 1993) (requirement of market power in patent misuse cases involving tying).

[36] As is true throughout these Guidelines, the factors listed are those that guide the Agencies' internal analysis in exercising their prosecutorial discretion. They are not intended to circumscribe how the Agencies will conduct the litigation of cases that they decide to bring.

patent, copyright, or trade secret necessarily confers market power upon its owner.

Package licensing—the licensing of multiple items of intellectual property in a single license or in a group of related licenses—may be a form of tying arrangement if the licensing of one product is conditioned upon the acceptance of a license of another, separate product. Package licensing can be efficiency enhancing under some circumstances. When multiple licenses are needed to use any single item of intellectual property, for example, a package license may promote such efficiencies. If a package license constitutes a tying arrangement, the Agencies will evaluate is competitive effects under the same principles they apply to other tying arrangements.

5.4 Exclusive dealing

In the intellectual property context, exclusive dealing occurs when a license prevents the licensee from licensing, selling, distributing, or using competing technologies. Exclusive dealing arrangements are evaluated under the rule of reason. See *Tampa Electric Co.* v. *Nashville Coal Co.*, 365 U.S. 320 (1961) (evaluating legality of exclusive dealing under section 1 of the Sherman Act and section 3 of the Clayton Act); *Beltone Electronics Corp.*, 100 F.T.C. 68 (1982) (evaluating legality of exclusive dealing under section 5 of the Federal Trade Commission Act). In determining whether an exclusive dealing arrangement is likely to reduce competition in a relevant market, the Agencies will take into account the extent to which the arrangement (1) promotes the exploitation and development of the licensor's technology and (2) anticompetitively forecloses the exploitation and development of, or otherwise constrains competition among, competing, technologies.

The likelihood that exclusive dealing may have anticompetitive effects is related, inter alia, to the degree of foreclosure in the relevant market, the duration of the exclusive dealing arrangement, and other characteristics of the input and output markets, such as concentration, difficulty of entry, and the responsiveness of supply and demand to changes in price in the relevant markets. (*See* sections 4.1.1 and 4.1.2.) If the Agencies determine that a particular exclusive dealing arrangement may have an anticompetitive effect, they will evaluate the extent to which the restraint encourages licensees to develop and market the licensed technology (or specialized applications of that technology), increases licensors' incentives to develop or refine the licensed technology, or otherwise increases competition and enhances output in a relevant market. (*See* section 4.2 and Example 8.)

5.5 Cross-licensing and pooling arrangements

Cross-licensing and pooling arrangements are agreements of two or more owners of different items of intellectual property to license one another or third parties. These arrangements may provide procompetitive benefits by integrating complementary technologies, reducing transaction costs, clearing blocking positions, and avoiding costly infringement litigation. By promoting the dissemination of technology, cross-licensing and pooling arrangements are often procompetitive.

Cross-licensing and pooling arrangements can have anticompetitive effects in certain circumstances. For example, collective price or output restraints in pooling arrangements, such as the joint marketing of pooled intellectual property rights with collective price setting or coordinated output restrictions, may be deemed unlawful if they do not contribute to an efficiency-enhancing integration of economic activity among the participants. *Compare NCAA* 468 U.S. at 114 (output restriction on college football broadcasting held unlawful because it was not reasonably related to any purported justification) *with Broadcast Music*, 441 U.S. at 23 (blanket license for music copyrights found not per se illegal because the cooperative price was necessary to the creation of a new product). When cross-licensing or pooling arrangements are mechanisms to accomplish naked price fixing or market division, they are subject to challenge under the per se rule. *See United States* v. *New Wrinkle, Inc.*, 342 U.S. 371 (1952) (price fixing).

Settlements involving the cross-licensing of intellectual property rights can be an efficient means to avoid litigation and, in general, courts favour such settlements. When such cross-licensing involves horizontal competitors, however, the Agencies will consider whether the effect of the settlement is to diminish competition among entities that would have been actual or likely potential competitors in a relevant market in the absence of the cross-license. In the absence of offsetting efficiencies, such settlements may be challenged as unlawful restraints of trade. *Cf. United States* v. *Singer Manufacturing Co.*, 374 U.S. 174 (1963) (cross-license agreement was part of broader combination to exclude competitors).

Pooling arrangements generally need not to open to all who would like to join. However, exclusion from cross-licensing and pooling arrangements among parties that collectively possess market power may, under some circumstances, harm competition. *Cf. Northwest Wholesale Stationers, Inc.* v. *Pacific Stationary & Printing Co.*, 472 U.S. 284 (1985) (exclusion of a competitor from a purchasing cooperative not per se unlawful absent a showing of market power). In general, exclusion from a pooling or cross-licensing arrangement among competing technologies is unlikely to have anticompetitive effects unless (1) excluded firms cannot effectively compete in the relevant market for the good incorporating the licensed technologies and (2) the pool participants collectively possess market power in the relevant market. If these circumstances exist, the Agencies will evaluate whether the arrangement's limitations on participation are reasonably related to the efficient development and exploitation of the pooled technologies and will assess the net effect of those limitations in the relevant market. *See* section 4.2.

Another possible anticompetitive effect of pooling arrangements may occur if the arrangement deters or discourages participants from engaging in research and development, thus retarding innovation. For example, a pooling arrangement that requires members to grant licenses to each other for current and future technology at minimal cost may reduce the incentives of its members to engage in research and development because members of the pool have to share their successful research and development and each of the members can free ride on the accomplishments of other pool members. *See generally United States* v. *Mfrs.*

Aircraft Ass'n, Inc., 1976–1 Trade Cas. (CCH) ¶ 60,810 (S.D.N.Y. 1975); *United States* v. *Automobile Mfrs. Ass'n*, 307 F. Supp. 617 (C.D. Cal 1969), *appeal dismissed sub nom. City of New York* v. *United States*, 397 U.S. 248 (1970), *modified sub nom. United States* v. *Motor Vehicle Mfrs. Ass'n*, 1982–83 Trade Cas. (CCH) ¶ 65,088 (C.D. Cal. 1982). However, such an arrangement can have procompetitive benefits, for example, by exploiting economies of scale and integrating complementary capabilities of the pool members, (including the clearing of blocking positions), and is likely to cause competitive problems only when the arrangement includes a large fraction of the potential research and development in an innovation market. *See* section 3.2.3 and Example 4.

Example 10

Situation: As in Example 9, two of the leading manufacturers of a consumer electronic product hold patents that cover alternative circuit designs for the product. The manufacturers assign several of their patents to a separate corporation wholly owned by the two firms. That corporation licenses the right to use the circuit designs to other consumer product manufacturers and establishes the license royalties. In this example, however, the manufacturers assign to the separate corporation only patents that are blocking. None of the patents assigned to the corporation can be used without infringing a patent owned by the other firm. *Discussion*: Unlike the previous example, the joint assignment of patent rights to the wholly owned corporation in this example does not adversely affect competition in the licensed technology among entities that would have been actual or likely potential competitors in the absence of the licensing arrangement. Moreover, the licensing arrangement is likely to have procompetitive benefits in the use of the technology. Because the manufacturers' patents are blocking, the manufacturers are not in a horizontal relationship with respect to those patents. None of the patents can be used without the right to a patent owned by the other firm, so the patents are not substitutable. As in Example 9, the firms are horizontal competitors in the relevant goods market. In the absence of collateral restraints that would likely raise price or reduce putout in the relevant goods market or in any other relevant antitrust market and that are not reasonably related to an efficiency-enhancing integration of economic activity, the evaluating Agency would be unlikely to challenge this arrangement.

5.6 Grantbacks

A grantback is an arrangement under which a licensee agrees to extend to the licensor of intellectual property the right to use the licensee's improvements to the licensed technology. Grantbacks can have procompetitive effects, especially if they are nonexclusive. Such arrangements provide a means of the licensee and the licensor to share risks and reward the licensor for making possible further innovation based on or informed by the licensed technology, and both promote innovation in the first place and promote the subsequent licensing of the results of the innovation. Grantbacks may adversely affect competition, however, if they substantially reduce the licensee's incentives to engage in research and development and thereby limit rivalry in innovation markets.

A non-exclusive grantback allows the licensee to practice its technology and license it to others. Such a grantback provision may be necessary to ensure that the licensor is not prevented from effectively competing because it is denied access to improvements developed with the aid of its own technology. Compared with an exclusive grantback, a non-exclusive grantback, which leaves the licensee free to license improvements technology to others, is less likely to have anticompetitive effects.

The Agencies will evaluate a grantback provision under the rule of reason, *see generally Transparent-Wrap Machine Corp.* v. *Stokes & Smith Co.*, 329 U.S. 637, 645–48 (1947) (grantback provision in technology license is not per se unlawful), considering its likely effects in light of the overall structure of the licensing arrangement and conditions in the relevant markets. An important factor in the Agencies' analysis of a grantback will be whether the licensor has market power in a relevant technology or innovation market. If the Agencies determine that a particular grantback provision is likely to reduce significantly licensees' incentives to invest in improving the licensed technology, the Agencies will consider the extent to which the grantback provision has offsetting procompetitive effects, such as (1) promoting dissemination of licensees' improvements to the licensed technology, (2) increasing the licensors' incentives to disseminate the licensed technology, or (3) otherwise increasing competition and output in a relevant technology or innovation market. *See* section 4.2. In addition, the Agencies will consider the extent to which grantback provisions in the relevant markets generally increase licensors' incentives to innovate in the first place.

5.7 Acquisition of intellectual property rights

Certain transfers of intellectual property rights are most appropriately analyzed by applying the principles and standards used to analyze mergers, particularly those in the 1992 Horizontal Merger Guidelines. The Agencies will apply a merger analysis to an outright sale by an intellectual property owner of all of its rights to that intellectual property and to a transaction in which a person obtains through grant, sale, or other transfer an exclusive license for intellectual property (i.e., a license that precludes all other persons, including the licensor, from using the licensed intellectual property).[37] Such transactions may be assessed under section 7 of the Clayton Act, sections 1 and 2 of the Sherman Act, and section 5 of the Federal Trade Commission Act.

Example 11

Situation: Omega develops a new, patented pharmaceutical for the treatment of a particular disease. The only drug on the market approved for the treatment of this disease is sold by Delta. Omega's patented drug has almost completed regulatory

---

[37] The safety zone of section 4.3 does not apply to transfers of intellectual property such as those described in this section.

approval by the Food and Drug Administration. Omega has invested considerable sums in product development and market testing, and initial results show that Omega's drug would be a significant competitor to Delta's. However, rather than enter the market as a direct competitor of Delta, Omega licenses to Delta the right to manufacture and sell Omega's patented drug. The license agreement with Delta is nominally nonexclusive. However, Omega has rejected all requests by other firms to obtain a license to manufacture and sell Omega's patented drug, despite offers by those firms of terms that are reasonable in relation to those in Delta's license.

Discussion: Although Omega's license to Delta is nominally nonexclusive, the circumstances indicate that it is exclusive in fact because Omega has rejected all reasonable offers by other firms for licenses to manufacture and sell Omega's patented drug. The facts of this example indicate that Omega would be a likely potential competitor of Delta in the absence of the licensing arrangement, and thus they are in a horizontal relationship in the relevant goods market that includes drugs for the treatment of this particular disease. The evaluating Agency would apply a merger analysis to this transaction, since it involves an acquisition of a likely potential competitor.

6. ENFORCEMENT OF INVALID INTELLECTUAL PROPERTY RIGHTS

The Agencies may challenge the enforcement of invalid intellectual property rights as antitrust violations. Enforcement or attempted enforcement of a patent obtained by fraud on the Patent and Trademark Office or the Copyright Office may violate section 2 of the Sherman Act, if all the elements otherwise necessary to establish a section 2 charge are proved, or section 5 of the Federal Trade Commission Act. *Walker Process Equipment, Inc.* v. *Food Machinery & Chemical Corp.*, 382 U.S. 172 (1965) (patents); *American Cyanamid Co.*, 72 F.T.C. 632, 684–85 (1967), *aff'd sub. nom. Charles Pfizer & Co.*, 401 F.2d 574 (6th Cir. 1968), *cert. denied*, 394 U.S. 920 (1969) (patents); *Michael Anthony Jewelers, Inc.* v. *Peacock Jewelry, Inc.*, 795 F. Supp. 639, 647 (S.D.N.Y. 1992) (copyrights). Inequitable conduct before the Patent and Trademark Office will not be the basis of a section 2 claim unless the conduct also involves knowing and willful fraud and the other elements of a section 2 claim are present. *Argus Chemical Corp.* v. *Fibre Glass-Evercoat, Inc.*, 812 F.2d 1381, 1384–85 (Fed. Cir. 1987). Actual or attempted enforcement of patents obtained by inequitable conduct that falls short of fraud under some circumstances may violate section 5 of the Federal Trade Commission Act, *American Cyanamid Co., supra*. Objectively baseless litigation to enforce invalid intellectual property rights may also constitute an element of a violation of the Sherman Act. *See Professional Real Estate Investors, Inc.* v. *Columbia Pictures Industries, Inc.* 113 S. Ct. 1920, 1928 (1993) (copyrights); *Handgards, Inc.* v. *Ethicon, Inc.*, 743 F.2d 1282, 1289 (9th Cir. 1984), *cert. denied*, 469 U.S. 1190 (1985) (patents); *Handgards, Inc.* v. *Ethicon, Inc.*, 601 F.2d 986, 992–96 (9th Cir. 1979), *cert. denied*, 444 U.S. 1025 (1980) (patents); *CVD, Inc.* v. *Raytheon Co.*, 769 F.2d 842 (1st Cir. 1985) (trade secrets), *cert. denied*, 475 U.S. 1016 (1986).

Bibliography

I BOOKS

R. Bork, *The Antitrust Paradox* (New York Basic Books, 2nd edn., 1978).

B. I. Cawthra, *Patent Licensing in Europe* (Butterworths, 2nd edn., 1986).

W. R. Cornish, *Intellectual Property: Patents, Copyright, Trade Marks and Allied Rights* (Sweet & Maxwell, 3rd edn., 1996).

S. Deakin & J. Michie, *Contracts, Cooperation and Competition* (OUP, 1997).

P. Demaret, *Patent Territorial Restrictions and EEC Law: A Legal and Economic Analysis* (Verlag Chemie, 1978).

R. Downing, *EC Information Technology Law* (J. Wiley, 1995).

T. Frazer, *Monopoly, Competition and the Law: The Regulation of Business Activity in Britain, Europe and America* (Wheatsheaf Books, 1988).

I. Govaere, *The Use and Abuse of Intellectual Property Rights in EC Law* (Sweet & Maxwell, 1996).

D. Goyder, *EC Competition Law* (OUP, 2nd edn., 1993).

D. Guy and G. Leigh, *The EEC and Intellectual Property* (Sweet & Maxwell, 1981).

R. Joliet, *Monopolization and Abuse of a Dominant Position: A Comparative Study of American and European Approaches to the Control of Economic Power* (Nijhoff, 1970).

C. S. Kerse, *EEC Antitrust Procedure* (Sweet & Maxwell, 3rd edn., 1994)

V. Korah, *Patent Licensing and EEC Competition Rules: Regulation 2349/84* (ESC, 1985).

—— *Know-how Licensing Agreements and the EEC Competition Rules: Regulation 556.89* (ESC, 1989).

—— *Franchising and the EEC Competition Rules: Regulation 4087/88* (European Competition Law Monographs, Oxford, 1990).

—— *An Introductory Guide to EEC Competition Law and Practice* (Sweet & Maxwell, 5th edn., 1994 and Hart Publishing, 6th edn., 1997).

—— *Technology Transfer Agreements and the EC Competition Rules* (OUP, 1996).

J. Lowe, N. Crawford, *Innovation and Technology Transfer for the Growing Firm* (Oxford, 1984).

M. Maresceau (ed.), *The European Community's Commercial Policy after 1992: the Legal Dimension* (Martinus Nijhoff Publishers, 1992).

OECD, *Competition Policy and Intellectual Property Rights* (Paris, 1989).

Oppenheim, Weston and McCarthy, *Federal Antitrust Laws Tenth Commentary* (4th edn., 1981).

R. Posner, *Antitrust Law: An Economic Perspective* (Chicago, 1976).

F. Scherer, *Innovation and Growth–Schumpeterian Perspectives* (Cambridge, 1984).

—— *Industrial Market Structure and Economic Performance* (Chicago, 2nd edn., 1980).

J. Schumpeter, *Capitalism, Socialism and Democracy* (George Allen & Unwin, 1976).

J. Schmokler, *Invention and Economic Growth* (1966).

L. A. Sullivan, *Antitrust Law* (West, 1977).

C. Taylor and Z. Silberstone, *The Economic Impact of the Patent System* (Cambridge, 1973).

G. Tritton, *Intellectual Property in Europe* (Sweet & Maxwell, 1995).

R. Whish, *Competition Law* (Butterworths, 3rd edn., 1993).

II ARTICLES

W. Alexander, 'Patent Licensing Agreements in the EC' [1986] *IIC* 1.

S. Anderman, 'Copyright, Compulsory Licensing and EC Competition Law' [1995] *Yearbook of Media and Entertainment Law* 215 (OUP).

—— 'The Aftermath of Magill' [1996] *Yearbook of Media and Entertainment Law* 530 (OUP).

—— 'Commercial Co-operation, International Competitiveness and EC Competition Policy' in S. Deakin and J. Michie, *Contract, Cooperation and Competitiveness* (OUP, 1997).

C. Baden Fuller, 'Article 86 EEC: Economic Analysis of the Existence of a Dominant Position' (1979) 4 *EL. Rev* 423.

—— 'Economic Issues Relating to Property Rights in Trademarks: Export Bans, differential Pricing, Restrictions on Resale and Repackaging' (1981) 6 *EL Rev* 162.

F.-K. Beier, 'The Significance of the Patent System for Technical, Economic and Social Progress' [1980] *IIC* 563.

—— 'Industrial Property and the Free Movement of Goods in the Internal Market' [1990] *IIC* 131.

—— 'The Future of Intellectual Property in Europe: Thoughts on the Development of Patent, Utility Model and Industrial Design Law' [1991] *IIC* 157.

B. Bishop, 'Price Discrimination under Article 86: Political Economy of the European Court' [1981] *Modern L Rev.* 282.

—— 'The Modernization of DGIV Analysis' [1997] *ECLR* 481.

C. Bright, 'Deregulation of EC Competition Policy: Rethinking Art. 85(1)' [1995] *Fordham Law Inst.* 505.

P. Demaret, 'Industrial Property Rights, Compulsory Licences and the Free Movement of Goods under Community Law' [1987] *IIC* 161.

J. Derbyshire, 'Computer Programs and Competition Policy' [1994] *EIPR* 379.

N. De Souza, 'The Commission's Draft Group Exemption on Technology Transfer' [1994] *ECLR* 338.

K. Ewing Jr., 'Antitrust Enforcement and the Patent System, Similarities in the European and American Approach' [1980] *IIC,* 279.

S. Farr, 'Abuse of a Dominant Position—The Hilti case' [1992] *ECLR* 174.

J. Flynn, 'Intellectual Property and Anti-trust: ECC Attitudes' [1992] *EIPR* 49.

I. Forrester and C. Norall, 'The Laicisation of Community law, Self help and the Rule of Reason' [1984] 21 *CMLRev.*

I. Forrester, 'Software Licensing in the Light of the Current EC Competition Law Considerations' [1992] *ECLR* 5.

—— 'Competition Structures for the 21st Century' [1994] *Fordham Corp. Law Inst.* 445.

E. Fox, 'The Modernization of Antitrust: A New Equilibrium', 66 *Cornell L. Rev.* 1140 (1981).

—— 'Monopolization and Dominance in the United States and the European Community: Efficiency, Opportunity, and Fairness', 61 *Notre Dame L. Rev* (1986).

T. Frazer, 'Vorsprung durch Technik: The Commission's Policy on Know-How Agreements' [1989] *Yearbook of European Law* 1.

G. Friden, 'Recent Developments in EEC Intellectual Property Law: the Distinction between Existence and Exercise Revisited' (1989) 26 *CML Rev.* 193.

D. Gerber, 'Law and the Abuse of Economic Power in Europe', 62 *Tulane L. Rev.* 57 (1987).

D. Glasl, 'Essential Facilities Doctrine in EC Anti-trust Law: A Contribution to the Current Debate' [1994] *ECLR* 306.

F. Gonzalez Dias, 'Some Reflections on the Notion of ancillary Restraints under EC Competition Law' [1995] *Fordham Corp. Law Inst.* 325.

Gotts and Bent, 'Comment' [1994] *EIPR* 245.

S. Guttuso, 'Know How Agreements' [1986] *Fordham Corp. Law Inst.* 483.

—— 'Technology Transfer Agreements under EC Law' [1994] *Fordham Corp. Law Inst.* 227.

B. Hawk, 'The American (Antitrust) Revolution: Lessons for the EEC?' [1988] *ECLR* 53.

W. Hoyng and M. Biesheuvel, 'The Know-how Group Exemption' [1989] *CML Rev.* 219.

H. James, 'Tetra Pak: Exemption and Abuse of Dominant Position' [1990] *ECLR* 267.

P. Jebsen and R. Stevens, 'Assumptions, Goals and Dominant Undertaking: The Regulation of Competition under Article 86 of the EU' [1996] *Antitrust Law Jnl* 4.

F. Jenny, 'Competition and Efficiency' [1993] *Fordham Corp. Inst.* 185.

R. Joliet, 'Patented Articles and the Free Movement of Goods within the EEC' [1975] *Current Legal Problems* 15

—— 'Territorial and Exclusive Trademark Licensing under the EEC Law of Competition' [1984] *IIC* 21.

A. Jones, 'Distinguishing Predatory Prices from Competitive Ones' [1995] *EIPR* 252.

L. Kaplow 'The Patent-Antitrust Intersection: A Reappraisal' [1983–N4] *Harvard Law Review* 1813.

T. Kauper, 'Article 86 Excessive Prices and Refusals to Deal' [1991] Vol. 59 *Antitrust Law Jnl.* 441.

C. Kerse, 'Block Exemptions under Article 85 (3): the Technology Transfer Regulation—Procedural Issues' [1996] *ECLR* 331.

S. Kon and F. Shaffer, 'Parallel Imports of Pharmaceutical Products: A New Realism or Back to Basics?' [1997] *ECLR* 331.

V. Korah, 'EEC Competition Policy—Legal Form or Economic Efficiency' [1986] *Current Legal Problems* 85.

—— 'No duty to License Independent Repairers to Make Spare Parts: the Renault, Volvo and Bayer & Hennecke Cases' [1988] *EIPR* 381.

—— 'The Preliminary Draft of a New EC, Group Exemption for Technology Licensing' [1994] *EIPR* 263.

N. MacFarlane, C. Wardle, J. Wilkinson, 'The Tension between Intellectual Property Rights and Certain Provisions of EC Law [1994] *EIPR* 525.

P. Lasok, 'Assessing the Economic Consequences of Restrictive Agreements: A Comment on the Delimitis Case [1991] *ECLR* 194.

F. Machlup, 'An Economic Review of the Patent System, Study of the Committee on Patents, Trademarks and Copyright', Senate Judiciary Committee, US 85th Congress, Study no 15, Washington DC, 1958.

G. Marenco, K. Banks, 'Intellectual Property and the Community Rules on Free Movement of Goods: Discrimination Unearthed' (1990) 15 *EL Rev.*

H. W. Moritz, 'EC Competition Aspects and Software Licensing Agreements'—A German Perspective', Part One [1994] *IIC* 357; Part Two [1994] *IIC* 515.

J. Ordover, 'A Patent System for Both Diffusion and Exclusion', *Jnl. Of Economic Perspectives* [1991] Vol. 5, No. 1, 430.

Jan Peeters, 'The Rule of Reason Revisited: Prohibitions on Restraints on Competition in the Sherman Act and the EEC Treaty', Vol. 37 *American Jnl. of Comparative Law* 521 (1989).

D. Price, 'The Secret of the Know-How Block Exemption' [1989] *ECLR* 213.

—— 'Abuse of a Dominant Position—The Tale of Nails, Milk Cartons, and TV Guides' [1990] *ECLR* 80.

T. Ramsay, 'The EU Commission's Use of the Competition Rules in the Field of Telecommunications: A Delicate Balancing Act' [1995] *Ford. Corp. Law Inst.* 561.

A. Reindl, 'The Magic of Magill: TV Program Guides as a Limit of Copyright Law?' [1993] *IIC* 60.

—— 'Intellectual Property and Intra-Community Trade' [1996] *Fordham Corp. Law Inst.* 453.

D. Ridyard, 'Essential Facilities and the Obligation to Supply Competitors' [1996] *ECLR* 438.

M. Schödermeir, 'Collective Dominane Revisited: An Analysis of the EC Commission's new Concept of Oligopoly Control' [1990] *ECLR* 28.

H. Schröder, 'The Application of Article 85 of the EEC Treaty to Distribution Agreements—Principles and Recent Developments [1984] *Fordham Corp. Law Inst.* 375.

S. Singleton, 'Intellectual Property Disputes: Settlement Agreements and Ancillary Licences under EC and UK Competition Law' [1993] *EIPR* 48.

M. Siragusa, 'The Application of Article 86 to the Pricing Policies fo Dominant Companies: Discriminatory and Unfair Prices' [1979] 16 *CML Rev.* 179.

—— 'EEC Technology Transfers—A Private View [1982] *Fordham Corp. Law Inst.* 116.

—— 'Notification of Agreements in the EEC: To Notify or not to Notify?' [1987] *Fordham Corp. Law Inst.* 243.

T. Skinner, 'The Oral Hearing of the Magill Case' [1994] *ECLR* 103.

P. Slot, 'The Application of Articles 3(f), 5 and 85 to 94 EEC' (1987) 12 *EL Rev* 179.

U. Springer, 'Borden and United Brands Revisited' [1997] *ECLR* 42.

—— 'Meeting Competition: Justification of Price Discrimination under EC and US Antitrust Law' [1997] *ECLR* 251.

J. Smith, 'Televison Guides: The European Court doesn't know there's so much in it' [1992] *ECLR* 135.

P. Smith, 'The Wolf in Wolf's Clothing: The Problem With Predatory Pricing' (1989) 14 *EL Rev.* 209.

R. Subiotto, 'The Right to Deal with Whom one Pleases under EEC Competition Law: A Small Contribution to a Necessary Debate' [1992] *ECLR* 234.

—— 'Moosehead/Whitbread: Industrial and No Challenge Clauses Relating to Licensed Trade Marks under EEC Competition Law' [1990] *ECLR* 226.

J. Temple Lang, 'Monopolisation and the Definition of Abuse of a Dominant Position under Article 86 EEC Treaty' [1970] 16 *CML Rev.* 345.

—— 'Defining Legitimate Competition: Companies Duties to Supply Competitors and Access to Essential Services' [1994] *Fordham Corp. Law Inst.* 216.

—— 'European Community Antitrust Law—Innovation Markets and High Technology Industries' [1996] *Fordham Corp. Law Inst.* 519.

Turner, 'Antitrust and Innovation' (1967) 12 *Antitrust Bulletin* 277.

H. Ullrich, 'Patents and Know How: Free Trade Interenterprise cooperation and Competition within the Internal European Market' [1992] *IIC* 583.

C. Vadja, 'The Application of Community Competition Law to the Distribution of Computer Products and Parts' [1992] *ECLR* 110.

B. Van der Asch, 'Intellectual Property Rights under EC Law' [1983] *Fordham Corp. Inst.* 539.

G. Van der Wal, 'Article 86 EC: The Limits of Compulsory Licensing' [1994] *ECLR* 230.

M. Van Kerchkhove, 'The Advocate General delivers his opinion on Magill' [1994] *ECLR* 276.

J. Venit, 'EEC Patent Licensing Revisited: The Commission's Patent Licence Regulation' [1985] *Antitrust Bulletin* 457.

—— 'The Commission's Opposition Procedure' (19850 22 *CML Rev.* 167.

—— 'In the Wake of Windsurfing: Patent Licensing in the Common Market' [1987] *IIC* 1, also in [1986] *Fordham Corp. Law Inst.* 521.

—— and J. Kallaugher, 'Essential Facilities: A Comparative Approach' [1994] *Fordham Corp. Law Inst.* 315.

T. Vinje, '*Magill*: Its Impact on the Information Technology Industry' [1992] *EIPR* 397.

—— 'The Final Word on *Magill*' [1995] *ECLR* 297.

P. Vogelenzang, 'Abuse of a Dominant Position in Article 86: The problem of Causality and Some Applications' (1976) 13 *CMI Rev.* 61.

M. Waelbroeck, 'The Effect of the Rome Treaty on the Exercise of National Industrial Property Rights' (1976) 21 *Antitrust Bulletin* 99.

—— 'Antitrust Analysis under Article 85 (1) and Article 85 (3)' [1987] *Fordham Corp. Law Inst.* Ch. 28.

M. Waelbroeck, 'Price Discrimination and Rebate Policies under EU Competition Law' [1995] *Fordham Corp. Law Inst.* 142.

D. Winn, 'The Commission Know-how Regulation 556/89: Innovation and Territorial Exclusivity, Improvements and the Quid Prop Quo' [1990] *ECLR* 135.

R. Whaite, 'Licensing in Europe' [1990] *EIPR* 88.

—— 'The Draft Technology Transfer Block Exemption' [1994] *EIPR* 259.

R. Whish and B. Sufrin, 'The Rule of Reason under Article 85' [1987] *Oxford Year Book of European Law* 1.

E. White, 'Research and Development Joint Ventures under EEC Competition Law' [1985] *IIC* 663.

L. Zanon, 'Price Discrimination under Article 86 of the EEC Treaty: A Comment on the UBC Case' (1982) 31 *ICLQ* 36.

L. Zanon, 'Price Discrimination and Hoffman La Roche' [1981] 15 *Jnl. World Trade Law* 305.

Index

abuse *see also* **Article 86**
  acquisitions 182, 189–90
  anti-competitive behaviour 181–7
  barriers to entry 174–5
  competition
    elimination, of 182–4
    normal 184–7
  copyright 200
  definition 147–8, 180
  discrimination 190
    pricing, in 232–43
  dominance 180–93, 246
  examples 180
  exclusive rights 188, 189–90
  expansion of concept 181–94
  exploitative 148
  indispensability 187
  innovation 185, 188, 246
  intellectual property rights 180–94
  invention 246
  Magill decision 188, 205, 208–11
  market definition 188
  monopolies 181, 182–3, 188, 246–7
  performance 184–5, 188–9
  predatory pricing 244–5
  pricing 181, 184–6, 224–31
  primary market 188–90
  prohibitions 186
  proportionality 186
  refusal to license 200, 203
  refusal to supply 195–220
  related markets 191–4
  relevant market 155, 163, 166, 188
  secondary market 188, 190–3
  specific 190–1
  structural 188–90
  technology 189
  tie-ins 186, 190, 221–3
access to markets 250
acquisitions 182, 189–90
agents 43
anti-competitive behaviour
  abuse 181–7
  Article 86 148
  best endeavours clauses 129
  block exemptions 77
  collusion 28
  exclusive rights 12–13
  investment 6
  licensing 30
  prohibitions 55

  technology transfer 84
  tie-ins 108
  United States 139
applicability test 63–6
appreciability test 72–3
Article 85
  block exemptions 35–40, 77
  clearances 36, 40–51, 141
  concerted practices 34–5
  fair competition 19
  improvements 112–12, 115
  innovation 102–3
  integration 21–2
  intellectual property rights 8–24
  licensing 13, 32–51
  market share 139
  market structure 16–17
  non-competition clauses 128
  non-territorial restraints 100–1
  patents 52–5, 77
  prohibitions 55–61
  refusal to licence 200
  royalties 120–1, 126
  structure 34–51
  technology 66–72
  territoriality 64
  text 256–7
  trade 34–5
  trade marks 15
  whitelists 140
Article 86, *see also* **abuse**, **dominance**
  anti-competitive behaviour 148
  barriers to entry 177–9
  block exemptions 77–8
  clearances 40
  competition 142
  compulsory licensing 215, 218
  discriminatory pricing 232–3, 235–43
  essential facility 242–3
  exclusive rights 9, 149–50
  fair competition 19
  innovation 246
  integration 21
  intellectual property rights 8–24
  investment 246
  licensing 12, 14–15
  Magill case 15, 205–6, 208–14
  market power 149
  market structure 16–19
  monopolies 150
  predatory pricing 244

Article 86 (*cont.*)
  pricing 215, 224–31
  prohibitions 197–8
  proportionality 186
  refusal to license 199–203
  refusal to supply 195–9
  regulation 147
  related markets 191–4
  relevant market 149, 154–7, 161–3, 165–6
  secondary markets 149
  text 257
  tie-ins 221–3
  trade marks 13
Assignment 68–9, 84, 104–5, 115, 117

barriers to entry
  abuse 174–5
  Article 86 177–9
  copyright 172
  dominance 172–9
  exclusive rights 172
  Magill case 177–9
  monopolies 173, 174–5, 177–8
  patent licensing 172
  product market 173, 177–8
  relevant market 177–8
  secondary markets 176
  separate markets 173
  software 175–6
  substitutes 173
  suppliers 174
  technology 182
best endeavours clauses 128–9
block exemptions
  anti-competitive behaviour 77
  Article 85 35–6
  Article 86 77–8
  blacklists 77–8, 80–1, 84, 87, 107, 117–18, 132, 134
  comfort letters 40
  competition policy 76–89
  copyright licensing 88, 133
  enforcement 37–8
  exclusions 86
  exclusive distribution agreements 86
  form A/B 39
  grant-back 116–18
  improvements 114–18
  innovation 102
  investigations 39–40
  joint ventures 38
  know-how 77, 78–81
  licensing 37–40, 76–89, 99, 133–4
  manufacturing 78
  market share 135, 140–2
  no-challenge clauses 123–4
  notification 140–1

  non-opposition procedure 38, 78
  non-territorial restraints 107
  notification 38–40, 87
  opposition procedure 87, 132, 139
  patent licensing 37, 55, 61, 76–89
  process 37–40
  prohibitions 58–63, 78
  royalties 126–7
  small and medium-sized enterprises 21
  technology 76–89
    transfer 37, 76, 81–9, 131, 134
  territoriality 77, 93–7
  tie-ins 108
  trademark licensing 88, 133
  whitelists 77, 83, 86, 114–15, 131, 135
  withdrawals 85–6, 132
brands 29, 56, 66–7, 72, 94

clearances
  agents 43
  agreements between independent
    undertakings 40–3
  appreciability 50–1
  Article 85 36, 40–51, 141
  Article 86 40
  competition
    distorting 48–51
    preventing 48–51
    restructuring 48–51
  concerted practices 41
  de minimis agreements 45–8
    horizontal 45
    networks 46–7
    vertical 45, 48, 50–1
  exclusive distribution agreements
    44–5, 49
  exclusive purchasing agreements 47
  freedom of action 49–50
  grant backs 112
  group 36, 41
  improvements 112
  integration 47
  joint ventures 44
  licensing 36, 40–51
  negative 36, 44, 141
  non-territorial restraints 100
  Notice on Agreements of Minor Importance
    44–8
  patents 54
  prohibitions 46, 58, 69
  relevant market 45
  small and medium-sized enterprises
    45–6
  subsidiaries 41–2
  trade 43–5
collusion 29
comfort letters 40

companies
  groups, of 36, 61
  small and medium-sized enterprises
    19–21, 45–6
  subsidiaries 41–2
competition *see also* **Article 85, Article 86,**
    competition policy
  distortion 17, 19, 21–2, 35, 48–51, 63, 74,
    147–8
  economic policy 1–2
  effective 16–19
  elimination 182–4
  exceptional circumstances test 246–7
  fair 19–21
  normal 184–7, 246–7
  preventing 48–51
  regulation 1–5
  restricting 48–75
  weakening levels 182–3
  workable 17–19
competition policy
  block exemptions 76–89
  improvements 110
  innovation 251
  integration 21–4
  intellectual property rights 4, 5–7, 27–33,
    52–75
  licensing 27–33, 52–89
  non-competition clauses 127–8
  objectives 16
  pricing 18
  prohibitions 57–63
  refusal to licence 204
  relevant market 158
  technology 76–89, 130
    transfer 82, 86
compulsory licensing
  Article 86 215, 218
  copyright 215
  dominance 215, 218
  essential facility doctrine 215, 217–19
  investment 216–17, 220
  innovation 215–16
  licensing 214–20
  Magill case 208, 210, 214–15
  monopolies 216–18
  pricing 214–20
  refusal to license 200
  refusal to supply 199
  royalties 215, 217
  secondary market 215
  telecommunications 215, 217–20, 248
concentrations 18, 30
concerted practices 34–5, 41
confidentiality 103–4, 113
copyright licensing
  abuse 200

barriers to entry 172
block exemptions 88, 133
compulsory licensing 215
exhaustion of rights 198–9
Magill case 204–8, 211–12
  refusal to licence 200
  refusal to supply 198–9
  technology transfer 88
  territoriality 92
customer allocation clauses 120

demand 169
dependence 20, 160–5, 202
designs 14, 160, 229–30
direct sales 90, 97–9
disclosure
  improvements 110
  inventions 251
discounts 233–5, 237
discrimination *see also* **discriminatory**
    pricing
  abuse 190
  exports 8–9
  imports 8–9
  refusal to supply 198
  secondary market 247
discriminatory pricing
  abuse 232–43
  Article 86 232–3, 235–43
  discounts 233–5, 237
  distribution 240
  dominance 233, 236–9, 242
  effects 235
  equivalent transactions 232–3
  essential facility doctrine 242–3
  geographic 239–42
  intellectual property rights 232–43
  licensing 236–7
  market power 240
  market share 241
  non-equivalent transactions 234–5
  parallel imports 239
  parallel trade 239
  patents 236
  performance 238
  prohibition 232
  quantities 234–5
  rebates 233–5
  relevant market 236
  royalties 236–7, 241
  separate markets 235–9
  single market 233–5
  technology transfer 236
  telecommunications 238
distribution 29, 240 *see also* **exclusive**
    distribution agreements

dominance
  abuse 180–93, 246
  access to markets 250–1
  Article 86 149–50, 168–9, 172
  assessment 170
  barriers to entry 172–9
  compulsory licensing 215, 218
  definition 149–50, 168
  demand 169
  discriminatory pricing 233, 236–9, 242
  exclusive rights 169, 172
  intellectual property rights 168–79
  innovation 171–2, 215
  investment 171–2
  know-how 172
  Magill case 169, 205–6, 208–14
  market power 246–7
  market share 170–1
  monopolies 168–9
  predatory pricing 244
  pricing 170–1, 224, 227, 229–30
  prohibitions 186
  refusal to licence 199, 203
  refusal to supply 195–9
  relevant market 151, 155–6, 159–64, 166,
       170–1
  research and development 172
  technology 171–2
  threshold 169
  tie-ins 221–2
dominant position *see* **Article 86,**
       dominance
dual markets 231

economic policy 1–2
entry barriers *see* **barriers to entry**
essential facilities doctrine 202–4, 212,
       215, 217–19, 242–3, 250–1
exceptional circumstances test 246–7
exclusive distribution agreements
  block exemptions 86
  clearances 44–5, 49
  integration 21–2
  patents 52–4
  prohibitions 59
  technology transfer 86
exclusive purchasing agreements 47
exclusive rights *see also* **exclusive**
       distribution agreements
  access to markets 250–1
  abuse 188, 189–90
  anti-competitive behaviour 12–13
  appreciability test 72
  Article 86 9, 149–50
  barriers to entry 172
  costs 249
  designs 14

  dominance 169, 172
  duration 251
  field of use provisions 118, 119
  innovation 5, 250
  inventions 249–50
  licensing 27, 57, 63, 65–9, 72, 90–9
  manufacturing 57, 59–60
  monopolies 6, 246
  non-competition clauses 127
  patents 52–4, 249, 251
  pricing 224
  prohibitions 57–60, 63, 66
  purchasing agreements 47
  refusal to supply 198–9
  relevant market 161
  royalties 126
  secondary market 248
  technology 66–9, 72
  territoriality 63–5, 90–9, 131
  tie-ins 223
  United States 137–8
exhaustion of rights 98–9, 198–9
exports 8, 10, 66, 92–3

field of use provisions 118–20
form A/B 39
franchising 70–2, 74–5
free movement of goods 8, 23–4, 57

Germany 52
grant-backs 109–18
groups of companies 36, 41
Grundig **decision** 55–7, 63

imports 8, 10–11 *see also* **parallel imports**
improvements
  Article 85 111–12, 115
  assignment 115, 117
  blacklists 117–18
  block exemptions 114–18
  clearances 112
  competition policy 110
  confidentiality 113
  disclosure 110
  extending relationships 118
  grant-back 111, 116–18
  innovation 118
  inventions 251
  know-how licensing 109–17
  non-competition clauses 128
  non-severable 115–18
  non-territorial restraints 109–18
  patent licensing 109–11, 114
  royalties 113, 115–16, 126
  severance 110–15, 117
  sub-licensing 113, 116–17
  technology transfer 110, 114–15, 117

territoriality 118
whitelists 114–15, 117
incentives 247–8
innovation
abuse 185, 188
Article 85 102–3
Article 86 246
assignment 104–5
blacklists 102–3
block exemptions 102
competition policy 251
compulsory licensing 215–16
costs 228
dominance 171–2, 215
efficiency 17–18
exclusive rights 5, 250–1
improvements 118
indispensability 102–7
intellectual property rights 3
investment 4, 5, 216
know-how 79–80, 103–7
licensing 29, 102–7, 130–1
low risk indispensable restraints 103–5
market power 249
market share 142
monopolies 18
no-challenge clauses 125
non-territorial restraints 102–7
patents 229
performance 185, 188–9
post-term use bans 105
pricing 227–9
prohibitions 62–3
quality controls 106–7
refusal to licence 199
sub-licensing 104–5
technology transfer licensing 102, 104–5, 107
whitelists 102, 107
integration 21–4, 33, 47, 56–7, 67, 92, 223
intellectual property rights
competition 1–5, 8–24, 52–75
policy 4, 5–7, 27–33
existence 11–12
grants 11–12
permitted exercise, of 12–16
prohibited exercise, of 12–16
refusal to supply 195–220
interbrand competition 29, 56, 66–7, 72, 94
internal market 233–5
inventions
abuse 246
access to markets 251
disclosure 251
exclusive rights 50 249
improvements 251
investment 5–6

market power 249
investment
anti-competitive behaviour 6
Article 86 246
innovation 4, 5, 216
inventions 5–6
licensing 29
research and development 5, 27, 247
technology 69–71
transfer 134
territoriality 90, 93

joint ventures 38, 44, 86, 127, 135

know-how licensing
blacklists 80
block exemptions 77, 78–81
confidentiality 103–4
dominance 172
field of use provisions 119–20
franchising 74–5
improvements 109–17
innovation 79–80, 103–7
no-challenge clauses 124–5
non-competition clauses 128
patents 77, 78–9, 96
post-term use ban 105
quality control 106–7
royalties 80, 120–2, 126–7
technology 79
transfer 79, 81, 87–8, 104
territoriality 79, 95–6
trade marks 74–5
whitelists 117

licensing *see also* **compulsory licensing, copyright licensing, know-how licensing, patent licensing, refusal to license, trade mark licensing, technology transfer licensing**
anti-competitive behaviour 30
appreciability test 72
Article 85 13, 32–51, 90–9
Article 86 12, 14–15
block exemptions 37–40, 99, 134
clearances 40–51
closed 66, 97–9
competition 6, 52–75
policy 27–33
compulsory licensing 214–20
concentrations 30
direct sales 98–9
discriminatory pricing 236–7
exclusive rights 27, 57, 63, 65–9, 72, 90–9
exemptible exclusive 93–5
exports 97–8
filtering mechanism 142

licensing (*cont.*)
horizontal 28–9, 31–2, 83
indispensability 102–18
information technology 28
innovation 29, 102–7, 130–1
integration 22–3, 33
intellectual property rights 27–33, 52–75
investment 29
Magill case 206–7, 209
manufacturing 29, 65
market sharing 6, 134–5
non-restrictive exclusive 91–3
non-territorial restraints 100–29
notification 63
open 65–6
parallel 57
parallel imports 97–8
prohibitions 46, 55–63
qualitative appreciability 64
quality controls 106
reform 142
refusal to grant licences 15
relevant market 32
research and development 29
restraints, in 31–2, 36
rule of reason 31–2
technology 66–73, 76–89
territoriality 64–5, 73, 90–9
United States 30–2
vertical 28–32, 83–4, 126–8, 141–2

Magill **case**
abuse 188, 205, 208–11
Article 86 15, 205–6, 208–14
barriers to entry 177–9
compulsory licensing 208, 210, 214–15
copyright 204–8, 211–12
dominance 169, 205–6, 208–14
essential facility case 212
information technology 212–13
licensing 206, 213–14
monopolies 206–7, 209
product market 213
proportionality 210
refusal to license 205, 207–8
refusal to supply 204–14
related market 207
secondary markets 209, 210, 213–14
software 213–14
manufacturing
block exemptions 78
exclusive rights 57, 59–60
licensing 29, 65
prohibitions 57–60
royalties 125–6
technology 67
territoriality 92

market share
Article 85 139
assessment 141
block exemptions 135, 140–2
de minimis 140
discriminatory pricing 241
dominance 170–1
flexibility 142
innovation 142
joint ventures 135
licensing 6, 134–5
market definition 143
prohibitions 55–6
relevant market 156
scrutiny 143
technology 142
transfer 86, 135–6
United States 135–6, 140
markets *see also* **market share, relevant
markets, secondary markets**
access, to 250
definition 143, 151, 160–5
dual 231
entry 172–9, 182
open testing 66–73
power 149, 240, 246–50
primary 90, 188, 250
product 153–65, 173, 177–8, 213, 222
related 181–4, 191–4, 203, 207
separate 152, 156–64, 173, 222, 235–9
structure 16–19, 32, 140
monopolies
abuse 181, 182–3, 188, 246–7
Article 86 150
barriers to entry 173–5, 177–8
compulsory licensing 216–18
de facto 150, 173, 174–5, 177–8, 209, 247
dominance 168–9
essential facilities doctrine 251
exclusive rights 6, 246
innovation 18
market power 246, 250
pricing 216–17
quasi-monopolies 188
secondary markets 250

national laws 11–12, 23
no-challenge clauses 101–2, 123–5
non-competition clauses 127–9
non-territorial restraints
Article 85 100–1
block exemptions 107
clearances 100
filed of use provisions 118–20
grant-backs 109–18
improvements 109–18
indispensability 107–18

innovation 102–7
licensing 100–29
minimum quantities 125–7
no-challenge clauses 101–2, 123–5
non-competition clauses 127–9
patent licensing 100–2
prohibitions 100
quality specifications 107–9
royalties 100–2, 120–3
    minimum 125–7
tie-ins 107–9
*Notice on Agreements of Minor
    Importance* 44–8
Notice on Patent Licensing 53–4
Notice on Sub-Contracting Agreements 59

oligopolies 135

parallel imports
discriminatory pricing 239
licensing 97
pricing 223
territoriality 63–6, 96
parallel trade 90, 239
patent licensing
Article 85 52–5, 77
barriers to entry 172
blacklists 77, 78
block exemptions 37, 55, 61, 76–89
clearances 54
Community Patent Convention 59
competition
    restrictions, on 52–5, 73
discriminatory pricing 236
exclusive rights 52–4, 249, 251
exhaustion of rights 98–9
field of use provisions 119–20
freedom of action 53, 54–5
Germany 52
imports 10–11
improvements 109–11, 114
innovation 229
inquiries 100
know-how 77, 78, 96
national laws 12
no-challenge clauses 123–5
non-competition clauses 128
non-territorial restraints 100–1
Notice on Patent Licensing 53–4
notifications 54
pricing 224, 228–30
prohibitions 53–4, 57–61
refusal to licence 200
royalties 61, 80, 101–2, 121–3, 126–7
technology transfer 79, 81, 87–8
territoriality 93–6
tie-ins 109

trade 54
United States 52, 61
whitelists 77, 131
performance
abuse 184–5, 188–9
discriminatory pricing 238
fair competition 20
innovation 184–5, 188–9
pricing 227–8
post-term use bans 105
predatory pricing 20, 244–5
pricing *see also* discriminatory pricing
abuse 181, 184–6, 224–31
Article 86 215, 224–31
comparisons 226
competition policy 18
compulsory licensing 214–20
costs 227–9
designs 229–30
dominance 170–1, 224, 227, 229–30
dual markets 231
excessive 224–31
exclusive rights 224
fair 229, 231
fixing 231
innovation 227–9
intellectual property rights 224–31
monopolies 216–17
parallel imports 225
patents 224, 228–30
performance 227–8
predatory 20, 244–5
reduction 171
refusal to supply 214–20
royalties 226–7
secondary market 231
unfair pricing 231
United States 227
primary markets 188–90, 250
product market 153–65, 173, 177–8, 213,
    222
prohibitions
abuse 186
anti-competitive behaviour 55
Article 85 55–61
Article 86 197–8
blacklists 132
block exemptions 58–63, 78
brands 56
clearances 46, 58, 60
competition policy 57–63
discriminatory pricing 232
dominance 186
exclusive distribution agreements 59
exclusive rights 57–60, 63, 66
exports 66
free movement of goods 57

prohibitions (*cont.*)
  Grundig decision 55–7
  innovation 62–3
  integration 56–7
  licensing 46, 55–63
    parallel 57
  manufacturing 57–60
  market share 55–6
  non-territorial restraints 100
  patents 53–4, 57–61
  per se 55–63, 78, 84, 132, 140
  quantitative appreciability 58
  refusal to supply 197–8
  rule of reason 62
  sub-contracting 59
  technology transfer licensing 63, 84, 132
  trade 57, 63
  United States 61–2, 140
proportionality 20, 186, 202, 210, 202
purchasing agreements 47

quality control 107–9

rebates 233–5
refusal to licence
  abuse 200, 203
  Article 85 200
  Article 86 199–203
  Commission decisions 201–2
  competition policy 204
  compulsory licences 200
  copyright 200
  dependence 202
  dominance 199, 203
  essential facility doctrine 202–4
  innovation 199
  Magill case 205, 207–8
  new entrants 201–2
  patents 200
  proportionality 202
  refusal to supply 199–204
  related markets 203
refusal to supply
  abuse 195–220
  Article 86 195–9
  copyright 198–9
  discrimination 198
  dominance 195–9
  exclusive rights 197
  exhaustion of rights 198–9
  intellectual property rights 195–220
  licensing 198–9
    compulsory 214–20
    refusal, to 199–204
  Magill case 204–14
  pricing 214–20
  prohibitions 197–8

  royalties 198
related markets 181–4, 191–4, 203, 207, 221
relevant market
  abuse 155, 163, 166, 188
  Article 86 149, 154–7, 161–3, 165–6
  barriers to entry 177–8
  clearances 45
  Commission practice 157–60
  competition policy 158
  dependence 160–5
  designs 160
  discriminatory pricing 236
  dominance 151, 155–6, 159–64, 166, 170–1
  essential facility 160–5
  exclusive rights 161
  identification 151
  intellectual property rights 151–67
  licensing 32
  market definition 151, 160–5
  market share 156
  products 151–65
    definition 153–7
    geographic market 165–7
    narrow markets 157–60
  separate markets 152, 156–64
  software 162–3
  substitutes 151–3, 156, 159–60, 167
  suppliers 152–3
  tie-ins 222
  United States 139
research and development 5, 27, 29, 128–9, 172, 247
royalties
  Article 85 120–1, 126
  block exemptions 121, 126–7
  calculation 122–3, 127
  compulsory licensing 215, 217
  discriminatory pricing 236–7, 241
  duration 120–2
  exclusive rights 126
  improvements 113, 115–16, 126
  know-how licensing 80, 120–2, 126–7
  manufacturing 125–6
  minimum 125–7
  no-challenge clauses 124
  non-territorial restraints 100–2, 120–3, 125–7
  patent licensing 61, 80, 101–2, 121–3, 126–7
  pricing 226–7
  refusal to supply 198
  regulation 120–3
  technology transfer 120, 122–3, 125, 127
  tie-ins 221
rule of reason 31–2, 62, 67, 136–7, 139–40, 143

secondary markets
  abuse 188, 1903
  Article 86 149
  barriers to entry 176
  compulsory licensing 215
  discrimination 247
  exclusive rights 248
  Magill case 209, 210, 213–14
  monopolies 250
  pricing 231
  tie-ins 221
separate markets 152, 156–64, 173, 222,
    235–9
severance 110–15, 117
single market 233–5
small and medium-sized competition
    19–21, 45–6
software
  barriers to entry 175–6
  information technology 4
  interoperability 250
  Magill case 213–14
  relevant market 162–3
state aids 20–1
sub-contractors 59
sub-licensing
  ban 104–5
  improvements 113, 116–17
  innovation 104–5
  severance 113
  technology 116
subsidiaries 41–2
substitutes 151–3, 156, 159–60, 167, 173
suppliers 152–3, 174 *see also* **refusal to
    supply**

technology *see also* **technology transfer**
  abuse 189
  access to markets 250
  appreciability test 72–3
  Article 85 66–72
  assignment 68–9
  barriers to entry 182
  blacklists 80–1
  block exemptions 76–89
  brands 66–7, 72
  competition policy 76–89, 130
  dominance 171–2
  exclusive rights 66–9, 72
  franchising 70–2
  integration 67
  investment 69–71
  licensing 66–73, 76–89
  manufacturing 67
  market opening testing 66–73
  market share 142
  rule of reason 67

sub-licensing 116
  territoriality 67–72
technology transfer
  ancillary restraints 133
  anti-competitive behaviour 84
  assignment 84
  blacklists 123
  block exemptions 37, 76, 81–9, 131, 134
  competition policy 82, 86
  copyright 88
  discriminatory pricing 236
  exclusive distribution agreements 86
  field of use provisions 118, 119–20
  improvements 110, 114–15, 117
  innovation 102, 104–5, 107
  investment 134
  joint ventures 86
  know-how licensing 81, 87–8, 104
  licensing 81–9
    mixed 81, 88
  market share 86, 135
  no-challenge clauses 124–5
  non-competition clauses 128
  patent licensing 81, 87–8
  prohibitions 63, 84, 132
  promotion 131
  regulation 143, 258–75
  restraint 87
  royalties 120, 122–3, 125–7
  territoriality 83, 86, 90–9
  tie-ins 107–9
  trademarks 87, 88
  United States 134–6
  whitelist 102, 107
telecommunications
  compulsory licensing 215, 217–20, 249
  discriminatory pricing 238
  information technology 4
territoriality
  appreciability test 72
  Article 85 64, 90–9
  block exemptions 77, 93–7
  brands 94
  copyright 92
  direct sales 90, 97
  duration 95–7, 131
  exclusive rights 63–6, 90–9, 131
    exemptible 91, 93–5
    non-exemptible 91
    non-restrictive 91–3
  exports 92–3
  freedom of action 63
  Grundig decision 63
  improvements 118
  integration 92
  investment 90, 93
  know-how licensing 79, 95–6

territoriality (*cont.*)
  licensing 64–5, 73, 90–9
  manufacturing 64, 92
  parallel imports 63–6, 96
  parallel trade 90
  patent licensing 93–6
  qualitative 63
  technology 67–72
    transfer 83, 86, 90–9
  trade 90–1
tie-ins
  abuse 186, 190, 221–3
  anti-competitive behaviour 108
  Article 86 221–3
  block exemptions 108
  definition 221
  dominance 221–2
  exclusive rights 223
  integration 223
  intellectual property rights 221–3
  non-territorial restraints 107–9
  patent licensing 109
  product markets 22
  quality control 108–9
  related market 221, 222
  royalties 221
  secondary market 221
  separate markets 222
  technology transfer licensing 107–9
trade
  Article 85 34–5
  clearances 43–5
  intellectual property rights 6
  interstate 34–5, 43–5, 57, 91
  parallel 90, 239
  prohibitions 57, 63

  quantitative dimension 43–4
trade mark licensing
  Article 85 15
  Article 86 13
  best endeavours clauses 128–9
  block exemptions 88, 133
  non-competition clauses 128
  exports 10
  franchising 74–5
  licensing 29, 74
  technology transfer 87–8
transfer of technology *see* **technology
  transfer**
Treaty on European Union 255–7

United States
  anticompetitive behaviour 136, 139
  Antitrust Guidelines 30–2, 135–40
    text 276–303
  competition 139–43
  exclusive rights 137–8
  licensing 30–2, 136–9
  manufacturing 136
  market share 135–6, 140
  market structure 32, 140
  patents 52, 61
  predatory pricing 245
  pricing 224
  prohibitions 61–2, 140
  relevant markets 139
  restraints 137
  rule of reason 31–2, 62, 136–7, 139–40
  safe harbour 139–40
  technology transfer 134–6

value, appropriation of 248–50